SAINT THÉRÈSE OF LISIEUX
Her Life, Times, and Teaching

SAINT THÉRÈSE OF LISIEUX
Her Life, Times, and Teaching

Edited by CONRAD DE MEESTER, OCD

Preface
GODFRIED Cardinal DANNEELS

Conclusion
ANASTASIO Cardinal BALLESTRERO, OCD

Photography
GIROLAMO SALVATICO, OCD

ICS Publications
Washington, DC
1997

General Editor of Project: Conrad De Meester, OCD
Photographic Editor: Girolamo Salvatico, OCD
Coordinator: Silvano Giordano, OCD

Text:
Tomás Alvarez, OCD
Anastasio Cardinal Ballestrero, OCD
Godfried Cardinal Danneels, archbishop of Malines-Brussels
Conrad De Meester, OCD
Pierre Descouvemont
Geneviève Devergnies, OCD
Roberto Fornara, OCD
Guy Gaucher, OCD, auxiliary bishop of Lisieux
Camillo Gennaro, OCD
Leopold Glueckert, O.Carm.
François-Marie Léthel, OCD
Stéphane-Marie Morgain, OCD
Emmanuel Renault, OCD
Federico Ruiz, OCD
Raymond Zambelli, rector of the basilica of Lisieux

Photographs:
Philippe Bannier: 32, 61, 62, 100
Edizioni San Paolo/Archivio: 106
Edizioni San Paolo/Max Mandel: 89, 94, 196
Felici: 190
Nils Loose/Cerf: 159, 180, 181, 184, 189
Office Central de Lisieux: 3, 8, 9, 10, 11, 14, 17, 38, 39, 63, 78, 114, 133, 139, 140, 141, 142, 163, 164, 165, 166, 167, 168, 169, 170, 171, 172, 173, 174, 183, 185

The authors express their lively and fraternal gratitude to the Discalced Carmelite nuns of the Lisieux monastery and to the Oblate Sisters of St. Thérèse, custodians of the Saint's birthplace in Alençon and of Les Buissonnets in Lisieux, for their sisterly contribution to the realization of this work.

General Editor of the English Language Translation: Steven Payne, OCD

Translators:
Susan Conroy (chaps. 1, 6, 7, 11)
John Grennon, OCD (introduction, boxed materials)
Kieran Kavanaugh, OCD (chaps. 8, 10, captions, conclusion, boxed materials)
Steven Payne, OCD (bibliography, chronology, boxed materials)
Salvatore Sciurba, OCD (chaps. 13, 14, boxed materials)
Kathryn Sullivan, RSCJ (chaps. 2, 3)
Mary Wogsland, OCD (chaps. 4, 5, 9, 12)

English Language Edition:
Copyright © Washington Province of Discalced Carmelites, Inc., 1997.

Italian Language Edition:
© Il Messaggero del Santo Bambino Gesù di Praga, Piazza Santo Bambino, 1, 16011 Arenzano (Genoa)
© Edizioni San Paolo s.r.l., 1996, Piazza Soncino, 5 20092 Cinsello Balsamo (Milan)

ICS Publications
2131 Lincoln Road, NE
Washington, DC 20002
800-832-8489

Library of Congress Cataloging-in-Publication Data

Teresa di Lisieux. English.
 Saint Thérèse of Lisieux: her life, times, and teaching / edited by Conrad De Meester;
preface, Cardinal Danneels; conclusion, Cardinal Ballestrero; photography, Girolamo Salvatico.
   p. cm.
 Includes bibliographical references.
 ISBN 0-935216-61-8
  1. Thérèse, de Lisieux, Saint, 1873–1897. 2. Christian saints—France—Lisieux—Biography.
3. Lisieux (France)—Biography I. De Meester, Conrad. II. Title
 BX 4700.T5T4413 1997
 282'.092—dc21   96–52134
 [B]   CIP

Table of Contents

Preface (Godfried Cardinal Danneels) 5

Introduction (De Meester, Salvatico, Giordano) 7

Abbreviations 8

Chapter 1:   **The Child of Louis and Zélie** (Conrad De Meester, OCD)...................9
     Catholic France in Thérèse's Time (Stéphane-Marie Morgain, OCD,
          and Leopold Glueckert, O.Carm.) 21
     Point d'Alencon (Guy Gaucher, OCD) 26
     Thérèse's Family Tree 34
     Thérèse Speaks: The Happy Days of Childhood 38
     Thérèse Speaks: Springtime Story of a Little White Flower 38

Chapter 2:   **Childhood in Lisieux** (Guy Gaucher, OCD) 39
     Les Buissonnets (Guy Gaucher, OCD) 50
     "Poor Léonie" (1863–1941) (Guy Gaucher, OCD) 53
     Thérèse Speaks: Family Life 67
     Thérèse Speaks: I Choose All 67

Chapter 3:   **Thérèse as a Young Laywoman** (Guy Gaucher, OCD) 69
     Thérèse Speaks: Toward the Eternal City 92

Chapter 4:   **Thérèse and Her Carmelite Community** (Geneviève Devergnies, OCD) 95
     The Origins and Spirit of Carmel in France (Stéphane-Marie Morgain, OCD)...... 98
     The Lisieux Carmel (Geneviève Devergnies, OCD) 100
     Plan of the Lisieux Monastery (Drawing by Renzo Restani) 104
     The Two "Teresas," Mother and Daughter (Tomás Alvarez, OCD) 108
     Thérèse and Saint John of the Cross (Federico Ruiz, OCD) 114
     Thérèse Speaks: Suffering Opened Wide Its Arms to Me 118

Chapter 5:   **"Suffering Opened Wide Its Arms to Me"** (Geneviève Devergnies, OCD) 125
     A Day in Carmel (Geneviève Devergnies, OCD)... 131
     Thérèse's Reading Material (Geneviève Devergnies, OCD) 137
     Thérèse Speaks: Like a Little Child 140
     Thérèse Speaks: The Triumph of My King 140
     Thérèse Speaks: I Know No Other Means but Love 140

Chapter 6:   **The Discovery of the "Little Way"** (Conrad De Meester, OCD) 147
     Thérèse Speaks: The Apostolate of Prayer 154
     Thérèse Speaks: Maintain Love 154

Chapter 7: **The Offering to Merciful Love** (Conrad De Meester, OCD) 155
  Thérèse Speaks: Living On Love 163

Chapter 8: **Thérèse Listening to the Word** (Roberto Fornara, OCD) 173
  Thérèse Speaks: I Take Up Holy Scripture 182

Chapter 9: **Thérèse and Love of Neighbor** (Pierre Descouvemont) 183
  Thérèse Speaks: A Lamp on a Lampstand 196
  Thérèse Speaks: Luminous Beacon of Love 196

Chapter 10: **Apostle and Missionary** (Camillo Gennaro, OCD) 197
  Thérèse Speaks: To Our Lady of Victories 208

Chapter 11: **Thérèse and the Mystery of Mary** (François-Marie Léthel, OCD) 215
  Thérèse Speaks: Why I Love You, O Mary! 222

Chapter 12: **Thérèse in the Night of Faith** (Emmanuel Renault, OCD) 223

Chapter 13: **The Final Illness** (Guy Gaucher, OCD) 235
  The Léo Taxil — Diana Vaughan Affair (Guy Gaucher, OCD) 236
  The "Last Conversations" (Guy Gaucher, OCD) 239
  Thérèse Speaks: To Sing the Mercies of the Lord 246

Chapter 14: **Thérèse's Universal Influence** (Pierre Descouvemont and Raymond Zambelli) 255
  Thérèse's Parlor (Raymond Zambelli) 256
  The Basilica of Lisieux (Pierre Descouvemont) 258
  Relics (Raymond Zambelli) 259
  Thérèse Speaks: I Will Be More Useful in Heaven Than on Earth 265
  Thérèse Speaks: I Shall Be Able to Make Him Loved 265

Thérèse Today (Guy Gaucher, OCD) 266

Thérèse: A Motive for Hope (Anastasio Cardinal Ballestrero, OCD) 283

Bibliography 284

Chronology 286

Preface

GODFRIED Cardinal DANNEELS

All of our postmodern difficulties can be summed up in the single problem of hope. Can we still hope? On every street, behind every other door, lives someone who is troubled, if not actually desperate. In our time, hope is truly that "little girl" between her two big sisters (of whom Péguy spoke), who is having problems growing. Everywhere existential anguish is in the air.

For a long time everyone has recognized that the economic crisis alone can hardly account for this situation. The real problem lies elsewhere: it is not that the times are bad, but that the human soul is sick. Like astronauts in their space capsules, we grab hold of everything presented to us in order to keep our balance.

Who will teach us hope? Where can we find a model, someone who has gone before us through the darkness and the throes of death? Is there somewhere a "Doctor of Hope"?

Thérèse herself has said: "Ah! Despite my littleness, I would like to enlighten souls like the prophets, the doctors; I have the vocation to be an apostle" (B 3r). "I sense within myself the vocation of doctor" (B 2v).

She identified the way of hope: it is the way of holiness. Our depressed society can only be saved by the saints.

This little girl from Normandy lived in a bourgeois society seemingly unmarked by our modern problems. Yet she lived, in a few short years and far from the world, the entire drama of the century that was to follow. How little importance the daily setting has for great souls!

Thérèse progressively marked the way that goes from the naive faith of childhood to the torments of those whom God so loves that he tests them as gold in the fire. She discovered that the ways of love pass through suffering, that Bethlehem is found very near Jerusalem, that the Nativity grotto (as shown in icons) strangely resembles the black sepulcher, that the Child Jesus is also the Holy Face. By the choice of her name, "Thérèse of the Child Jesus and the Holy Face," she was forever identified with this mysterious shortcut between hope and suffering, between the crib and the cross.

Thérèse is the saint of hope. At a time when no one spoke of it, in a society where this theme was absent, Thérèse lived what so many would live after her: the night of unbelief of all anxious seekers, the night of those with bad faith or no faith. Thérèse was already "seated at the table of sinners" long before certain Catholic literature—of Bernanos, Mauriac, Graham Greene—would treat it in a way which has never since been equalled. The drama in this little Carmelite's soul reverberates in the souls of innumerable men and women, Christians and unbelievers alike. Thérèse's drama was nothing less than a prophecy at the dawn of this century of things to come.

She lived the drama in her soul within the silence of her Carmel. She never drew attention to herself as someone to be noticed. There was nothing theatrical, pathetic, or spectacular in her life, not even enough to write an obituary that would interest readers in other Carmels, according to her Sisters. Thérèse climbed her own Mount Carmel anonymously. She was satisfied to be, without wanting to be seen. She let God take care of disclosing the secret of her little way. She was and remained a "child."

Her dreams were immense, however, and her gaze limitless. Within this little Carmel of Lisieux, she embraced the whole church, all missionary lands, all times, and all people—saints and sinners alike. For the one who loves embraces all. The measure of love is without measure, according to St. Bernard's beautiful saying.

Thérèse is certainly a saint of faith. Through the thick darkness of her nights, she clung to the naked word of God. She is also a saint of love, for according to her own testimony, she chose love in order to be at the heart of the church.

Yet she is first and foremost the saint of hope. Certainly faith, hope, and charity are the three great sisters that cannot do without each other. Faith sees what already is, hope sees what is yet to come. Charity loves what already is, hope puts its trust in what is not yet here. But for our times, isn't hope the greatest virtue? And the most necessary? And the rarest?

In Péguy's "Le porche du mystère de la seconde vertu," God says that "faith does not surprise me so much" because "I am so evident in my creation." Love, we might add, should not astonish God either; God might say that if we love each other, it is entirely to our advantage. "What surprises me," God says, "is hope." It is the least obvious of the three. It has the greatest need of being cultivated, for it is only a little girl that needs to grow.

Hope is essential. It is not found somewhere at life's margins. It is its heart muscle, the miocardia. If it stops, we die.

This fine book on Thérèse is like a Christmas tree. In the wintertime of our era, it reminds us that nature remains green, looking forward to the colors of spring and the abundance of summer. Go through this book, look at it, read it: it bears the colors of hope.

Godfried Cardinal Danneels
Archbishop of Malines-Brussels

Introduction

A century has passed since Thérèse Martin "entered into life" on September 30, 1897, the day of her death. For the love of Christ and the salvation of the human race, she left a comfortable situation in the bosom of a well-to-do family, to bury herself, so young, in the austere Discalced Carmelite monastery of her town, Lisieux.

Seed that fell to the ground, to disappear before bearing fruit. "To love is to give everything [and] to give oneself," sang Thérèse a few months before her death at the age of twenty-four. Apparently the fallen grain had completed its task. God alone would know its hidden fruitfulness.

Yet by a destiny exceptional in Carmelite history, the seed would spring up in plain sight. During the last months of her illness, Thérèse of the Child Jesus had a prophetic presentiment. In the infirmary, they brought her a spray of wheat. She took from it the fullest and most beautiful stalk, and said: "This ear [of wheat] is the image of my soul. God has entrusted me with graces for myself and for many others" (DE 4.8.3; HLC 131).

She spoke of a heavenly "mission" to accomplish, a "little way" to teach, of her desire to help priests and missionaries, to make Love loved. Ardently she begged the Lord to choose a legion of souls who would dare to believe without hesitation in God's ineffable mercy. In fact, Thérèse's influence has been extraordinary, and it is far from fading away.

This is why we must let Thérèse speak for herself. One of the many means, we hope, will be this Album, which tries through image and written word to place the experience and thought of this young saint in their developmental and historical context.

We have no wish to redo the work of Père François de Saint-Marie in his *Le Visage de Thérèse de Lisieux* (Lisieux: Office central de Lisieux, 1961) [*The Photo Album of Saint Thérèse of Lisieux,* reprint ed. (Westminster, MD: Christian Classics, 1990)]. Nor have we yielded to the temptation to imitate the admirable research of Pierre Descouvemont and Helmuth Nils Loose in *Thérèse et Lisieux* (Paris: Cerf, 1991) [*Thérèse and Lisieux* (Grand Rapids, MI: Wm. B. Eerdmans, 1996)] and *Sainte Thérèse de Lisieux: La vie en images* (Paris: Cerf, 1995). Rather, we wished to do what these authors expressly avoided: to illustrate the life of Thérèse and to clarify it with the help of a detailed study, following the thread of her life story. Thus we have conceived our work as complementary to theirs, in inner dialogue with these friends, and drawing upon the best experts. These three projects constitute a kind of trilogy.

Nevertheless, the initial idea came from within the Discalced Carmelite Order, with the encouragement of its Father General, Camilo Maccise, OCD. It is a very limited and sketchy tribute to our saintly little sister who for a century has been, for all our religious family and for the whole church, a sacrament of countless graces and an abyss of contemplation and apostolic inspiration. By herself, Thérèse no longer appears to us as a single well-laden stalk but as a vast field of wheat that feeds us abundantly. Thank you, Thérèse!

The Carmelite Province of Genoa (Italy) has especially borne this project. The friars of the Shrine of the *Infant Jesus* in Arenzano, with the illustrated magazine *Messaggero del Bambino Gesú di Praga,* felt prompted to offer this tribute to Thérèse of the *Infant Jesus.* This book takes its place alongside their previous albums on Saint Teresa, Saint John of the Cross [*God Speaks in the Night*], and *Carmel in the Holy Land,* whose respective editors (Tomás Alvarez, Federico Ruiz, and Silvano Giordano) all participated in this new work.

With all our hearts we thank the distinguished collaborators involved in this Album, the Carmelite nuns of Lisieux, and the publishing houses responsible for the versions in Italian, English, German, Spanish, Dutch, Polish, and Catalan.

Through the pages you hold in your hands, dear reader, may Thérèse continue speaking her words of grace to you, bringing to greater life the reality and beauty of Him whom she wished to honor in the humility of his childhood and the beauty of his face, radiant with mercy and fidelity.

Conrad De Meester, OCD
Girolamo Salvatico, OCD
Silvano Giordano, OCD

ABBREVIATIONS

All quotations from St. Thérèse are taken from ICS translations of the French critical edition of the works of St. Thérèse of Lisieux; their sometimes unusual punctuation follows Thérèse's own distinctive use of exclamation points, majuscules, emphases, suspension points, etc. Unless otherwise noted, the abbreviations and referencing system used in the ICS Publications volumes follow that of French critical editions. More complete bibliographical information appears at the end of this volume.

"Mgr." is an abbreviation for "Monseigneur," a French title of honor for members of the Catholic episcopacy (and thus not precisely equivalent to the word "Monsignor" in American usage). The term "Sisters" is used here to refer to religious women, some of whom in the Lisieux Carmel were also Thérèse's blood "sisters."

St. Thérèse's Writings

A, B, C: Thérèse's autobiographical manuscripts, ordinarily with indication of page number and recto or verso side. (C 3v, for example, refers to the verso side of the third page of manuscript C.) This referencing system is incorporated into the ICS Publications third edition of SS.

DE: *Derniers entretiens.* The numbers indicate day, month, and entry, e.g., DE 31.8.9 indicates the ninth saying on August 31.

DE II: Synopsis of DE published as *Dernières Paroles* (followed by date or page numbers).

HLC: *Her Last Conversations,* translated from DE (followed by page numbers in ICS Publications edition).

LT: Thérèse's *Letters.*
PN: Thérèse's *Poetry.*
Pri: Thérèse's *Prayers.*
RP: Thérèse's *Pious Recreations* (i.e., *Plays*).
SS: *Story of a Soul* followed by page number in ICS Publications edition.

Other Works Frequently Cited

CF: Zélie Martin's *Correspondance familiale.*
CSG: Sr. Geneviève's *Conseils et Souvenirs.*
MSG: Sr. Geneviève's *A Memoir of My Sister, St. Thérèse* (translation of CSG).
PA: Procès Apostolique, 1915–1917 (Rome, 1976).
PO: Procès de l'Ordinaire, 1910–1911 (Rome, 1973).

CHAPTER ONE

The Child of Louis and Zélie

CONRAD DE MEESTER, OCD

Alençon, 36 rue Saint-Blaise. It was June 25, 1874, a Thursday, and Zélie Martin had just met with her workers. She was the head of her "Point d'Alençon" business and every Thursday, when they went to the weekly market, the lacemakers brought their finished work—little pieces of lace about fifteen by twenty centimeters (roughly six by eight inches), which Zélie then had to assemble according to the sizes ordered by Parisian homes.

Zélie was as skilled at writing as she was at needlework, and in her leisure time she would write to her oldest daughters, Marie and Pauline, who were attending boarding school at the Visitation Convent in Le Mans, where her only sister, Marie-Louise Guérin, was a nun.

Five children was a lot. But too few! How Zélie would have cherished the two little boys and the two girls whom an early death had snatched away from her. Of the five remaining children, Marie and Pauline were respectively fourteen and thirteen years old, with very promising futures. Léonie, the third child, was eleven years old, and because of her unsociable and obstinate temperament, was the cause of unending worries. Then there was Céline, who was five, and Thérèse, the baby of the family, one and a half years old, the jewel of her mother's heart.

Zélie's heart was constantly with her children. One day the two youngest were playing in the garden with their Papa, her husband Louis. "Your Father just installed a swing," she wrote.

> Céline's joy knows no bounds. But you should see the little one using it; it's funny to see her trying to conduct herself as a big girl. There is no danger of her letting the rope go. When the swing doesn't go fast enough, she cries! We attached her to it with a rope, but in spite of this I'm still uneasy to see her perched so high. (A 5r)

Thérèse didn't share this worry. How could she? Wasn't her Papa, her "king," pushing her? She could feel his strong hands pushing too gently from behind with each return of the swing. And upsadaisy! Higher! She wanted to go even higher!

She was like that, this little one. Always wanting to go higher! One day she would compare holiness to a mountain top. Higher! Up to heaven, if possible! In their house on rue Saint-Blaise, the Martin family spoke often about heaven. It was the express purpose of their life. The Martins were a practical family in the long run. They were spiritual realists.

Louis smiled when he saw the joy and confidence of the baby, his ninth child. How much he agreed with what Zélie had written in her long letters to Marie and Pauline, or to her sister at Le Mans, and to her brother Isidore Guérin, who was a pharmacist in Lisieux. "She appears to be very intelligent. She will be beautiful and she is already graceful" (CF [*Correspondence familiale*, Office central de Lisieux, 1958] 117). She "is becoming more and more amiable, she babbles from morning to night" (CF 118). "She is very intelligent and we have quite amusing conversations. She already knows how to pray to the Good Lord" (CF 130).

Higher! Finally, little Thérèse grew weary, since she could never go as high as she would like. And suddenly, a whole new universe opened up before the eyes of her "warm and affectionate" heart (A 4v): her mother!

Louis the Pilgrim

She was right, Louis thought, to look for her mother. What a wife! How could he ever have imagined her sixteen years ago! He was thirty-five years old at that time and no longer considering marriage, being well settled in the single life.

He was born on August 22, 1823 in Bordeaux where the battalion of his father, Pierre Martin, was stationed. His father was a captain in the French army, and at the time of Louis's birth was stationed in Spain, where he was taking part in the Spanish campaign. The servicemen and their families were often on the move.

At four and a half years old, the young Louis was living on the other side of France, in Strasbourg. Then, at seven and a half, he reached Alençon, in his father's Normandy. Certainly he had studied under the Brothers of Christian Schools, but his studies seem to have been less those of an academic scholar than of a self-taught man who loved literature and learned German.

Louis Martin is above all known by his daughter Thérèse's description in her autobiography: a venerable and very pious old man who adored his children, was somewhat of a dreamer, and who lived off his investments. That was "Louis Martin II"! Louis Martin I, by contrast, was the young man who with perseverance and a gentle stubbornness made his way in life, patiently carried out a project, and earned his place in society. At nineteen years of age, he left Alençon and completed an extensive apprenticeship as a watchmaker, staying with relatives and friends: one year in Rennes, four years in Strasbourg, three years in Paris where he lived through the turbulent revolution of 1848, with the abdication of King Louis Philippe and the election of the president of the republic, Louis-Napoléon Bonaparte.

As the son of a serviceman, Louis was a man of order and duty, a courageous man always ready to intervene and to make decisions. "From an idea to its execution is not a long distance for me," he later wrote to his friend Nogrix. Meditative and deeply religious, he carried within him the dream of a monastic life. At the same time, all his life he had a taste for traveling. When he was twenty years old he visited the Great Saint Bernard Hospice (in the Swiss Alps), and at twenty-two he returned there asking for admission to the Order of Canons Regular of Saint Augustine. "I have always thought," his daughter Céline later shared,

> that in his attraction to the religious life, in his choice of the Great Saint Bernard to live in the heights far from the commotion of the cities, there was also an attraction to taking risks such as running to the help of travelers in distress on the glaciers.

Louis wasn't refused by the monks; they simply asked him to complete his studies. As a result, he was going to pursue Latin courses with a private tutor. After a year and a half, he stopped his difficult studies. He began to concentrate on his future as a watchmaker. At twenty-seven, in November of 1850, he purchased a house at 15 rue du Pont-Neuf in Alençon, where he set up a watchmaking and watch-repair shop, soon adding a jewelry shop. He brought his parents into his home; they had already lost three children, aged nine, twenty-five, and twenty-six years.

His business prospered. In seven years, he paid off all his debts and bought a piece of land at the edge of town that had a garden and a little hexagonal tower with a ground floor and two stories above. It was called the "Pavilion," and it became his place of prayer and reading. After work, his fishing parties, his meetings with friends from the Vital-Romet Club, the parish work, and daily Mass, this solitude seemed to offer all that his soul could desire.

But his mother had other plans. She was worried to see her single son alone and was anxious to marry him off. Was it she who proposed to him a marriage with Pauline Romet, a proposal that clearly ended up in a refusal because of the rather "liberal" ideas of the Romet family, as Céline would explain? In any case, Fanny Martin had better success on her second try. At the lacemaking school of Alençon, which she frequented while attending classes in her free time, she noticed Zélie Guérin, the diamond whom she insistently promoted to her son the jeweler.

This Strange, Blessed Marriage!

Filled with emotion, on Thursday, June 25, 1874, in his garden on rue Saint-Blaise, Louis smiled while remembering the past. Indeed, Zélie was different from the others! He had noticed it from their first arranged meeting: in Zélie, one couldn't go wrong. An energetic girl, with a clear heart, practical mind, and active hands, she was deeply Christian.

In keeping with her religious soul and her desire for an active devotion to the poor, one day (when she was eighteen or nineteen years old), Zélie asked for permission to enter the Daughters of Charity—the Sisters of Saint Vincent de Paul who consecrated their lives to God in serving the sick in hospitals at the Hôtel-Dieu of Alençon. The superior didn't recognize a vocation in her. Zélie didn't insist on it and took this to mean that her vocation was to become the mother of children whom, if God willed, she would consecrate to him. We read more than once in her later letters of this desire to have a "saint" among her children—particularly a priest, a missionary.

On July 13, 1858, in the Church of Notre Dame, at midnight (the custom was not uncommon at that time), Louis Martin, aged thirty-five years, and Zélie Guérin, who was twenty-seven, were united in marriage before God. They exchanged their vows of faithfulness that the ring symbolized, and exchanged their hearts in a first glance as bride and groom.

It seems incredible today, though it was certainly common with many young women of that era when sexuality was often surrounded by total silence: Zélie, with her scrupulously pure heart, in desiring to become a mother, didn't know the "facts of life."

It must have been a serious emotional shock to her when she learned of these realities of marriage. Louis proved to be tactful. By common consent and with a common ingenuousness, this married couple decided to live as brother and sister in a union of heart and prayer and by sharing their possessions. Hadn't they both dreamed in the past of a consecrated life? They were not looking for the ease of a tranquil life, however, and very soon they welcomed into their home on rue du Pont-Neuf a little boy from a very poor family. After ten months, the time of a long maturation, and after having spoken to a priest again, they decided to have many children: they ended up having nine of them.

We struggle to understand. It is so naive and beautiful at the same time. One the one hand, where is the logic of a marriage that Zélie had contracted in such an unprepared manner? On the other hand, what respect there was in the heart and body of Louis, what strength of soul in the waiting and renunciation. With their eyes fixed on God, they wanted to consecrate themselves to him, and it was in listening to the Lord that they made their decision to have many children. Thérèse, the ninth, saw the dimension of Providence who governed her birth: "It was He who had her born in a holy soil, impregnated with a *virginal perfume*" (A 3v).

Zélie the Generous

Almost twenty years later, just days after the death of her sister who was a nun at the Visitation Convent, whom they had visited on their wedding day and who fifteen days later had alluded to their "secret," Zélie remembered while writing to her daughter Pauline:

> Your father and I had similar inclinations; I even think that our mutual affection has grown. We always thought alike, and he has always been my comfort and my support. But when we had our children, our ideas changed somewhat. From then on we lived only for them; they made all our happiness and we would never have found it save in them. In fact, nothing mattered more to us; the world was no longer a burden to us. As for me, my children were my great compensation, so that I wished to have many in order to raise them for heaven! (CF 192)

Let us go back to little Thérèse, on that Thursday, June 25, 1874, getting tired of the swing and looking for her mommy, her world of warmth and security. "Here's our little Baby coming to stroke my face with her little hand and hug me," wrote Zélie.

> The poor thing never wants to leave my side, she is constantly with me. She loves going into the garden, but if I

am not here, she doesn't want to stay and she cries until someone brings her back to me. I am very glad that she is so fond of me, but sometimes it's inconvenient! Especially on Thursdays, when my workers come to bring their lacework!

Late in the evening, Zélie would still be writing to her sister-in-law in Lisieux, her beloved Céline Fournet who, after her marriage with Isidore, had become Madame Guérin:

> Thérèse is beginning to say almost everything. She is becoming more and more sweet, but this is not a small difficulty, I assure you, because she is continually around me and it's difficult to work! What's more, in order to make up for lost time, I continue my lacework until ten o'clock in the evening and I wake up at five o'clock. It's necessary for me to get up once or twice during the night for the baby. In short, the harder it gets, the better I feel!

Zélie loved her children. Thérèse, the ninth, was a great blessing. Two weeks before the birth of the baby, the happy mother confided to her sister-in-law:

> I am now waiting every day for my little angel. If God gives me the grace to be able to nurse her, it would be but a pleasure to bring her up. As for me, I love children to a fault; I was born to have them. (CF 83)

Expecting little Thérèse was like carrying deep music within her. Mother and child resounding in unison, she hardly dared to confess to her sister-in-law:

> While I'm carrying her, I have noticed something that never happened with my other children: When I sing, she sings with me. I tell you this in confidence, as no one would believe it! (CF 85)

Three years later, she wrote: "How happy I am to have her! I believe that I love her more than all the others, it is certainly because she is the youngest" (CF 158).

Zélie's Family

Having children to love consoled Zélie very much from her own unhappy childhood. She did not treat her own children as her mother had treated her. Three years after their marriage, Isidore Guérin, a serviceman, then a gendarme, and his wife, Louise-Jeanne Macé, daughter of a wheelwright, had a first child, Marie-Louise, the future Visitation nun. Two and a half years later, Zélie was born on December 23, 1831, almost a Christmas baby. Nine and a half years after that, the younger son, Isidore, was born. All the children were born in Saint Denys-sur-Sarthon, two kilometers (a mile and a quarter) northwest of Alençon. But in 1844, the family moved to Alençon, to 36 rue Saint-Blaise, where little Thérèse was born.

The *Summarium* (II, 91) of the Cause for Zélie's beatification describes the Guérin parents as follows:

> They were strongly marked types, both in their own way. They were rough, authoritative, hard to please. Contrary to what one would imagine, there was more kindness in the husband than in the wife, and the children born of their union were the first to feel the effects of this contrast. Moreover, the demanding will of the Guérin couple asserted itself in a fortunate way in their concern for moral integrity and religious fidelity. Great would be the influence of this in the education of their children.

There is no doubt: Zélie had suffered a lot from this "demanding will" of her parents. "Although she wanted one very badly," tells her daughter Céline, "never in her childhood did she have a doll, even the most little one. She suffered from frequent migraines that only added to the painful climate." It's true that the affections of Mother Guérin were geared more toward her oldest daughter and her son Isidore than toward Zélie.

Zélie, who would have loved so much to have owned a little doll, loved her brother Isidore very much. Ten years younger than she, he was like her only doll. Later, when Isidore, who had become a pharmacist, decided to set up his practice in distant Lisieux instead of nearby Le Mans where they could easily have visited and where their Visitandine sister already lived, Zélie allowed herself to complain bitterly—a complaint that did not interfere with her great happiness of being a mother. She wrote on November 7, 1865, to her independent brother:

> I am totally disappointed. I would have been able to see you in Le Mans and I would have treated myself to making little visits with you from time to time; it would have been a joy to me, to my laborious and monotonous life. But since you want this, we must give up everything; I have never had pleasure in my life, no, nothing that can be called pleasure. My childhood and my youth were shrouded in sadness because, while our mother spoiled you, she was much too severe with me, as you know; good as she was, she didn't know how to treat me, so I suffered very much in my heart.

If the details are hardly known, the obituary Circular of her religious sister outlined a familial atmosphere where the figure of the austere Madame Guérin dominated, "simple and a little bit rustic, but of a sturdy faith." What was said about Marie-Louise could also apply to Zélie. "A certain atmosphere of austerity, constraint, and scrupulosity" reigned in the family.

> The phrase "that's a sin" stopped the poor child [Marie Louise] in her strongest inclinations.… Madame Guérin, who taught her daughters this excessive fear of offending God, used to harp on the phrase "that's a sin" to curb their least imperfections. Marie-Louise worked a lot and played too little.

We are told in particular how the little Marie-Louise, in games or dances with the other children, "had feared to commit the grave sin of finding herself near a little boy; she would slip away trembling, as skillfully as possible, sometimes bringing malicious teasing upon herself because of what others interpreted as her wild temperament."

Given this climate, we can better understand the perplexity and reservations of her sister Zélie, who was so uninformed on her wedding night. The tact of her husband, his peaceful presence, and also a better understanding of the work of the Creator helped her to honor her marriage even in all its implications. Later the beauty of fruitful love and the joy of children would continue to make Zélie blossom.

Intuitions

Let's return again to Zélie's past. For some years, the financial situation of the retired gendarme's household was seriously compromised; the work of his daughters had to bring some relief. In 1848 (when Zélie was going to be seventeen years old) the house on rue Saint-Blaise went through some modifications in view of opening a little café on the ground floor and a billiard room on the second floor. While the retired man applied himself as an amateur to woodworking, his wife tended the café. The couple had hoped that this café would generate some much-needed supplemental income. But that didn't happen. Inclined by her strict character, Madame Guérin chided the customers. The patrons didn't find her moralizing remarks to their liking and went looking elsewhere for less austere places to relax (cf. *Summarium* II, 91).

Zélie seemed to have the gift of intuition, without being able to explain it herself. The facts are there. When she first turned twenty, she made a novena to the Immaculate Virgin to guide her in her choice of a profession; suddenly she knew clearly, on December 8, 1850, as if it had been dictated to her by the Mother of the family of Nazareth: "See to the making of Point d'Alençon." For her, December 8 would remain "a memorable day." "I obtained great graces twice on this day," she wrote (CF 16); "it's a great feast for me" (CF 147).

Zélie's idea was in fact not just to *make* "Point d'Alençon," which is among the most beautiful and refined lacework, but (at twenty years old!) to *see to the making*, that is, to employ other workers in her service and reserve for herself the assembly of different pieces, corrected as needed. "When necessary, [she] carried out the invisible joining of pieces, a task that is both the snare and the triumph of the craftswoman," wrote Fr. Piat (*Story of a Family* [New York: P. J. Kenedy & Sons, 1947], p. 36).

Her mother approved of Zélie's plan, on the condition, however, that the older daughter, Marie-Louise, manage the business. The young women didn't have any connections with the rich families of Alençon, in such a small city; therefore they had to find some outlets in Paris. After some tenacious proceedings, they gained the confidence of the Maison Pigache of which Zélie became the appointed supplier of Point d'Alençon. During the industrial Exposition of Alençon, Zélie received special praise from the jury for "the beauty" of her lace, "the richness of her designs," and "her intelligent direction." That was June 20, 1858. One month later Zélie got married.

The actual decision to marry was also made after an unusual intuition. Her children gathered confidence from it. One day while crossing the St. Leonard Bridge in Alençon, a bridge that runs over the Sarthe River, as she passed by a distinguished young man who was Louis Martin, Zélie's heart knew "that one" was chosen for her. Over the course of three months in the springtime, Zélie and Louis met each other, spoke to each other, assessed each other, and loved each other with a pure and deep love. They decided to unite their hearts and minds in a common destiny as yet unknown, which they believed to be willed and guided by God.

Once married, Zélie transferred her lace–making business to the home of her husband at 15 rue du Pont Neuf, where the Martin parents lived in the apartment on the first floor. By their zealous work, crowned with success, they were already comfortable enough. Louis owned his house with the garden as well as the little property, the "Pavilion"; in the watchmaking business, he earned 11,000 francs (approximately $75,000

American dollars at the beginning of 1995). Zélie brought approximately 5,000 francs as a dowry and as a result of her personal savings.

Happiness and Sorrow of the Parents

Oh, no! Zélie's children wouldn't suffer as she had suffered, she guaranteed it! But life dictated otherwise. The joyous expectation of the first baby blended with the sadness of the brief illness and death of Madame Guérin, on September 9, 1859.

The focus, however, was on the life that Zélie felt blossoming inside her for the first time. On February 22, 1860, Marie-Louise was born (named after Zélie's sister who, three days later, made her profession at the Visitation convent). The little one would be called "Marie" for short. All of Zélie's nine children would bear the name "Marie" as a first name. On September 7, 1861, little Pauline was born. Then on June 3, 1863, little Léonie. These first three children, whom she could breastfeed herself, lived to be eighty, ninety, and seventy-eight years old respectively.

Deep sorrow came when she could no longer manage adequately to feed her fourth child, Hélène, who was born on October 13, 1864, and for whom it was necessary to find a wet nurse. Already Zélie began to "suffer a little" from "a breast tumor" (CF 13) that would ultimately develop into a cancer of which she would die thirteen years later.

Let's look for a few moments at Zélie's maternal love for the baby who was away from home. Zélie wrote on January 12, 1865: "Little baby Hélène is growing very well, she is beautiful, like an angel. I am going to see her at the first of the year, I assure you that I miss her so much, I think of her continually. She has a good nurse, full of health" (CF 11). On March 5 she wrote:

Last Tuesday, I went to see my little Hélène. I set off alone at seven o'clock in the morning, in rain and wind

2

3

4

1. Lisieux. Carmel. Statue of St. Thérèse in the inside cloister.

2. Pond at Saint-Denis-sur-Sarthon. Zélie Guérin was born at Pont, a village situated in the township of Gandelaine and in the parish of Saint-Denis-sur-Sarthon.

3. Zélie Guérin (1831–1877), Thérèse's mother. A charcoal drawing by Céline Martin from a photo of her mother.

4. Saint-Denis-sur-Sarthon. Parish church, exterior.

5. Saint-Denis-sur-Sarthon. Parish church, interior.

6. Saint-Denis-sur-Sarthon. Baptismal font where Zélie was baptized on December 24, 1831, the day after her birth.

7. Saint-Denis-sur-Sarthon. Property of the Vital Romet family, visited by Thérèse at the age of ten (cf. A 32v).

5

6

7

8

9

10

11

12

13

8. Isidore Guérin (1789–1868), Zélie's father, former soldier of the gendarme.

9. Pierre Martin (1777–1865), Thérèse's paternal grandfather.

10. The three Guérin children. From left to right: Zélie (1831–1877), Isidore (1841–1909) and Marie-Louise (1829–1877), who became a Visitandine nun.

11. Thérèse's father Louis Martin (1823–1894) at the age of forty.

12. Hospice of the Great Saint Bernard, visited by Louis Martin in 1843 and in 1865.

13. Great Saint Bernard Pass.

14. Alençon. Louis Martin's jewelry and watchmaker's shop at 15 rue Pont-Neuf.

15. Alençon. Cathedral and typical houses.

16. Alençon. Pont Saint-Léonard on the Sarthe, where Zélie, encountering Louis by chance, had a definitive intuition of her marriage with him.

Catholic France in Thérèse's Time

Stéphane-Marie Morgain, OCD, and Leopold Glueckert, O.Carm.

Although the "big" French Revolution, which began in 1789, had ended long before Thérèse Martin's birth in 1873, it was anything but a distant memory. The Revolution had unleashed political, religious, and social concerns that persisted as hot issues during the lifetime of Thérèse, as indeed they still do.

The ideals of Liberty, Equality and Fraternity were good and noble. But they had also been accompanied by the excesses of the Reign of Terror, and a wave of ferocious anticlericalism. Legislation had swept away the privileged position and institutions of the French church: not just the complacent prince-bishops, but schools, religious orders, and a multitude of charitable organizations as well. When the monarchy was restored in 1815, Catholics hoped to re-establish the link between "altar and crown" that had existed before the revolution.

Fortunately for the church, the purging effects of the crisis had improved the quality of the clergy and renewed the vigor of many lay people dedicated to the service of others. A renewed sense of mission persuaded Catholic leaders to rebuild what had been lost, beginning with the sense of community that had always been the basis for the best works of mercy.

It is genuinely unfortunate that so many high-minded reformers outside the ranks of the church failed to note the healthy improvements in lay and clerical attitudes. For many critics of the restored monarchy, the church was still an antiquated symbol of superstition and misrule; it had to be totally destroyed if liberty were to be revived in the modern world. Throughout the rest of the nineteenth century, anticlericalism would continue to taint all dealings between Catholics and other Frenchmen. Conversely, most devout Catholics had come to associate the Revolution with terror, and the Republic with injustice. For them, freedom for the church required the protection of a monarch; even a bad king was better than none!

In the first years of the Restoration, there were two kings of the stodgy but safe Bourbon dynasty. Most devout people were content to worship freely once again, and there were few open disagreements within the Catholic community. But in 1830, a change of government provoked a debate between those who hoped to reconcile liberalism with Christianity, and those who felt the primary need was to defend the church from unjust assaults.

The so-called July Monarchy of King Louis-Philippe (1830–1848) coincided with the industrial revolution in France, and promoted rapid technical advancement. This development caused a growing polarization between an increasingly wretched caste of factory workers and a wealthy commercial class of investors and industrialists, dedicated to unrestrained development and profit. The primary supporters of the new government were bourgeois liberals. In their view, the church represented a curb on liberty and an outdated remnant of medieval morality. Their assault on surviving Catholic institutions was more subtle than in previous years, but just as dedicated and deadly. So after 1830, France suffered from a wave of anticlericalism that was especially strong in some country areas.

A movement of "social Catholics" arose to establish a social and democratic program to meet the liberals halfway. The republican Catholic newspaper *l'Ère nouvelle* attracted several noted figures. One was Frédéric Ozanam (1813–1853), who practiced self-denial and love of neighbor through the St. Vincent de Paul Society. Another was Henri Lacordaire (1802–1861), renowned Dominican preacher and head of the liberal Catholic movement with Charles de Montalembert (1810–1870). Félicité de Lamennais (1782–1854) founded the newspaper *L'Avenir* in 1830, and Philip Buchez (1796–1865) inspired Christian Socialism through his newspaper *L'Européen*.

Unfortunately, many Catholics saw their own liberal movement as a dangerous attempt to justify the godless elements of popular democracy. Pope Gregory XVI condemned Lamennais's ideas as too close to those who were violently anti-Catholic. Montalembert, on the other hand, was elected to parliament in 1837, and pressed the single issue of freedom for Catholic schools. By 1846, the Catholic party he had organized saw 140 deputies elected by the voters. Although another revolution in 1848 interrupted his plans, his perseverance led eventually to the Falloux Law, which allowed the foundation of separate Catholic schools.

The same year of 1846 saw the election of Pius IX, who succeeded Gregory XVI. Pius is the last pope who would rule the papal states, since the movement to unify Italy would soon wrest his provinces away by force. The so-called "Roman question" proved troublesome for France as well, since most French Catholics were convinced that the pope needed political freedom to remain truly impartial in the world arena.

After the Revolution of 1848, Catholics put their trust in Louis-Napoléon Bonaparte (1808–1873) because he promised to defend religious interests, educational freedom, and the freedom of the pope. On December 10, 1848 he was elected president of the Second Republic, supported by the Party of Order (monarchists and conservative republicans).

He allowed the conservatives in parliament to set the political tempo at first. France sent an expedition to

Rome in July 1849 to restore the Pope's temporal power, but did not really settle the Roman question. The Falloux Law finally granted the church freedom in secondary education, and would be modified in 1882 and 1896. There were limits placed on universal suffrage and the freedom of the press in May 1850.

The crisis of 1848 had allowed divisions to burst forth among the many currents of French Catholicism. Disputes arose between Montalembert and Lacordaire, and disagreements between *l'Ère nouvelle* and *l'Ami de la Religion* of Felix Dupanloup (1802–1878). Both the bishops and journalist Louis Veuillot (1813–1883) criticized the Falloux Law, which they considered too modest. After 1850, there were two strong tendencies within the Catholic community, with various intermediate blocs. One group strongly favored submission to the pope's leadership and reclaiming of church's rights; their vigorous spokesman was Veuillot and his paper *l'Univers*. The other group sought harmony between Catholic tradition and contemporary aspirations; Montalembert and Dupanloup were their most prominent leaders.

But much of the church's vitality had nothing to do with factional disputes. Numerous provincial councils allowed clergy to establish creative pastoral methods to counter religious indifference. Popular faith was energized by the rhythm of eucharistic processions, pilgrimages, and parish missions. Retreats for men became common, especially after 1871. Clubs and organizations for young people touched all levels of the population, such as the "Catholic Circle" which meant so much to Thérèse's father Louis. French Catholics nourished their spiritual life with readings from the Bible (which saw twenty editions between 1781 and 1850), the *Imitation of Christ,* and liturgical books, such as Dom Gueranger's *The Liturgical Year.*

Worried about social and religious preservation, many Catholics came out in favor of the new regime established by Louis-Napoléon's coup d'etat at the end of 1851. A new plebiscite and a new constitution allowed the restoration of the empire, proclaimed on December 2, 1852. Louis-Napoléon, now Napoléon III, began with a true dictatorship, pursuing a military policy in the Crimea and later in Italy in 1859, which drew hostility from the Catholics. Napoléon had stumbled into one of the century's insoluble problems. On one hand, he was committed to protect the pope's secular domain; on the other hand, he supported the unification of at least some of Italy's northern states. In the end, he released a tidal wave that both he and Pius failed to survive. After a tentative liberalization of the regime (1859–1860), Napoléon III tried to establish a parliamentary empire at the beginning of 1870, which produced fresh opposition.

During this time, diplomatic relations with Prussia continued to deteriorate. Napoléon III decided in July 1870 to declare war on Prussia. But his army was defeated and Napoléon himself was captured at Sedan (September 2, 1870), marking a milestone in Europe's history. The Second French Empire collapsed, a powerful Germany emerged and annexed the former French provinces of Alsace and Lorraine, and the Kingdom of Italy occupied Rome and what was left of the papal states. In the face of these events, the First Vatican Council, which Pope Pius IX had assembled in Rome on December 8, 1869, had to suspend itself in September 1870.

At the end of 1871, a starving and exhausted Paris accepted a truce. France held elections that gave a large majority to the conservatives, grouped around Louis-Alphonse Thiers (1797–1877). The Parisians revolted and set up the revolutionary Commune of Paris as an alternative government. The Commune was violently suppressed during the "Bloody Week" of May 22–28, with the loss of thousands of lives. Catholics were shocked by the violent anticlericalism that brought 10,000 Freemasons to Paris on April 29, 1871, to support the Commune and *écraser l'infâme,* i.e., "crush the infamy" (= the church). They were even more shocked by the hatred that pushed the Communards to shoot Archbishop George Darboy of Paris, along with fifty-three other clerics.

The disastrous loss of Alsace and Lorraine in 1870 aroused a chauvinistic patriotism which exalted national glory and grandeur. This atmosphere stirred national unity around the memory of Alsace-Lorraine during the first years of the Third Republic. Thiers was later turned out of office by the Assembly's conservative majority. He was replaced by army commander Patrice Mac-Mahon, who hoped to restore the monarchy. But republicans carried the elections twice in a row (1876 and 1877), and Mac-Mahon resigned out of frustration in January 1879.

Pope Leo XIII (1878–1903) tried every means to rally Catholics to the Republic. He certainly hoped for French diplomatic support, but he also understood that secularization was an established fact. The church simply could no longer embrace an anti-republican policy without harming evangelization. Cardinal Lavigerie's allocution in Algiers (December 12, 1890), and Leo XIII's direct interventions, show his genuine desire for a working relationship. The 1893 elections took place against the background of this attempted "Rallying" as well as a strong wave of socialist voting strength.

Within this fragile and ever-shifting political and social environment, Christian life still managed to flourish. There was plenty of fertile ground for worship, piety, devotion, publishing, and creative thought.

France's colonial empire, begun by Napoléon III, continued to grow under the Third Republic, and provided an impetus to the country's missionary enthusiasm. The expanding mission fields in Indochina were joined by impressive results in the islands of the Pacific. Thérèse was fascinated by the missionary congregations, and the work of the Propagation of the Faith promoted by Pauline Jaricot (1799–1862).

The teaching orders grew with the democratization of teaching, and the freedom effected by the Falloux Law. The encyclical *Rerum Novarum* promoted church involvement in workers' rights and social questions, as seen in the accomplishments of Léon Hamel, or the Saint Vincent de Paul Conferences. Jeanne Jugan (1792–1879), who founded the Little Sisters of the Poor, personified the dedication of so many Christians to the service of the impoverished.

Marian devotion in France was particularly rich, marked by apparitions scattered throughout the century: the Miraculous Medal, rue de Bac (1830), Our Lady of Victories (1836), La Sallette (1846), Lourdes (1858), and Pontmain (1871). Pius IX defined the dogma of the Immaculate Conception in 1854. Many new congregations were naturally placed under the Virgin's mantle. Louis-Marie Grignion de Montfort's *True Devotion to Mary* was in every hand.

Devotion to the Sacred Heart became a bone of contention between some Catholics opposed to the Republic and Freemasons who considered themselves enemies of the church. The appeal for France's consecration to the Sacred Heart represented a wish for the restoration of the monarchy (even if this desire was not universal), and for a renewal of the faith. The construction of the Sacré-Coeur basilica on Montmartre was a public penance by Catholic France to atone for the bloodshed of 1871, and to reconcile itself with God. "Save France in the name of the Sacred Heart." The many pilgrimages to Rome organized during this era expressed a hope for the restoration of the papal states. Thérèse made such a journey with her family in 1887.

This vital and flourishing spectrum of Christian life opened new and fresh horizons, all sustained by the silent prayers of contemplatives, those people who produce saints. Thérèse saw and understood the vitality of her beloved French church, with its many exciting ministries. Yet she, one frail individual, elected to make her own contribution as one of those robust contemplatives. Given the results, who can question the wisdom of her choice?

that accompanied me there and back. You can imagine how tired I was along the way, but I was encouraged by the thought of soon holding my treasure in my arms. She is a dainty little jewel, that little Hélène. She is enchantingly pretty. (CF 12)

Two weeks ago, I went to see the little one who is being nursed; I never remember experiencing such a thrill of happiness as when I took her into my arms, and she smiled at me so sweetly that I seemed to be looking at an angel. Really, I can't describe it. I don't think that I have ever seen, nor will I ever see again, such an enchanting little girl. O my baby Hélène, when will I have the happiness of possessing you entirely? I cannot believe that I have the honor of being the mother of such a delightful little creature! Oh! How I do not regret being married. (CF 13)

On June 26, 1865, grandfather Pierre Martin died. "He had a holy death," wrote Zélie, "and died as he had lived." As a presentiment of all that followed, she remained very moved:

I could never have imagined that this could affect me so much: I am overwhelmed. My poor mother-in-law spent her nights nursing him for two and a half months, without allowing anyone to help her.... I confess that I am terrified of death. I have just been to see my father-in-law. His arms were so stiff and his face so cold! And to think that I shall see my loved ones like that, or that they will see me! (CF 14)

And the maternities continued, one after the other! There was great joy, on September 20, 1866, at the birth of little Marie-Joseph, at last the boy who could become a priest and missionary. Alas, he too had to be entrusted to a wet nurse, a young farmer's wife in Semallé, a village ten kilometers from Alençon. Her name was Rosalie Taillé, whom the Martin family called "the little Rose," and to whom they would one day entrust their little Thérèse.

"I went to see my little Joseph," wrote the proud mother on November 18, 1866. "Oh! He is a lovely little boy, so big and strong! I could not wish for better. I have never had a child who has come along so well, except for Marie. Oh! If you knew how I love him, my darling little Joseph! I think my fortune is made!" (CF 19).

But what anguish soon came!

I had the happiness of seeing my little Joseph at the first of the year. As a New Year's gift, I dressed him like a little prince.... The next day at three o'clock in the morning we heard a very loud knock at the door; we got up to open it and someone said to us 'Come quickly, your little boy is very sick. They are afraid that he is dying.' You can be sure that I didn't take long to get dressed and get on my way to the countryside, on such a cold night, in spite of the snow and the thin coating of ice on the ground. I did not ask my husband to come with me, because I was not afraid and I would have crossed a forest alone, but he would not let me go without him. The poor little one had a severe erysipelas, and his face was in a pitiful state. The doctor told me that he was in great danger. In fact, I saw him already dead! But the Good Lord didn't have me waiting for a boy in order to take him away so soon, He wanted to leave him for me, he is now in full health. (CF 21)

Alas, one month later, on February 14, Zélie's and Louis's first son died. One can imagine the wound in these parents' hearts.

This would not be the only sorrow this household would experience. After a difficult birth and some constant sicknesses, a second son, another "Joseph" (Joseph-Jean-Baptist)—who was likewise entrusted for nursing to "little Rose"—died on August 24, 1868, at the age of eight months. "My dear little Joseph died this morning, at seven o'clock," wrote Zélie to her brother. "I was alone with him. He had a night of cruel suffering and I asked with tears for his deliverance" (CF 36). Nine days later Monsieur Guérin died, the retired gendarme, Zélie's papa.

> My heart is broken with grief and, at the same time, filled with heavenly consolation. If you knew in what holy dispositions he prepared himself for death!… His grave will be very near those of my two little Josephs. (CF 38)

On April 28, 1869, the seventh child, Céline (the future Sr. Geneviève) was born. But, to the deep anguish of Zélie and Louis, their little Hélène died unexpectedly on February 22, 1870. She was only five years and four months old.

> As soon as I held her, her little head fell on my shoulder, her eyes closed, then five minutes later she was dead. That left an impression on me which I will never forget. Neither I nor my husband expected this sudden end. When he came in and saw his poor little daughter dead, he burst out sobbing and crying 'My little Hélène! My little Hélène!' Then together we offered her to God…. I dressed her myself and laid her in her coffin. I thought I was going to die then and there, but I did not want others to touch her. (CF 5)

> There is not a moment of the day when I do not think of her…. Indeed, she is in heaven and much happier than here below, but for me, it seems as though all my happiness has flown away. (CF 54)

In the midst of all this, Zélie became newly pregnant. The death rate was a merciless scourge in an era when medicine had not yet taken wing, and this first little Thérèse (Marie-Mélanie-Thérèse), who was born August 16, 1870, died fifty-three days later. Nine months after this death for which "she could never console herself," Zélie wrote "I will be so happy to have another," and this other child will be called "Thérèse, like my last little one" (CF 85).

And the trials didn't stop. Even in the last months of her life, Zélie was filled with worries about her little Léonie, the child who was different from the others, less gifted, the little "ugly duckling" who avoided all good counsel: the one and only Léonie, the unexpected, who later, after three failed attempts at religious life, became a religious at the Visitation Convent, where she lived to perfection the "little way" that Thérèse had taught her.

In the Confidence of Each Day

The year 1870 was very upsetting for the Martin family. The death of little Hélène. The birth and death of little Mélanie-Thérèse. The sale of Papa's watchmaking business to his nephew Adolf Leriche, who had come into a rich inheritance. The ensuing series of worries about the move (in July 1871) from 15 rue Pont-Neuf to 36 rue Saint-Blaise. The Franco-German War with the occupation of France. Louis was ready to defend his country:

> It is still quite possible that men between the ages of forty and fifty will have to go. I am almost expecting as much. My husband isn't upset at all. He wouldn't ask for exemption and often says that if he were a single man, he would soon join the sharpshooters. (CF 62)

There was the constant threat of an invasion at Alençon by the Prussians, who were effectively occupying the city in January 1871. They were: "25,000 in number. I couldn't describe our anxieties to you…. My husband is upset; he can neither eat nor sleep." The Martins had to lodge nine Prussian soldiers in their home, "not malicious, nor pillagers," but horribly "gluttonous like I have never seen, they eat everything without bread. They swallow a mutton stew like soup" (CF 110).

At a distance, we can smile. For the Martins, it was a continuous worry, transformed only by "the firm confidence that they were supported from on high" (CF 65). The political events in the country deeply upset these benevolent and sincere Catholics: "All that is happening in Paris," wrote Zélie on May 29, 1871, "fills my soul with sorrow, I have just learned of the Archbishop's death and of the sixty-four priests who were shot yesterday by the Communards. I am utterly dismayed" (CF 66).

If the family didn't know poverty ("We have more than what is necessary to live and raise our children well; besides, I will continue the Point d'Alençon" [CF 54]), their material worries were never lacking. They were inherent in the business that must "keep going" to avoid losing one's place; inherent in the sicknesses of the children, in problems of education, in the future of these five little girls whom Louis and Zélie scarcely encouraged to enter the convent and for whom it was necessary to prepare a future dowry.

But worries and efforts were integrated by the Martins in a profoundly Christian way. Abandonment to God and trust in God's providence, daily prayer and church fasts, keeping the Sabbath holy and the liturgical life, honesty in business and esteem for their workers, aid to the deprived and solid commitment to the disadvantaged; all this was sacred to them.

And in 1872 they were awaiting their ninth baby, the first to be born in the house on rue Saint-Blaise facing the prestigious Prefecture where Thérèse would later go to play with Genny Bechard, "the Mayor's little daughter" (cf. A 9v). Here also she would take her first family walks across to the parish church of Notre Dame, to the convent of the Poor Clares on rue de la

Demi-Lune, and to the train station where Marie and Pauline would come and go while they were boarding students at the Visitation Convent at Le Mans. A little later, the family excursions would go toward the surrounding villages and to the Pavilion, where Papa relaxed and enjoyed fishing in the Sarthe River while Thérèse looked for strawberries. But let's not anticipate too much.

The Little Flower Threatened

What a blessing when, on January 2, 1873 at 11:30 P.M., two and a half years after Mélanie-Thérèse died, this other Thérèse was born, arriving like a gift, a last fruit of their mutual love. Louis was in his fiftieth year, while Zélie was about to begin her forty-second year ("the age when one is old enough to be a grandmother" [CF 83]), and she already counted on "having no more" children (CF 66). Thus it was a gift and at the same time a "surprise, because I was expecting to have a boy. I imagined this for two months, because I felt very much that this child was stronger than my other children" (CF 84). How Zélie had prayed for her little boy to become a good priest, a good missionary!

On January 3, 1873, Marie-Françoise-Thérèse was baptized at the Church of Notre Dame. Her older sister Marie was the godmother, and the young son of a family friend, Paul-Albert Boul, was the godfather, both aged thirteen. (Thérèse's godfather died six years later.) A child who was apparently "very strong" (CF 84–85), "beautiful," and who "already smiled" after twelve days (CF 85), Thérèse was "always cheerful" and "good natured" (CF 88).

The new happiness always present at the birth of a child was soon eaten away by "a continual agony. I doubt that Purgatory could be worse than this" (CF 89). When Mélanie-Thérèse died through the fault of "her unworthy nurse" who left her "to die of hunger," Zélie

Point d'Alençon

Bishop Guy Gaucher, OCD

The production of the lacework known as "Point d'Alençon" began in Alençon around 1664, under the administration of Colbert. The minister brought some thirty clothworkers from Venice to launch the enterprise.

Point d'Alençon is made with extremely fine threads of flax, using barely perceptible needles matching the thread. It is made entirely by hand.

This lacework is made out of pieces roughly six by eight inches, on a green parchment perforated according to the design to be reproduced, and lined with linen. One begins by making the outline of the work on the parchment, using projecting threads. The various stitches ("points") of the design are then executed over the outline. There are nine different stitches; each piece including these stitches (not all designs have them) must pass successively through the hands of nine lacemakers, each a specialist in one of the stitches. They all work at home, and one of them is the assembler, responsible for joining all the finished pieces together in a way that makes the connection invisible. This is the most difficult part. But before beginning the assembly, it is necessary to detach the piece, and once finished, to cut from the reverse side the numerous threads attaching it to the outline, then to lift the lacework carefully. With the same care, one must remove the unnecessary threads, and also pull away, with pincers, the ends of the threads still hooked to the parchment, in order to be able to reuse the same design.

In Alençon there were professional schools to teach the young women the different stitches. In the boarding schools and academies, courses were given for the same purpose, to develop this industry that made the city's reputation. Unfortunately, because the cost of the handwork required too high a sale price, this remarkable lacework had to be greatly simplified.

In running her business, Madame Martin hired the workers, distributed the work, and controlled it; she personally worked the netting, skillfully repairing the tears inevitably produced in the course of all the aforementioned handling, and taking on the role of assembler as needed.

Monsieur Martin was very artistic, and so his role was to choose the designs and arrange to have them done tastefully. This required frequent trips to Paris, where he also took care of supplies and orders placed by the shops. In addition, he reserved to himself the perforation of the designs into the parchment, very hard work, done over a cushion with a specially mounted needle.

---

told herself "never again." The children yet to come "would not leave the house" (CF 61). She thus tried to breastfeed her new infant, but fearing that this wasn't sufficient, she tried to "make use of a feeding bottle," after which "it was impossible to make her return to breast-feeding."

At first, Thérèse "drank perfectly" (CF 85). But at the end of February she suffered "from enteritis," and was "very pale" (CF 88). On March 11, Doctor Belloc's orders were explicit: "It was necessary to breast-feed this infant immediately, only this could save her." Louis was on a trip. At daybreak, Zélie left for Semallé to look for "little Rose," the nurse who "suited them in everything." She had earnestly wished that Rose would come to live temporarily at their house, but she was only allowed to stay with the Martins for "eight days"—that is, if the child even survived. They departed for Alençon.

When Rose saw Thérèse, she shook her head: all was lost. The child was doomed and it looked as though the end was near. Zélie went up to her room to pray before the statue of Saint Joseph. When she came back down again, she could hardly believe her eyes: "The child was feeding greedily," but then she lay "like one dead on the nurse's lap." "I felt my blood grow cold," wrote Zélie, "the baby did not seem to be breathing." After a quarter of an hour, "my little Thérèse opened her eyes and began to smile" (CF 89). Saved! But she had to resign herself to seeing her baby leave again with the nurse.

The Little Peasant of Semallé

Thérèse slowly recovered while remaining susceptible to colds. For more than a year, she lived in the country in the humble cottage of Moyse and Rosalie Taillé, together with their four children (of which one, Eugene, was the "foster-brother" of Thérèse), the cow named "Rousse" (Redskin) and the

17. Thérèse Martin at age three. Her mother writes: "The little one was afraid of the photographer [covered by the black veil]. She who is always smiling pouted as though ready for tears; we had to reassure her" (CF 164).

18. Alençon. 36 rue Saint-Blaise. Thérèse's birthplace.

19. Alençon. Bedroom of Thérèse's parents, where she was born and Zélie died.

20. Alençon. Thérèse's birthplace. Hall and staircase.

21. Alençon. Thérèse's birthplace. Louis Martin's desk.

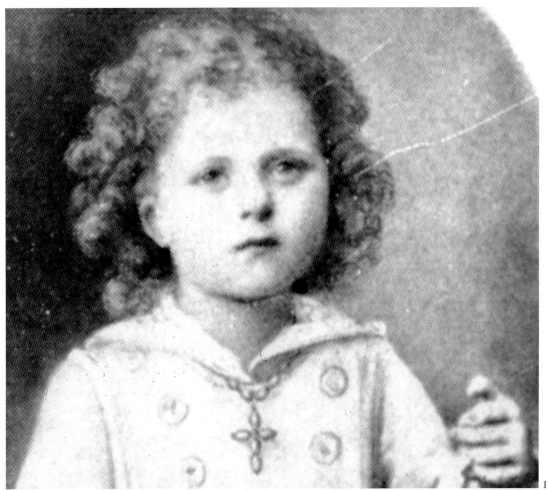

17

18

19

20

22. Alençon. Thérèse's birthplace. A clock repaired by Louis Martin.

23. Alençon. Thérèse's birthplace. Louis Martin's eyeglasses.

24. Alençon. Thérèse's birthplace. Louis Martin's binoculars.

25. Alençon. Thérèse's birthplace. Zélie Guérin's work table.

26. Alençon. Thérèse's birthplace. Alençon lace and Zélie's work tools.

27–28. Alençon. Thérèse's birthplace. Samples of Alençon lace.

29. Alençon. Church of Notre-Dame, where Louis and Zélie were married and Thérèse was baptized. Baptismal font.

30. Alençon. Church of Notre-Dame. Stained-glass window depicting Thérèse's baptism.

21

22

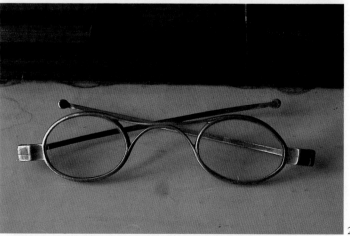

23

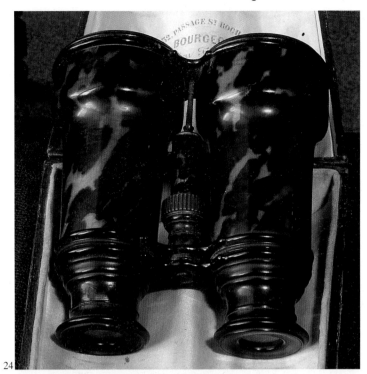

24

25

26

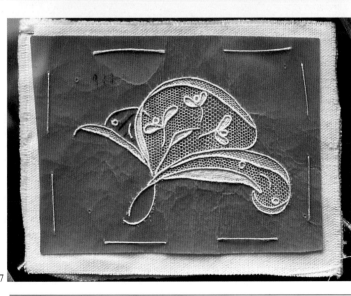

27

28

29

30

THÉRÈSE PRIANT
SUR LES GENOUX DE SA MÈRE

31

32

33

31. Alençon. Chapel at Thérèse's birthplace. Fresco of Thérèse in her mother's arms.

32. Semallé. Parish church. Stained-glass window of St. Thérèse. On the upper right is a cow representing "Rousse" (Redskin), on whose back the wet nurse Rose Taillé sometimes placed little Thérèse.

33. Semallé. The house of Moyse and Rose Taillé, Thérèse's wet nurse. Inset pictures of Moyse and Rose Taillé drawn by Renzo Restani from a photo of the time.

34. Alençon. The prefecture, in front ot the Martin house.

35. The Pavilion, acquired by Louis Martin before his marriage.

36. Sées. Basilica of Notre-Dame de l'Immaculée Conception, pilgrimage site for the Martins.

37. Alençon. Chapel at Thérèse's birthplace. Fresco of the death of Zélie Guérin (1877).

38. Thérèse with her mother. Painting by Céline Martin.

34

35

36

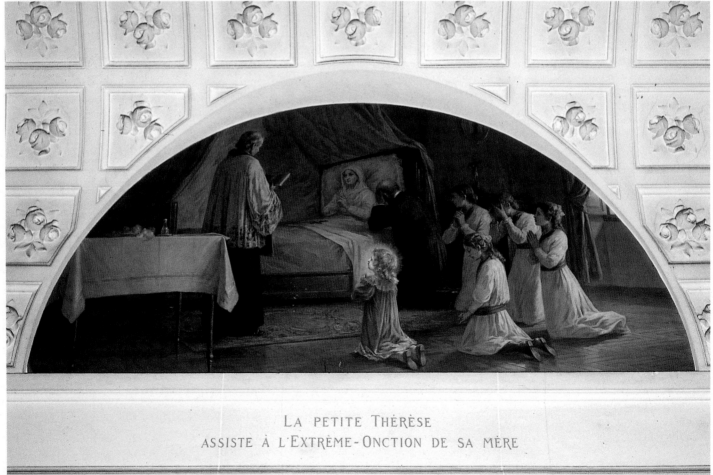

LA PETITE THÉRÈSE
ASSISTE À L'EXTRÊME-ONCTION DE SA MÈRE

37

38

Thérèse's Family Tree

A. Paternal Branch

Grandfather: Captain Pierre-François Martin, born in Athis-de-l'Orne (Orne) on April 16, 1777; married in Lyon on April 4, 1818;.died in Alençon on June 26, 1865.

Grandmother: Marie-Anne-Fanie Boureau, born in Blois on January 12, 1800; died at Valframbert (Orne) on April 8, 1883.

Their Children:

1) Pierre Martin, born at Nantes on July 29, 1819; disappeared in a shipwreck (date unknown).

2) Marie-Anne Martin, born in Nantes on September 18, 1820; married to François-Marie Burin on October 8, 1838; died in Argentan on February 19, 1846.

3) **Louis-Joseph-Aloys-Stanislaus Martin** (Thérèse's father), born in Bordeaux on August 22, 1823; married to Zélie Martin on July 13, 1858 in Alençon; died in Saint-Sébastien-de-Morsent (where the estate of La Musse is located) on July 29, 1894.

4) Anne-Françoise Fanny Martin, born in Alençon on March 10, 1826; married on March 11, 1842, to François-Adolph Leriche (who died on May 25, 1843); remarried on February 26, 1849, to her brother-in-law, François-Marie Burin (by then a widower); died in Fécamp on October 9, 1853.

5) Anne-Sophie Martin, born in Alençon on November 7, 1833; died on September 23, 1842.

Thérèse knew none of her paternal aunts and uncles, and knew her paternal grandmother only until the age of six.

B. Maternal Branch

Grandfather: Isidore Guérin, born in Saint-Martin-l'Aiguillon (Orne) on July 6, 1789; married in Pré-en-Pail on September 5, 1828; died in Alençon on September 3, 1868.

Grandmother: Louise-Jeanne Macé, born in Pré-en-Pail on July 11, 1804; died in Alençon on September 9, 1859.

Their Children:

1) Marie-Louise-Pétronille Guérin, born in Gandelain on May 31, 1829; died as a Visitation nun (Sr. Marie-Dosithée) in Le Mans on February 24, 1877.

2) **Azélie-Marie (Zélie) Guérin** (Thérèse's mother), born in Gandelain on December 23, 1831; married in Alençon to Louis Martin on July 13, 1858; died in Alençon on August 28, 1877.

3) Marie-Victor-Isidore Guérin, born in Gandelain on January 2, 1841; died on September 28, 1909. In Lisieux on September 11, 1866, Isidore married Elisa (Céline) Fournet, born in Lisieux on March 15, 1847; died in Lisieux on February 13, 1900. Their children were:

    1) Jeanne, born in Lisieux on February 24, 1868; married to Francis La Néele (1858–1916) on October 1, 1890. They had no children.

    2) Marie, born in Lisieux on August 22, 1870; entered the Lisieux Carmel (becoming Sister Marie of the Eucharist); died on April 14, 1905.

    3) Paul, born dead in Lisieux on October 16, 1871.

C. Thérèse's Brothers and Sisters

1) Marie-Louise, born on February 22, 1860; entered the Lisieux Carmel (becoming Sister Marie of the Sacred Heart); died on January 19, 1940.

2) Pauline, born on September 7, 1861; entered the Lisieux Carmel (becoming Sister, and then Mother, Agnes of Jesus); died on July 28, 1951.

3) Léonie, born on June 3, 1883; entered the Visitation convent at Caen (becoming Sister Françoise-Thérèse); died on June 16, 1941.

4) Hélène, born on October 13, 1864; died on February 22, 1870.

5) Joseph-Louis, born on September 30, 1866; died on February 14, 1867.

6) Joseph-Jean-Baptiste, born on December 19, 1867; died on August 24, 1868.

7) Céline, born on April 28, 1869; entered the Lisieux Carmel (becoming Sister Geneviève of the Holy Face); died on February 25, 1959.

8) Mélanie-Thérèse, born on August 16, 1870; died on October 8, 1870.

9) Marie-Françoise-Thérèse, born on January 2, 1873; entered the Lisieux Carmel on April 9, 1888 (becoming Sister Thérèse of the Child Jesus and the Holy Face); died on September 30, 1897.

All of the Martin children were born in Alençon at 15 rue du Pont-Neuf, except Thérèse who was born at 36 rue Saint-Blaise. All carried "Marie" as a first name.

fowls. Her stay in the country included one springtime, a summer, an autumn, a winter, and the beginning of another spring. Familial gaiety, the cries of children, the singing of birds and wind, the scenery and scent of fruits, flowers, grass, and animals, little walks to the parish church in the arms of Rose. In the summertime, the little "Martin-Taillé" was sunburnt as she was wheeled in a wheelbarrow into the fields, carried on top of bundles of grass. Sometimes they would even mount her on the back of Rousse, the cow!

We gather most of these details from the letters of Zélie, the mother at a distance, who visited her little one almost every two weeks, her heart filled with a thousand thoughts and sentiments ("I have already suffered much in my life," she said after Thérèse's departure [CF 90]). Or sometimes it was Rose who brought the baby to Alençon, for the weekly market where she sold her produce.

While Thérèse must have felt deeply attached to the house of her birth, to her Mama and Papa, and to her young sisters, she was also strongly attached to "little Rose," whom she undoubtedly called "Mama," like the other children. This is clear from passages in Zélie's often amusing letters.

> We saw little Thérèse last Sunday. We weren't expecting her; the nurse arrived with her four children. She put the baby in our arms and left immediately to go to Mass. Yes, but the little one didn't want that at all, and she cried uncontrollably! All the house was upset by it. We had to send Louise [the servant of the house] to beg the nurse to return immediately after Mass…. The nurse left in the middle of Mass and came running; I was not pleased about that, as the baby wouldn't die of crying. In the end, at last, she was instantly consoled; she is very strong, everyone is surprised by it. (CF 99—Thérèse was four months old.)

> We will go by carriage to see little Thérèse next Monday; she is doing so well right now. I saw her last Thursday, her nurse brought her, but she didn't want to stay with us and threw herself into a fit of tears when she didn't see

her nurse. So, Louise had to carry her to the market where little Rose was selling her butter, as there was no other way of keeping her here. As soon as she saw her nurse, she looked at her laughing, and then didn't make another sound; she stayed like that all day, while her nurse sold her butter with all the good country women, until noontime! (CF 102—Thérèse was almost six months.)

Thérèse had become a little country girl and her tastes were conformed to that lifestyle! Here was her reaction when, at the age of eleven months, she spent some time in her house in the town of Alençon.

> The baby wanted neither to look at Louise nor to go with her, I was very upset by it; my workers came to me at each instant, I entrusted her to them, one after another. She was very willing to see them, even more so than I, and kissed them repeatedly. The working women who were dressed like her "Little Rose" were all the society she wanted! A lady with fancy clothes came into the room while one of the workers was holding her. As soon as I saw her, I said to her: "Let's see whether the baby will want to go with you." Completely surprised, she replied: "Why not? Yes, let's try!"… She held out her arms to the little one, but the baby hid her face, crying out as if she had been burnt. She would not even let Madame T. look at her. We had a good laugh at that; in short, she is afraid of people dressed fashionably! (CF 112.

"I reason with myself," wrote Mama:

> …and try to master the feeling. I am with you in spirit all day and I tell myself: "Now you are doing such-and-such a thing." I long so much to be with you; I love you with all my heart, and I feel my affection doubled by being deprived of your company; it seems impossible for me to live apart from you. (CF 108)

It was not to Thérèse, but to her "dear Louis," that Zélie addressed these words, from Lisieux where she was visiting her brother Isidore and her sister-in-law, while Thérèse was in Semallé. Louis was this "saintly man" with whom she was "always very happy." He "made [her] life very sweet," he was a husband such as she "wished every woman had." Since this confession after four and a half years of married life (LT 1) nothing had changed even eleven years later, but how much she desired to "become a saint, which will not be easy; there is much to burn up and the wood is as hard as stone" (CF 110).

They "longed to have their little Thérèse at home" (CF 114). A second time the child's homecoming was intensely awaited. Zélie set out everything in blue and white, as for a new birth and a new baptism. "I already have a sky-blue dress planned for her to wear, with little blue shoes, a blue sash and a pretty white bonnet. She will be charming. I am rejoicing in advance in dressing this little doll!" (CF 115). Thérèse eventually returned home, on the second of April, 1874: "a delightful child," "very sweet and very advanced for her age" (CF 116), "I admire her little mouth" (CF 117).

"A Little Girl Not Without Faults"

Very sweet? We need to look again. The child had certainly experienced a new period of uprooting, this time from Semallé and from her "little Rose;" but she quickly rediscovered her Martin roots in reattaching herself strongly to her mother: we recall the pages where Zélie, herself strongly attached to the "little baby," described her sitting on the swing or "stroking her mother's face with her little hand" (CF 119). But at other moments Thérèse also showed herself to be capable of "frightful furies" (CF 147), and she "would break everything" that was a little delicate (CF 125). At the age of three, "the little imp" who was "so heedless" proved that "her stubbornness was almost unconquerable" (CF 159). And her cute "little mouth" could cry to the point of "suffocating" (CF 147).

Her tenderhearted mother would go so far as to say the "little imp who is the joy of all the family" (CF 157) had "a choice nature" (CF 195) and a "little angelic nature" (CF 201). But later the Saint would discern "excessive self-love" in a "nature such as my own."

"How far I was from being a faultless little child!" (A 8r–v). Besides this, pointing out her "love of the good" ("It was enough for one to tell me a thing wasn't *good* and I had no desire to repeat it twice" [A 8v]), she agrees implicitly with her mother's praise of the "heart of gold" (CF 159) of her youngest daughter, who "would not tell an untruth for all the gold in the world" (CF 195).

Thérèse was also a fine observer who grasped the meaning of life. She listened "very attentively" (A 4v, 17v). "Without appearing to do so, I paid close attention to what was said and done around me. It seems to me I was judging things then as I do now" (A 4v). With growing years, she observed that her natural "pride" and her innate "love of the good," which inspired her to react positively to the advice she received, bore the secret work of Jesus, who "willed that all turn out for her good, even her faults that, corrected very early, stood her in good stead to make her grow in perfection" (A 8r–v).

Thérèse's confessions concerning the "sunny years" of her childhood are surprising: "Virtue had its charming qualities for me, and I was, it seems to me, in the same dispositions then as I am now, enjoying a firm control over my actions." The Saint added that she had "got into the habit of not complaining ever, even when they took what belonged to her or when she was accused unjustly. She preferred to be silent and not excuse herself. There was no merit here but natural virtue" (A 11v). The exceptions would prove the rule.

Let us acknowledge that the little Martin girl found in her mother a spiritual teacher of the first class, raising the heart of her child "to God from the dawn of reason" (A 40r). Zélie guided Thérèse's freedom, again and again placing this little being full of energy on good paths. These good seeds would flourish abundantly: "I loved God very much and I offered my heart to Him very often, making use of the little formula that mother had taught me" (A 15v).

Thérèse was conscious of all that she owed to her "parents without equal" (A 4r) whom she, filled with veneration, would judge "more worthy of Heaven than of earth" (LT 261).

> God was pleased all through my life to surround me with *love,* and the first memories I have are stamped with smiles and the most tender caresses! But although He placed so much *love* near me, He also sent much love into my little heart, making it warm and affectionate. I loved Papa and Mama very much and showed my tenderness for them in a thousand ways. (A 4v)

And what exchanges of love the house at rue Saint-Blaise witnessed!

The Sun Sets

It would take us too far ahead to relate in detail the illness that drove Zélie to the grave. For more than twelve years (CF 13) she had suffered from a breast tumor, which slowly developed into an extremely painful cancer. She consulted a doctor and learned quickly the cruel truth of her imminent death and the futility of any surgical intervention.

The family was overwhelmed. Zélie still wanted to live several more years to finish her educational work, especially with Léonie, the child of her endless worries whom she still saw making great progress. She went on a pilgrimage to Lourdes with Marie, Pauline, and Léonie, but the miracle didn't happen. With realism and abandonment to God, the mother understood that she was invited elsewhere, by another Mother. "What do you want? If the Holy Virgin does not cure me, it is because my time is done and the good Lord wants me to rest someplace other than the earth" (CF 217). Silently, Thérèse recorded "all the details of my Mother's illness" (A 12v). On August 28, 1877, Zélie became "our dear Mother, now in heaven" (A 12v). She was missed terribly by her child on earth.

Thérèse herself noted later the deep wound that the disappearance of this "matchless Mother" (A 4v) left in her, at such a vulnerable age of four years and eight months. The combined tenderness of her Papa and her sisters could never truly cure it.

At the same time, Thérèse writes, "I don't recall having cried very much, neither did I speak to anyone about the feelings I experienced" in the face of this supreme goodbye (A 12v). But what was not expressed in words or tearful eyes, would express itself psychologically in tears from her depths. "My happy disposition completely changed after Mama's death. I, once so full of life, became timid and retiring, sensitive to an excessive degree" (A 13r).

The soil where Zélie and Louis had planted would still be watered for a long time by tears of sorrow and the dew of grace, before the little Martin girl became Saint Thérèse of the Child Jesus and of the Holy Face.

Thérèse Speaks

The Happy Days of Childhood

How happy I really was at that age, dear Mother! I had already begun to enjoy life; virtue had its charming qualities for me, and I was, it seems to me, in the same dispositions then as I am now, enjoying a firm control over my actions.

Ah! how quickly those sunny years passed by, those years of my childhood, but what a sweet imprint they have left on my soul! I recall the days Papa used to bring us to the *pavilion;* the smallest details are impressed in my heart. I recall especially the Sunday walks when Mama used to accompany us. I still feel the profound and *poetic* impressions that were born in my soul at the sight of fields enamelled with *cornflowers* and all types of wild flowers. Already I was in love with the *wide open spaces.* Space and the gigantic fir trees, the branches sweeping down to the ground, left in my heart an impression similar to the one I experience still today at the sight of nature.

We frequently met poor people on these long walks, and it was always little Thérèse who was put in charge of bringing them alms, which made her quite happy. (A 11r–v)

Springtime Story of a Little White Flower

It is to you, dear Mother, to you who are doubly my Mother, that I come to confide the story of my soul.... Before taking up my pen, I knelt before the statue of Mary (the one that has given so many proofs of the maternal preferences of heaven's Queen for our family), and I begged her to guide my hand that it trace no line displeasing to her. Then opening the Holy Gospels my eyes fell on these words: "And going up a mountain, he called to him men of his *own choosing,* and they came to him" (Mk 3:13). This is the mystery of my vocation, my whole life, and especially the mystery of the privileges Jesus showered on my soul. He does not call those who are worthy but those whom He *pleases....*

I wondered for a long time why God has preferences, why all souls don't receive an equal amount of graces.... Jesus deigned to teach me this mystery. He set before me the book of nature; I understood how all the flowers He has created are beautiful, how the splendor of the rose and the whiteness of the Lily do not take away the perfume of the little violet or the delightful simplicity of the daisy. I understood that if all flowers wanted to be roses, nature would lose her springtime beauty, and the fields would no longer be decked out with little wild flowers.

And so it is in the world of souls, Jesus' garden. He willed to create great souls comparable to Lilies and roses, but He has created smaller ones and these must be content to be daisies or violets destined to give joy to God's glances when He looks down at his feet. Perfection consists in doing His will, in being what He wills us to be.

I understood, too, that Our Lord's love is revealed as perfectly in the most simple soul who resists His grace in nothing as in the most excellent soul; in fact, ...the nature of love is to humble oneself.... He created the child who knows only how to make his feeble cries heard; He has created the poor savage who has nothing but the natural law to guide him. It is to their hearts that God deigns to lower Himself. These are the wild flowers whose simplicity attracts Him. When coming down in this way, God manifests His infinite grandeur. Just as the sun shines simultaneously on the tall cedars and on each little flower as though it were alone on the earth, so Our Lord is occupied particularly with each soul as though there were no others like it.

Perhaps you are wondering, dear Mother, with some astonishment where I am going from here.... It is not, then, my life, properly so-called, that I am going to write; it is my *thoughts* on the graces God deigned to grant me. I find myself at a period in my life when I can cast a glance on the past; my soul has matured in the crucible of exterior and interior trials. And now, like a flower strengthened by the storm, I can raise my head and see the words of Psalm 22 realized in me: "The Lord is my Shepherd...." To me the Lord has always been "merciful and good, slow to anger and abounding in steadfast love." (A 2r–3v)

CHAPTER TWO

Childhood in Lisieux

Bishop GUY GAUCHER, OCD

When little Thérèse was four and a half years old her mother died. So great was this shock that she was unable to recover for ten years. At first she could only throw herself into the arms of her favorite sister Pauline and say: "It's Pauline who will be my Mama." This was a turning point in her life. "How quickly those sunny years passed by, those years of my childhood" (A 11v).

Louis Martin was now forty-four years old. He had five little girls to raise. Alençon had always been his home but the family ties with Lisieux, less than fifty-five miles from rue Saint-Blaise, were very close. The Guérin family was firmly settled there. Their pharmacy was prospering in Place Saint-Pierre. Isidore was a well-known Catholic. His wife Céline, always very gentle and motherly, had two daughters, Jeanne and Marie. She believed it was her duty to help her brother-in-law.

After extensive investigations, Isidore Guérin wrote to Louis telling him that he had found an ideal spot for the Martins. It was just outside the city, near a large park on a slight elevation. The house was a beautiful dwelling with a big garden, surrounded by walls. The girls at once named it "Les Buissonnets" (the little thickets). The father resigned himself for their sakes to leave his friends. He sold the Alençon lace business, and in November 1877 the family moved into their new home whose lease was already signed.

Thérèse was to live there for eleven years. "I experienced no regret whatsoever at leaving Alençon; children are fond of change, and it was with pleasure that I came to Lisieux" (A 13v). Nevertheless, the move marked a profound change in her life. She arrived in mid-winter. The unknown town was small, with a mere 18,600 inhabitants. It was an industrial center for the manufacture of fine cotton fabrics and the conversion of skins or hides into leather, and there were many distilleries, etc. The streets were lined with old houses with their columbaria, unchanged since the Middle Ages. These homes were overshadowed by the fine old cathedral built during the thirteenth and fourteenth centuries.

The 119th Infantry Regiment of 1,200 men had a cheerful band that provided lively music in the public gardens. The industrial situation was not good. The working class knew the meaning of poverty. Many were unemployed.

For the moment, little Thérèse was unaware of these realities. What a contrast with their home in Alençon! It had faced the Prefecture where all day and often into the night horses and carriages passed constantly. Les Buissonnets was like an enclosed garden. They knew no one except the Guérins. The family, deprived of the mother's dynamic presence, depended entirely on the father. He took no active part in the town but lived quietly on his savings and investments. He took charge of the garden, spending his days reading, meditating, and praying in the belvedere, a spacious piece of land on the highest part of their property. It overlooked the town. He liked to take walks with his youngest daughter. They would go fishing in the little villages around Lisieux at Ouilly-le-Vicomte, Rocques, Hermival. The oldest girls, with the help of maids and nurses, were responsible for the house and the education of the two youngest children, Céline and Thérèse.

A Long Road to Freedom

Much later Thérèse was to write that she had now begun the second period of her life, the long period of purification that was to last until her fourteenth year. In fact she admitted that after Mama's death her character was totally changed.

> I, once so full of life, became timid and retiring, sensitive to an excessive degree. One look was enough to reduce me to tears, and the only way I was content was to be left alone completely. I could not bear the company of strangers and found my joy only within the intimacy of the family. (A 13r)

Life was fairly smooth as long as she was sheltered in the warmth of her family. She did not go to school. Marie and especially Pauline took their responsibilities seriously. They gave her a solid foundation for future studies, stressing all that concerned religion. The last and youngest of the Martin sisters was not spoiled. Prayer was an important part of her formation. Morning and evening prayers were said together. Nearby churches were part of her daily walks with her father. The liturgical feasts were "the little Queen's" delight and gave a pattern to life at Les Buissonnets.

There were few peak moments in this simple life. Yet this sensitive child found wonders: the first discovery of the sea during a day's visit to Trouville (August 8, 1878), afternoons enjoyed in the flower-filled fields of Normandy, long vigils seated beside her father who was an avid fisherman, games with the inseparable Céline who was her elder by three and a half years.

Céline's First Communion on May 13, 1880, was an important event for her little sister. "It seemed it was I who was going to make my First Communion. I believe I received great graces that day and I consider it one of the most *beautiful* in my life" (A 25r). Indeed Thérèse already had a great hunger for the Eucharist and she now began to prepare herself for her First Communion, which was to take place four years later. Her confession made to Abbé Ducellier this same year brought her great joy. She so identified the priest with Jesus that she wanted to tell him that she loved him with her whole heart. She was persuaded not to do so. At home she continued to be lively. One day she lost her temper with Victoire Pasquier, the nurse who liked to tease her, calling her "a little brat." This was typical of her quick reactions at this time (A 16r).

One unexpected episode occurred during this period: She had "a prophetic vision" on a summer day in 1879 or 1880. She saw a man, "dressed exactly like Papa," and "his *head* was covered with a sort of apron of indistinct color" (A 20r). He crossed the garden and disappeared behind a hedge. Thérèse was looking from a window in the back of the house. Monsieur Martin was then away, visiting in Alençon. To reassure the child, her sisters and the nurse made a thorough but fruitless search of the shrubbery. Recalling this mysterious experience much later, she would see in it the premonition of her beloved father's illness, the great trial of her life.

She had grown very close to him after the death of her Mama, for he treated her with a tenderness that was not only paternal but also maternal. She feared that she would one day lose him, too. A spiritual bond united the child with the patriarch of Les Buissonnets who knew so well how to make each one happy when they came together as a family. She had only to look at him to know how the saints pray. She would always hold him in great veneration.

At School

It was time to go to school. On October 3, 1881, when she was eight years and nine months old, Thérèse Martin went to the Benedictine Abbey school in the district of Saint-Denis. "I have often heard it said that the time spent at school is the best and happiest of one's life. It wasn't this way for me. The five years I spent in school were the saddest in my life" (A 22r).

Unaccustomed as she was to contacts with anyone other than the Guérins, the little school girl discovered, with a certain distress, the social life she had to share with older students. They were frequently jealous—she was often the first in the class—and now and then they would tease her. Thérèse would cry in secret. She could not enjoy the loud, rough games that they played during recess. She preferred to tell stories and help the younger children bury dead birds (A 37r). Her teachers found her docile and quiet, somewhat scrupulous, at times a little sad. Catechism was her moment of triumph.

39. Thérèse Martin at age eight with her sister Céline.

40. Lisieux. Panorama. In the center, the Discalced Carmelite chapel and monastery.

41. Lisieux. The Cathedral of Saint-Pierre. Twelfth-century facade. The Martins attended daily Mass there.

42. Lisieux. Cathedral of Saint-Pierre. Interior.

43. Lisieux. The Touques river where Louis Martin often went fishing.

44. Lisieux. The Orbiquet river which flowed alongside the garden of the Carmel.

45. Lisieux. Church of Saint-Jacques.

39

40

41

42

43

44

45

46

46. Lisieux. Les Buissonnets. The house leased by the Martins. Facade.

47. Lisieux. Les Buissonnets. The kitchen fireplace where Thérèse received her Christmas grace of 1886.

48. Lisieux. Les Buissonnets. Garden in the backyard.

49. Lisieux. Les Buissonnets. Dining room.

47

48

49

50. Lisieux. Les Buissonnets. *The Liturgical Year* by Dom Guéranger, a book read faithfully by the Martin family.

51. Lisieux. Les Buissonnets. The bedroom where Thérèse was cured by Our Lady's smile on Pentecost Sunday, May 13, 1883.

52. Statue of Mary, later called Our Lady of the Smile, placed above the casket containing Thérèse's remains in the Carmelite chapel of Lisieux. It belonged to Louis Martin before his marriage and was kept in the family. Each evening the Martins gathered to pray before this statue.

53. Lisieux. Les Buissonnets. Thérèse's cure. Painting by a Carmelite nun, Sr. Marie of the Holy Spirit.

54. Lisieux. Les Buissonnets. Thérèse's birdcage (cf. A 42v).

55. Lisieux. Les Buissonnets. Thérèse's doll.

52

53

54

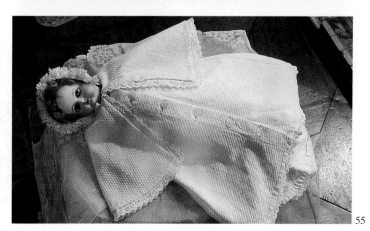

55

56

56. Lisieux. Les Buissonnets. Objects belonging to Thérèse.

57. Lisieux. Les Buissonnets. A little boat called "Abandonment," a gift from Céline to Thérèse on Christmas Day, 1887 (cf. A 68r): "I sleep but my heart watches."

58. Lisieux. Garden of the Benedictine boarding school for girls where Thérèse went to school (October 1881 to March 1886). Photo from the time.

59. Lisieux. Les Buissonnets. Dress worn by Thérèse for her First Communion.

60. Lisieux. Chapel built on the site where Thérèse made her First Communion. The Benedictine monastery was destroyed in 1944.

57

58

59

60

The House of Les Buissonnets

Bishop Guy Gaucher, OCD

On November 16, 1877, the Martin daughters moved into Les Buissonnets, a house found for them by their uncle, Isidore Guérin, a Lisieux pharmacist. Thérèse would live here until April 9, 1888, the date of her entry into Carmel.

The house was then on the outskirts of Lisieux, in a quiet quarter called "New World Village." The house was a century old but in perfect condition. Surrounded by high walls, it had a flower bed in front and a garden with trees behind. The garden gate opened onto a small uphill walk that M. Martin called "the path to paradise."

The basement is divided into a small vault and a fruit cellar. On the ground floor are four rooms, including a beautiful dining room with oak panelling. On the second floor are three bedrooms, and a smaller one level with the garden behind. The third floor has a belvedere overlooking the town, and three small attics.

Near the house was a well with a pulley for drawing water, a cistern, a shed, a wash house, a greenhouse, and an aviary.

Very close by is the splendid Jardin de l'Étoile, which required a ticket for admission. The Martins went there often.

The Martins were only tenants at Les Buissonnets. With their father's illness and confinement, the lease was cancelled on December 31, 1889. The furniture was divided up, some of it going to Carmel.

In December 1909, Doctor La Néele—cousin by marriage, as the husband of Jeanne Guérin—bought Les Buissonnets. Pilgrims were already coming in great numbers. In 1913 the house was set up and opened for regular pilgrimage visits. In 1922, the widowed Jeanne La Néele sold the house to the building society for pilgrims. Today it is maintained for visitors by the Oblates of St. Thérèse.

When classes were over she returned to Les Buissonnets ready to explode with joy. She needed the warmth and love she found there where she could expand and blossom forth. On Thursdays when there were no classes, she played with Céline and her cousin Marie. She did not enjoy a visit to her Maudelonde cousins, where she was expected to dance quadrilles. She preferred to read and to study pictures. The heroic exploits of French heroines, especially those of the Venerable Joan of Arc, left her burning with zeal. She decided that she was born for glory, the glory of "becoming a great *saint!*" (A 32r).

The Loss of Pauline

Another dramatic separation was about to affect her. Pauline Martin had just decided to become a religious. Because of her school days with her aunt, Sister Marie-Dosithée, at the Visitation convent of Le Mans, her first thoughts turned toward this order founded by Saint Francis de Sales and Jeanne de Chantal. But during the celebration of the third centenary of the death of Saint Teresa of Avila (1882) she assisted at a Mass in the Church of Saint-Jacques. Pauline felt an inspiration to become a Carmelite. Their monastery was near. "The Fine Pearl," as her Father had named her, told her family of her vocation. Thérèse only learned of this by chance. "It was as if a sword were buried in my heart" when she heard that she was going to lose her second mother. "How can I express the anguish of my heart? In one instant, I understood what life was; until then, I had never seen it so sad; but it appeared to me in all its reality, and I saw it was nothing but a continual suffering and separation. I shed bitter tears"(A 25v).

Pauline at once explained the meaning of the Carmelite life. The child of nine years listened avidly: this life with Jesus alone, for Jesus alone, attracted her. "I felt that Carmel was the *desert* where God wanted me to go also to hide myself. I felt this with so much force that there wasn't the least doubt in my heart." She was convinced that she had received a divine call. It might be objected that she wanted to be reunited with the mother whom she had just learned she was about to lose. Thérèse declared categorically: "I wanted to go to Carmel, not for *Pauline's sake,* but for *Jesus alone*" (A 26r).

She confided her secret to Pauline and even to the prioress of the Carmel, Mother Marie de Gonzague, who received her in the speakroom but did not accept the nine-year-old postulant. She would have to wait until she was sixteen years old. What did it matter? Thérèse now knew toward whom to orient her life.

On Monday October 2, 1882, the Martins and the Guérins accompanied Pauline to Mass. Then the heavy door of Carmel closed. All the girls were in tears, especially Thérèse. It was also the first day of school. Going to the speakrooms on Thursday for the family visit with Pauline gave her more distress than joy. At the end of the prescribed half hour, she was allowed only a moment alone with her "little mother"—more sadness and tears.

In December her classes were interrupted by headaches, pains in different parts of her body, all of which affected her disposition. She snapped at Marie who had replaced Pauline and become her third mother. She argued constantly with Céline who was now fourteen and found her little charge "excessively teary."

A Serious Illness

All these symptoms were the prelude to a grave illness that appeared suddenly at Eastertide 1883. Louis Martin wanted Marie and Léonie to spend Holy Week in Paris. The Guérins agreed to take care of the two little ones during the short vacation.

Unfortunately the conversation at the Guérins centered on Madame Martin and memories of life in Alençon. Thérèse could not endure these reminders of the past. She was put to bed. But when her uncle returned from the Catholic Circle meeting she was shivering from the cold and moved restlessly. The pharmacist was so anxious that the next day he called his friend Dr. Notta. His diagnosis was not reassuring. "He judged, as did Uncle, that I had a very serious illness and one which had never before attacked a child as young as I" (A 27v). He did not identify it by name.

The Martins were panic-stricken when they were summoned from Paris. Thérèse could not be moved; she stayed at the Guérins. The disturbing symptoms increased: hallucinations, uncontrolled movements of the body, periods of weakness, anorexia. All her thoughts were focused on her Carmelite sister who was to take the habit on April 6. Obviously there was no question of her being able to go to the ceremony. However, on that day she got up and declared that she was cured. Before services she was allowed to sit on Pauline's knees. This dear sister had now become Sister Agnes of Jesus.

Thérèse was able to return to Les Buissonnets. But the next day she had a still more serious relapse. She was delirious, her words were incoherent, her cries for help were incessant. Would she die or remain an "idiot?" The cold baths that Doctor Notta prescribed helped her not at all.

The family and Carmel prayed ardently for this child who seemed lost. Would she die like her other sisters? A novena of masses was offered at the Parisian shrine of Our Lady of Victories, so dear to the Guérins and the Martins. Thérèse was not in her own room but in that of her sister Marie on the first floor. On the chest beside her they had placed the statue of the Blessed Virgin given to Louis Martin by a devout single woman before his marriage. Our Lady was the protectress of the family. She had given graces to Zélie Martin.

An Inexplicable Cure

The feast of Pentecost, May 13, 1883, arrived. Léonie had kept her sister in her room. Thérèse continued to moan, ceaselessly crying out "Mama, Mama," wishing that Marie would come to her. At last the older sister came from the garden but Thérèse did not recognize her. All her sisters were kneeling around her bed. Then the unexpected happened. "All of a sudden the Blessed Virgin appeared *beautiful* to me, so *beautiful* that never had I seen anything so attractive; her face was suffused with an ineffable benevolence and tenderness, but what penetrated to the very depths of my soul was the *'ravishing smile of the Blessed Virgin.'* At that instant, all my pain disappeared, and two large tears glistened on my eyelashes, and flowed down my cheeks silently, but they were tears of unmixed joy" (A 30r).

Thérèse was cured. The Blessed Virgin's smile had instantaneously restored the invalid. She got up. Except for two slight incidents, absolutely nothing ever recurred, not a single symptom.

Carmel received her as someone miraculously cured. The sisters' questions troubled and disconcerted the child. How did the Blessed Virgin look? Thérèse had promised to keep the secret to herself, but her sister Marie who had seen the cure taking place had made her speak. How could she refuse? Alas, the older sister had spoken to the Carmelites. Thérèse felt an inner discomfort that would last a very long time—four years—because what should have been a joy became a torment. Hadn't she betrayed the secret of the Blessed Virgin? Another doubt was added to this one: Had she pretended to be sick? This was a pertinent question because she was aware of having experienced a kind of dual personality! This suffering was to last five years. "Ah! What I suffered I shall not be able to say except in heaven!" (A 30r).

Naturally in the course of time psychiatrists were questioned about this strange sickness. The diagnoses did not always agree. They did agree about the cause: the shock of the brutal departure of her second mother, Pauline, renewed the unhealed wound of the loss of her Mama. Nor had she recovered from the deep blow that had marked her affective personality, which brought about changes in her character, transforming the happy, strong, outgoing child into a hypersensitive, self-conscious, and timid pre-adolescent.

In 1959 Doctor Guayral declared that "Thérèse displayed a delayed growth in affectivity as a consequence of the regression caused by the loss of her mother and not compensated for by a sufficiently comprehensive education" (*Carmel* 1959, p. 93).

The question remains open. But these various explanations should not preclude Thérèse's own evaluation. When giving an account of her life in 1895—she was twenty-two years old—she would then see this illness as caused without a doubt by the devil enraged at Pauline's entry into Carmel. She declared: "He wanted to take his revenge on me for the wrong our family was to do to him in the future" (A 27r).

With the passage of time we can in our turn recognize that in this "future" Thérèse herself would be a redoubtable adversary of the Prince of Darkness. Who can say with complete insight what an illness of this kind that requires the help of psychiatry denotes on the spiritual plane? Later Thérèse realized that in "this strange illness" (A 28v) there was at stake a spiritual value in which she was both the agent and the field of battle.

On the other hand in these two "spiritual trials" that were to torture her for years (it is possible to see in them John of the Cross's purifications of the senses), the only startling element is her youth. But the Lord has plans that escape human inquiry. Thérèse would not lose sight of the fact that God had saved her from a hopeless situation.

The convalescent would not be asked to go to school after such emotional upheavals. Her family believed she was very delicate and they were concerned about her health for a long time; they made every effort to avoid anything that might disturb her.

What better way to forget these dark days than to travel? From August 20 until September 3, 1883, Thérèse (now ten and a half years old) made her "entrance into the world" by returning to Alençon and visiting family friends. She had left when she was six years old and never gone back. She was entertained. She was coddled. Louis Martin wrote to a friend: "She is now a fine figure of a girl." Her long blond hair reached her waist, her beautiful eyes were clear. Zélie Martin had always dressed her daughters elegantly, and this won the admiration of the bourgeois families of Alençon and neighboring towns. The beautiful convalescent went

"Poor Léonie" (1863–1941)

Bishop Guy Gaucher, OCD

Marie-Léonie Martin was born on June 3, 1863, at Alençon, the third of the Martin daughters (after Marie and Pauline), but ahead of the six that followed, of whom four died.

Thus she found herself quite alone between the two oldest and the two youngest (Céline and Thérèse). With delicate health and a temperament less graceful than the others, she caused her mother constant concern. Despite their best efforts her aunt, Sister Marie-Dosithée, was not able to keep her at the Visitation girls' school at Le Mans. At Alençon the housemaid tormented her, making Léonie more withdrawn.

She had a good heart and was avid in her affections, but proved less gifted than her sisters. On a sudden impulse, she entered the Poor Clares in Alençon after her mother's death, but remained there only a few weeks (October 1886). Yet the call to religious life stayed with her. On July 16, 1887, at twenty-four years, she entered the Visitation monastery in Caen. On January 6, 1888, she returned to Les Buissonnets, just as Thérèse was preparing to enter the Lisieux Carmel.

Five years passed during the illness of M. Martin. What would become of the one whom all the world called "poor Léonie"? On June 24, 1893, she presented herself once more at the Visitation monastery in Caen. She took the habit, but left again two years later, on July 20, 1895. Thérèse tried to encourage her, and before her death, reassured Léonie that she would become a Visitandine.

In fact, on June 28, 1899, Léonie returned forever to the Visitation monastery of Caen. She died there, humble and hidden, on June 17, 1941, at seventy-eight years of age.

From afar, she had witnessed the growing "storm of glory" that crowned her little sister. She had become a disciple of the little way of childhood, perfectly suited to her own weakness. This is why so many friends of Thérèse love Léonie very much.

Since 1970 the Visitation monastery has received letters and pilgrims from all over the world. The nuns have opened the crypt of Sister Françoise-Thérèse—Léonie—who said of her youngest sister, "The more I see her raised in glory, the more I feel the need to humble myself."

---

from "house to house," she rode horseback. "I must admit this type of life had its charms for me.… At the age of ten the heart allows itself to be easily dazzled" (A 32v).

After her brush with the madness of death, the lucky convalescence revived her enthusiasm for living. Would the austere Carmel where her sister lived remain in her heart, even though she had an inkling that another way could open up before her: a happy marriage, children, a big house, an easy life? No she was attentive to where the gravity of her heart was drawing her. This earthly experience would indeed be useful: "Perhaps Jesus wanted to show me the world before His *first visit* to me in order that I may choose freely the way I was to follow" (A 32v). Note this clarity in the freedom of her decision that removes all suspicion that her entrance into Carmel was a consequence of her ignorance of the world.

First Communion

After this pleasant and brilliant life, the return to Lisieux was a shock. She had to go to school in

October 1885; the pupil Thérèse Martin entered the second division of the same class. One joy that shone brightly in this darkness was the possibility of making her First Communion this year. This desire remained deeply rooted in her heart. Her realistic love of Jesus incarnate enabled her to see the Eucharist as the sacrament of the Real Presence.

The instructions were given by Father Domin, who had been chaplain of the Benedictines for forty-one years. He was satisfied with his pupil whom he called "his little doctor." She had trouble following him when he said that children who died without baptism were deprived of heaven. Thérèse thought that the omnipotence of divine love would never allow such a misfortune, because nothing was worse than not seeing God. An all-powerful God could surely draw them to himself!

In Carmel Sister Agnes of Jesus also helped to prepare her sister for the great day: for four months she wrote each week to Thérèse and made a little book that would help her to pray and make daily sacrifices. Thérèse responded with an exceptional generosity. From March 1 to May 7, 1883, she performed 1,949 sacrifices and repeated the prayers suggested by Pauline

2,773 times. She continued this mathematical accounting, much practiced at that time, but the day would come much later when she would write: "When one loves one does not calculate" (PN 17, 5).

The great day was to be May 8, a happy date that coincided with Pauline's profession at Carmel. The two sisters were also united in the gift they were to make to Jesus.

For the first time in her life she did not sleep at home. During the three days of preparatory retreat she was required to sleep at the Abbey. The family made a thousand suggestions to the sisters in charge. They were reminded that the little Martin girl was still very delicate. The rules must be modified in certain ways for her. Her father and sisters could visit her every day.

Father Domin preached the retreat to the little girls who were ten and eleven years old. The conferences were strongly marked with the Jansenism then prevalent. In her little notebook Thérèse merely made a few notes. The second instruction was on death, the third on hell and the tortures to be endured there, and that of May 7 on sacrilegious Communions. She later wrote: "Father told us many things that filled me with fear." But the death of the Benedictine prioress prevented the chaplain from giving all the instructions and no doubt from terrifying the young retreatants still more.

On May 7 she made a general confession that left her in great peace. The next day she knew a joy that was unmixed. The vocabulary she used to describe it in 1895 was utterly unlike that of the instructions given by Father Domin:

Ah, how sweet was that first kiss of Jesus! It was a kiss of *love;* I *felt* that I *was loved,* and I said, 'I love You, and I give myself to You forever!' There were no demands made, no struggles, no sacrifices; for a long time now Jesus and poor little Thérèse *looked at* and understood each other. That day, it was no longer simply a *look,* it was a fusion; they were no longer two, Thérèse had vanished as a drop of water is lost in the immensity of the ocean. Jesus alone remained; He was the Master, the King. (A 35r)

This is the language of one who loves and who has made the total gift of herself. The Eucharistic hunger that she had experienced for several years was seeking satisfaction. She would mark twenty-two Communions in her little notebook in the coming year, because daily Communion was not yet permitted.

In the afternoon she recited the Act of Consecration to the Blessed Virgin, her Mother, in the name of her companions. She was not indifferent in any way to family feasts and the gifts she had been given, but to receive holy Communion once again was what attracted her. This would not be possible until two weeks later, on the feast of the Ascension, May 22. This second Communion would mark Thérèse very deeply, but in a very different way. "What a sweet memory I have of this second visit of Jesus." The words of Galatians 2:20 were engraved, as it were, on her heart. "It is not I who live, it is Jesus who lives in me!" But above all, she received insight into the meaning of suffering: "I felt born within my heart a *great desire* to suffer, and at the same time the interior assurance that Jesus reserved a great number of crosses for me. I felt myself flooded with consolations so *great* that I look upon them as one of the *greatest* graces of my life" (A 36r).

These thoughts are surprising in so young a child, but are presentiments of her youth and of her life to come.

Why be surprised that she felt a great desire to deepen her prayer? But her sister Marie did not allow her to make half an hour of mental prayer a day, not even a quarter of an hour, because she found that Thérèse was already sufficiently pious.

Confirmation

She received another great grace on June 14, 1884. Bishop Hugonin confirmed her after two days of retreat. Thérèse was amazed that people did not attach sufficient importance to "the sacrament of Love." The visit of the Holy Spirit came like a "light breeze." She wrote that on that day she received strength to suffer. Later Céline testified:

> Thérèse, usually so calm, was no longer the same: a kind of enthusiasm and ecstasy was apparent exteriorly. On the day of preparatory retreat when I expressed my astonishment that I found these dispositions in her, she explained to me that she understood that by this sacrament the Spirit of Love had taken possession of her whole being. Her words were spoken with such vehemence and ardent fervor that I was penetrated with an impression wholly supernatural. I left her very much moved. This incident was fixed so deeply in my memory that I can still recall her gesture, her attitude, the place where she was, and this memory has never left me. (PO 226–227)

In August she spent her vacation at Saint-Ouen-le-Pin (Calvados) some ten kilometers (6.2 miles) from Lisieux, on the way to Caen, in the home of Madame Fournet (the Guérin grandmother) in the heart of the Auge. Thérèse loved this part of the country with its little valleys, its apple orchards, the streams and pools, its groves of trees. She made a detailed drawing of the dovecotes. The family wandered the countryside where the Guizot castle stood, on the estate of the old Cistercian Abbey of Val-Richer. She was very happy there; she was able to care for a child suffering from whooping cough. Was she accompanied by her dog Tom, a white spaniel, the gift her father gave her in June? No matter, she would find him again at Les Buissonnets, when school began. This was always a painful time for her. She met the other students, about thirteen to fourteen years old, frivolous and quarrelsome. She continued to love history and compositions; her zeal for the catechism never lessened, on the contrary! But her sensitivity to failure was great and led to many tears.

Her teacher, Mother Saint-Léon, found her too delicate and scrupulous. Her "sensitive and loving" heart craved affection. But her attempts to make friends failed; her love was not understood.

From May 3 to 10 she again enjoyed a vacation with the Guérins, but this time they went to the "Chalet des Roses," 17 quai de la Touques in Deauville. Aunt Guérin was hostess to the four young girls who enjoyed the sea air: Jeanne (seventeen years old), Marie (who was almost fifteen), Thérèse (twelve and a half years), and Marcelline, the maid (nineteen). They spent their days walking along the seashore as far as Roches Noires, or going to Mass at Notre-Dame-des-Victoires and Notre-Dame-de-Bon-Secours. Sometimes they were busy with needlework or making drawings for the Guérins. Thérèse tried but failed again to show her love. She missed her mother and found it difficult to establish real balance in human relations. In spite of all these distractions she missed her sister Marie who had remained at Les Buissonnets.

"Second" Communion

Moreover, she had to return home because she had to begin the retreat for her "Second" Communion, that is, the solemn renewal of her first. Father Domin preached to them at the Abbey from May 17 to 21, 1885. The retreatant took a few notes in the same notebook. The terrifying tone of the instructions had not changed from the preceding year. "What Father said to us filled us with fear. He spoke about mortal sin." Thérèse wrote nothing about his conference on death. Later in her memoirs she would say: "It was during my retreat for the second Communion that I was assailed by the terrible sickness of scruples. One would have to pass through this martyrdom to understand it well, and for me to express what I suffered for *a year and a half* would be impossible" (A 39r).

In fact this long crisis lasted seventeen months. The "two spiritual trials" that followed her sickness of 1883 returned and reinforced the scruples that troubled her, at that age, from her anxieties about chastity. Her only relief came when she confided her inner sufferings to her sister Marie, who was able to help her to see more clearly when she went to confess. She was also disturbed enough that after this second Communion she would soon leave school.

Let us note that once again she made the same three resolutions that she had made before her First Communion. "1. I will not be discouraged. 2. I will say every day a *Memorare* to the Blessed Virgin. 3. I will try to humble my pride."

In July 1885 she visited Saint-Ouen-le-Pin. No one who saw her "openly happy, charming, and gay" could suspect the weight of her interior sufferings. At the end of September she enjoyed another holiday at the seashore. This time Céline and she were at Trouville, staying at the "Villa Rose," on rue Charlemagne. Thérèse had a very good time. One day she received from her Aunt some pretty sky-blue ribbons that she put in her beautiful hair. Fearing this was a sin she accused herself in confession of being a flirt.

The beginning of the school year of 1885 was to be the last for Thérèse. Céline, who was sixteen years old, had completed her years of studying. Her cousin Marie, who was often ill, also left the Abbey. This was too much for Thérèse, who found herself alone once again as the only day-student in the family. This was a great solitude for the young adult, accentuated all the more by the absence of her father, who was away for two months traveling to the East, going as far as Constantinople.

The retreat for the opening of school was preached by a priest who had replaced Father Domin. Unfortunately he did not succeed in helping the troubled student. The terrifying truths he proposed were so unlike the idea she had of the love of Jesus.

In 1886 Thérèse was thirteen. On February 2, she was received as an aspirant in the Children of Mary at the Abbey, where Céline "the Intrepid" was president. Her teacher could not understand why Thérèse was so sad. At this time she suffered from constant headaches. Monsieur Martin decided to take her out of school.

Like her cousin Marie Guérin, she would follow special classes given by Miss Valentine Papinau, who lived with her mother and her cat on Grande-Rue, near the cathedral of Saint-Pierre.

This was a great change for Thérèse: her school life had ended. Three or four times a week she went for her lessons, always accompanied. The work was light because her teacher received many visits. When they said she was very pretty, she would blush with confusion and pleasure.

These days gave her plenty of leisure. She arranged a room for herself in one of the attics on the top floor of Les Buissonnets that she described as "a real bazaar, an assemblage of pious objects and curiosities, a garden, and an aviary…the portrait of Pauline" (A 42v).

At the end of June she again went to Trouville. This time she stayed at the Chalet des Lilas. But it was a short stay because she did not feel well. She was homesick for Les Buissonnets. This little incident confirmed that she had not yet fully recovered.

Marie's Departure

It was at this time that she learned that her sister Marie was going to enter Carmel. This was a new tragedy for Thérèse who now had only Céline to help her. At the age of seventeen Céline was in charge of the house. Léonie, aged twenty-three, was still thinking of religious life. The world turned upside down for the last little sister. She decided that life is nothing but a succession of separations. She no longer took any pleasure in her old room, and began once again with Marie the life she had led with Pauline: covering her with kisses, preparing little gifts for the great departure.

Was she helped by a trip to Alençon at the beginning of October, giving her a change of air and some distractions? No. She wept at her mother's grave because she had forgotten to bring a bouquet of flowers.

61

61. Saint-Ouen-le-Pin, about six miles from Lisieux. House of Madame Fournet, mother of Thérèse's aunt Céline Guérin. Thérèse spent long vacations here in 1884 and 1885. She slept on the first floor in the room on the right.

62. Saint-Ouen-le-Pin. Building connected to the Fournet house. Thérèse did a drawing of it in 1884.

63. Thérèse's drawing.

64. Ouilly-le-Vicomte, about two miles from Lisieux. The church.

62

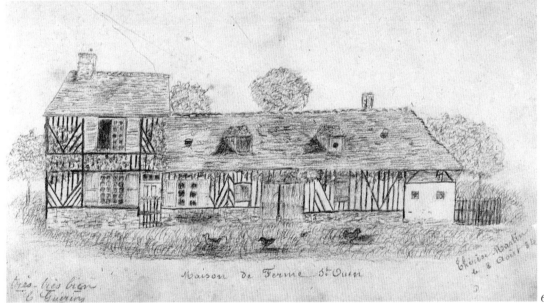

63

65

65. La Paquine, a river that borders the church of Ouilly-le-Vicomte, where Louis Martin used to fish while Thérèse gathered flowers in the meadow.

66. The sixteenth-century mansion of Saint-Hippolyte, two miles from Lisieux. Thérèse passed by it on walks with her father.

67. Thérèse at age five saw the ocean for the first time at Trouville. The impression it left was unforgettable: "a luminous trail" of grace (A 21v).

68. Deauville, by the sea. Chalet des Roses, where Thérèse stayed during May 1885.

69. Trouville. The Chalet des Lilas where Thérèse vacationed in 1886 and 1887. One has a view of the ocean from the balcony.

70. Trouville. Church of Notre-Dame des Victoires, where Thérèse attended Mass.

71. Honfleur. Church of Notre-Dame de Grace, visited by Thérèse in June 1887.

66

67

68

69

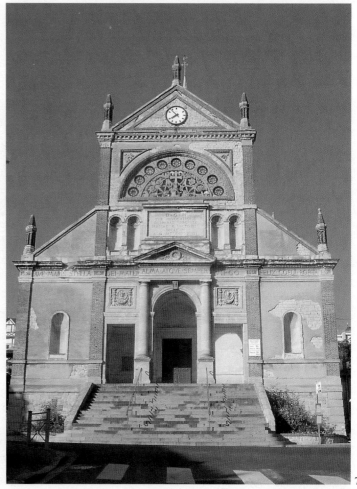

70

71

72

72. Lisieux. Les Buissonnets. Statues in the garden representing the scene in which Thérèse on Pentecost Sunday, May 29, 1887, requested permission from her father to enter Carmel.

73: Bayeux. Diocesan museum. Portrait of Bishop Hugonin (1823–1898).

74. Honfleur. Côte de Grâce. The crucifix erected by Bishop Hugonin of Bayeux on August 3, 1873. Le Havre in the background.

75. Bayeux. The cathedral.

76. Bayeux. The old episcopal palace, today a diocesan museum. The room in which Thérèse was received by Bishop Hugonin (cf. A 54v).

77. Bayeux. Diocesan museum. The bishops' portraits of which Thérèse speaks (cf. A 54v).

73

74

76

77

And suddenly Léonie entered the Poor Clares of rue de la Demi-Lune. This was the end of the family.

Marie, her "only support," left on October 15. She would now have to struggle alone with her scruples. Pauline could no longer help her. The rare contacts in the speakroom, separated by the double grille, did not suffice for a true exchange.

Here was a beautiful young girl, nearly fourteen years old, with long hair going down her back to her waist. What a contrast to what was going on within. She was hypersensitive, weepy, "unbearable because of my extreme touchiness," sometimes crying "for having cried" (A 44v), tortured by her scruples. This was the lowest point of her life. She felt the solitude of an adolescent who still dreamed of entering Carmel. But with such emotional problems would this ever be possible? She had no attraction for practical things. She was unable to make a bed correctly. Everything became a cause of suffering (A 44v).

In the depths of her grieving she reacted with a cry to heaven. Curiously she did not turn to God, nor to the Blessed Virgin who had once cured her. The poor abandoned child turned to her little brothers and sisters who had died very young. Being the last of the family she implored them "with the simplicity of a child" (A 44r). The answer came immediately. This prayer brought peace and she had the consolation of knowing that in her interior solitude she was loved in heaven.

This sudden cure put an end to her scruples but did not solve all her problems. Her hypersensitivity remained unchanged. She always had a tendency "to cry like a Magdalene." The situation seemed hopeless. How could this adolescent be definitively cured?

The "Miracle" of Christmas 1886

At this time an interior experience of capital importance occurred in the life of Thérèse Martin. It was not spectacular because, except for her sister Céline, no one knew anything about it.

The facts are very simple. Returning from midnight Mass at the cathedral, Monsieur Martin, who was very tired after the ceremonies, saw that Thérèse had placed her shoes as usual at the chimney-corner, and regretted that a fourteen-year-old would continue this custom. He declared: "Well, fortunately, this will be the last year." Thérèse heard his words and tears started to flow as she went upstairs to remove her hat. Céline begged her not to go back to her father immediately.

But Thérèse made a great effort to force back her tears, and went down to open her gifts. Monsieur Martin had regained his cheerfulness and seemed very happy. Céline did not refer to the incident.

Grace had touched Thérèse's heart. "In an instant" she had received great interior strength. No more tears. She was no longer the same; her hypersensitivity had disappeared. She was transformed, strong, without "the swaddling clothes of a child," no longer an adolescent but a woman. She was "armed for war," ready for every struggle, especially for all that would enable her to enter Carmel as quickly as possible.

Nine years later when writing her first autobiographical manuscript she made a synthesis of the events of Christmas 1886. It seemed to her to have been a "little miracle," a "conversion," an "admirable exchange" between the strength of God who had made himself little in the crib and the weakness of little Thérèse who had become strong. The liturgical and Eucharistic grace—for Thérèse had received Communion at the Midnight Mass—had transformed her completely (A 45–46).

She had "grown." She had hoped for this obscurely, while maintained in a certain childish atmosphere by her family. "Céline wanted to continue treating me as a baby because I was the youngest of the family" (A 45r). But the father's words suddenly put an end to the family ritual and had enabled her to escape from herself.

This was a lasting conversion that opened "the third period of her life, the most beautiful and the most filled with graces from heaven" (A 45v). She could, as she said, begin "to run as a giant" (Ps 18, 6).

With remarkable clarity she realized that she had now recovered the character she had when she was four and a half years old, but which she had lost ten years ago when her mother died. At last she had done her mourning and was at peace. This was a grace of interior healing, deep and lasting. But this grace worked on a nature with its own story. The psychological wound had not been indelible. "God is the health of the soul" (John of the Cross).

A year after the text of her autobiography, Thérèse spoke again about her "conversion" in a letter to Father Roulland (LT 201) on November 1, 1896. The synthesis is perfect.

> The *night* of Christmas 1886 was, it is true, decisive for my vocation, but to name it more clearly I must call it: the night of my conversion. On that blessed night about which it has been written that it sheds light even on the delights of God Himself, Jesus, who saw fit to make Himself a child out of love for me, saw fit to have me come forth from the swaddling clothes and imperfections of childhood. He transformed me in such a way that I no longer recognized myself. Without this change I would have had to remain for years in the world. Saint Teresa, who said to her daughters: "I want you to be women in nothing, but that in everything you may equal strong men," would not have wanted to acknowledge me as her child if the Lord had not clothed me in His divine strength, if He had not Himself armed me for war.

Thus "in an instant" she was freed from a powerlessness that had lasted for ten years. She now knew from experience what the divine mercy was that had rescued her from an abyss. She would never forget this, and on every Christmas that followed she celebrated her "conversion."

During the last days of her life she would return to this decisive Christmas of 1886 to make very clear that divine grace never acts without human freedom.

> Today, I was thinking of my past life, about the courageous act I performed formerly at Christmas, and the praise directed to Judith came into my mind: "You have acted with manly courage, and your heart has been strengthened." Many souls say: I don't have the strength to accomplish this sacrifice. Let them do, then, what I did: exert a great effort. God never refuses that first grace that gives one the courage to act; afterwards, the heart is strengthened and one advances from victory to victory. (DE II, 8.8.3; HLC 142)

In this way the second part of the life of Thérèse Martin came to an end, according to the divisions that she herself made: ten years of sufferings and struggles, but also of very special graces. As a child and adolescent she experienced purifications that matured and deepened her. This long period of powerlessness lasting for ten years was followed by three supernatural healings that, one after the other, finally led to a permanent liberation. She had made this personal discovery: that she had been saved. She knew that she had come a long way and that her life would have turned out badly had it not been for these many graces, of which the most efficacious was that of Christmas 1886.

It is easy to understand why 1887 was a very beautiful year for her. It was a year of human, intellectual, artistic, and above all spiritual development. This was the year of her great struggle to enter Carmel as soon as possible. Thérèse herself had decided the date of her entrance: it would be Christmas 1887, the anniversary of her conversion.

Thérèse Speaks

Family Life

I experienced no regret whatsoever at leaving Alençon; children are fond of change, and it was with pleasure that I came to Lisieux. I recall the trip, our arrival at Aunt's home; and I can still picture Jeanne and Marie [Guérin] waiting for us at the door. I was very fortunate in having such nice little cousins. I loved them very much, as also Aunt and especially Uncle [Isidore]; however, he frightened me, and I wasn't as much at ease in his home as I was at Les Buissonnets, for there my life was truly happy.

In the morning you [i.e., Pauline] used to come to me and ask me if I had raised my heart to God, and then you dressed me. While dressing me you spoke about Him and afterward we knelt down and said our prayers together. The reading lesson came later and the first word I was able to read without help was "heaven." My dear godmother [Marie] took charge of the writing lessons and you, Mother, all the rest. I enjoyed no great facility in learning, but I did have a very good memory. Catechism and sacred history were my favorite subjects and these I studied with joy. Grammar frequently caused me to shed many tears. You no doubt recall the trouble I had with the masculine and feminine genders!

…Each afternoon I took a walk with Papa. We made our visit to the Blessed Sacrament together, going to a different church each day, and it was in this way we entered the Carmelite chapel for the first time. Papa showed me the choir grille and told me there were nuns behind it. I was far from thinking at that time that nine years later I would be in their midst! (A 13v–14r)

What shall I say of the winter evenings at home, especially the Sunday evenings? Ah! how I loved, after the *game of checkers* was over, to sit with Céline on Papa's knees. He used to sing, in his beautiful voice, airs that filled the soul with profound thoughts, or else, rocking us gently, he recited poems that taught the eternal truths. Then we all went upstairs to say our night prayers together and the little Queen was alone near her King, having only to look at him to see how the saints pray. When prayer was ended we came according to age to bid Papa good night and receive his kiss; the *Queen* naturally came last and the *King* took her by the two *elbows* to kiss her and she would cry out in a high-pitched tone: "Good night, Papa, good night and sleep well!" (A 18r–v)

I Choose All

One day, Léonie, thinking she was too big to be playing any longer with dolls, came to us with a basket filled with dresses and pretty pieces for making others; her doll was resting on top. "Here, my little sisters, *choose;* I'm giving you all this." Céline stretched out her hand and took a little ball of wool that pleased her. After a moment's reflection, I stretched out mine saying: "I choose all!" and I took the basket without further ceremony. Those who witnessed the scene saw nothing wrong and even Céline herself didn't dream of complaining (besides, she had all sorts of toys, her godfather gave her lots of presents, and Louise found ways of getting her everything she desired).

This little incident of my childhood is a summary of my whole life; later on when perfection was set before me, I understood that to become *a saint* one had to suffer much, seek out always the most perfect thing to do, and forget self. I understood, too, there were many degrees of perfection and each soul was free to respond to the advances of Our Lord, to do little or much for Him, in a word, to *choose* among the sacrifices He was asking. Then, as in the days of my childhood, I cried out: "My God *'I choose all!'* I don't want to be a *saint by halves*, I'm not afraid to suffer for You, I fear only one thing: to keep my *own will;* so take it, for '*I choose all'* that You will!" (A 10r–v)

CHAPTER THREE

Thérèse as a Young Laywoman

Bishop GUY GAUCHER, OCD

On January 2, 1887, Thérèse was fourteen years old. She was transformed, even in her physical appearance. Céline gave her drawing lessons. Her desire to read was insatiable. She was interested in everything. Some books made a deep impression on her, such as Canon Arminjon's *The End of the Present World and the Mysteries of the Future Life*. Her favorite pages were in the seventh conference on "Heavenly Happiness." Longing for spiritual knowledge, she received here an important supplement to the inadequate catechism presentation on final perseverance, which seemed too academic to her. Arminjon quoted frequently from Scripture and the Fathers, and opened to her the infinite dimensions of the Christian mystery.

But above all else her thoughts were centered on her goal: to enter Carmel. She decided to break the news to her father on the feast of Pentecost (May 29). He was seated in the garden of Les Buissonnets. She found him perfectly ready for every sacrifice: willing to offer his daughters to God, even the one he loved best, the "little Queen." Plucking a little white flower growing on a wall of the garden, he gave it to her as a symbol of her life, enlightened by the sun of God. Thérèse kept it until her death.

The grace of Christmas was to yield abundant fruit. She described the opening of her heart to the sorrows of the world: "I felt *charity* enter into my soul, and the need to forget myself and to please others; since then I've been happy!" (A 45v). Freed from herself by the divine *agapé* within, Thérèse went out to others. Leaving her ego behind, she tried to love in truth. She wanted "to please others." As a result she was filled with joy, because the secret of happiness is the gift of self. At the end of her life, in her last poem about the Virgin Mary, she wrote: "To love is to give everything. It's to give oneself" (PN 54).

Among the many graces of this year 1887, there is one that would prove decisive for her vocation. Once again the occasion was almost trivial. Probably in July, when she was at Mass in the cathedral of Saint-Pierre,

she came upon a picture in her missal of Jesus on the cross. She was struck by the blood flowing from the hands of the Crucified. No one was there to gather the sacred drops. She was so grieved that she resolved to stand at the foot of the cross and gather this divine blood so that she might apply it to the needs of souls. She heard Jesus say: "I thirst" (Jn 19:26). This was a physical thirst, but even more, a thirst for souls. She too felt this thirst for souls, after the opening of her heart at Christmas. She felt that she was a "fisher of souls." She wanted to work for the conversion of sinners, "to snatch them from the eternal flames."

> I was resolved to remain in spirit at the foot of the cross and to receive the divine dew. I understood that I was then to pour it out upon souls. The cry of Jesus on the cross sounded continually in my heart: 'I thirst!' These words ignited within me an unknown and very living fire. I wanted to give my Beloved to drink and I felt myself consumed with a thirst for souls. (A 45v)

In a priestly attitude, this young girl of fourteen and a half stood fixed at "the foot of the cross" of Jesus, to share in the salvation of the world. Her whole vocation was there. Already, it was the intense desire she would so often later express: "To love Jesus and to make him loved" (Pri 6; SS 276).

Circumstances were soon to provide an opportunity to put her resolutions into action (A 46–47). During the night of the sixteenth and seventeenth of March, three women were murdered at 17 rue Montaigne in Paris: Marie Regnault, a woman well-known in the Paris world, her maid, and a little girl of thirteen. Robbery was the motive. Horror of the crime enraged the press against the man arrested in Marseilles on March 20: Henri Pranzini, originally from Alexandria. Having tried various professions, he took up gambling and began stealing in order to survive. His women victims were numerous. The charges against him were overwhelming (the stolen jewels were found in Marseilles). His trial opened on July 9 and was avidly followed by the whole country. But Pranzini insisted that he was innocent. Despite his denials he was condemned to death on July 13.

Had Monsieur Martin talked about this incident at Les Buissonnets in the presence of his daughters, as Céline claims? Or isn't it more likely that Thérèse had learned about it when she was with the Guérins, whose pharmacy on the Place Thiers was very popular and where such subjects were openly discussed? Or perhaps from Madame Papinau?

In any case, quite contrary to the opinions of her contemporaries, Thérèse's immediate reaction was a great desire to save Pranzini. She began to multiply her prayers and sacrifices, to have Masses said for him. So great was her confidence that she was sure she would be heard, and that God would show mercy to this poor unfortunate man even if he gave no sign of repentance. Nevertheless she asked the Lord for a sign for herself.

Driven by a need that knows no law, she did not think that she was disobeying her father's prohibition against reading the newspapers when she read on the first of September in *La Croix* the account of the public execution of Pranzini in the Roquette prison. He had first refused the offers of the chaplain, Father Faure, but he suddenly called him and kissed the crucifix before he was guillotined.

As soon as she read this detail in the paper, Thérèse hid herself, crying tears of joy. She had been given the hoped-for sign. Pranzini was saved! She did not doubt for a moment that he had received "the merciful sentence" from the One who forgives repentant sinners, such as the Good Thief.

This sign was a powerful encouragement on her road to Carmel. If the Lord had given her such a great sinner, how many others would follow! This young girl did not hesitate to call him her "first child" in spite of the fact that the press, including the Catholic papers, was vilifying him. Her vocation was clear: She was to be a "Carmelite, spouse, and mother" (B 2v) because consecrated virginity is not sterility but spiritual maternity.

Great graces enlightened her during the summer of 1887. With her sister Céline, eighteen at the time, she lived her ideal of a life of happiness. In the evening in the belvedere they shared many thoughts and received great graces. "It appears we were receiving graces like those granted to the great saints.... How *light* and *transparent* the veil was that hid Jesus from our gaze! Doubt was impossible, faith and hope were unnecessary, and *Love* made us find on earth the One whom we were seeking." They were "spiritual sisters" realizing the words of St. John of the Cross (*Canticle*, stanza 25): they ran "lightly along the way," following the footprints of Jesus. Thérèse did not hesitate to write that they had received graces as lofty those granted to Monica and her son Augustine at Ostia (A 48r)!

Moreover, her confessor allowed her to receive Communion four times a week, something rare in that era. She wanted throughout her whole life to receive daily Communion, but was never able to do so.

After asking her father's permission to enter Carmel, she would have to overcome even greater obstacles.

The Struggle to Enter Carmel

First she had to obtain the permission of her uncle, Isidore Guérin, the surrogate guardian of his nieces who were still minors. Four months after speaking to her father she approached the pharmacist. He felt that she was too young to lead the life of a "philosopher"! Not before she was seventeen! So distinguished a citizen, he feared the criticism and gossip of the city. He was intransigent.

Thérèse was in tears when she left him, and her desolation lasted three days. For the first time—it would not be the last—she entered into the night, declaring the sleep of Jesus in which he was silent, apparently having forsaken her (A 51r–v). This was her first powerful purification, three days of agony that reminded her of Gethsemane. This trial came to an end thanks to a little "miracle." In fact it was Pauline who made this possible. She wrote a persuasive letter to her uncle in which she said she believed in the vocation of her little sister, as did the prioress, Mother Marie de Gonzague.

On Saturday, October 22, Uncle Isidore received Thérèse affectionately and gave her his permission. Thérèse believed that she had reached her goal. Alas, at Carmel she learned that the ecclesiastical superior, Canon Delatroëtte, was adamantly opposed to her entrance before she was twenty-one. She was crushed by this "insurmountable opposition." Canon Delatroëtte had just had a difficult experience with the Fleuriot family whose daughter Jeanne had to leave Carmel after some problems. He did not want to face such criticisms once again, especially because the little Martin girl had been sick. She was said to be delicate, and Carmel's physician, Doctor de Cornière, agreed with this opinion: he did not approve her entrance. Despite a visit from Monsieur Louis Martin accompanied by Thérèse and Céline, the Father Superior remained inflexible.

Again Thérèse shed more tears and resolved to go to Bayeux to call on Bishop Hugonin. But already in her heart, knowing that she was going on a pilgrimage to Rome, she hoped to speak to the pope. On October 31, in a heavy rainstorm (this was a bad sign for Thérèse), Monsieur Martin brought her to the episcopal residence in Bayeux to meet the bishop. The cathedral was packed. It was a funeral Mass for Madame Octavie-Félicité Quesnault de Grondière. In his simplicity Monsieur Martin had led his daughter, clothed entirely in white, to a little chapel behind the main altar!

After a cheerless meal in a very good restaurant in the city, the Martins were received by Father Révérony, the Vicar General, and brought to Bishop Hugonin. Thérèse was wearing a white dress and had fixed her hair in a bun so as to seem older. She explained the purpose of her visit, but the bishop thought that she had plenty of time. He believed that he was pleasing Monsieur Martin by the delay because two of her sisters were already in Carmel, but he marveled to see that the generous father was ready for this new sacrifice. When he learned that the Martins were going on the pilgrimage to Rome to visit Pope Leo XIII, the bishop said he would give his answer while they were in Italy. What a disappointment on leaving the episcopal palace to know it had been a futile attempt! Tears flowed abundantly. But it was time to think of the great trip to Rome. The departure date was set for the fourth of November.

An Eventful Pilgrimage

This pilgrimage had been organized by the diocese of Coutances under the direction of Bishop Germain. The diocese of Bayeux and Lisieux also joined, and Father Révérony was chosen to represent Bishop Hugonin. The occasion was the celebration of the golden jubilee of Pope Leo XIII's ordination to the priesthood. This was all the more significant because the Holy Father had just suffered the anticlerical spoliations of the Crispi government. This was an opportunity to comfort the Holy Father with the faith of those from beyond the Alps.

The pilgrimage began on November 7 and ended December 2, 1887. It included visits to many Italian cities and a ten-day stay in Rome with a papal audience. This would give the young Thérèse an ideal opportunity to speak to the pope about her desire to enter Carmel at Christmas.

The pilgrimage included 197 pilgrims, of whom nearly one-fourth belonged to the nobility. Obviously the price of the trip, 660 francs for first class, was a limiting factor. Sixty-five priests accompanied the group. Because this pilgrimage was rather exceptional, the French and Italian press gave it plenty of publicity, not to mention all the reports published later in the weekly papers of the dioceses involved.

This month away from Calvados was going to be decisive in the formation and vocation of the young Thérèse. Even on her deathbed she would recall memories of this great trip, exceptional at that time for a young girl of her age.

First of all, there was the discovery of other regions, other countries, other landscapes so novel for a young Normandy girl: Switzerland, Italy with its prestigious towns (Milan, Padua, Venice, Bologna, Pompeii, Naples, Florence, Pisa, Genoa), treasures of art and history. There was so much to learn about religion: the papacy in Rome, the many saints honored in all these places (Agnes, Cecilia, Francis of Assisi, Charles Borromeo). These were indelibly engraved in the memory of the young Carmelite. The pilgrimage began with three days spent in Paris. There were many who could see in the capital nothing more than a "modern Babylon" full of terrible dangers. The two Martin girls concentrated on the historic monuments, rode up the elevators of the big Printemps department store, and walked down the Champs-Elysées.

Contact with different classes of society had an effect on Thérèse. At the close of the nineteenth century, sharp distinctions were still clearly preserved in French society. The Martins came from a working-class family who had managed by their own efforts and careful economy to increase their holdings. But they did not move in aristocratic circles. Thérèse, timid by nature, found herself in a society to which she was not accustomed. As a simple commoner she discovered that "true greatness is to be found in *the soul,* not in a *name*" (A 56r). She was perfectly at ease at the evening parties in the hotels of Venice or Rome. The cure of Christmas 1886 had yielded lasting fruits.

Another discovery, more troubling, involved men. Surrounded by sisters and female cousins (the Guérins and the Maudelondes), Thérèse had few contacts with boys. On the pilgrimage she met many. The two Martin girls, elegantly dressed and in the charm of their youth (they were fifteen and eighteen), could not pass unnoticed. Céline remembers that "there was talk of marriages." Thérèse was well aware that she could easily have made a brilliant match. She realized that this trip could affect her vocation.

The attentions men paid her grew more insistent. When she wrote that her memories of Bologna were not pleasant, the reason was that the French pilgrims' train was met by a swarm of Italian students. On the platform, one of them grabbed her in his arms and tried to drag her away, but Thérèse gave him such a look that he released her (VT no. 81, p. 38).

Another experience, which would touch the future Carmelite more profoundly, was living in such proximity to priests. Before this she had always seen them exercising their priestly duties at the altar, in the confessional, teaching catechism. She thought of them as "angels" and she could not understand why St. Teresa of Avila asked that the reformed Carmelites pray for priests. Thérèse Martin thought it right that they should pray for sinners, but why pray for priests? She was to say later that she discovered her vocation in Italy. "I lived in the company of many *saintly priests* for a month and I learned that, though their dignity raises them above the angels, they are nevertheless weak and fragile men" (A 56r).

What did she see that could have scandalized her? Probably nothing very serious. But their life together showed her realistically that priests have their own defects, their taste for fine Italian food and excellent wine. She could also suffer—as we see later—from their lack of fervor in the celebration of the sacraments, especially the Eucharist.

All these new experiences, concentrated in less than a month, were enormously instructive for the young Thérèse. She wrote that this trip "taught more than long years of studies."

But even more, it was for her an interior experience of the first importance. From the start, she knew that

78

79

80

81

78. Thérèse Martin at age fifteen, some days before entering Carmel.

79. Paris. Church of Our Lady of Victories. Facade.

80. Paris. Church of Our Lady of Victories. The statue of Our Lady.

81. Paris. Basilica of the Sacré-Coeur in Montmartre. Crypt. In 1887 the basilica was not yet finished.

82. Switzerland. Panorama between Lucerne and Saint Gotthard (cf. (A 57v–58r).

83. Switzerland. Flüelen on Lake Lucerne along the railroad route.

84. Switzerland. Precipices and waterfalls in the vicinity of Saint Gotthard.

82

83

84

85

86

87

85–86. Milan. The Campo Santo (cemetery). "One would almost be tempted to console these imaginary personages who were all around us" (A 58v).

87. Milan. Cemetery. "Campo Santo attracted us even more than the cathedral" (A 58v).

88. Milan. The Cathedral. Thérèse climbed to the very top of the highest belltower (cf. A 58r–v).

89. Venice. San Marco. "Venice was not without its charms" (A 58v).

90. Padua. Basilica of Saint Anthony. Belltower.

88

89

90

91

92

93

91. Loreto. Basilica of the Holy House. Facade. (cf. A 59v).

92. Loreto. Basilica of the Holy House. Thérèse receiving communion in the Holy House (A 59v). Fresco by Cesare Peruzzi.

93. Loreto. Basilica of the Holy House. The "little bowl of the Child Jesus," in which Thérèse placed her rosary (cf. A 59v).

94. Loreto. The Holy House, interior. Thérèse received communion here with Céline: "Our greatest consolation was to receive Jesus *Himself* in His *house* and to be His living temple" (A 60r).

94

95

96

97

98

95. Rome. St. Peter's Square.

96. Rome. Albergo del Sud, on the Via Capo le Case (first building on the right), the hotel where Thérèse stayed.

97. Rome. Basilica of the Holy Cross. Relics of the cross, venerated and touched by Thérèse (cf. A 66v).

98. Rome. The arena in the Colosseum (cf. A 60v–61r).

99. Rome. Catacombs of St. Callistus. Statue of St. Cecilia (cf. A 61r–v).

99

100

101

IL 17 NOVEMBRE DEL 1887
PELLEGRINA AI PIEDI DI·LEONE XIII
PER IMPLORARNE QUINDICENNE L'INGRESSO AL CARMELO
IN QUESTO CONVENTO E CHIESA DI
S.MARIA DELLA VITTORIA
SOSTÒ IN PREGHIERA
L'ANGELICA TERESA MARTIN
QUASI AD ARCANO PRESAGIO
CHE QUESTO STESSO CONVENTO
SCELTO A SEDE DELLA POSTULAZIONE
DOVEVA PROMUOVERE
L'INCOMPARABILE APOTEOSI DI COLEI
CHE IL 17 MAGGIO DEL 1925
ALLA PAROLA INFALLIBILE DI PIO XI
IL GRIDO DI TUTTO IL MONDO ACCLAMAVA
SANTA TERESA DI GESÙ BAMBINO

I CARMELITANI SCALZI
A TESTIMONIANZA DI PERENNE DEVOZIONE
IL 2 GENNAIO DEL 1962

102

103

104

105

106

100. Rome. Santa Maria della Vittoria, church of the Discalced Carmelite friars. Facade.

101. Lisieux. Carmelite chapel. Stained-glass window of Thérèse Martin and Leo XIII (cf. A 62r–64r).

102. Rome. Santa Maria della Vittoria. Inside the cloister, memorial plaque of Thérèse's visit.

103. Rome. Santa Maria della Vittoria. Cloister. Thérèse by mistake "advanced into the inner cloisters." ("Ah! poor women" who "are so easily excommunicated in Italy.") A "good old Carmelite friar," instead of chasing her away "smiled at me kindly" (cf. A 66v).

104. Rome. Santa Maria della Vittoria. Interior.

105–106. Pompei. Ancient ruins: "I would have loved to walk all by myself in these ruins, meditating on the fragility of things human" (A 64v).

107

108

107. Assisi. Basilica of St. Francis.

108. Lisieux. Basilica of St. Thérèse. Mosaic of St. Francis of Assisi: "Blessed are the poor in spirit."

109. Pisa. Piazza dei Miracoli. The tower.

110. Florence. Panorama.

111. Florence. Monastery of the Carmelite nuns. St. Mary Magdalen de' Pazzi, venerated by Thérèse (cf. A 66r).

112. Genoa. The old city and the port (cf. A 66v).

113. Lyon. Shrine of Notre-Dame de Fourvière. Here on December 1 the last leg of Thérèse's pilgrimage ended: "Ah! what poetry flooded my soul at the sight of all these things I was seeing for the first and last time in my life!" (A 67r).

110

111

112

113

in a sense it would be a test of her vocation, because of the various temptations already related and also because she knew that Father Révérony had been charged by Bishop Hugonin to study the young candidate and report to him her suitability for cloistered life.

At the beginning of the pilgrimage she had a special privilege. Louis Martin had reserved rooms in a hotel near Our Lady of Victories, the famous sanctuary venerated by the Guérin and Martin families. There the young girl received a great grace. Kneeling before the statue of the Blessed Virgin, she understood that she had been wrong to harbor her "spiritual trial" for four years. Mary was not displeased because she had spoken of the grace received on May 13, 1883. Thérèse had not betrayed Mary's secret. No, Thérèse had not imagined anything. "The Blessed Virgin made me feel it was really herself who smiled on me and brought about my cure" (A 56v). What a consolation and liberation! Anticipating the possible dangers of the trip, she entrusted her purity to Mary and St. Joseph (A 57r).

On Sunday, November 6, the pilgrims assembled in the crypt of Montmartre (the basilica was not yet completed). They were consecrated to the Sacred Heart. They could now depart.

To Speak With the Pope!

The spiritual high point of the pilgrimage was obviously the expected audience with Pope Leo XIII! The exact date was not yet known. The intense correspondence between Rome and Lisieux (at that time mail between France and Italy traveled very quickly) shows their impatience and uncertainty: Should she speak to the pope or not? Pauline directed the proceedings, wavering. Finally, the answer was "Yes."

The great day finally arrived, Sunday, November 20. The ceremony was long and complicated. After two Masses, Leo XIII received the long line of pilgrims. First

he welcomed the women, then came the priests, followed by the men. The emaciated pope was exhausted. Father Révérony, the Vicar General, standing beside His Holiness, forbade anyone to speak to him. Thérèse, who was about to pass him, hesitated. But the intrepid Céline pushed her: "Speak!"

Kneeling at his knees, poor Thérèse said: "Most Holy Father, I have a great favor to ask you…to enter Carmel at the age of fifteen." The old man did not understand. Father Révérony interrupted and explained. Thérèse continued: "Oh! Holy Father, if you say yes, everybody will agree!" The pope fixed his piercing eyes on her: "You will enter if God wills it." Thérèse hung on. Two noble guards had to lift her and carry her weeping to the door (A 62–63). Céline, on her knees, begged the Holy Father to bless the Lisieux Carmel.

Father Révérony grew impatient: these young Martin girls are very persistent! Nevertheless a few moments later when Louis Martin was presented in his turn (he had seen nothing of the incident) the Vicar General was most gracious and told Leo XIII that this gentleman was the father of two Carmelites. The pope placed his hand on his head and blessed him. But Father Révérony made no attempt to explain that he was the father of the two insistent young ladies who had preceded him.

Céline was disconsolate, declaring that the audience was a "fiasco." That very evening Thérèse wrote to Pauline about her grief and her tears. But she gave herself to the Child Jesus as his toy. She added that "the good pope is so old that one would say he is dead; I would never have pictured him like this. He can hardly say anything. It is M. Révérony who talks" (LT 36).

The latter never held the incident during the audience against the future postulant. All the pilgrims who learned of her experience spoke sympathetically about "the little Carmelite." On November 24 *l'Univers* reported the story. It was from this paper that her confessor in Lisieux, Father Lepelletier, learned about the incident. She had never spoken to him about it. Jesus alone was her real director. "I went to confession only a few times, and never spoke about my interior sentiments. The way I was walking was so straight, so clear, I needed no other guide but Jesus" (A 48v).

Under the careful scrutiny of the Vicar General who was evaluating the capabilities of the future Carmelite, Thérèse could have adopted a formal attitude, a pious expression, and lowered eyes. On the contrary, she behaved perfectly naturally, full of life, curious about the wonders of the trip even after November 20. Father Révérony was very discerning. Finally he believed in her vocation. On the road to Nice he promised to plead the cause with Bishop Hugonin.

The return was less joyful, but no less interesting. They stopped at various sanctuaries: Notre-Dame de la Garde at Marseilles and Fourvière at Lyons. On the second of December they were at Lisieux. It is easy to imagine the tales they told in the Carmelite speakroom. But about the essential point there was no information: Bishop Hugonin had not revealed himself in Italy. With only twenty-two days until Christmas, would Thérèse's dream be fulfilled to the letter?

The battle resumed but Father Delatroëtte remained intransigent. Thérèse wrote to Father Révérony, then to the bishop. There was nothing to be done but to wait. Every day until December 24 Louis Martin accompanied his daughter to the post office. No answer!

At last the long-awaited Christmas of 1887 arrived. What a contrast with the previous year, which had been so full of light and happiness. At Midnight Mass Thérèse meditated on this trial of faith, without losing hope and despite her tears. No doubt she also understood that one did not dictate dates to the Lord: he remained the Master. She was only a "little ball" in his hand. On that day Céline gave her a tiny boat; the sail bore the word "Abandonment." During this long period this was Thérèse's attitude.

She began her fifteenth year in 1888. A letter from Pauline brought the news that on December 28, the feast of the Holy Innocents, Bishop Hugonin authorized her entrance at the Lisieux Carmel. There was a "but." The Carmelites, considering the candidate too young to face entry during the Lenten fast, decided on a three-month delay! Her joy was also a bitter disappointment. But Thérèse was willing to accept this trial, which would enable her to "grow very much in abandonment and the other virtues" (A 68r).

To complete her training she followed several classes with Madame Papinau. But above all she prepared herself for the life she was about to begin. This did not involve great penances but fidelity in little things, mortifying her will, "always so ready to impose itself on others," "rendering little services without any recognition." "It was through the practice of these nothings that I prepared myself to become the fiancée of Jesus" (A 68v). At last these three months passed quickly, leaving her with a happy memory.

Her father, always ready to travel, proposed a pilgrimage to the Holy Land. Her first impulse was to know the places where Jesus lived. She had a realistic sense of the Incarnation! But this would mean a delay of two or three months before she could enter. This she could not accept, having struggled so much to enter as soon as possible. Did she have some doubts about her decision? This seems unlikely. The return of Léonie, who left the Visitation of Caen on January 6 (this was her second departure after leaving the Poor Clares), reminded her that her new life would not be easy. Her sister had told her to reflect seriously before entering religion. This was not a step to be taken lightly. But Thérèse's resolution was firm. She said she was acting "without any illusions" (A 69v).

Despite appearances to the contrary, she already had a profound experience of a life lived with Jesus, and of the graces and sufferings that this required. She had known and endured multiple purifications, learning by experience what it means to be saved by grace. Only one thing mattered: to live hidden with her future Spouse "to love him and to make him loved." Even if she had presentiments about the brevity of her life, she couldn't have known that her time in this place would last no longer than nine years, time enough to "run as a giant" (A 44v).

map
Itinerary of the French pilgrimage in which Thérèse, her father, and her sister Céline participated (drawn by Renzo Restani).

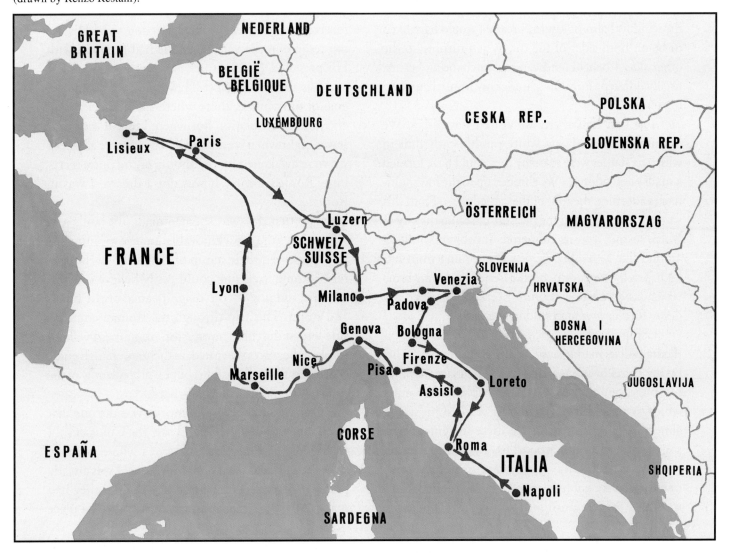

Thérèse Speaks

Toward the Eternal City

After our solemn consecration to the Sacred Heart in the Basilica at Montmartre, we departed from Paris on Monday [November 7]. We very quickly became acquainted with the different people on the pilgrimage. So timid that I usually dared not speak, I was surprised to find myself completely freed from this crippling fault. I was talking freely with the great ladies, the priests, and even the Bishop of Coutances. (A 57r)

Before reaching the "Eternal City," the goal of our pilgrimage, we were given the opportunity of contemplating many marvels. First, there was Switzerland with its mountains whose summits were lost in the clouds, its graceful waterfalls gushing forth in a thousand different ways, its deep valleys literally covered with gigantic ferns and scarlet heather. Ah! Mother, how much good these beauties of nature, poured out *in such profusion,* did my soul. They raised it to heaven which was pleased to scatter such masterpieces on a place of exile destined to last only a day. I hadn't eyes enough to take in everything. Standing by the window I almost lost my breath; I would have liked to be on both sides of the car. When turning to the other side, I beheld landscapes of enchanting beauty, totally different from those under my immediate gaze. (A 57v)

The first Italian city we visited was Milan. We examined minutely its white marble cathedral in which its statues were so many they could have formed a small population.... We climbed up to the lower pinnacles adorning the roof of the cathedral.... From this vantage point, we had the pleasure of seeing the city of Milan at our feet, its numerous inhabitants milling around like *so many tiny ants.* Descending from our high perch, we commenced a series of driven tours which lasted a whole month. I certainly satisfied my desire forever *to ride* around in comfort!

Campo Santo attracted us even more than the cathedral. All its marble statues, seemingly brought to life by the chisel of some great genius, are placed around the huge cemetery in a sort of haphazard manner which to me added greatly to their charm. One would almost be tempted to console these imaginary personages who were all around us. The expression on the faces is so real, the sorrow so calm and resigned, one can hardly fail to recognize the thoughts of immortality which must necessarily have filled the

hearts of the artists creating these masterpieces. One saw a small child scattering flowers on the grave of its parents; the marble seemed to lose its heaviness as the delicate petals slipped through the child's fingers and the breeze scattered them. (A 58v–59r)

At Venice, the scene changed completely; instead of the noise of the great cities, one heard in the solitude nothing but the cries of the gondoliers and the murmur of the waves agitated by their oars. Venice was not without its charms, but I found this city sad. The palace of the Doges is splendid, however it too is sad where gold, wood, the most precious statues and paintings of the masters are on display. (A 58v)

And what shall I say about the Holy House [of Loreto]? Ah! how deep was my emotion when I found myself under the same roof as the Holy Family.... I beheld the little room in which the angel had appeared to the Blessed Virgin. I placed my rosary in the little bowl of the Child Jesus. What ravishing memories! Our greatest consolation was to receive *Jesus Himself* in His *house* and to be His living temple in the very place He had honored with His presence. (A 59v–60r)

It is about Rome I still have to speak, Rome the goal of our voyage, there where I believed I would encounter consolation but where I found the cross! It was night when we arrived and as we were all asleep we were awakened by the shouts of the porters crying: "Rome! Rome!" It was not a dream, I was in Rome!

The first day was spent outside the walls and was perhaps the most enjoyable, for the monuments have preserved their stamp of antiquity. In the center of Rome itself one could easily believe one was in Paris, judging by the magnificence of the hotels and stores. This trip through the Roman countryside left an indelible impression upon me. I will not speak of the places we visited, as there are enough guide books describing these fully, but I will speak only of the *principal* impressions I experienced.

One of my sweetest memories was the one that filled me with delight when I saw the Colosseum. I was finally gazing upon that arena where so many martyrs had shed their blood for Jesus. I was already preparing to kneel down and kiss the soil they had made holy, but what a disappointment! The place was nothing but a heap of ruins, and the pilgrims were expected to be satisfied with simply looking at these. A barrier prevented them from entering the ruins. No one would be tempted to do so. But was it possible to come all the way to Rome and not go down into the Colosseum?... I cried to Céline: "Come quick! We can get through!" We crossed the barrier where there was an opening, the fallen masonry hardly reaching up to the barrier, and we were climbing down over the ruins that rumbled under our feet.

Papa stared at us, surprised at our boldness. He was calling us back, but the two fugitives no longer heard anything. Just as warriors experience an increase in courage in the presence of danger, so our joy increased proportionately to the trouble we met with in attaining the object of our desire. Céline had listened to the guide and remembering that he had pointed out a tiny bit of pavement marked with a cross as the place where the martyrs fought, we began looking for it. We soon found it and threw ourselves on our knees on this sacred soil, and our souls were united in the same prayer. My heart was beating hard when my lips touched the dust stained with the blood of the first Christians. I asked for the grace of being a martyr for Jesus and felt that my prayer was answered! (A60r–61r)

The Catacombs, too, left a deep impression on me. They were exactly as I had imagined them when reading the lives of the martyrs. After having spent part of the afternoon in them, it seemed to me we were there for only a few moments, so sacred did the atmosphere appear to me. (A 61r–v)

On the morrow of that memorable day [of the papal audience], we had to leave early for Naples and Pompeii. In our honor, Mount Vesuvius made a lot of noise all day long.... The traces it has left upon the ruins of Pompeii are frightening and are a manifestation of God's power....

I would have loved to take a walk all by myself in these ruins, meditating on the fragility of things human, but the number of travelers took away a great part of the charm of the destroyed city. At Naples it was just the opposite. The trip to the monastery of San Martino, placed on top a hill dominating the whole city, was made magnificent by the *great number* of carriages drawn by two horses. Unfortunately, the horses took the bit into their own

mouths and more than once I was convinced I had seen my last hour. (A 65r–v)

At Florence, I was happy to contemplate St. Magdalene de' Pazzi in the Carmelite choir. They opened the big grille for us. As we did not know we would enjoy this privilege and many wanted to touch their rosaries to the Saint's tomb, I was the only one who could put my hand through the grating which separated us from the tomb. And so everybody was carrying rosaries to me and I was very proud of my office. I always had to find a way of *touching everything.* At the Holy Cross Church in Rome, we were able to venerate several pieces of the true Cross, two thorns, and one of the sacred nails. The nail was enclosed in a magnificent golden reliquary which *did not have a glass covering.* I found a way of placing my *little finger* in one of the openings of the reliquary, and could *touch* a nail bathed in the blood of Jesus. (A 66r–v)

One day when we were visiting a Carmelite monastery [in Rome], not content with following the pilgrims in the *outer* galleries, I advanced into the *inner* cloisters, when all of a sudden I saw a good old Carmelite friar at a little distance making a sign for me to leave. But instead of going, I approached him and showing him the cloister paintings I made a sign that they were beautiful. He undoubtedly understood by the way I wore my hair and from my youthful appearance that I was only a child, so he smiled at me kindly and left. He saw he was not in the presence of an enemy. Had I been able to speak Italian I would have told him I was a future Carmelite, but because of the builders of the Tower of Babel it was impossible for me.

After visiting Pisa and Genoa once more, we returned to France. On the return trip the scenery was magnificent. We travelled at times along the side of the sea and the railroad was so close to it that it seemed the waves were going to come right up to us. This impression was created by a tempest which was in progress. It was evening and the scene became all the more imposing. We passed through fields full of orange trees laden with ripe fruit, green olive trees with their light foliage, and graceful palm trees. It was getting dark and we could see many small seaports lighted up by many lights, while in the skies the first *stars* were beginning to sparkle. (A 66v–67r)

CHAPTER FOUR

Thérèse and Her Carmelite Community

GENEVIÈVE DEVERGNIES, OCD

Her trousseau had been prepared long in advance, and the painful leave-taking of all the familiar objects about her was complete. After one last walk around the family garden with her faithful dog Tom at her side, Thérèse was ready at last, and on the next day she would be entering Carmel. It was Low Sunday, April 8, 1888. The family attended morning Mass together in their beautiful parish church, the Cathedral of Saint-Pierre, where they sat, as was their custom, in a side chapel to the right of the main altar. In late afternoon, they returned there for the celebration of vespers.

Then Evening Came…

Monsieur Martin had invited all the close relatives to the family dinner: affectionate and wise Uncle Isidore, refined and thoughtful Aunt Céline, their daughters Jeanne and Marie, and of course Léonie, Céline, and Thérèse.

This small group, which had remained so closely knit since Madame Martin's death, assembled in the peaceful dining room. When the blessing was over, they seated themselves on the ornate, high-backed chairs around the old oak table, reserved for just such special occasions. Then came the breaking of bread together and the sharing of the best wine. A blazing fire was roaring on the hearth and warmth circulated in the room. The light from the candelabra played on the soft hair of the "Benjamin" of the family, while the buffet, the mirrors, the paintings on the wall, the fine porcelain on the embroidered tablecloth, were all animated by a strange play of shadows.

Unrelentingly time rushed on, consuming the evening. Now and again happy memories were recalled, but very soon everyone was once more lost in deep thought. Silence descended on the group, broken only by the measured tick-tock of the clock on the mantle. "Ah! how heartrending these family reunions can really be," Thérèse would later write. "When you would like

to see yourself forgotten, the most tender caresses and words are showered upon you, making the sacrifice of separation felt all the more" (A 68v).

Farewell childhood! Farewell sheltered nest! The hour for parting has arrived. Farsighted Thérèse, with her face resolutely turned to the future, was about to embark on the road leading to her own Jerusalem (cf. Lk 9:51): the Carmel, where Someone who loved her was awaiting her.

The Desert Will Flower

On Monday, April 9, the day on which the transferred feast of the Annunciation was to be celebrated, Thérèse got up at the crack of dawn. She got dressed quickly, putting on a light-blue woolen outfit that matched the color of her eyes. Casting one last glance over her familiar surroundings, she contemplated for a moment, through the window of the belvedere, the beloved landscape that was so often blurred by mists rising from the valleys of the Orbiquet, the Touques, and the Cirieux. From this vantage point, she took in the picturesque view of Lisieux, with its narrow streets lined with wooden houses of medieval design.

Leaving "that beautiful cradle of my childhood which I was never to see again" and the garden all pearled with dew, she set out "on my dear King's arm to climb Mount Carmel" (A 69r). The walk to the Carmel was a very short one: the budding Carmelite and her family went down the gravel path that ends at Les Buissonnets, passed in front of the old gray church of Saint-Jacques, crossed the little bridge that spans the Orbiquet, and filed down the narrow rue de Livarot (today called "rue de Carmel").

The chapel of the Carmel is a building of simple and modest proportions. At the altar, it is divided laterally by a grille, which separates the part reserved for the nuns from the space open to the public.

It was in this "public" section that Thérèse, surrounded by her loved ones, knelt to participate in the seven o'clock Mass. At Communion time, she could hear sobbing all around her. "I was the only one who didn't shed any tears" (A 69r), she would write. But Thérèse's heart was pounding. "Ah! what a moment that was! One would have to experience it to know what it is!" (A 69r).

The eucharistic celebration over, everyone walked to the door leading to the enclosure. There Thérèse embraced the whole family and knelt before her father to receive his blessing, but he himself knelt down and blessed his youngest, his "Benjamin," through his tears.

About ship! The anchor is weighed! The new postulant crossed the threshold of Carmel with a firm, determined step. The heavy oaken door, with its double locks and bolts, closed tightly behind her. Papa, Léonie, Céline, the Guérins would from now on be on the outside.

But Sister Marie of the Sacred Heart and Sister Agnes of Jesus, Marie and Pauline, were waiting for her within: "and there I was received by the *dear Sisters* who…had acted as mothers to me…. My desires were at last accomplished; my soul experienced a *PEACE* so sweet, so deep, it would be impossible to express it" (A 69v).

The following day Louis Martin would tell his friends, the Nogrix: "My little Queen entered Carmel yesterday. Only God could ask such a sacrifice of me; but he is helping me so powerfully that, in the midst of my tears, my heart is overflowing with joy" (CG 1142).

What is this "land of Carmel" where Thérèse was putting down her roots? The Order of the Blessed Virgin Mary of Mount Carmel began at the end of the twelfth century in the Holy Land, south of Haifa. There, in the Crusader kingdom, on the slopes and in the caves of Mount Carmel, a colony of Latin hermits settled down with the desire to imitate the prophet

Elijah, that man so attentive to the presence of the living God and zealous for God's glory.

The Rule of Life for this little group was drawn up by Albert, Patriarch of Jerusalem, around 1210, calling them "Hermit Brothers." This Rule was revised on June 8, 1245, by Pope Innocent IV and ratified by him on October 1, 1247. The feminine branch of Carmel with its contemplative vocation, however, did not come into existence until 1452.

Eventually the Order developed in the West, but after suffering a serious decline, due to an excessive mitigation of the Rule, it underwent a rebirth through the "reform" inaugurated by St. Teresa of Jesus. She began in 1562 with the founding of the Carmel of San José in Avila, Spain. Soon she was assisted in this reform by St. John of the Cross.

Teresa of Avila, along with a group of other Carmelites, wished to return to the "primitive" Rule of Carmel which, according to general opinion, contained a maximum of *spirit* with a minimum of *letter*. The Teresian "reform" spread to France, where the Discalced Carmelite nuns and friars lived in the spirit of *La Madre*, St. Teresa of Avila.

Discalced Carmelites are hermits who, paradoxically, live as brothers and sisters in small communities, "meditating day and night on the law of the Lord and keeping watch at prayer," as the Rule prescribes, in the heart of the church. As the "Order of the Virgin Mary," Carmel is totally Marian. With her and following her example, one is led to Carmel to hear the Word, receive it, and let it germinate within.

And what about the Carmel of Lisieux? Without hesitation Thérèse engulfed herself in it, knowing with an unshakable certitude on which bank to moor: it was there, beyond the wall of the visible world, that a boundless love, God himself, would break like a wave upon her.

Thérèse was embraced by all the nuns, now her sisters in Jesus Christ, "a new family whose devotion and tenderness could never be imagined by the outside world," according to the words of Mother Agnes of Jesus. Thérèse recounts:

> I was led, as are all postulants, to the choir…. What struck me first were the eyes of our holy Mother Geneviève which were fixed on me. I remained kneeling for a moment at her feet, thanking God for the grace He gave me of knowing a saint. (A 69v)

The young girl followed Mother Marie de Gonzague to the different parts of the community. The interior of the monastery was unfamiliar to her. Certainly her visits to the speakroom had given her a hint of the decor of this other side. She knew the eloquent significance of the grilles, armed with spikes, dating back to the time of the Spanish conquistadors. Besides, her two older sisters, already cloistered for several years, had informed her about the spirit and letter of Carmelite life.

Everything she saw pleased her then and there: the silent cloisters, the sparsely furnished rooms, the plain white walls on which were inscribed solemn quotations from Scripture. In fact, Thérèse was pleasantly surprised on her tour of this Carmel that her sister Marie had described, when she entered, as "small and poor." Thérèse concluded: "Everything thrilled me; I felt as though I was transported into a desert" (A 69v).

A Space for Sanctification

The entry rites completed, Thérèse was led down a long dormitory corridor (running past the doors of the cells) until she came to the door of her own cell. To foster a spirit of detachment, the Carmelites used to speak of the various things given to them for their use in the first person plural. Thus Thérèse would write: "*Our* little cell, above all, filled me with joy" (A 69v). Her glance seemed to caress each detail of this relatively small room—roughly ten by eight-and-three-quarters

feet (83.1 meters by 2.65 meters)—which would be hers for at least five years. In August of 1894 she would move to a cell in St. Elias dormitory, one with a small antechamber to serve as a workroom for her painting.

There was very little furniture in her cell. A bed resting on the bare clean floor, consisting of a plank on two trestles with a straw mattress on top, covered with brown blankets. No table. No running water. On a small stand, a water pitcher, an hourglass, and an oil lamp. A wicker basket containing sewing materials. A wooden "cell bench," very crudely made, on which rested a portable desk that the young Thérèse would later use while composing her autobiographical manuscripts and her correspondence.

On the white plaster wall hung a wooden cross, without the figure of Christ, which secretly invited the occupant to an oblation of self. No electricity nor heat. No horizon for Thérèse to see. Although the window, nearly ten feet high, let in a lot of sunshine all afternoon, the view was obstructed by the slate roof of an adjacent building. Thérèse experienced a feeling of calm: "Ah! I was fully recompensed for all my trials. With what deep joy I repeated those words: 'I am here forever and ever!'" (A 69v). It was with jubilation that she signed her first letter written to her father: "Your little Queen" who is "at last pulled from under the cart," an expression from that part of Normandy meaning, in Thérèse's case, "Here you are sheltered from the dangers of the world!" (LT 46).

Actually, an immense peace flooded her soul, a peace that she would maintain throughout her severest trials. This was the definitive affirmation of the Lord's call, Alleluia! Now, in the desert of her own cell, Thérèse would meditate continually on the Word and would be watchful in prayer. Another element would be worked out in this solitude: her relationship with the community. She would live it, above all, as the ecclesial perfection of love and as the daily call to union with her Sisters.

The Origins and Spirit of Carmel in France

Stéphane-Marie Morgain, OCD

The arrival in Paris on October 15, 1604, of six Discalced Carmelite nuns from Spain ended the difficult birth of the first foundation of the Teresian Carmel in France and inaugurated an extraordinary adventure. The six nuns included four Spaniards (Anne of Jesus [de Lobera], Anne of St. Bartholomew [Garcia], Isabel of the Angels [Márquez Mexia], and Beatrix of the Conception) and two Flemish (Léonor of St. Bernard and Isabel of St. Paul [de Chavaira]).

The idea of founding a monastery of the Teresian Reform in France was not new. It was born by chance in the speakroom of Seville, between Mother Maria de San José (Salazar) and Jean de Quintanadueñas de Brétigny, a young man of Spanish extraction from Rouen. The project, encouraged in October 1585 by Nicolas of Jesus and Mary (Doria), then provincial of the discalced, came up against France's internal conflicts. Torn by religious wars, France was anxiously looking for a Catholic king who could reestablish the kingdom's unity and manage the bad relations with Spain.

Between 1601 and 1602, rather than definitely renouncing his foundation plan, Jean de Brétigny bided his time by translating the writings of Saint Teresa, published in Spain in 1588. Three volumes appeared in succession: the *Autobiography,* the *Way of Perfection*, and the *Interior Castle.* Finally, he published in French the life of Mother Teresa of Jesus written by Francisco de Ribéra in 1590. Preceding her daughters, Teresa conquered the heart of France. The impact was immediate.

A group of Parisian Catholics, close to the Catholic League and hostile to the Edict of Nantes, united by convictions and often by blood, endeavored to promote the spiritual renewal of a France exhausted by religious quarrels. Barbe Avrillot, the wife of Peter Acarie, was the mainspring. In the salons of her mansion on rue des Juifs she used to gather about herself men and women—aristocrats, members of parliament, ecclesiastics, doctors of the Sorbonne, students—all driven by the same reforming zeal. Michel de Marillac mingled there with René Gualtier, André Duval, Philippe de Gamaches, François Tremblay, Dom Richard Beaucousin, Benet of Canfield, Philippe de Cospeau, the Marquise de Maignelay, and the young Pierre de Bérulle.

Sensitive to Saint Teresa's intuition, the little "areopagus" decided, with Francis de Sales's temporary assistance, to undertake the steps necessary for a foundation. In Paris, Madame Acarie was in charge of forming candidates who were already pressing to enter; meanwhile Catherine of Orleans, princess of Longueville, was looking for some buildings for the future monastery. In Spain, Jean de Brétigny was trying to convince the Discalced Carmelite friars to allow Sisters to leave who had known Mother Teresa and would be able to introduce into France the Reform from across the Pyrenees. In Rome, Denis de Santeuil obtained the bull for the foundation, a bull inspired by the one governing the monastery of Carmelite nuns in Rome, founded in 1597. On July 18, Henry IV granted the patent letters for the establishment of the Carmelite nuns, and on November 13, 1603, the papal bull was dispatched. In accord with French demands, the Carmelite nuns would be governed by three ecclesiastical superiors (Jacques Gallemant, André Duval, and Pierre Bérulle); visitations would be done by the prior of the Carthusians while awaiting the arrival of the Carmelite friars. (This arrangement would be modified in 1606 and in 1616 when Paul V named Pierre de Bérulle perpetual visitator to the Discalced Carmelite nuns of France. The Discalced Carmelite friars of the Italian Congregation, arriving in Paris in 1611, were unable according to their *Constitutions* to take charge of directing the nuns.)

All was ready. Only the Carmelite nuns were missing! After many procrastinations, difficulties, subterfuges, and impatient moments that required the direct intervention of Pierre de Bérulle and repeated consultations with Madame Acarie, the nuns arrived in Paris, happy to bring there the Teresian ideal.

The clash of mentalities, habits, and spiritualities was brutal yet without becoming violent. The Spanish Discalced Carmelite nuns, convinced that they were going to die as martyrs in this heretical

This community of nuns formed a vibrant and rather homogeneous group whose median age was about forty-seven. They were of average intelligence with an evident lack of culture and education—the prioress, the Martin sisters, and three or four others being the exception.

For the most part, a spirit of good will was evident among them. Their piety was sincere, if not always enlightened. There was a fair amount of awkwardness and austerity in the practice of the common life, with a somewhat narrow observance of the Rule, but an authentic charity, practiced by limited intelligences.

land, were amazed at the welcome accorded them. For their "viaticum," they brought with them the 1582 *Constitutions* of Alcalá (as modified by Anne of Jesus in 1588) as well as their exuberant and colorful baroque piety. They discovered the austere and classic devotion of the French, lacking in spontaneity but not in grace. The aristocratic iconography of the French School contrasted with the striking [Spanish] images of Christ or the Madonna covered with embroideries and brocades.

After the forced departure of the Jesuits (1594), the French candidates to the Order were placed under the direction of the Capuchins. The mystical orientation of Laurent de Paris, Archange de Pembrocke, Honoré de Champigny, Joseph de Tremblay, but especially Benet of Canfield left a strong impression on this period. They formed the future Carmelites in "experiential unity of the spirit" and "the essential will of God." This mysticism of essence, derived chiefly from the *Mystical Theology* of Harphius and the writings of Ruysbroeck, prepared the French candidates badly for entering the world of Teresian spirituality, marked by the humanity of Christ, the "friendly conversation" of prayer, the simple and unceremonious relation between the soul and God. Neither did Pierre de Bérulle, formed in this same school but with an independent mind imbued with the theology of the Church Fathers and the writings of Pseudo-Dionysius, have the means to grasp at first what the Spanish foundresses wanted to make him understand. Nevertheless, Anne of St. Bartholomew, with the help of other Carmelites, would lead Pierre de Bérulle to the contemplation of the mystery of the Word Incarnate. In exchange, he would give to Saint Teresa's Christology a new and more expanded interpretation.

The spiritual difficulties could have been surmounted easily. Bérulle worked for the spread of the nuns and they collaborated freely with him. Anne of St. Bartholomew and Madeleine of St. Joseph (de Fontaines Marans) encouraged the prelate to found a congregation of priests, the Oratory of Jesus and Mary (1611), which could have looked after the Carmelite nuns. But Bérulle gave his congregation another mission. The conflict between Bérulle and some monasteries of Carmelite nuns flared up violently over juridical questions. The Discalced Carmelite friars of the Italian Congregation, in France since 1611, thought they could obtain governance of the nuns by virtue of the first article of the Alcalá *Constitutions.* They were supported in their claim by certain prioresses who wished to see the letter of Saint Teresa's wishes enforced on this point. But the *Constitutions* of the Italian Congregation of the friars, the bulls and papal briefs, the pope and the head of the Italian Congregation, favored Bérulle and confirmed him in his office. The dispute then shifted to a theological problem.

One June 5, 1615, Bérulle imposed on the Carmelites of Chalon a vow of absolute servitude to the Blessed Virgin Mary. Ignorant of theological distinctions and frightened by the formula's complexity, the nuns were alarmed. Persuaded to introduce the Sisters for whom he was responsible into his Marian spirituality, Bérulle became aware too late of his blunder. The scandal was immense. The ordinance was annulled. The Carmelite friars seized upon the defective formula in order to have it condemned and thus prove Bérulle's incapacity to govern the Carmelite nuns. The affair divided the monasteries, troubled the king, disturbed the pope who counted on the French Oratorians to reform the clergy, and provoked the bishops who were jealous of their authority over strictly enclosed monasteries. This devotion later spread more discreetly. Weighed down with calumnies, Bérulle nonetheless won the case, and the Discalced Carmelite friars were punished.

Bérulle was unable to contribute to an authentic Teresian Carmelite formation. He had come to know the spirit of "Madre" Teresa too late. On the other hand, he had favored the introduction of the Order into France, and stimulated its growth despite the crises. It was in the cloister that the Carmelite nuns came to know their foundress. The role of the Spanish Mothers was irreplaceable. Moreover, Thérèse of the Child Jesus would dream of Anne of Jesus many years later, and would recognize her immediately.

It was, therefore, the mediocrity of human nature bathing in an atmosphere of courage, and of joy mixed with shadows, where one could be sanctified without being unhappy.

The community Thérèse entered was definitely fervent and united on essentials: to save souls, to intercede for humanity, to pray for priests, for the church, and to give glory to God. Such are the great motives proposed to every Carmelite. Each one, according to personal temperament and grace, endeavors to respond to them under the promptings of the Spirit.

The Lisieux Carmel

Geneviève Devergnies, OCD

The inauguration of the Lisieux Carmel could find a place in Saint Teresa of Avila's *Book of Foundations,* so dramatic were its beginnings. Two young ladies from Pont-Audemer, Athalie and Désirée Gosselin, aspiring to Carmelite religious life, decided to dedicate their rather modest fortune to the building of a Carmel. Mgr. Dancel, bishop of Bayeux, directed them toward Lisieux, giving them as future superior a Sulpician priest from Lisieux, Pierre Sauvage, curate of the church of Saint-Jacques.

Thus on March 16, 1838, the coach deposited at the little town's inn four novices from Normandy and two professed Carmelite nuns from Poitiers: Sister Elizabeth of Saint Louis, who would assume the office of prioress, and Sister Geneviève of Saint Teresa, named subprioress and mistress of novices. Mother Elizabeth died four years later. Sister Geneviève then became prioress in 1842. She would hold this office, except during the periods provided for in the Constitutions, until 1886. She was considered the true foundress of the Lisieux Carmel.

The Carmel was under construction. There was no question of conveniently settling there within a few weeks. In a driving rain, a canvas-covered cart took the travellers to Chausseé Beuvillers, the home of Madame Le Boucher, a hospitable and generous widow who offered to lodge them in her cottage.

On August 24, 1838, the new bishop of Bayeux, Mgr. Robin, blessed the oratory under the title of "Mary conceived without sin." Later it would receive the additional titles of "the Sacred Heart of Jesus" and "Saint Thérèse of the Child Jesus."

On September 5, the embryonic community moved to a slightly larger dilapidated house on rue de Livarot, which would give way to the present Carmel. On September 16, the two Gosselin sisters and Caroline Guéret made their profession. On March 19, 1839, the feast of Saint Joseph, the first postulant presented herself.

The community lived in real poverty, bordering on destitution. Trials came but the monastery quickly took on a beautiful spiritual vigor, so much that by 1861 Sister Philomène of the Immaculate Conception

was able to leave Lisieux accompanied by three other Sisters of her community to go to Saigon and found the first Carmel in the missions of the Far East. Ties would always remain strong between these two monasteries.

Father Sauvage himself gathered throughout France the necessary donations for the construction of Carmel's chapel. On September 6, 1852, Mgr. Robin blessed the new sanctuary. Father Sauvage died a few months later in April 1853. The Carmelite nuns buried him near the choir grille, in their little chapel built by his efforts. A few months later, while still pastor of Saint-Jacques, Canon Delatroëtte would claim the title of superior of the Carmel, from 1867 to 1895.

It was only in 1858 that Mother Aimée of Jesus, who replaced Mother Geneviève for three years as head of the Lisieux Carmel, was able to build the first big monastery wing. Mother Marie de Gonzague, who succeeded Mother Geneviève of St. Teresa, set herself from 1876 to giving the monastery its definitive shape. When Thérèse entered the Carmel in 1888, the monastery had only been finished for eleven years. Some forty years were necessary for its completion. Situated at the bottom of a basin near the Orbiquet, the monastery, rising above the rue de Livarot in the center of old Lisieux, presents a unity of geometric construction in dark red brick.

The cloister square is constituted along one side by the length of the chapel and the nuns' choir; from one side to the other two wings of the building take shape; and the fourth side puts the finishing touches on the whole, with the harmoniously proportioned cylindrical vaulted arcades of a cloister in the most austere style.

A large granite crucifix, built in 1877, dominates the inner courtyard. The garden is narrow, squeezed between the course of the Orbiquet with its muddy waters and the neighboring properties. A lovely little alley of chestnut trees borders a small piece of hayfield, "the meadow" planted with some pear trees. The young Discalced Carmelite nun will love this familiar little landscape.

Thérèse Among Her Sisters

At noon, for her first recreation, Thérèse again greeted all her new Sisters, with whom she was going to live in solidarity from this moment on until her death. Very quickly she got to know the twenty-six nuns who formed the community of the Lisieux Carmel in 1888. Here are brief biographical sketches of each of the Sisters.

Mother Geneviève of St. Teresa (1805–1891)

Claire-Marie-Radegonde Bertrand, born in Poitiers on July 19, 1805. Entered the Carmel of that city on March 26, 1830. Became novice mistress in 1837, and was sent as foundress to Lisieux on March 16, 1838. Subprioress and then elected prioress for five terms. She was venerated by her Sisters, who were edified by her activity totally permeated with prayer.

Thérèse only knew her as an invalid and would pay tribute to her unfailing abandonment: "On more than one occasion I received great consolations from her.... Jesus was living in her and making her act and speak" (A 78r). There was a real spiritual rapport between these two Sisters. In the course of an extremely rigorous winter, Mother Geneviève died on December 5, 1891, in her eighty-seventh year. It was the first time Thérèse had assisted at a death, and to her it was a "ravishing" sight. She gathered up the last tear of the saintly Mother, and shortly thereafter heard Mother Geneviève say to her in a dream: "To you I leave my *heart*" (A 79r).

In the sanctuary of the Carmelite chapel, even to this day, Mother Geneviève of St. Teresa rests under the same tombstone as Abbé Sauvage. Three weeks prior to her death, the Carmelites asked Doctor de Cornière to remove Mother Geneviève's heart when she died, so that they would have a first-class relic to venerate of the one they considered their saintly foundress.

Mother Marie de Gonzague (1834–1904)

Marie-Adèle-Rosalie Davy de Virville, born in Caen on February 2, 1834, of a family of seven children. Her father was a magistrate. She was educated at the Visitation of Caen, where she acquired solid principles of morality. Welcomed to the Lisieux Carmel on September 29, 1860, by Mother Geneviève of St. Teresa, she made her profession in 1862. Elected prioress in 1874, Mother Marie de Gonzague remained in that position for twenty-seven years, apart from the intervals prescribed by the Rule (a prioress was elected each time for a three-year term and at the end of six years in office was obliged to step down, leaving the office to another religious).

After the flood of July 7, 1876, which left the ground floor of the monastery covered with a layer of mud nearly six feet deep, she courageously undertook the restoration and extension of the monastery, soliciting financial aid from her relatives. This permitted her to complete, in eighteen months, the construction of the two wings of the cloister: the one that comprises the infirmary and the other that opens to the garden.

When Thérèse Martin entered in 1888, Mother Marie de Gonzague was fifty-four years old. She had lost nothing of her tall stature, her distinguished bearing, and her natural charm, despite the domineering expression on her face. Her sound judgment was deeply appreciated by the clergy of Lisieux. Very approachable, her numerous qualities of intelligence, heart, and good manners attracted the sympathies of outsiders. On the other hand, being rather touchy by nature and jealous of her authority, it was very painful for her to see the leadership of the monastery pass, one day, into the hands of another. An energetic woman and of good judgment, efficient and alert, she most often treated community matters according to the mood of the moment and as her fancy dictated. Mother Marie de Gonzague held an extremely important position in Carmel and she marked the community with her forceful personality. She died on December 17, 1904, in a terribly pathetic state, of cancer of the tongue, humbly confessing her faults, lovingly surrounded by the three Martin sisters, and putting all her trust in the intercession of "her" little Thérèse, who had died seven years before her.

Without the benevolent authority of Mother Marie de Gonzague, the four Martin sisters (and their cousin Marie Guérin) would never have been admitted into the same community. With Thérèse she was very strict, sometimes unjust. At the same time, sizing up with a rare intuition the profound spiritual capacity of this very young girl, she was ingenious in testing her in a thousand ways. This was done, undoubtedly, to spur Thérèse on to greater virtue. Mother Marie de Gonzague actually esteemed Thérèse very highly, as is seen in a letter written to Madame Guérin on May 17, 1888: "I would never have believed such an advanced judgment in a fifteen-year-old; I don't have to say a word to her, she is perfect."

As for Thérèse, she will remark tersely: "Our Mother Prioress, frequently ill, had little time to spend with me. I know that she loved me very much and said everything good about me that was possible, nevertheless, God permitted that she was VERY SEVERE *without her even being aware of it*.... What would have become of me if I had been the 'pet' of the community?" (A 70v).

Mother Agnes of Jesus (1861–1951)

Marie-Pauline Martin, sister and "little mother" of Thérèse; born in Alençon (Orne), on September 7, 1861. Second child of the Martin family; had her uncle Isidore Guérin as a godfather. Did her studies at the Visitation of Le Mans (1868–1877).

Entered the Carmel of Lisieux on October 2, 1882; received the habit on April 6, 1883; and made her profession on May 8, 1884—the same day on which Thérèse received her First Communion! Elected prioress on February 20, 1893 for three years. Re-elected prioress on April 19, 1902 for six years. Except for an interruption of eighteen months (1908–1909) she was

to remain in office until her death, at the express command of Pope Pius XI (May, 1923). She died on July 28, 1951, almost ninety years old.

Mother Agnes of Jesus was Pauline, the favorite daughter of Madame Martin and the one who most closely resembled her mother in character. She was also her father's "fine pearl," gifted in everything, of an eminently rich nature that was lacking in nothing, so much in harmony were her intelligence and sensitivity.

When Thérèse, the "Benjamin" of the Martin girls, arrived as a postulant, Sister Agnes of Jesus had already been in Carmel for six years and was then twenty-seven years old. She held herself very erect, to compensate, no doubt, for her small stature: at just over five feet, she was the shortest of the family (1.54 meters) while Thérèse, at roughly five foot three and three quarters inches (1.62 meters), was the tallest. Fine featured, serious, her face (sometimes with a worried look) radiated an intense spiritual life. Very perceptive and down to earth, she faced all situations with intelligence and tact. With great integrity, she performed the many austerities of the time.

When Sister Agnes was elected prioress in 1893, it was Mother Marie de Gonzague who had steered the votes in her direction, secretly hoping to be able to continue ruling the monastery through her. This was a very big mistake! It did not take long to realize that the new one in charge fully intended to direct the Carmel herself. She did it, moreover, with brilliance: enterprising, versatile, capable, clever, persevering, and tenacious, Mother Agnes showed herself to be invincible and always on top. Had she not been the "first" of the Martin girls to enter Carmel, even before Marie, her older sister?

Mother Marie de Gonzague, however, did not back down so easily, especially during Mother Agnes's first term as prioress. Thérèse witnessed the confrontations between them and suffered in silence on this account. With extreme delicacy, she threaded her way between these two domineering personalities, respecting what was best in each one, but never taking sides by seeking the maternal protection of one or the other. This enabled her to maintain her interior freedom with regard to these "mothers" and also to create her own way.

In this conflict in the cloister, Thérèse was able to keep the confidence of both parties, but at the same time to assume a detached attitude and maintain her own peace of mind. Thérèse always remained neutral because she loved them both; love alone guided her. Very intuitive, the young Sister knew how to bandage wounds. To Mother Marie de Gonzague, embittered because she was re-elected prioress in 1896 only after seven deliberations and not unanimously as in former elections, she would say "that all this happened to you because God loves you more" (LT 190).

Sister Marie of the Angels (1845–1924)

Jeanne-Julie de Chaumontel was born in Montpinçon (Calvados) on February 2, 1845. A lively spitfire, her brothers nicknamed her "Lady Tempest." Entered the Lisieux Carmel in 1860, despite the pained disapproval of her parents. Subprioress for three terms, from 1883 to 1886, from 1893 to 1899, and from 1903 to 1909. In charge of the novitiate from October 1886 to February 1893, and from 1897 to 1899. She was forty-three years old when Thérèse Martin entered Carmel.

Thérèse said regarding her: "Our Novice Mistress was *really a saint*, the finished product of the first Carmelites. I was with her all day long since she taught me to work. Her kindness to me was limitless and still my soul did not expand under her direction" (A 70v).

The reality was that, guessing the worth of this young girl, Sister Marie of the Angels made it her duty to deliver interminable spiritual talks to her while they were doing the laundry together. Thérèse would have preferred silence but she put up as best she could with the pious chatter and questioning of her novice mistress. One day, not knowing how to respond, the postulant threw her arms around her and hugged her! This

communication block lasted for two years. Then, little by little, the tension relaxed, giving way to a confident dialogue. Sister Marie of the Angels died on November 24, 1924, several months before the canonization of her former novice.

Mother Hermance of the Heart of Jesus (1834–1898)

Madeleine Pichery, born in Honfleur (Calvados) on February 12, 1834. A former teacher. In 1866 she participated in the founding of the Carmel of Coutances. Returned to Lisieux in 1882, where she suffered until her death (October 30, 1898) from a chronic cerebral anemia, which tried the patience of the infirmarians. Mother Hermance showed great esteem for Thérèse.

Sister St. Joseph of Jesus (1809–1892)

Marie-Eugénie Larbourg, born in Saint-Méen (Ille-et-Vilaine) in 1809. She entered Carmel on March 19, 1838 and was the first postulant of the Lisieux foundation. Contemporary of Mother Geneviève of St. Teresa. She died a victim of the influenza epidemic on January 2, 1892, Thérèse's nineteenth birthday.

Sister Fébronie of the Holy Childhood (1819–1892)

Born in Paris in November, 1819, Marie-Julie Malville lost her mother at the age of five. Her father, a tailor, re-married and moved to Lisieux. Mother Geneviève welcomed her to Carmel on January 15, 1842.

Sister Fébronie was over sixty-eight years old when Thérèse entered Carmel and was subprioress at the time. A victim of the influenza epidemic, she would die on January 4, 1892. The subprioress saw very clearly into the soul of the new postulant, as the following dialogue testifies. It is related by Thérèse herself, who found it difficult to open up to her novice mistress:

One good old Mother understood one day what I was experiencing, and she said laughingly during recreation:

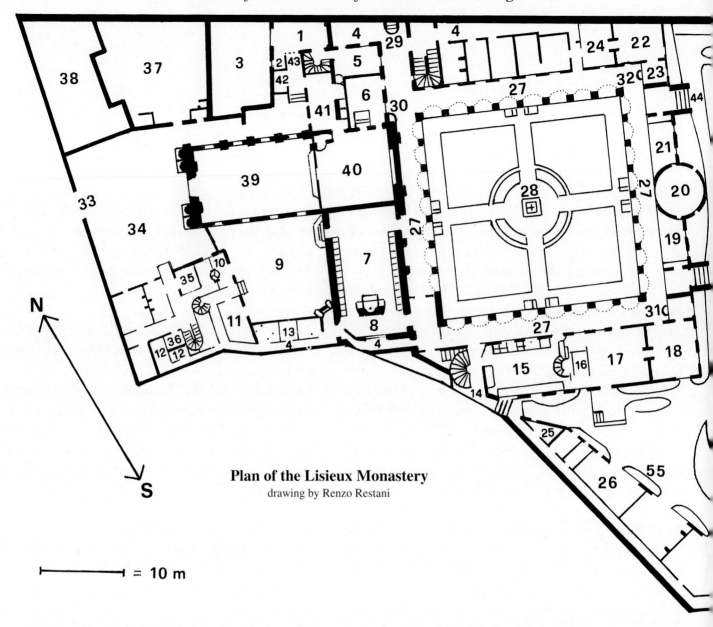

Plan of the Lisieux Monastery
drawing by Renzo Restani

= 10 m

Inside the Cloister

1. Vestibules
2. Confessional (nuns' side)
3. Sacristy courtyard
4. Hallways
5. Sacristy
6. Oratory
7. Choir
8. Entrance room to choir
9. Lourdes courtyard
10. Inner turn
11. Turn sisters' workroom
12. Sisters' side of parlors (speakrooms)
13. Storeroom
14. St. Alexis (refectorian's workroom)
15. Refectory

16. Procurature (pantry)
17. Kitchen
18. Recreation room
19. Hermitage of St. Joseph
20. Hermitage of the Sacred Heart
21. Room for making altar breads
22. Infirmary of the Holy Face
23. Infirmarian's cell (Sr. Geneviève)
24. Infirmary of Our Lady of Lourdes
25. Lamp storeroom (?)
26. Cellar
27. Cloisters
28. Large cross in cloister courtyard
29. Statue of Immaculate Virgin
30. Thérèse's statue of the Infant Jesus
31. Statue of Our Lady of Mount Carmel
32. Statue of St. Teresa of Avila

Outside the Cloister

33. Entrance door
34. Chapel courtyard
35. Extern sisters' house
36. Visitors' side of parlors (speakrooms)
37. Chaplain's garden
38. Chaplain's house
39. Chapel
40. Sanctuary
41. Sacristy
42. Confessional (priest's side)
43. Door into enclosure

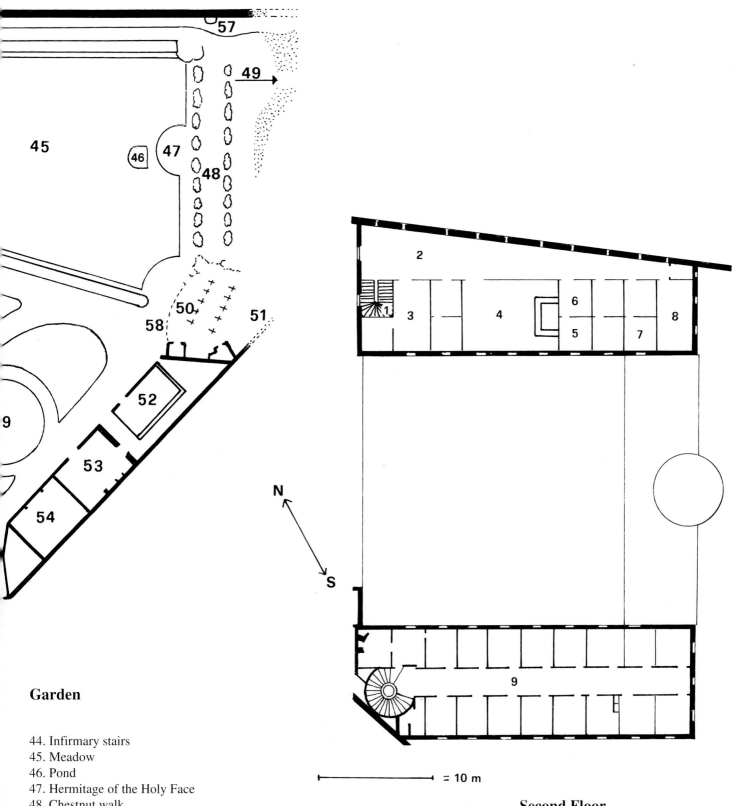

Garden

44. Infirmary stairs
45. Meadow
46. Pond
47. Hermitage of the Holy Face
48. Chestnut walk
49. Lower yard
50. Cemetery
51. Grotto of St. Mary Magdalen
52. Laundry
53. Washhouse
54. Shed
55. Statue of the Heart of Mary
56. Carriage gate
57. Statue of St. Joseph
58. Medlar tree
59. Flower garden

≅ 10 m

Second Floor

1. Stairs to the St. Elias corridor
2. St. Elias corridor
3. Storeroom
4. Chapter room
5. Thérèse's cell (of St. Eliseus)
6. Antechamber
7. Sr. Geneviève's cell
8. Library
9. Corridor of Thérèse's first cell

"My child, it seems to me you don't have much to tell your Superiors." "Why do you say that, Mother?" "Because your soul is extremely *simple,* but when you will be perfect, you will be even *more simple;* the closer one approaches to God, the simpler one becomes." (A 71r).

As subprioress, Sister Fébronie saw to the observance of the Rule of Carmel, being herself a model of silence and recollection. She felt that Thérèse exalted the Lord's mercy a little too much to the detriment of the divine justice. While discussing this together one day, Thérèse retorted: "You want God's justice? You will have God's justice. The soul receives exactly what it expects from God."

Sister St. Stanislaus of the Sacred Hearts (1824–1914)

Marie-Rosalie Gueret, born May 4, 1824; entered Carmel on April 6, 1845, being, therefore, one of the first Carmelites of the Lisieux foundation. Thérèse helped her in the sacristy from 1891 to 1893. At the time of the influenza epidemic, Sister St. Stanislaus, "first sacristan," fell gravely ill, so Thérèse replaced her in the sacristy as best she could. When the epidemic was over, Sister St. Stanislaus found herself the oldest member of the community. Sister Marie of the Angels described her as "the accomplished type of the perfect religious. Declining in years but still young at heart, her inexhaustible goodness and heroic devotion produced a sprightliness in her that edified the youngest, while being for all the most beautiful example of abnegation and charity" (CG 1172). On February 1896 she became first infirmarian. (She served in several offices: bursar, sacristan, infirmarian.) In the spring of 1897, she delegated her powers of infirmarian to "Céline," so that she might take care of Thérèse.

As a patient, Thérèse was touched by the delicate attentions of Sister St. Stanislaus: "She bandages wounds with so much gentleness! I see her choose with care the finest linens and apply them with a hand of velvet!" The infirmarian, for her part, admired the patience of her sick one: "Never a complaint!" Sister St.

Stanislaus survived Thérèse by seventeen years, dying on May 23, 1914.

Sister Marie Emmanuel (1828–1904)

Virginie-Bathilde Bertin, born in Sables d' Olonne (Vendée) on September 10, 1828. Wife of Auguste Bérèze. A widow at thirty-five, after having lost her three children in their infancy. Entered Carmel on January 3, 1879. From the biographical sketches of the Sisters written by Sister Marie of the Angels, we learn: "Sister Marie Emmanuel made the stockings for the community. A Vendéen widow, she possessed the ardor of the Vendéens and the heart of a fifteen-year-old. 'Life of the party' during recreations; knowing how to tell stories to perfection to amuse the Sisters. Always at everyone's beck and call, even for the smallest service." She died on June 21, 1904.

Sister Teresa of Jesus (1839–1918)

Léonie-Anastasie Jezewska was born on August 6, 1839. Entered May 6, 1873. We know nothing about her except what we glean from one of Thérèse's letters, dated September 3, 1890, where Thérèse asks Sister Agnes of Jesus if she has to do the pictures that this Sister has just requested her to paint, even though Thérèse is in the middle of her profession retreat (LT 114). She often tried Thérèse's patience by asking her to carry out various art projects for her. "Because this poor sister was rather eccentric, she used to ask for subjects that were very grotesque—really bizarre and in poor taste" (CG 567). In June 1897, Thérèse used her brushes for the last time to paint two little pieces for her. Sister Teresa of Jesus had very poor eyesight, although "she loved to make Sacred Heart scapulars." Final note: "she had a cheerful and friendly personality" (cf. CG 1174). She died on October 31, 1918.

Sister Marie Philomène of Jesus (1839–1924)

Noémie Jacquemin, born in Langrune (Calvados) on October 10, 1839, third in a family of six children.

Entered the Lisieux Carmel in 1874, but had to leave the following year to care for her mother who was gravely ill. In 1884, she obtained permission from Mother Marie de Gonzague to re-enter, resuming her life as a Carmelite at the age of forty-five. Put to the test, she was to become a hidden saint, humility itself.

Three and a half years later, Thérèse joined her in the novitiate. Despite the big difference in their ages, they felt a great deal of sympathy for each other. Thérèse rather quickly upbraided the older one for her excessive fear of purgatory: "You do not have enough trust. You fear God too much." For her part, Marie-Philomène reproached the young Sister for her hope of dying soon: "One does not ask to rest before completing her work!" (*Circulaire Nécrologique*). Thérèse retorted that in heaven she would not rest.

Tall and strong, Sister Marie-Philomène did not spare herself. She was often chosen to perform the heavier tasks of the community. For a long time she made hosts, the "altar breads." Occupying the cell next to Thérèse, she would remember this little gesture all her life: Every evening, after Matins, before closing her cell door, Thérèse would wait in the hall and give Sister Marie-Philomène her most gracious smile. At the beginning of November 1896, Thérèse wrote in her honor the poem, "The Sacristans of Carmel" (PN 40). Sister Marie-Philomène died January 5, 1924.

Sister St. Raphael of the Heart of Mary (1840–1918)

Laure-Stéphanie Gayat, born February 18, 1840. She was portress (receptionist) at the turn, where Thérèse assisted her from 1893 to 1896. Gentle and good, but with a multitude of little irritating ways. Great devotion to St. Anthony of Padua. One day, filled with compassion for Thérèse's chilblains, Sister St. Raphael bound up all of Thérèse's fingers, leaving only the little finger on each hand free! While deploring the fact that the provisor didn't serve Thérèse enough in the refectory, she failed nevertheless to share her bottle of cider with Thérèse as she should have, since she sat next to her. In order not to humiliate her thirsty neighbor, however, Thérèse contented herself with water. Sister St. Raphael died August 27, 1918.

Sister St. John the Baptist of the Heart of Jesus (1847–1917)

Marie-Estelle Dupont, born on October 10, 1847. Entered October 7, 1871. In charge of the linen room. With a spirituality totally opposite to that of Thérèse, who regarded her as the *image of God's severity* (LT 230). She wanted to conquer sanctity by sheer hard work and thought that Thérèse counted too much on divine mercy. Considering it a mistake to entrust the formation of the novices to such a young Sister, she said to her one day during recreation: "You should be tending to your own direction instead of directing others!" Thérèse, claiming the shabbiest garments for herself, would always be given those that were most mended, to give her pleasure! A fervent devotee of Cardinal Bérulle, Sister John the Baptist went about with her head in the clouds, forgetful of the things of earth. One day, when it came time to serve the soup in the refectory, she could not remember where she had put it. It was later discovered in a cupboard! (cf. CG 1174). She died on October 27, 1917.

Sister Anne of the Sacred Heart (1850–1920)

Maria de Souza, born in Macao (a Portuguese colony of China) in 1850, daughter of a Portuguese father and a native mother. At her own request, she had transferred from the Saigon Carmel for her psychological well-being. She remained in the Lisieux Carmel from June 1883 to July 29, 1895 and then returned to Saigon. Very gifted intellectually and artistically, with a very pronounced Chinese way of doing things. She was, according to Sister Marie of the Angels: "filled with spirit, knowledge, talents, working marvelously, but her lack of strength did not permit her to have many duties. Fervent as an angel and a source of edification by her courage and piety." Thérèse lived with her then, in the Lisieux Carmel, for more than seven years, and her

The Two "Teresas," Mother and Daughter

Tomás Alvarez, OCD

More than once the question has been raised whether Teresa and Thérèse resemble each other in anything more than their name and vocation to Carmel. It's a banal question at first sight, as though formulated not about two persons and their history but about pictures of them. We do in fact have the portrait of Teresa done in Seville by Fray Juan de la Miseria and the photos of Thérèse taken with Céline's camera. As a matter of fact, the Teresa of sixty-one long years poorly painted by the lay brother, and the Thérèse of twenty-three years, in a somewhat ecstatic pose before a nineteenth-century camera, do not look alike in any other respect than their habit and name.

Nonetheless, the question is not as superficial as it seems. In what is essential we are all alike. Yet it is in what is essential that we are most different, that is, in the secret and profound nucleus that decides our personality and makes us unique and unrepeatable. Proceeding from this center are the radial lines with which God shapes the existential mission and salvation history of each individual.

Viewed from this theological perspective, the persons and stories of Teresa and Thérèse converge in the deepest part of their being and mission. Both, impelled by a mysterious inner spring, wrote their own stories, discovered and bore witness to the passing of God through their lives, and presented them as a lower staff accompaniment to the song of God's mercies. An autobiography is the first book that each wrote. And the two are alike in giving their life stories the force of prophecy: not a simple narrative of their own human adventure, but a prophetic word with a strong message as an aid to any reading or rereading of our own lives.

Within Their Families

The two families do not run along parallel lines. Thérèse's home was set in beautiful Normandy, and Teresa's on the harsh plateau of Castile. Yet between the two we find an ample interweaving of coincidences and contrasts. The two were very much loved in their homes. Without any lack of affection in their infancy, they both had to undergo the bitter experience of the death of a mother: Thérèse lost hers when still a very little girl; Teresa lost her mother at age fourteen. The figure of their fathers then increased to the point of becoming transfigured. For Teresa, Don Alonso is the image of the perfect man. With Thérèse, Louis Martin is the reflection of God's countenance. Going against the prevailing ascetical tendencies and certain pseudomystical conceptions about flight from the world, both Madre Teresa and her Carmelite daughter of Lisieux maintain deep family connections throughout their religious lives. Both come from large families. Teresa of Avila has nine brothers; Thérèse of Lisieux, two. But Thérèse never knew her brothers because they had died before she was born. Teresa is present as all of hers leave their homeland to make their way to the West Indies. Left at their father's side were only his daughters, as was the case in the home at Alençon and Lisieux.

There is still another pair of coincidences in these pictures of home life. On the maternal level, the two orphans find refuge in the motherly care of the Blessed Virgin Mary. On the paternal level, however, the shadows of war come close to them: Teresa is born at the time her father returns from the war in Navarre. Thérèse is born when M. Martin suffered at home from the extended shadow of the Franco-German War. Teresa and Thérèse inherit, if not a warrior spirit, certainly a vigorous frame of mind, a fortitude that will accompany them in life. Recalling some typical instructions of the Saint from Avila, Thérèse writes: "Saint Teresa, who said to her daughters, 'I want you to be women in nothing, but that in everything you may equal strong men,' would not have wanted to acknowledge me as her child if the Lord had not clothed me in His divine strength, if He had not Himself armed me for war" (LT 201).

Within Carmel

For Teresa and Thérèse Carmel is the soul's family. Here one is not dealing with coincidences, affinities, or approximate comparisons, as with family ties of blood. In the soul's family everything is transferred to profound levels of another order and magnitude.

By different paths, the vocational choice of Carmel was for both the outcome of an intimate little drama. Uprooted from the paternal hearth, they were planted anew in the hearth of the spirit, with all the accompanying human poignancy. For the Saint of Avila it will be the community life of the Incarnation that defines and decides her sense of her religious vocation. On the other hand, the Saint of Lisieux enters Carmel already with clear ideas and a well-defined choice. To clarify these and arrive at her positions, it helped Thérèse to approach the one who was to become her Holy Mother Teresa. Before entering Carmel, Thérèse undertook a thorough reading of a biography of Teresa.

A cluster of features that characterize Teresa's personality left their mark on Thérèse, who quickly incorporated them into her own human and spiritual makeup. It should be sufficient to enumerate them.

— *First of all, high ideals.* "Lofty thoughts," urged Madre Teresa. "I have always had great desires," she writes. Thérèse had written in her private notes: "The desire to practice virtue in a heroic degree in imitation of the saints, or to long for martyrdom, is not presumption" (cf. *Life* 13, 4).

— *Disposition to give one's life for others, as Christ did.* Among her private notes, Thérèse also preserved this thought of her Holy Mother: "I would have given a thousand lives to save one soul" (*Way of Perfection,* 1, 2). This was repeated by Teresa with all kinds of nuances and variations and also by Thérèse. Another saying of Teresa's left its mark on Thérèse: "What does it matter to me to remain until the end of the world in purgatory if through my prayers I save a single soul?" (quoted from the *Way of Perfection,* 3, 6, in a letter to P. Roulland [LT 221]).

— *An intense apostolic sense of contemplative vocation.* "You know that a Carmelite who would not be an apostle would separate herself from the goal of her vocation and would cease to be a daughter of the Seraphic Saint Teresa" (LT 198). And how happily she endorsed this ideal at the end of her life: "I shall not be sorry for having worked solely for the salvation of souls. How happy I was to learn that our holy Mother, St. Teresa, thought the same way" (DE 4.6.1; HLC 56).

— *Feeling of love.* The Saint of Avila had insisted greatly on not confusing love with the feelings of love. Thérèse reflects deeply along these lines: "How well I understand Our Lord's words to St. Teresa, our holy Mother: 'Do you know, my daughter, who are the ones who really love me? It's those who recognize that everything that can't be referred to me is a lie'" (DE 22.6; HLC 67).

— *To be friends of the Crucified.* Thérèse recalls at various times one of the little stories about Teresa: "St. Teresa was very right in saying to Our Lord, who was loading her with crosses when she was undertaking great works for Him: 'Ah! Lord, I am not surprised that You have so few friends; You treat them so badly!'" (LT 178).

— *The guidepost of the contemplative ideal: God alone!* In her private notes Thérèse transcribed in its entirety Teresa's poem "Let nothing trouble you…, God alone suffices."

On a deeper level, in narrating their own lives Teresa and Thérèse sum them up in a doxological key, as a hymn to God's mercies. Both of them center all their longings for sanctity on the bridal love of Christ, appropriating for themselves the nuptial symbolism of the Song of Songs, and they become enamored of Christ's Gospel. They both have a refined sense of the church. Thérèse herself testifies to this convergence of spirit: "Finally, I want to be a daughter of the Church as our holy Mother St. Teresa was" (C 33v). As a result she thinks that she who was her Holy Mother "sent me my first little [missionary] brother" (C 31v).

Within the Church

In the closing pages of her *Story of a Soul,* tacitly comparing her ecclesial mission with that of her holy patroness, Thérèse writes: "O Mother, how different are the ways through which the Lord leads souls! In the life of the saints, we find many of them who didn't want to leave anything of themselves behind after their death, not the smallest souvenir, not the least bit of writing. On the contrary, there are others, like our holy Mother St. Teresa, who have enriched the church with their lofty revelations, having no fears of revealing the secrets of the King in order that they may make Him more loved and known by souls. Which of these two types of saints is more pleasing to God? It seems to me, Mother, they are equally pleasing to Him, since all of them followed the inspiration of the Holy Spirit and since the Lord has said: 'Tell the just man ALL is well.' Yes, all is well when one seeks only the will of Jesus" (C 2v).

Thérèse had no foreknowledge—or perhaps she did—that her mission in the church was going to take paths similar, almost parallel, to those of her Holy Mother. For she also had been called mysteriously to "reveal the secrets of the King." Like the *Mater Spiritualium* (Mother of Spiritual Seekers), she too had been called to exercise a teaching mission of incomparable universality.

Certainly, we can never underscore the difference enough. Teresa and Thérèse embody two statements irreducible to a common denominator. And this, precisely because their ideologies are born of two human experiences profoundly diverse, within two irreducible cultural and ecclesial contexts.

The distances are shortened—according to the passage Thérèse just quoted—in the unique "movement of the Holy Spirit," which echoes the Pauline text: "There are different kinds of spiritual gifts but the same Spirit" (1 Cor 12:4). Both Teresa's and Thérèse's gift for teaching have their point of origin in the Spirit who enlivens the autobiographical narrative of them both. The two began by writing their own autobiographies. To grasp the profound meaning of life as it is lived is, as it were, the wellspring of their doctrinal message and ecclesial service. This is so not only because they manage to understand and expound their existence in a kind of micro-salvation-history account but also because through it they proclaim to the reader the Gospel of Jesus.

This explains, perhaps, the great impact produced by the writings of the two Carmelites. These writings have spread rapidly even beyond ecclesial frontiers and Western cultural boundaries. The works of both are translated and read in countless languages. They remain fresh and timely, going against the grain of cultural-religious changes and the breaks in continuity characteristic of the last decades. Although so many authors fade away through the lapse of any number of ideologies and messages, the writings and teachings of these two saints continue in their dialogue with readers and cultures both inside and outside the Church, in concert with the demands of the new evangelization.

This undoubtedly is the basic motive in joining Teresa and Thérèse in the fulfillment of an identical service in the Church, that of their doctorate: the saint of Avila already proclaimed a doctor, the "first woman doctor of the Church"; the saint of Lisieux waiting to be the next one proclaimed a doctor.

presence certainly stimulated Thérèse's own missionary desires. Sister Anne died on July 24, 1920.

Sister Marguerite Marie of the Sacred Heart (1850–1926)

Léa-Adolphine Nicolle, born in Colombiers-sur-Seulles (Calvados) on May 11, 1850. Entered the Lisieux Carmel on July 15, 1873. Second seamstress (habit maker) and also helper in the making of altar breads. Simple and devout.

In 1890, she was found to have mental problems and, after a serious attack, was hospitalized from March 14 to June 9, 1896, in the "Bon Sauveur" in Caen, the very institution where Monsieur Martin had been confined. Better but not cured, she left the hospital and returned to her family. Her last years were spent with the Little Sisters of the Poor in Caen. "One of those who make community life sweet and agreeable," Sister Geneviève would say of her (n. 1948). She died on June 12, 1926.

Sister Aimée of Jesus (1851–1930)

Marie-Léopoldine Féron, born on January 24, 1851, of a family of rural origin. Robust and helpful, she always aimed for what was practical: she wanted potatoes, for example, to be planted around the Calvary in the cloister instead of rose bushes, which, according to her, were "good for nothing." The Martin sisters, with their "petite bourgeois" manners, got on her nerves. She was also opposed for a long time to Céline Martin's entrance into Carmel: "Carmel has no need of artists," she used to say, "it has a much greater need of good nurses and good menders."

Thérèse recounted how Sister Aimée's opposition suddenly ceased: "When the difficulties seemed insurmountable one day, I said to Jesus during my act of thanksgiving: 'You know, my God, how much I want to know whether Papa went *straight to heaven;* I am not asking you to speak to me, but give me a sign. If Sister A. of J. consents to Céline's entrance or places no obstacle to it, this will be an answer that Papa went *straight to You!'*... God...changed this Sister's dispositions. The first one to meet me after my thanksgiving was Sister Aimée, and she called me over to her with a friendly smile.... She spoke to me about *Céline* and there were tears in her eyes" (A 82v).

As infirmarian, she cared for her Sisters with devotion. In September 1897, when Thérèse was so weak that she had to be placed on a temporary bed while her own bed was being made, Sister Aimée lifted the little patient as though she were a light burden, without giving her the slightest jolt. Thérèse thanked her with such a smile of affectionate gratitude that it would be a compensation for her regrets at having been the only one not to hear the infirmary bell summoning the Sisters at the moment of Thérèse's death. Sister Aimée's own death was on January 7, 1930.

Sister St. John of the Cross (1851–1906)

Alice-Émilie Bougeret was born on July 25, 1851 and entered Carmel on April 25, 1876. Second portress, always leaving her post at the first stroke of the bell. Passionately fond of prayer and reading, with a great devotion to the Blessed Sacrament. Rigid, rather secretive, but willingly seeking advice from Thérèse. She died on September 3, 1906.

Sister Teresa of St. Augustine (1856–1929)

Julia-Marie-Elise Leroyer, born in La Cressonière (Calvados) on September 5, 1856. Entered the Lisieux Carmel on May 1, 1875. Very short of stature. Sister Marie of the Angels will testify of her that "she never lost any occasion to practice an act of virtue or fidelity to the smallest things." She loved Thérèse very much, who for her part, felt a strong antipathy for this stiff and virtuous Sister:

> There is in the Community a Sister who has the faculty of displeasing me in everything, in her ways, her words, her character, everything seems *very disagreeable* to me. And still, she is a holy religious who must be *very pleasing* to God. Not wishing to give in to the natural antipathy I was experiencing, I told myself that charity must not consist in feelings but in works; then I set myself to doing for this Sister what I would do for the person I loved the most…. I wasn't content simply with praying very much for this Sister who gave me so many struggles, but I took care to render her all the services possible, and when I was tempted to answer her back in a disagreeable manner, I was content with giving her my most friendly smile, and with changing the subject of the conversation, for the Imitation says: "It is better to leave each one in his own opinion than to enter into arguments."
>
> Frequently, when I was not at recreation (I mean during the work periods) and had occasion to work with this Sister, I used to run away like a deserter whenever my struggles became too violent. As she was absolutely

unaware of my feelings for her, never did she suspect the motives for my conduct and she remained convinced that her character was very pleasing to me. One day at recreation she asked in almost these words: "Would you tell me, Sister Thérèse of the Child Jesus, what attracts you so much towards me; every time you look at me, I see you smile?" Ah! what attracted me was Jesus hidden in the depths of her soul; Jesus who makes sweet what is most bitter. I answered that I was smiling because I was happy to see her (it is understood that I did not add that this was from a spiritual standpoint. (C 14r.)

Only a month before her death on July 22, 1929 did Sister Teresa of St. Augustine discover how tiresome she had been to the other Sisters and especially to Thérèse.

Sister Marie of St. Joseph (1858–1936)

Marie-Joséphine-Lucie Campain, born in Valognes (Manche) on January 29, 1858. Entered Carmel on April 28, 1881. Very attached to Thérèse. Highly gifted, able to make use of anything and make whatever she wished with her hands. Unfortunately, she was of a highly nervous temperament with sudden mood changes, which accounted for her being isolated from the community. Impulsive one minute, exalted or depressed the next, subject to violent rages, she was feared by the others and nobody wanted to work with her. Thérèse, however, found the way to her heart and, from time to time, Sister Marie of St. Joseph would even ask for permission to go and seek counsel from her younger Sister.

In March 1896, Thérèse volunteered to work under her in the linen room. One day Thérèse remarked: "If you only knew how she is to be pardoned! How she is to be pitied!" Sharing the work of this poor neurasthenic, she also tried to help keep her from falling asleep, saying that it was part of her own missionary zeal. Sister Marie of St. Joseph was forced to leave the cloistered life in 1909 because of her severe psychological problems. She died in Gavray (Manche) on November 26, 1936.

Sister Marie of the Sacred Heart (1860–1940)

Oldest sister and godmother of Thérèse, Marie Martin was born in Alençon on February 22, 1860. After Pauline's entrance into Carmel, Marie in particular looked after her youngest sister. Having entered Carmel on October 15, 1886, she was still a novice with Thérèse for a short time. She carried out the office of provisor or refectorian from 1894 to 1933.

Of a very assertive and independent character, Sister Marie of the Sacred Heart had a truly loyal nature. Although lively and tenacious of her own ideas, fond of teasing—sometimes annoyingly so—she had a heart of gold and discharged all of her duties with love. In speaking of her, Sister Marie of the Angels affirms:

> She is a soul of faith, with a humility that knows no touchiness. As a flower gardener, her favorite get-up is a rustic canvas apron, large hobnailed shoes, a spade, a rake, a wheelbarrow, a watering can and pruning shears. Her gardening, however, does not prevent her from being marvelously successful at very delicate pieces of needlework.

Sister Marie of the Sacred Heart was without question one of those who best discerned the mystery of grace in Thérèse. It was at her insistence that Mother Agnes asked Thérèse, at the end of 1894, to write her childhood memoirs (Manuscript A) and it was at her request that Thérèse, in 1896, addressed to her the splendid letter that makes up Manuscript B. Speaking of her godchild who was beginning her novitiate, Sister Marie of the Sacred Heart affirmed: "From the very first days, I saw to what extent she would be faithful to the Rule."

Around 1920, Sister Marie contracted arthritis which, in the end, confined her either to her bed or to a wheelchair. She died on January 19, 1940.

Sister Marie of Jesus (1862–1938)

Eugénie-Henriette-Amélie Courceau, born in Rouen on September 13, 1862. Entered Carmel April 26, 1883. Seamstress, part-time infirmarian, having for a continual refrain: "I can never do too much; I will never do enough." She tried Thérèse's patience all during prayer by making a clicking sound on her teeth with her fingernail (C 30r–v). She died November 25, 1938.

Sister Geneviève of St. Teresa and of the Holy Face (1869–1959)

Marie-Céline Martin, born in Alençon on April 28, 1869, sister of Thérèse. After six years of separation, and the opposition of Sister Aimée of Jesus overcome, Céline joined Thérèse in Carmel on September 14, 1894: "The most intimate of my desires, the greatest of them all…my dear Céline's entrance into the same Carmel as ours" (A 82r). Thérèse was already assistant mistress of the novitiate, and, although younger than Céline by three years, found herself in charge of forming her sister in the religious life. This would call for a great deal of tactfulness and sensitivity on her part, for Céline was far superior to her from a practical standpoint. Céline, first called "Marie of the Holy Face," would in the future be known as "Geneviève of St. Teresa and of the Holy Face," following the suggestion of Canon Delatroëtte who wished, in this way, to perpetuate the memory of the Foundress. In the fall of 1896, there was a serious question of Sister Geneviève and another novice leaving for Saigon. Thérèse suffered in silence over this possibility, but did not intervene. In the end, the project was not realized and the two novices continued to be sanctified in Lisieux. Very talented in painting and photography, Céline, with the authorization of the prioress, had brought along with her to Carmel her photographic equipment (a 13/18 Darlot).

During the last months of her sister's life, Sister Geneviève was the infirmarian. Thérèse, very ill, went down to the infirmary on July 18, 1897 and "Céline" moved into an adjoining cell. Thérèse's last glance would be for her infirmarian who had just placed a little piece of ice on her parched lips. It was a glance full of tenderness and also of encouragement and of promise. Sister Geneviève of St. Teresa died on February 25, 1959.

Sister Marie of the Eucharist (1870–1905)

Marie-Louise-Hélène Guérin, born on August 22, 1870. First cousin of Thérèse. Scrupulous, she freely confided in her. Entered Carmel on August 15, 1895. The prioress at the time was Mother Agnes of Jesus, and Thérèse was the "senior of the novitiate." Sister Marie of the Eucharist helped in the refectory and in the sacristy with Thérèse, who often had to curb her companion's lively chatter. Gifted with a lovely voice, very musical (she had brought a whole repertory of popular tunes that would later serve as melodies for Thérèse's poems). The mistress supported the novice in her efforts and encouraged her with her advice, recommending, for example, that during recreation she not take her place next to the Sisters she liked best. The training was a bit severe and one day Sister Marie of the Eucharist answered her with a rebellious look: "I promise you that I will be a saint when you have gone to heaven!" But in response, Thérèse explained to her the value of time.

From June 1896 on, she alerted her parents concerning the deterioration of their niece's health. For all the countless remedies, tonics, and sweets that they sent over, she was charged with sending them thank-you notes. At the same time, her letters beginning with April 1897 are a precious source of information about Thérèse's last illness. Sister Marie of the Eucharist died April 14, 1905.

Sister Marie of the Trinity and of the Holy Face (1874–1944)

Marie-Louise-Joséphine Castel, born on August 12, 1874 in Saint-Pierre-sur-Dives (Calvados). First entered Carmel in Paris, Avenue de Messine, but was forced to leave for health reasons. She joined the Lisieux Carmel on June 16, 1894. "The 'Little Mischief' of the Carmel was never at a loss for anything and knew perfectly well how to get herself out of any scrape." That is the way Sister Marie of the Angels depicted young Sister Marie-Agnes of the Holy Face, who would become, two months before her profession, Sister Marie of the Trinity and of the Holy Face.

Sister Thérèse was delighted to no longer be the youngest, the "Benjamin" of the novitiate, thanks to this new novice, younger by a year. She looked so young that Thérèse affectionately called her "my little doll," but she never gave into the temptation to mother "her doll." On the contrary, she treated her rather severely, letting no caprice of hers pass by unnoticed. The new recruit had a good voice, which consoled Thérèse whose own voice was rather weak for the recitation of the Office in choir. The novice accepted the lessons of her mistress, such as the episode when Thérèse gave the "weepy" young Sister a mussel shell in which to shed her tears.

Thérèse's strictness did not prevent a privileged relationship from developing between these two souls, a real "complicity" in the best sense of the word. Their exchanges deepened. In 1897, Thérèse confided to her novice: "I sing what I want to believe, but it is without any feeling." It was during this same time that Sister Marie of the Trinity was relieved of the task of assistant infirmarian, out of fear of contagion. She herself would die of cancer of the face on January 16, 1944.

The community also had five Lay Sisters, that is, religious who were assigned to the domestic service of the community (cooking, housekeeping, etc.). They attended the Office in choir, but the breviary was replaced for them by the recitation of a certain number of "Our Fathers." After their profession, they kept the white veil.

Sister Madeleine of the Blessed Sacrament (1817–1892)

Victoire-Désirée Toutain saw the light of day on May 27, 1817, in St. Hippolyte-des-Près (Calvados). Entered the Lisieux Carmel as a Lay Sister and made her profession on July 14, 1844. On January 7, 1892, Thérèse found her dead in her cell, the third victim of the influenza epidemic.

Thérèse and Saint John of the Cross

Federico Ruiz, OCD

Thérèse's Affinity with John

After she entered Carmel Thérèse openly admitted her debt to John of the Cross: "Ah! how many lights have I not drawn from the works of our holy Father, St. John of the Cross! At the ages of seventeen and eighteen I had no other spiritual nourishment" (A 83r). But these lights began earlier and continued increasing until her death. When in a period of dryness she focused on the Gospels in her prayer, and left aside spiritual books, John of the Cross remained the exception, perhaps the only one. She continued reading and quoting from him with the same fondness as before. In the last months of her life, she frequently relived and repeated words from the *Living Flame of Love.* Explicit references to John of the Cross appear throughout her writings. Direct testimonies abound that she continually mentioned his life and doctrine in her conversations and oral teachings.

Contrasts in Life and Culture

The attraction is surprising. Given the differences in origin, family, epoch, life, temperament, and education, the harmony between the two is unexpected. In Thérèse we find a childhood surrounded by affection and bounty, a temperament sensitive and emotional; she was the center of attention for her whole family, isolated from the world and its suffering. In John of the Cross, on the other hand, we find a childhood of suffering and privation, hard and humble work, study, and care of those with contagious diseases. Within Carmel the life of the two manifests little in common. Thérèse writes at age twenty in a narrative, autobiographical, and anecdotal style. John at forty writes in a clean, essential, and symbolic language.

But beyond the differences, there prevails a kind of preestablished harmony. When Thérèse was twelve or thirteen years old her father hid the works of St. John of the Cross from her for fear that his rigorous teachings would warp her spiritual growth. Precisely from those years of growth an autograph has been conserved, in which she repeats in a handwriting exercise the strong motto of John of the Cross: "Lord, to suffer and be despised for you."

The Type of Relationship

Her interest in her Carmelite father and master was not a matter of simple devotion or of recalling luminous passages. What we find is a convergence in key points of their teaching. Thérèse experienced a profound and spontaneous communion with the very person of the saint, and not merely with his writings. He is "Our Holy Father," the spiritual father of the Teresian Carmelite family. Attitudes and sentiments of veneration, affection, and discipleship were mingled: he is the saint, the father, the master, a brother and friend. Her admiration was spontaneous for this mature man, this experienced and sure witness to God, who was also a theologian of keen insight. She feels she is his disciple, sister, reader, daughter. In him she finds a spiritual model who empowers, strengthens, inspires, and offers her sometimes even the exact word for expressing her own experience.

Toward the Nucleus

An unerring instinct guides her directly to the nucleus of John of the Cross's experience: love, vocation in the church, dark and sure faith, the cross, hope, death and glory. She discovers the dynamics of the theological virtues in John's synthesis at a time when the theological-spiritual study of his doctrine had not yet come to a similar precision. All her quotations and all that strikes a chord in her are connected with the life of the theological virtues: union of love, intimate experience (in intensity and extension) of union with God in faith, love, and hope. This tri-dimensional relationship with God has from the beginning to the end the same axis for both saints: love, the life and death of love. We know that among the few books Thérèse kept in her room for personal use are the *Spiritual Canticle* and the *Living Flame of Love,* bound in one volume. Love is her center, but not her boundary. Impelled by an expanding love, Thérèse takes upon herself the demands and experience of the *todo–nada* (the "all–nothing") found in the *Ascent,* as well as the "night of faith" found in the *Dark Night.*

Love

By grace, vocation, and temperament, Thérèse from the beginning centers on love and takes the *Spiritual Canticle* as her preferred book. Here she sees portrayed John of the Cross himself, "the saint of love par excellence," and she finds herself portrayed as well in her most intimate aspirations. For her, stanzas 25–29 form the heart of the work: young souls in love with Christ, the inner wine cellar, the total gift through love, the contemplative vocation, service of the church. John here shows Thérèse how to love, the plenitude of Christian, ecclesial, and Carmelite life, and how to be contemplatives so as to love. Now she wants no other office, only to devote herself to love: to love and be loved.

She encounters the supreme value of the church and the meaning of her own vocation in one of John's classic phrases that fills her with enthusiasm: "A little of this pure love is more precious to God and the soul and more beneficial to the church, even though it seems one is doing nothing, than all these other works put together" (*Canticle,* 29, 2).

All and Nothing

Love, for Thérèse as for John of the Cross, is not an isolated feeling but the total gift of one's entire life, a renunciation of all that is not love of God. The experience of love uncovered for her the demands of an unconditional vocation. She entered, then, into the rhythm of the *Ascent of Mount Carmel:* "To love is to labor to divest and deprive oneself for God of all that is not God" (*Ascent,* 2, 5, 7).

From the time she was a child, she chose "all," not love by half measures. Her vocation of love asserted itself with markedly Sanjuanist colors. Marie of the Trinity tells us that she insisted that "her little way of humility and love was none other than that of St. John of the Cross: the nothing that we are, the all that God is." She does not reject the harshest expressions of her master: *it is necessary to suffer, to suffer much; I suffered before, but I didn't love suffering.*

Night of Faith

Unexpectedly, a final discovery of faith, pure and dark, came over her. It was a painful experience that pressed upon and precipitated her into an abyss of darkness. She entered into the world of suffering for which she was not psychologically predisposed and converted it into a supreme form of union of love. It is the mark of her interior and exterior life during her last months. The fraternal word of her brother John was both spiritual company and a precious help. In her desolation, she and her sisters referred to the experience with terms taken from the "dark night of faith" of St. John of the Cross.

It was an all-encompassing problem regarding life and meaning. She spoke with the same words

and examples of the master: temptations toward blasphemy, scruples, and even the sense that death would be a relief. And we find also the same positive elements: interpretation of the experience in the key of faith, trust in God who never abandons us, and solicitude about serving him, at least materially, with gestures that seemed to her of little value.

Hope and the Death of Love

All her life and work resonated with the virtue of hope: great desires and certitude about their fulfillment. Two of John's principles form the basis for this: "The more he wants to give, the more he makes us desire" (Letter 15); "for in relation to God, the more a soul hopes the more it attains" (*Ascent,* 3, 7, 2). God does not inspire us with unrealizable desires.

She identified with the *Living Flame of Love,* especially the verse of the first stanza, "tear through the veil of this sweet encounter": to live by and die of love. "With what longing and what consolation I repeated from the beginning of my religious life these other words of St. John of the Cross: 'It is of the highest importance that the soul practice love very much in order that, being consumed rapidly, she may be scarcely retained here on earth but promptly reach the vision of her God face to face'" (DE 26.7.5; HLC 113). During the last months of her life, Thérèse and her sisters seemed to be reliving this scene from the *Flame.*

Personal and Cultural Adaptation

The benefit Thérèse sought to derive from the Sanjuanist corpus was limited by her simplicity of thought and life. The selection was not guided by criteria such as gentleness or rigor, love or renunciation. She accepted without reserve the master's most exalted expressions as well as his most austere.

One notes her silence in certain areas, or at least the absence of explicit references to them: the mystical life, its graces and phenomena; the prayer of loving attention; the purifying of all mediations through faith and love; the transcendence of God in the *Ascent;* and the trinitarian perspectives of the *Canticle* and *Flame.* Carried along by her own experience or under the influence of some other source, she modified many of the things taken from her father and master. Regarding love, she enlarged and went deeper into the meaning of the reference to the church in stanzas 27–29 of the *Canticle.* She developed her own ideas about abandonment and victimhood, words that John of the Cross never used. As for the image of night, she introduces into the living experience of the dark night shades of atheism and materialism, unthinkable in John of the Cross's time and environment; she lives the dark night at the end, not as an earlier phase of the journey. One could add many other divergences.

Common Grace

We all benefit from this spiritual kinship and affinity. The reader of John of the Cross's works will encounter new stimuli and orientations in Thérèse's simple and profound rereading of John: 1) She confirmed what John foresaw, that these matters will be understood better through the affinity gained from mystical experience than through the study of scholastic theology. 2) She identified from the outset the essential nucleus of the Sanjuanist doctrine without getting lost in minutiae of style or contrasting viewpoints. 3) She engaged in an authentic reading, open to the reality of grace and her personal experience, a faithful, dynamic, and original reading.

In the final analysis Saint Thérèse did not take the word of Saint John of the Cross as a book or doctrine, norm or project. Hers was a personal story about the common life of grace: this is what John of the Cross lived, and this very same thing is what is now happening to me.

Sister Marie of the Incarnation (1828–1911)

Zéphyrine-Joséphine Lecouturier. Born in Firfol (Calvados) on July 14, 1828. Entered Carmel August 10, 1852. Always sickly. She was very responsible in caring for the poultry yard. Without specifically naming her, Thérèse spoke of her later, as one of the Sisters who used to constantly bother her during her illness, several months before her death, while she was busy writing in her notebook in the garden:

> In order for me to translate my thoughts, I have to be *like the solitary sparrow,* and this is rarely my lot. When I begin to take up my pen, behold a Sister who passes by, a pitchfork on her shoulder. She believes she will distract me with a little idle chatter: hay, ducks, hens, visits of the doctor, everything is discussed; to tell the truth, this doesn't last a long time, but there is *more than one good charitable Sister,* and all of a sudden another hayworker throws flowers on my lap, perhaps believing these will inspire me with poetic thoughts. I am not looking for them at the moment and would prefer to see the flowers remain swaying on their stems. (C 17v)

Sister Marie of the Incarnation died February 23, 1911.

Sister St. Pierre of St. Teresa (1830–1895)

Louise-Adélaïde Lejemble, born in Saint-Laurent-de-Cuves (Manche), on January 20, 1830. Entered Carmel as a Lay Sister, October 22, 1866 and led there a life of untiring devotion. In the last years of her life, she was struck down with extremely painful crippling arthritis that continually grew worse. By sheer willpower, she managed to drag herself on crutches to the choir where she sat on a bench. She had to be helped to get to the refectory, but was not easy to please. Thérèse offered to perform this little service for her:

> Then a ritual was set in motion. I had to remove and carry her little bench in a certain way, above all I was not to hurry, and then the walk took place. It was a question of following the poor invalid by holding her cincture; I did this with as much gentleness as possible. But if by mistake she took a false step, immediately it appeared to her that I was holding her incorrectly and that she was about to fall. "Ah! my God! You are going too fast; I am going to break something." If I tried to go more slowly: "Well, come on! I don't feel your hand; you've let me go and I'm going to fall! Ah! I was right when I said you were too young to help me." … I gained her entire good graces, and this especially (I learned later) because, after cutting her bread for her, I gave her my most beautiful smile before leaving her alone. (C 29r)

Sister St. Pierre prayed continually, and always had a sermon ready for every occasion, generally on her favorite topic, the Apocalypse. She died on November 10, 1895.

Sister St. Vincent de Paul (1841–1905)

Zoé-Adèle Alaterre was born on August 13, 1841 in Cherbourg (Manche). Lost both father and mother in 1849, during a cholera epidemic. Brought up in Caen by the Sisters of St. Vincent de Paul, she became an excellent embroideress. Entered Carmel as a Lay Sister on February 2, 1863. Very short of stature and of fragile health. A veritable living encyclopedia! Had great devotion to the Blessed Sacrament, but, alas, sang terribly off-key, and with a booming voice.

Sister Vincent de Paul did not have a very sisterly attitude in her dealings with Thérèse: she was very ingenious in her desire to humiliate the "big kid goat," as she called her, finding her too slow and clumsy when it came to manual work. Thérèse suffered a great deal from her "pin-pricks." Without holding a grudge, however, the young religious responded to Sister Vincent de Paul's wishes and composed four poems for her on her cherished theme, Eucharistic devotion. Sister Vincent de Paul wondered what they would be able to say about Thérèse after her death. That is why she would be one of the first to benefit from Thérèse's miracles: the cure of her grave cerebral anemia. Sister Vincent de Paul died on April 13, 1905.

Sister Martha of Jesus (1865–1916)

Florence-Marthe-Cauvin, born in Giverville (Eure) on July 16, 1865; lost her parents at the age of six and grew up in various orphanages. Having been deprived of affection, she was excessively attached to her prioress and would show herself rather aggressive all her life. Entered Carmel December 23, 1887, and was twenty-two years old when Thérèse arrived three months later. A Lay Sister, not very tall, but very strong—a little Hercules! She merits special mention insofar as she tried her young companion's patience to the limit. While admiring Thérèse, she used to suffer from repeated violent attacks of jealousy in her regard. Thus it was very hard for her to endure seeing the younger Thérèse admitted to profession two weeks ahead of her.

It was only after 1897 that Sister Martha became aware of the delicate charity that the "Servant of God" had demonstrated toward her: "She was always calm and composed," she would testify. Sister Martha died September 4, 1916.

Sister Marie Madeleine of the Blessed Sacrament (1869–1916)

Mélanie-Marie Françoise Le Bon, born in Plouguenast (Côtes-du-Nord) on September 9, 1869. Entered Carmel as a Lay Sister on July 22, 1892. A very sullen and withdrawn character. Refused to confide in Thérèse: Feeling that Thérèse saw through her and could read her thoughts, she avoided the meetings her mistress set up for her. As for Thérèse, she never lost patience with her novice, but still loved her in a disinterested manner. Sister Marie Madeleine died on January 11, 1916.

Two "Turn" Sisters (Externs) complete the group. They lived outside the enclosure in the exterior part of the monastery. They were in charge of business with persons from the outside and managed the "turn" on which things brought by them were passed. What is a "turn"? It is a cylindrical cupboard, turning on a pivot and embedded in the wall, on which items coming in or going out are passed. In the Lisieux Carmel, turns are found at the main entrance, in the sacristy, and in the speakrooms.

Sister Marie Elizabeth of St. Teresa (1860–1935)

Marie-Antoinette-Eugénie Hamard, born October 13, 1860 at Couterne (Orne). Entered Carmel as an Extern on October 15, 1891. Witty and intelligent, delicate of heart and health, a soul of prayer and very devout, she merited the confidence and attachment of the community. She knew Thérèse in her offices as portress and sacristan, and several times during Thérèse's last illness she watched over her during Mass. On October 4, 1897, Sister Marie Elizabeth represented the community at Thérèse's burial. She died on February 13, 1935.

Sister Marie Antoinette (1863–1896)

Marie-Antoinette Blanc, born in Granville (Manche) on February 12, 1863. Entered the Lisieux Carmel as an Extern on July 9, 1890. Struck down by tuberculosis, her state grew worse in the spring of 1895 when Thérèse was the assistant turn-sister on the inside. They called Sister Marie Antoinette "the little lark of the turn" because of her cheerfulness and her good, devout, and loving heart. She died on November 4, 1896.

Sister Thérèse of the Child Jesus and of the Holy Face

And finally we have Thérèse. This whole book speaks of her. But isn't it normal to ask ourselves the question: what did her community think of Thérèse?

Here is the testimony of Sister Marie of the Angels:

> Sister Thérèse of the Child Jesus, novice and jewel of the Carmel, its dear Benjamin. Office of painting in which she excels without having had any other lessons than those of seeing our Reverend Mother, her dear sister, at work. Tall and strong, with the appearance, the tone of voice, and the expression of a child, hiding within her a wisdom, a perfection, and insight of a fifty-year-old. Soul always calm and in perfect possession of itself in all things and with everybody. Little innocent thing to whom one would give God without confession, but whose head is full of mischief to play on anyone she pleases. Mystic, comic, everything…she can make you weep with devotion and just as easily split your sides with laughter during our recreations. (CG 1176)

With her Sisters, Thérèse Martin discovered that community life is a perilous and difficult enterprise! How many differences of temperament, gifts, social backgrounds, education, scale of values, ways of dealing with one's companions! Each one is a little world in herself; fortunately, a united vision brings hearts together and leads to a constantly renewed reconciliation because Jesus Christ is *the* point of reference.

Thérèse would explain: "No doubt, we don't have any enemies in Carmel, but there are feelings. One feels attracted to this Sister, whereas with regard to another, one would make a long detour in order to avoid meeting her…. Well, Jesus is telling me that it is this sister who must be loved" (C 15v). Love? That's what Thérèse did from the moment of her arrival in Carmel.

Thérèse Speaks

Suffering Opened Wide Its Arms to Me

This happiness was not passing. It didn't take its flight with "the illusions of the first days." *Illusions*, God gave me the grace *not to have* A SINGLE ONE when entering Carmel. I found the religious life to be *exactly* as I had imagined it, no sacrifice astonished me and yet, as you know, dear Mother, my first steps met with more thorns than roses! Yes, suffering opened wide its arms to me and I threw myself into them with love. I had declared at the feet of Jesus-Victim, in the examination preceding my Profession, what I had come to Carmel for: "I came to save souls and especially to pray for priests." When one wishes to attain a goal, one must use the means; Jesus made me understand that it was through suffering that He wanted to give me souls, and my attraction for suffering grew in proportion to its increase. This was my way for five years; exteriorly nothing revealed my suffering, which was all the more painful since I alone was aware of it. Ah! what a surprise we shall have at the end of the world when we shall read the story of souls! There will be those who will be surprised when they see the way through which my soul was guided!

CRUX
AVE,
CARMELI.

114

115

116

117

118

119

114. Thérèse as a novice in January 1889, at age sixteen.

115. Lisieux. The monastery of the Discalced Carmelite nuns on the right; on the left the Fleuriot house, today the chaplain's quarters.

116. Carmel of Lisieux. Facade of the chapel.

117. Carmel of Lisieux. Interior of the chapel.

118. Carmel of Lisieux. The main altar of the chapel in Thérèse's time, now conserved in the sacristy.

119. Carmel of Lisieux. Side chapel dedicated to St. John of the Cross.

120. Carmel of Lisieux. Entrance to the cloister. Thérèse crossed the threshold on April 9, 1888.

121. Carmel of Lisieux. Thérèse entering the cloister on her clothing day (January 10, 1889) with her father's blessing. Stained-glass window.

122. Carmel of Lisieux. The inside sacristy, within the cloister, where Thérèse worked.

123. Carmel of Lisieux. The turn through which Thérèse passed things from the inside sacristy to the outside.

124. Carmel of Lisieux. The inside part of the confessional. Thérèse went to confession once a week.

125. Carmel of Lisieux. The oratory for the sick. Thérèse painted this fresco during the summer of 1893 (retouched by Sr. Geneviève). She represented herself as the little angel, upper left, leaning its arm on the tabernacle while dozing off.

120

121

122

123

124

"Suffering Opened Wide Its Arms to Me"

GENEVIÈVE DEVERGNIES, OCD

Postulancy is the first stage of formation in the Carmelite life. From the very beginning, Thérèse seemed at ease in Carmel: "Everything thrilled me. This happiness was not passing. It didn't take its flight with 'the illusions of the first days'" (A 69v).

She lived in this Carmel until her death, that is to say, a total of five hundred weeks—less than ten years—without ever leaving it.

First Steps

The new postulant felt totally herself, right at home. What others might call a prison, she looked upon as the ultimate place of freedom. This hard and austere life delighted her. To realize this, one only had to see her as she passed through the silent cloisters with an even gait, unhurried, with a firm and peaceful step.

Thérèse's conduct, moreover, surprised her community. Aware of her young age, they expected to see her act like a child. Quite the contrary! The Sisters felt a certain respect in Thérèse's presence, appreciating her dignified and reserved bearing, her rapt and determined expression. Of course, some of the Sisters must have been curious, and some had preconceived ideas: How was this precocious postulant going to conduct herself? Let us observe the beginner in action....

The novice mistress was to testify later: "From the first moment of her entrance, she set about performing her duties with a charming grace." In fact, from April on, Thérèse was busy. "In her case, manual work was reduced to three hidden tasks: mending in the linen-room; sweeping a dormitory, staircase, and cloister; and a little weeding in the garden for physical exercise" (PA 348). The postulant was learning that "the humble life with its monotonous and simple tasks is," as Paul Verlaine says, "a choice work that demands a great deal of love."

"Those beautiful festivities of the month of May" began on May 22, 1888, Pentecost Monday, when Thérèse was chosen to adorn with roses her godmother Marie, who had just made her profession: "The *oldest* of the family being crowned on her wedding day by the *youngest*" (A 71v). On the following day, Monsieur Martin attended the veiling of his "diamond," his favorite daughter. It was on this occasion that Thérèse, filled with gratitude and bursting with happiness, had a meeting with the one whom her father called the "director of the entire family," Père Almire Pichon.

This somewhat eccentric but amiable Norman Jesuit was born of a family of cattle-raisers, on February 3, 1843, in Sainte-Marguerite-de-Carrouges, near Alençon. He was asked to preach at the veiling of Sister Marie of the Sacred Heart on May 23, 1888. The fiftieth anniversary of the foundation of the Lisieux Carmel was also commemorated at the same ceremony.

From May 24 to 28, Père Pichon conducted some days of recollection for the nuns. In a lively and pleasing manner, he spoke on his favorite topics: prayer, humility, love of God, fraternal charity, and sanctification through suffering. It was the latter that made the biggest impression on Thérèse: "Sanctity! We must conquer it at the point of the sword. We must suffer, we must agonize," she would say later, quoting Père Pichon.

For Thérèse the crowning event of these days was her interview with Père Pichon. In a general confession, she disclosed to him the inner distress, the "interior martyrdom," that she had been enduring for the past five years and that at times was still agony for her: a terrible malady of scruples.

I can't describe this strange sickness, but I'm now convinced it was the work of the devil. For a long time after my cure, however, I believed I had become ill on purpose.... God, willing no doubt to purify and especially to *humble me,* left me with this *interior martyrdom* until my entrance into Carmel when the *Father* of our souls, as with the wave of his hand, removed all my doubts. Since then I am perfectly calm. (A 28v)

The Jesuit listened for a long time to the confidences of the postulant: her fear of having committed a mortal sin by pretending to have been sick, her sufferings, and her aspirations. After putting her soul at peace, Père Pichon added these words: "In the presence of God, the Blessed Virgin, and all the Saints, I declare that you have never committed a mortal sin…. May Our Lord always be your Superior and your Novice Master." Thérèse comments: "He was this in fact and he was also *'my Director' '*(A 70r), for very quickly Père Pichon left again for Canada and she found herself spiritually alone once more.

Papa's Visits

From time to time Monsieur Martin and Céline came to visit their Carmelites in the speakroom. A typical "speakroom" in those days was a place where a Carmelite could meet the members of her family and her friends and speak to them through a double grille. For persons outside the immediate family, an opaque curtain remained drawn in front of the grilles. A third person, called the "tierce," was present during the conversation, without taking part in it or being seen from the outside section of the speakroom. The normal length of a visit in the speakroom was half an hour. The nuns refrained from seeing visitors during the hours of the liturgical Office and during the seasons of Advent and Lent.

Now, especially since Thérèse's entry into Carmel, the exchanges in the speakroom were going to become the family treat for Monsieur Louis Martin; he already had three of his daughters there and he intensely appreciated those conversations, which were mostly on spiritual matters. Within the four cold and bare walls of that room, facing the grille that stood as a challenge hurled

at the world, he felt in himself the soul of a monk…. In any case, the "Benjamin" behind the criss-crossed bars seemed radiant to him. Now that she had joined the inside speakroom, it would always be the same for the youngest: brief encounters, only a few seconds given to her for little confidences. The half-hour measured by the hourglass slipped by quickly and her older sisters always had so much to share with the visitors. From her postulancy on, when the allotted time was up, Thérèse took leave on her own, not wishing to stay a second longer than obedience allowed her.

After Thérèse entered Carmel, Monsieur Martin showed a lavish generosity to the monastery. Scarcely a day went by without gifts pouring in from Les Buissonnets, especially gifts of food. Some special treat, left at the turn, relieved the ordinary frugal meals of the community. Monsieur Martin especially enjoyed going fishing for the nuns. He caught pike for them at Saint-Martin-de-la-Lieue; trout at Saint-Ouen-le-Pin; and at Touques, not far from Deauville, the stream furnished him with flounder.

Some marvelous catches were attributed to him, notably a carp measuring just under two feet that Sister Agnes sketched life-size, and about which Thérèse wrote: "If you only knew the pleasure your carp, *your monster*, gave us! The dinner was held back for half an hour. Marie of the Sacred Heart made the sauce, and it was delicious" (LT 58).

From then on, Thérèse received the assignment of thanking *the* benefactor. Thus she would write to her father: "I still have a sweet mission to carry out, and it is that of thanking you…for an avalanche of pears, onions, plums, and apples which came from the turn as from a horn of plenty" (LT 63).

Monsieur Martin's Illness

The nine-month period of Thérèse's postulancy was especially full of trials; a veritable overdose of tribulations of all kinds fell upon her. Exteriorly nothing revealed the sufferings that already constituted her lot. "My first steps met with more thorns than roses! Jesus made me understand that it was through suffering that he wanted to give me souls" (A 69v).

What underlined the truly sharp insight of this "young one" was that, from very early on, she perceived religious life "*exactly* as I had imagined it…no sacrifice astonished me" (A 70r). Thérèse felt that she was where she belonged, where Christ wanted her to be: "Here I am, Lord, I come to do Your will" (Ps 39). The human heart, however, never lacks some sorrow.

First of all, Monsieur Martin's health became the source of many anxieties. On May 1, 1887, he had already suffered a rather strong attack of cerebral congestion, but had been quickly freed of a paralysis on his left side. At the beginning of 1888, arteriosclerosis resumed its ravages: he had moments of great fatigue and memory loss. One day he became brutally aware of his state when, owing to uncustomary negligence, he let his favorite parrot die of thirst. A few days later, in the speakroom at Carmel, he confided his prayer to his daughters: "My God, it is too much! Yes, I am too happy, it isn't possible to go to heaven this way. I want to suffer something for you! I offer myself…!" (LT 261).

Two family events helped disturb Thérèse's father. First was the problem of Léonie, who after entering the Visitation of Caen on July 16, 1887, could not adapt herself to the life; so her father was forced to bring her back to Lisieux on January 6, 1888. Then Céline, on whom he depended totally, having just reached her nineteenth birthday, informed him on Saturday, June 16 of her desire to be a religious.

This announcement came as a great shock to Monsieur Martin, so soon after the entrance of his "little Queen" into the Lisieux monastery. He felt the loneliness of old age. On the morning of June 23, without informing anyone of his plans, he set out unnoticed on an adventure. There was panic at Les Buissonnets: Who

had seen him? Who knew his whereabouts? They searched in vain. His flight was extremely distressing for his children, left with no news of him! On the following morning, a telegram arrived from Monsieur Martin asking for some money to be sent to him in Le Havre, general delivery. This enabled Céline and her uncle Isidore Guérin eventually to track down the fugitive. They immediately left for Le Havre, found Louis Martin there three days later, and brought him back home to Lisieux.

Even more than the rest of the family, Thérèse, who loved her father so dearly, was shaken to the core by this event.

Then came a lull for several months. Some humiliating remarks, however, were circulating about her father's illness. "Outside the monastery, many persons made us responsible for the misfortune, caused, they said, by his extreme sorrow, especially when Thérèse entered the Carmel" (LT 81).

We can guess Thérèse's distress, stricken in what she held most dear! Even her handwriting shows the effects of the blow. At the moment when her father needed his "Benjamin" the most, she could not rush to his aid! The inability to have daily contact with her family was not the least of her renunciations in Carmel. Her loved ones remained deep in her heart. Later on Thérèse would say: "I don't understand the saints who don't love their family" (DE 21.5.1; HLC 46–47).

But Thérèse was strong. She astonished her novice mistress who had come to comfort her: "I am suffering very much, but I feel I can still bear greater trials," she said to her (A 73r). When the occasion arose to reinforce family ties with Sister Agnes of Jesus and Sister Marie of the Sacred Heart, Thérèse gently told the latter, who was trying to keep her near her: "Thank you. I would be happy to stay with you, but it is better that I deprive myself, for we are no longer at home!" (CG 367).

Thérèse even found the strength to overcome her own anxiety in order to boost Céline's courage:

Life is burdensome. What bitterness…but what sweetness. Yes, life is painful for us. It is hard to begin a day of work…. If we feel Jesus present, oh! then we would really do all for Him…. What annoying company when Jesus is not there. But what is this sweet friend doing then? Doesn't He see our anguish, the weight that is oppressing us?… He is there, very close…*begging* this sorrow…. Let us raise ourselves above what is passing away…. Jesus is hiding Himself, but we can see Him. When shedding tears, we are drying His. (LT 57)

And again:

What a grace when, in the morning, we feel no courage, no strength to practice virtue; that is the moment to put the axe to the root of the tree…. It is true that sometimes…we are tempted to leave all behind, but in one act of love, even *unfelt love*, all is repaired…. Love can do all things…. Jesus does not look so much at the grandeur of actions or even their difficulty as at the love which goes to make up these actions. (LT 65)

The Reed That Bends Without Breaking

We cannot enter into the joy of loving without entering into the suffering of loving. By lovingly seeking the truth about what God wanted for her, Thérèse would arrive at the truth about love.

The process of adapting to community life was strewn with contradictions. The "little reed" experienced her weakness, but her generosity was unfailing: "Yes, I desire them, these agonies of the heart, these pinpricks…. What does it matter to the little reed if it bends? It is not afraid of breaking, for it has been planted at the edge of the waters…. Its weakness gives rise to all its confidence" (LT 55).

First of all, it was Mother Marie de Gonzague who was going to pose a problem for her. During the first months of her postulancy, Thérèse had to struggle not to yield to a too natural affection for her:

I remember when I was still a postulant that I had such violent temptations to satisfy myself and to find a few

crumbs of pleasure that I was obliged to walk rapidly by your door and to cling firmly to the banister of the staircase in order not to turn back. There came into my mind a crowd of permissions to seek…. I found a thousand reasons for pleasing my nature. (C 22r)

However, "our Mother," as the prioress was called, showed an unaccustomed severity toward her. Thérèse discovered a Marie de Gonzague totally different from the one who was formerly so kind to her during the speakroom visits. Now she often received from her nothing but humiliations and an affected indifference, which was most painful to Thérèse's extreme sensitivity. Thérèse, however, held no grudge against her: "You will see, dear Mother, in the copybook containing my childhood memories, what I think of the *strong* and maternal education I received from you. From the bottom of my heart I want to thank you for not sparing me" (C 1v).

At the same time, as winter approached, Thérèse was to undergo an apprenticeship in another harsh penance: the cold. She had never spent a winter without heat and she was always freezing. In her cell, penetrated by the icy dampness from the outside, she shuddered from the cold. The nights were especially hard to bear and she sometimes shivered until morning without ever being able to get warm. She could easily have obtained a mitigation of the rules on her behalf, but she did not ask for one. To endure this suffering was for her an opportunity to prove her love for Jesus. Only on her deathbed did she admit to Mother Agnes of Jesus: "I've suffered from the cold in Carmel even to the point of dying from it." And Mother Agnes commented: "I was astonished to hear her speak in this way, because in the winter time her conduct revealed nothing of her suffering. Not even in the coldest weather did I see her rub her hands together or walk more rapidly or bend over more than was her usual habit, as all of us do naturally when we are cold" (DE 1178; HLC 258).

The novice mistress will later be grief-stricken at this revelation of Thérèse: "If only I had known, what I would not have done to remedy this matter! Today I say to myself: 'How heroic was that dear girl's virtue.' Her mortification can be summed up in these words: to suffer everything without ever complaining, neither about food nor about clothing" (PO 2022).

Another source of mortification for Thérèse was the food. Sister Marie of the Sacred Heart, who was "provisor" at the time (that is, the Sister in charge of meal planning and everything dealing with food supplies), will relate: "I never succeeded in knowing her tastes and, without meaning to, I made her practice great mortifications. On days, for example, when the dinner consisted of beans, not knowing that they made her sick, I would fill her plate and as she had been advised to eat everything, she would always be sick" (DE 535). It was a fact that "seeing her so sweet, never complaining, they passed all the leftover food to this child who needed something more nourishing; several times all she had on her plate were a few herring heads or leftovers already reheated several times" (PO 272).

Thérèse touched on this topic: "Love for mortification was given me, and this love was all the greater because I was allowed nothing by way of satisfying it.... The penances they did allow me consisted in mortifying my self-love, which did me much more good than corporeal penances" (A 74v).

If through all of this the young postulant held her own, it was because of the fact that "the little reed" was always "faithful to the lightest breeze of grace" (LT 55): It bent without breaking because in Thérèse, "God himself was her Peace" (Mi 5:4).

The Martyrdom of Father and Daughter

It was time for the community to decide whether to admit Thérèse to the "clothing" or reception of the habit. Thérèse should have been clothed with the Carmelite habit in October, 1888, after a postulancy of

six months. Her wedding finery was ready. Her father had insisted on sending her some exquisite Alençon lace in memory of her deceased mother. According to his wishes, the young postulant was to wear a bridal dress of white velvet, trimmed with swansdown and Alençon lace.

Louis Martin suddenly suffered a relapse that forced the Sisters to delay the ceremony. In fact, on October 31, on his way to Le Havre to see Père Pichon off for Canada, he suffered a second attack at Honfleur. The month of November was heavy with anxiety for his daughters because of their father's mental impairment. On November 15, Thérèse wrote to him: "How good God is, then, for having cured you!... The whole Carmel was in prayer.... Above all, take care of yourself" (LT 66). In December, the patient's state of health improved. Thus the temporary "cure" enabled them finally to set the date for Thérèse to receive the habit.

The clothing was to take place on January 9, 1889, nine months to the day from her entrance into Carmel on the feast of the Annunciation. The postulant was delighted at the prospect: It was the Virgin Mary who, for nine months, had carried her in her heart as she had carried Jesus in her womb. So it was with joy that Thérèse looked toward the dawning of her sixteenth birthday on January 2. On December 28, she wrote to her aunt:

> How quickly life passes; it's already sixteen years since I have been on earth.... I love these words of the psalms very much: 'A thousand years in the eyes of the Lord are like yesterday that has passed already.' What rapidity! Oh! I want to work during the day while it is still light, for afterwards will come the night when I shall be able to do nothing. (LT 71)

As the year 1888 closed, her postulancy was coming to an end. In her autobiography, Thérèse drew up a sort of balance sheet for it: "Yes, suffering opened wide its arms to me and I threw myself into them with love" (A 69v). The postulant aspired to this interior suffering, in order to give to her Beloved the proof of her great love for him alone: "Jesus, I would so much like to love Him!... Love Him more than He has ever been loved!" (LT 74). And that is what she would try to live in its fullness during her nine years in Carmel, as long as the hourglass of her life would run.

On the evening of January 5, 1889, Thérèse entered into retreat for the first time in Carmel. It would last for three full days according to the custom of the time; but the postulant would see her solitude prolonged for a day due to an unforeseen event. During her retreat, she was only allowed to speak to the prioress or to her novice mistress. Any other necessary communication she did through notes, written on scraps of paper, already used on one side (out of a spirit of poverty). Thus she wrote to her sister Agnes of Jesus: "You cannot imagine how much I am deprived by not being able to talk with you" (LT 76). She also confided to her: "When I go to Our Mother, I am continually interrupted [by the Sisters who come to speak to her], and then when I do have a moment, I can't tell her what is taking place in my soul, and I go away without joy after having entered without joy!" (LT 78).

The change in plans in the middle of her retreat caused another disappointment: The funeral of Abbé Voisin, honorary Vicar General, presided over by the Bishop, was arranged for Wednesday, January 9, the very date already set for Thérèse's reception of the habit. Bishop Hugonin advised the Lisieux Carmel that the clothing ceremony would be postponed until the 10th. Thérèse supernaturalized her disappointment: "Do you understand something regarding Jesus' conduct?... He has undoubtedly found that the date of the 9th was too ravishing" (LT 76).

The aridity that she had been suffering for several months was increased: "Today more than yesterday, if that were possible, I was deprived of all consolation" (LT 76), especially during the three or four hours of her daily prayer: "Nothing near Jesus. Aridity!... Sleep!...

But at least there is silence!" (LT 74). She "wants to be as Jesus wills [her] to be; that is [her] joy, otherwise, all is sadness" (LT 78).

Moreover, one of the Sisters in the community, although Thérèse was on retreat, directed many biting remarks at her while fitting her with the *alpargata* (hemp sandals with corded soles) that she had made for Thérèse: "This morning, I had trouble with Sister St. Vincent de Paul; I went away with a heavy heart" (LT 76). And Thérèse concluded: "I believe that the work of Jesus during this retreat has been to detach me from all that is not Himself" (L78). "Well, then, all will be for Him, all, even when I feel am able to offer him nothing; so...I will give him this nothing!" (LT 76).

Reception of the Habit

What a radiant interlude was Thérèse's reception of the habit on January 10, 1889! Monsieur Martin, humiliated by his diminished lucidity, recovered enough calm and strength to be able to participate in the celebration.

Much simplified today, the clothing ceremony at that time was carried out with great solemnity: Thérèse left the enclosure dressed in a bridal gown with a long train; a wreath of lilies (a gift from her aunt) crowned the veil covering the long blond curls that fell down over her shoulders. At the vestibule to the chapel, she joined her family and relatives. Then, as for a wedding, the young girl entered the chapel on the arm of her father. "We made our solemn entrance into the Chapel.... This was really his day of *triumph* and it was his last celebration on this earth" (A 72r).

The entire family followed in procession down the aisle and assisted at the Mass. After the first part of the ceremony was completed, the nuptial procession formed again and went to the sacristy. There Thérèse kissed her father, who had never looked "so handsome, so *dignified*" (A 72r), and all her loved ones for the last

A Day in Carmel

Geneviève Devergnies, OCD

What made up the schedule of a Carmelite day in the Lisieux Carmel, at the time of "little Sister Thérèse"? Apart from a slight alteration in the summer horarium (Easter to September 14) and the winter horarium (September 14 to Easter), the ordinary day was almost always the same. The following is a copy of the daily schedule, according to Sister Geneviève's notes.

4:45 A.M.	Rising
5:00	Mental Prayer
6:00	Little Hours of Office (Prime, Terce, Sext, None)
7:00	Mass & Thanksgiving (Sunday: 8:00 A.M.)
8:00	Breakfast: soup (nothing on fast days) Work
9:50	Examination of Conscience
10:00	Meal
11:00	Recreation (dishwashing for Sisters assigned, for about thirty minutes)
12:00	Silence (siesta, free time)
1:00 P.M.	Work
2:00	Vespers
2:30	Spiritual Reading (or meeting of the novices in the novitiate)
3:00	Work
5:00	Mental Prayer
6:00	Supper
6:45	Recreation (dishwashing)
7:40	Compline
8:00	Silence (free time as at noon)
9:00	Matins and Lauds (length: an hour and a quarter; an hour and forty minutes on feast days) Examination of Conscience (ten minutes) Reading of meditation points for next day's prayer
10:30–11:00	Retire

During the winter schedule (beginning September 14), everything in the morning schedule started an hour later, recreation included. Since there was no siesta in winter, the afternoon schedule remained the same as in summer.

The time was thus divided into six and a half hours of prayer (two hours of mental prayer and four and a half hours for Mass and the recitation of the Office in choir); a half hour of spiritual reading; about five hours of work; two hours of community recreation; forty-five and thirty minutes for meals in common (eaten in silence but accompanied by reading at the lectern); an hour of free time before

Matins ("grand silence"); six hours of sleep in summer (with an additional hour of siesta) and seven continuous hours in winter.

The Diet in Carmel

Here are some details concerning the diet in the Lisieux Carmel in Thérèse's day. The Rule of Carmel prescribed perpetual abstinence from meat, but authorized eating meat in cases of sickness or infirmity. Bread was the basic element of the diet, which also included a lot of milk and starches. The meals were served as follows:

a) Summer diet, without fasting
— After Mass (around 8 A.M.) : thick soup, eaten standing at one's place in front of the table.
— Midday meal (10:00 A.M., actually): fish or eggs, vegetables (generous serving), dessert (cheese or fruit); the portions were dished out in advance on earthenware plates.
— In the evening (at 6:00 P.M.): soup, a vegetable, dessert.
Nothing between meals, but Sisters had permission to take a drink of water at 3:00 P.M. and after Matins.
Some Sisters found this regime, of two morning meals two hours apart, more painful than the fast.

b) Fast of the Order
— Nothing in the morning.
— Main meal at 11:00 A.M.: soup and the rest as usual.
— Collation at 6:00 P.M.: bread weighed out (average of seven ounces, around 215 grams), butter or cheese, fruit, sometimes jam. No broth or soup: nothing hot.

c) Ecclesiastical Fast (Lent, Forty Hours, and Vigils)
— Nothing in the morning.
— Main meal at 11:30 A.M.: same as during the fast of the Order, but eggs and all milk products entirely excluded from the diet; the food boiled or prepared with oil.
— Collation at 6:00 P.M.: six ounces of bread, no jam, fresh or dried fruit (apples, figs, nuts, etc.).

Thérèse did not fast before her twenty-first birthday (January 1894), but she was bound by the law of abstinence from meat, unless dispensed because of illness.

time. Finally, she once again crossed the threshold of the enclosure, this time for good.

Preceded by all the Sisters carrying candles, the heroine of the day was led into the nuns' choir by the prioress, where the clothing rites, properly so-called, took place. Her family followed the ceremony at the grille. The mother prioress then clothed Thérèse in the rough, homespun habit and matching brown scapular and a white choir mantle. On her head she placed the short white veil that the novice would keep until her profession. The celebrant, Mgr. Hugonin, Bishop of Bayeux and Lisieux, pronounced the liturgical formulas. The novice officially received her name in religion: Sister Thérèse of the Child Jesus and of the Holy Face.

As was the custom, at the conclusion of the ceremony while the *Te Deum* was sung, Thérèse lay prostrate on the earth-colored carpet that was spread out for her in the nuns' choir and ornamented with artificial lilies. Then everyone went to the speakroom. From behind the grille, Thérèse greeted her radiant father one last time. In fact, he would only see his Carmelite daughters once more on earth.

Reentering the cloister, "the first thing that struck my eye," said Thérèse, "was the statue of 'the little Jesus' smiling at me from the midst of flowers and lights" (A 72v). This statue of the Infant Jesus, painted with a rose-colored robe, was the one Thérèse would be in charge of decorating until her death. She herself declared that the ceremony had been a real feast where nothing was missing, not even *snow*, for which the mild temperatures of the season had not given much hope. "What a beautiful celebration it was! Nothing was missing, not even the *snow!* I had always wished that on the day I received the Habit, nature would be adorned in white just like me" (A 72r).

That evening, Thérèse gave Sister Martha of Jesus a holy card in remembrance of her clothing. On the back she had written: "Ask Jesus that I become a great saint; I will ask the same grace for my dear little companion!" (LT 80).

Thérèse of the Child Jesus and "of the Holy Face"

In community, she would still be called "Sister Thérèse of the Child Jesus" even though, in January 1889, she had added to her title the phrase "of the Holy Face." Ever since she was ten years old, Thérèse had been preoccupied with the name she would bear in religion. Mother Marie de Gonzague, whom she visited in the speakroom, used to call her by the diminutive 'Thérésita', alluding to the niece of Saint Teresa of Avila, who had entered the monastery very young. Thérèse, for her part, reflected: "I wondered what name I would be given in Carmel.... All of a sudden I thought of *Little* Jesus whom I loved so much, and I said: 'Oh! how happy I would be if they called me Thérèse of the Child Jesus!' I *said nothing* during the visit about the *dream* I had while wide awake" (A 31v). How great was her joy when the prioress herself proposed it to her.

From her earliest youth, Thérèse had been accustomed to venerating the Holy Face of Jesus as it is reproduced on Veronica's veil, found in the Basilica of Saint Peter in Rome. She would discover a picture of the Holy Face in the choir of Carmel, with a light burning before it day and night. Since April 26, 1885, the adolescent had been enrolled in the register of the Archconfraternity of the Holy Face of Tours, a devotion resulting from the private revelations received by a nun at the Carmel of Tours, Sister Marie de Saint-Pierre, and thanks also to the "Holy Man of Tours," Monsieur Dupont, who would spend the rest of his life in spreading devotion to the Holy Face in the same spirit.

In the Holy Face, Thérèse contemplated the love of Jesus for humanity. It was not so much the "reparation" aspect that attracted her. She considered rather the element of love: "Jesus is on fire with love for us.... Look at His adorable Face!... There you will see how He loves us" (LT 87). She also considered all the humiliations endured by our Savior: "Ah! I desired that, like the Face of Jesus, my face be truly hidden" (A 71r).

"Until my coming to Carmel, I had never fathomed the depths of the treasures hidden in the Holy Face" (A 71r). *Sister Thérèse of the Child Jesus and of the Holy Face:* She was the first one in the Lisieux Carmel to choose this title. "I understood what real glory was.... I desired that, like the Face of Jesus, 'my face be truly hidden, that no one on earth would know me' (Is 53). I thirsted after suffering and I longed to be forgotten" (A 71r). Thérèse also said: "The glory of Jesus, that is all; as for my own glory, I abandon it to Him" (LT 103).

Then came the cruel day of February 12, 1889. Louis Martin's health deteriorated sharply; he lost his memory, he imagined all kinds of dramatic episodes, and his hallucinations took a disquieting turn for those around him. On February 18, Céline wrote to her friend, Pauline Romet:

> It is very sad that the paralysis settled in his brain, otherwise we would still have our very-much-loved Father at home. He is incredibly good; he was far from wanting to do us any harm with his revolver; on the contrary he wanted to defend us. In his imagination, he was seeing frightful things, slaughter, battles; he was hearing the sounds of the cannon and the drum. I tried in vain to correct his mistake. An attempted robbery in the town served only to confirm him in his ideas, so he took his revolver and wanted to carry it with him in case of danger for, he said, 'I would not want to harm even a cat.' In fact, I don't believe that he would have made use of it; it was just an idea that was passing and it would have vanished. Perhaps they should have waited before acting, and should have tried ways of taking it away from him.

But this was not the opinion of Monsieur Guérin, who feared for his nieces' lives and that of the maid, Maria Cosseron. Without any hesitation, he called in their mutual friend, a tall, vigorous man, to help disarm Monsieur Martin. Uncle Isidore Guérin made the decision to have him confined to the asylum of Bon Sauveur at Caen. He was placed in the good care of Sister Costard, who was in charge of one section of the establishment; 500 sick men were under her supervision.

Monsieur Martin was to remain at the Bon Sauveur for three years. A few days after his admission, Léonie and Céline moved in nearby as boarders with the Sisters of St. Vincent de Paul. From February 19 to May 5 they went every day to the hospital to inquire about their father, although they were only permitted to visit with him once a week.

The Martin family was crushed, bewildered, devastated with sorrow. Thérèse wrote regularly to Céline at Caen, and in the Carmel she buried herself in silence, nourished by the Word of God.

> I didn't know that on February 12, a month after my reception of the Habit, our dear Father would drink the *most bitter* and *most humiliating* of all chalices. Ah! that day, I didn't say I was able to suffer more! Words cannot express our anguish, and I'm not going to attempt to describe it. One day, in heaven, we shall love talking to one another about our *glorious* trials; don't we already feel happy for having suffered them? Yes, Papa's three years of martyrdom appear to me as the most lovable, the most fruitful of my life; I wouldn't exchange them for all the ecstasies and revelations of the saints. My heart overflows with gratitude when I think of this inestimable *treasure.* (A 73r)

What added even more to the affliction of the family was the gossip: The "holy Patriarch" is living with the insane! Will this mental defect show up in his children?

How did Thérèse react to this trial that touched her to her very depths? By keeping her eyes fixed more than ever on the Holy Face of Jesus. Her entire novitiate bore the stamp of this great suffering.

But her father's sorrowful face was gently transformed into a Veronica's veil. "Just as the adorable Face of Jesus was veiled during His Passion, so the face of His faithful servant had to be veiled" (A 20v). Through her tears, Thérèse discovered in the face of her humiliated father the features of the Suffering Servant: "He was without beauty and without majesty; he appeared to us an object of scorn, a Man of Sorrows" (Is 53). In the evening of her life, Thérèse confided: "These words of

Isaias…have made the whole foundation of my devotion to the Holy Face, or, to express it better, the foundation of all my piety. I, too, have desired to be without beauty, alone in treading the winepress, unknown to everyone" (DE 5.8.9; HLC 135).

And Jesus was going to show her that "true wisdom consists in being unknown and counted as nothing—in putting one's joy in forgetting self" (*Imitation* 3, 49). Thérèse wrote to Sister Marie of the Sacred Heart: "Ask that your little daughter always remain a little grain of sand, truly unknown, truly hidden from all eyes, that Jesus alone may be able to see it, and that it may become smaller and smaller, that it may be reduced to *nothing*" (LT 49).

And to Sister Agnes of Jesus, she wrote:

Pray for the poor little grain of sand, that the grain of sand be always in its place, that is to say, under the feet of all, that no one may think of it, that its existence be, so to speak, *unknown*. The grain of sand does not desire to be *humbled;* that is still too glorious since one would be obliged to be occupied with it. It desires only one thing, to be FORGOTTEN, counted for *nothing!*… May, at least, the blood-stained Face of Jesus be turned towards it…. It desires only one look, one look!… If it were possible for a grain of sand to console Jesus, to wipe away His tears, there really is such a grain of sand that would like to do it…. May Jesus take the poor grain of sand and hide it in His adorable Face. There, the poor atom will no longer have anything to fear, it will be sure of *no longer sinning!* (LT 95)

In Silence and Trust Will Be Your Strength (Is 30:15)

With the reception of the habit, Thérèse's canonical year of novitiate began. It was, in fact, to last twenty months. Normally, at the end of one year she should have been able to pronounce her perpetual vows (at that time there was no temporary profession). In January 1890, she had just reached the seventeen years required by the Constitutions for making a life commitment. But seeing she was so young, her superiors,

Canon Delatroëtte and Mother Marie de Gonzague, thought it best to delay her profession. *More waiting,* just as it had been for her clothing. Thérèse confided: "I found it difficult, at first, to accept this great sacrifice" (A 73v).

During the novitiate, the Carmelite continued to receive formation in every area, but she still did not take part in the chapter of the nuns. Thérèse, in fact, would never participate in the chapter; she never voted because she always remained in the novitiate. "For that matter, she would not have been able to enjoy her rights as a capitular nun with active and passive voice [i.e., with the right to vote and be voted into office] because of her two older sisters in the conventual chapter" (CG 725). The novitiate was a time of real "religious" apprenticeship: of interior growth, of initiation into the life of prayer and communal sharing. Thérèse trained herself to assume her part in the community workload, with all its inherent joys and difficulties.

This period of her life was uneventful: "I applied myself to practicing little virtues, not having the capability of practicing the great. For instance, I loved to fold up the mantles forgotten by the Sisters, and to render them all sorts of little services" (A 74v).

"I Work Simply for His Pleasure"

The novice was getting more and more accustomed to her milieu. Marie of the Sacred Heart, Thérèse's "angel," initiated her in the customs of Carmel. During the recitation of the Office in choir, Thérèse intoned the antiphons, recited the verses, read the lessons for Matins—all in Latin. She also took her turn at the various weekly assignments: ringing the bells, serving or reading in the refectory during meals, and so on.

Household chores were also a part of the daily Carmelite routine. Some of the tasks were done by the community as a whole, such as the weekly wash. The Sisters all took turns washing, pounding, and rinsing the clothes in the laundry rooms. Thérèse always worked diligently, but she never forgot the essential: "Your task in this life must only be: 'Love!' "(PN 13).

In her autobiography, Thérèse often speaks of the "first" or "second" person in charge of an "office" or job (*emploi*). Two Sisters were usually given the responsibility of an "office" such as the sacristy. The one directly in charge, or head of the sacristy, was "first" sacristan; the one assisting her, usually a novice or a young professed, was "second" sacristan. Sister Thérèse of the Child Jesus would remain "second" throughout her religious life.

The department was the place where the task or office was performed: the sewing room, the linen room, the altar bread room, the turn room, the art room, and so on. When Thérèse was slowly dying in the infirmary, Mother Agnes of Jesus, in one of the last conversations, asked her to enumerate her offices in Carmel:

> At my entrance into Carmel, I was placed in the linen-room, working with Mother Sub-prioress, Sister Marie of the Angels; besides, I had to sweep the staircase and the dormitory. I recall how much it cost me to ask our Mistress permission to perform acts of mortification in the refectory, but I never gave in to my repugnances; it seemed to me that the Crucifix in the courtyard, which I could see from the linen-room window, was turned towards me, begging this sacrifice. It was at this time that I was going out to weed the garden in the afternoon at 4:30; this displeased Mother Prioress very much. After I received the Habit, I was put in charge of the refectory until I was eighteen; I swept it and set out the water and the beer. During the Forty Hours devotion in 1891, I was assigned to the sacristy with Sister St. Stanislaus. From the month of June of the following year, I went for two months without any assignment.... After these two months I was assigned to the turn with Sister St. Raphael, while still being in charge of painting. I had these two assignments until the elections of 1896, when I asked if I could help Sister Marie of St. Joseph in the linen-room, under the circumstances about which you are aware.

Mother Agnes remarked:

> She then told me how others found her slow, little devoted to her duties, and how I myself believed it; and in fact, we both recalled how much I scolded her for a refectory tablecloth which she had kept in her basket for a long time without mending it. I accused her of negligence, and I was wrong, for she didn't actually have time to do it. On that occasion, without excusing herself, she had cried very much, when she saw that I was sad and very much displeased. Is this possible? She told me, too, how she had suffered in the refectory with me (I was in charge), not being able to speak with me about the little affairs as she had formerly, because she didn't have permission and for other reasons. 'You had come to the point where you no longer knew me,' she added. She spoke to me, moreover, about the violence she had to do to herself to remove the spiders' webs from the alcove of St. Alexis under the stairs (she had a horror of spiders), and a thousand other details which proved to me how faithful she had been in her tasks, and what she suffered from them without anyone's being aware of it. (DE 13.7.18; HLC 95–96)

And there was another task that awaited Thérèse: "How happy I would be if I were able to paint.... To the greatest astonishment of the Sisters I was told to paint, and God permitted that I profit by the lessons my dear Mother [Agnes] gave me" (A 81r).

Little by little, after her sister was elected prioress, Thérèse devoted herself to the office of painting. She continued quietly to illuminate and to paint religious pictures and church decorations. During the summer of 1893, she painted a fresco on the wall of the oratory for the sick. This fresco encircled the tabernacle where the chaplain, on days of adoration, exposed the monstrance.

When Sister Agnes of Jesus was elected prioress on February 20, 1893, she was no longer able to organize the feast day celebrations as she had done formerly—especially since the principal celebrations were for the prioress! Mother Agnes handed this task over to her sister, Thérèse. God "willed also that I write poems and compose little pieces which were considered beautiful" (A 81r–v). According to the testimony of her most serious critics, the young religious had a real poetic gift although she had no formal literary training. Thérèse explained: "Our Beloved has no need of our beautiful thoughts and our dazzling works.... It is not, then, intelligence and talents that Jesus has come to seek here below." In fact, she gave God first place in her life. Sanctity? That was her masterpiece!

Thérèse, then, followed an old tradition in Carmel: that of transcribing in a poetic form the sentiments of the soul, the profound movements of the interior life. Teresa of Avila and John of the Cross with their spiritual "glosses" had given the example. In this same spirit, Thérèse was called on to write poems to celebrate the feasts of the church, anniversaries, and professions.

In the Service of the Liturgy

Little Sister Amen" (as the first sacristan, Sister St. Stanislaus, called her) helped in the sacristy from February 1891 until February 1893. When her cousin, Marie Guérin, became a Carmelite in March 1896, Thérèse was reassigned there.

Thérèse was delighted with this activity, which was the closest she could get to the priestly ministry: Here she was a priest without being one, she who so envied their vocation! "I feel in me the *vocation of* the PRIEST. With what love, O Jesus, I would carry You in my hands when, at my voice, You would come down from heaven. And with what love would I give you to souls! But alas! while desiring to be a *Priest*, I admire and envy the humility of St. Francis of Assisi" (B 2v).

How she loved to prepare the host and fill the chalice! "I was very fortunate, too, to touch the sacred vessels.... I felt that I should be very fervent and recalled frequently these words...: 'You are to be holy, you who carry the vessels of the Lord!'" (A 79v). After a First Mass, eleven days before her death, Thérèse asked to be able to look at herself mirrored in the bottom of the chalice of the newly ordained: "My reflection is there;

when I was sacristan, I used to love to doing this. I was happy to say to myself: My features are reflected in the place where the Blood of Jesus rested" (DE 9.19.4; HLC p. 192).

On the day after Christmas 1891, the influenza epidemic that had been raging in Europe (claiming nearly 70,000 victims) broke out in the monastery. In a week's time the "grim reaper" claimed the lives of three of the oldest Sisters in the community: eighty-three-year-old Sister St. Joseph of Jesus, on January 2, 1892; Sister Fébronie, the subprioress, on January 4; Sister Madeleine, the senior Lay Sister, whom Thérèse found dead in her cell, on January 7.

Most of the nuns were confined to their beds. Thérèse, Sister Marie of the Sacred Heart, and Sister Martha (a Lay Sister) were the only ones left on their feet. "At this time I was all alone in the sacristy because the first in charge was seriously ill; I was the one who had to prepare for the burials, open the choir grilles for Mass, etc." (A 79r). Thérèse calmly gave herself to the task at hand; she saw to the burying of the dead and cared for the sick. Community life became disorganized: no bells, no offices, no meals in the refectory. The superior, M. Delatroëtte, who formerly had shown himself to be so doubtful of the vocation of "little Sister Amen," as she was nicknamed at times, was forced to shake off his prejudice against her when he saw how she handled the situation: "She is a great hope for the community," he would say from then on.

During this period, since there was no thought of endlessly bothering the sick prioress for permissions, Thérèse took the opportunity to fulfill one of her deepest desires: "All through the time the community was undergoing this trial, I had the unspeakable consolation of receiving Holy Communion *every day*" (A 79v).

Thérèse, who "loved the *feasts*" (A 17r), would not be deprived of them in Carmel. So many liturgical and community feasts are celebrated there. The entire year is mapped out according to the liturgical feasts. St. Teresa of Avila had already placed the liturgy at the

Thérèse's Reading Material

Geneviève Devergnies, OCD

The spiritual education Thérèse received at home powerfully aided her in achieving spiritual integration. Her formation continued in Carmel through personal readings or those she heard in community.

As a postulant, Thérèse had at her disposal *The Christian Manual* containing some psalms and the New Testament, the Rule and Constitutions, a book of spiritual direction, and the "Papier d'Exaction" brought to France by the Spanish Carmelite foundresses, a work that served as the basis for novice formation in Thérèse's time. This book included all the regulations dealing with the "external disposition" that the Carmelite should acquire. There was also the Glaire translation of the psalter, and a Little Office of the Sacred Heart.

Among the books Thérèse certainly consulted most often were: *The Imitation of Christ,* which the youngest Martin girl knew practically by heart; Père Surin's *Foundations of the Spiritual Life,* an authoritative commentary on the doctrine of renunciation; Bishop de Ségur's *Nos Grandeurs en Jésus* (Our Grandeurs in Jesus) as well as *La Piété et la Vie Intérieure* (Piety and the Spiritual Life); some works of Father Faber, especially *The Foot of the Cross,* from which Thérèse borrows the legendary subject for her pious recreation, "The Flight into Egypt" (RP 6).

Certain books were put at the novices' disposal. Others were placed outside the choir; the religious could borrow them or consult them there. Thérèse became acquainted with Henry Suso's *Avis spirituels* (Little Book of Spiritual Wisdom); she also loved the commentaries on certain verses of Isaiah by Père Louis d'Argentan. She had already appreciated for a long time the conferences of Abbè Arminjon, as a reliable treatise on the last things.

This list is not exhaustive. Far from it! Nevertheless, it is interesting to note that the young Carmelite nun became particularly attached to the basic writings of the Carmelite reformers. In the Lisieux Carmel, Teresa of Avila was better known and more influential than John of the Cross. Thérèse did not read the complete works of "La Madre"; nevertheless in her own words she in turn liked to call herself "a daughter of the church," to declare that "God alone suffices," and to claim "I would give a thousand lives to save one soul."

The effect of John of the Cross on this youngest child was far more profound: "Ah! how many lights have I not drawn from the works of our holy Father, St. John of the Cross! At the ages of seventeen and eighteen I had no other spiritual nourishment" (A 83r). It is mainly from him that Thérèse obediently received the lessons of interior detachment, living in her turn "without support and with support."

In fact, the "Mystical Doctor" was little known in France, and studied even less. In 1888 the library of the Carmelite monastery on rue de Livarot contained only the three volumes of his works and life, related by an anonymous author. In addition, when the Carmel of the avenue de Messine translated and edited the works of John of the Cross in 1876 under the auspices of the prioress, Mother Teresa of Jesus (of Andalusian origins), it was not a Carmelite friar but a Dominican, Very Rev. Père Chocarne, who was asked to write the introduction. Before Sister Thérèse of the Child Jesus, we find no trace of any systematic use of the writings of the Spanish Carmelite friar. No periodicals popularized or commented on them. The rather superficial religious climate did not welcome fathoming the mysteries of a teaching judged to be reserved for rare initiates. So much was this the case that John of the Cross at the end of the nineteenth century still appeared as an obscure author; he was little read and no one appealed to his authority.

Thérèse would conclude: "But it is especially the *Gospels* that sustain me during my hours of prayer, for in them I find what is necessary for my poor little soul" (A 83v).

summit of the life of prayer; she gave a very important place to the Eucharist and to the rhythm of the Liturgy of the Hours. The Eucharist is the heart of the day, for it is essentially at Mass that the community relives the mystery of the Passion and encounters the Risen Christ. The entire day in Carmel is structured by the Liturgy of the Hours; all the great intentions of humanity are brought together and interceded for during its recitation. In addition, the entire day is marked by contemplative prayer: "the exchange of love with the One who we know loves us," as the Saint of Avila used to say. The morning and evening hours of mental prayer are periods of *silent listening* to the "true Friend."

The great liturgical feasts of Christmas, Easter, Pentecost, and Our Lady of Mount Carmel were celebrated with jubilation and were followed by "free" days (three at Christmas), during which the Sisters could freely converse among themselves. Community feasts, such as clothings, professions, and jubilees, began with a public celebration and continued with the Sisters' private festivities within the cloister. The community feasts in the Lisieux Carmel were enhanced by "special" recreations, consisting of plays and skits composed by Sister Agnes of Jesus and later by Thérèse.

The prioress's name day was celebrated with special fanfare. Not only was it stretched out over two days, but the Sisters also put on a play carefully prepared for the occasion. On January 21, 1894, Thérèse wrote and directed the play "The Mission of Joan of Arc" (RP 1), honoring the Maid of Orléans. The following year, on the same date, she presented "Joan of Arc Accomplishing Her Mission" (RP 3).

In winter, "ordinary" recreations were spent in the "chauffoir"—the only heated room in the monastery—where the Sisters chatted while doing some little piece of handwork. In summer the garden provided a verdant gathering place. During haying season, all who were able set about the task with delight.

Mother Marie de Gonzague loved the gaiety of these recreations. On one occasion she even allowed one of the novices to get a letter from her cell on the first floor by climbing out of a window and down a ladder that happened to be leaning there against the wall!

I Am My Beloved's and My Beloved Is Mine (Song 6:3)

The time finally arrived for Thérèse to make her irrevocable commitment through the vows of religious life, sealing the total gift of her being to the God of love by following a path of daily fidelity. Already consecrated to God through her baptism, the novice desired to deepen this union. For this, she chose to live a life of poverty, chastity, and obedience, surrendering herself to the Holy Spirit, so that her life might be offered with Christ to the Father for the church and for all humanity.

As for the practical observance of the vows, Thérèse had, to a high degree, the spirit of regularity and renunciation. Several quotations speak volumes on this subject:

> One evening, after Compline, I was looking in vain for our lamp on the shelves reserved for this purpose. It was during the time of the Great Silence and so it was impossible to complain to anyone about my loss. I understood that a Sister, believing she was taking her lamp, picked up ours which I really needed. Instead of feeling annoyed at being thus deprived of it, I was really happy, feeling that Poverty consists in being deprived not only of agreeable things but of indispensable things too. (A 74v)

On the subject of spiritual poverty: "I rejoiced at being *poor*, I wanted to become this more and more each day" (LT 176). "Do not fear, the poorer you are, the more Jesus will love you" (LT 211).

As for the vow of chastity, she says: "The Heart of my Spouse is mine alone, just as mine is His alone" (LT 122).

For Thérèse, the vow of obedience went hand in hand with interior freedom: "What anxieties the Vow of Obedience frees us from!… But when [we] cease to look upon the infallible compass…then [we] soon wander into arid paths (C 11r). Finally, "I am not writing to produce a literary work, but only through obedience, and if I cause you any boredom, then at least you will see that your little child has given proof of her good will" (C 6r). "I am obeying you…. Do not believe I am trying to discover what use my poor work can have; since I am doing it under obedience, it is enough for me, and if you were to burn it before my eyes without having read it, it would cause me no pain" (C 33r).

Thérèse was about to pronounce her vows. The profession ceremony was set for September 8, 1892, with the preparatory retreat beginning on August 29. On August 30, Thérèse wrote to Sister Agnes:

> The little hermit must tell you the itinerary of her trip and here it is. Before she left, her Fiancé seemed to ask her in what country she desired to travel, what route she desired to follow…. The little fiancée answered that she had but one desire, that of being taken to the summit of the *mountain of Love*.… Then Jesus took me by the hand, and He made me enter a subterranean passage where it is neither cold nor hot, where the sun does not shine, and in

which the rain or the wind does not visit, a subterranean passage where I see nothing but a half-veiled light, the light which is diffused by the lowered eyes of my Fiancé's Face.... The route on which I am has no consolations for me, and nevertheless, it brings me all consolations since Jesus is the one who chose it, and I want to console Him alone, alone! (LT 110)

The same day she confided to Sister Marie of the Sacred Heart: "She [Thérèse] is happy to follow her Fiancé because of her love for *Himself alone* and not because of his gifts.... He alone is so beautiful, so ravishing!... even when He *is silent* ...even when He *hides Himself!"* (LT 111).

At the time of the canonical examination on September 2, she responded to M. Delatröette, the superior: "I came to save souls and especially to pray for priests" (A 69v).

But on the eve of her profession, a sudden tempest shook the retreatant: "The darkness was so great that I could see and understand one thing only: I didn't have a vocation!... I made the Mistress come out of the choir, and filled with confusion, I told her the state of my soul. Fortunately, she saw things much clearer than I did, and she completely reassured me" (A 76r–v).

On Monday morning, September 8, in the chapter room, Thérèse made her profession in the presence of the assembled community: "I felt as though I were flooded with a river of peace and it was in this peace 'which surpasses all understanding' that I pronounced my Holy Vows.... I offered myself to Jesus in order to accomplish His will perfectly in me without

creatures ever being able to place any obstacle in the way" (A 76v).

In a letter that Thérèse carried on her heart on the day of her profession, she had written: "O Jesus...give me the grace to fulfill my Vows in all their perfection, and make me understand what a real spouse of Yours should be. Never let me be a burden to the community, let nobody be occupied with me, let me be looked upon as one to be trampled under foot, forgotten like Your little grain of sand, Jesus. May Your will be done in me perfectly, and may I arrive at the place You have prepared for me" (Pri 2; SS 275).

On September 24, 1890, the ceremony of Thérèse's veiling took place: She exchanged the novice's white veil for the black veil of the professed.

The day was veiled in tears. Papa was not there to bless his Queen; Father Pichon was in Canada; the Bishop, who was supposed to come and dine with Uncle, did not come at all since he was sick. In a word, everything was sadness and bitterness. And still *peace,* always *peace,* reigned at the bottom of the chalice. That day, too, Jesus permitted that I was unable to hold back my tears and these were misunderstood. (A 77r)

In her testimony at the beatification process, Mother Agnes of Jesus wrote: "Instead of consoling her, I said to her: 'I can't understand your crying!...'"

Thérèse was now fully a Carmelite. What was Carmel for her? A way of life that is austere, demanding, filled with trials, but continually illuminated from within by the presence of the God of love, to whom Thérèse fully intended to refuse nothing.

Thérèse Speaks

Like a Little Child

I understood what *real glory* was. He whose Kingdom is not of this world showed me that true wisdom consists in "desiring to be unknown and counted as nothing," in "placing one's joy in the contempt of self." Ah! I desired that, like the Face of Jesus, "my face be truly hidden, that no one on earth would know me." I thirsted after suffering and I longed to be forgotten. How merciful is the way God has guided me. *Never* has He given me the desire for anything which He has not given me, and even His bitter chalice seemed delightful to me. (A 71r)

Really, I am far from being a saint, and what I have just said is proof of this; instead of rejoicing, for example, at my aridity, I should attribute it to my little fervor and lack of fidelity; I should be desolate for having slept (for seven years) during my hours of prayer and my *thanksgivings* after Holy Communion; well, I am not desolate. I remember that *little children* are as pleasing to their parents when they are asleep as well as when they are wide awake; I remember, too, that when they perform operations, doctors put their patients to sleep. Finally, I remember that: *"The Lord knows our weakness, that he is mindful that we are but dust and ashes."*

Just as all those that followed it, my Profession retreat was one of great aridity. God showed me clearly, however, without my perceiving it, the way to please Him and to practice the most sublime virtues. I have frequently noticed that Jesus doesn't want me to lay up *provisions;* He nourishes me at each moment with a totally new food; I find it within me without my knowing how it is there. I believe it is Jesus Himself hidden in the depths of my poor little heart: He is giving me the grace of acting within me, making me think of all He desires me to do at the present moment. (A 75v–76r)

The Triumph of My King

The [clothing ceremony] was wonderful. The most beautiful, the most attractive flower of all was my dear King; never had he looked so handsome, so *dignified*. Everybody admired him. This was really his day of *triumph* and it was to be his last celebration on this earth. He had now given *all* his children to God, for Céline, too, had confided her vocation to him. He had *wept tears of joy*, and had gone with her to thank Him who "bestowed such honor on him by taking all his children."

…After embracing my dear King for the last time, I entered the cloister once more, and the first thing that struck my eye was the statue of "the little Jesus" smiling at me from the midst of flowers and lights. Immediately afterward, my glance was drawn to the snow, the monastery garden was white like me! What thoughtfulness on the part of Jesus! Anticipating the desires of His fiancée, He gave her snow.… This accentuated even more the *incomprehensible condescension* of the Spouse of virgins, of Him who loves *Lilies white* as *SNOW!*

…January 10, as I have just said, was my King's day of triumph. I compare it to the entry of Jesus into Jerusalem on the day of the palms. Like that of our Divine Master, Papa's glory of *a day* was followed by a painful passion and this passion was not his alone. Just as the sufferings of Jesus pierced His Mother's heart with a sword of sorrow, so our hearts experienced the sufferings of the one we cherished most tenderly on earth. (A 72r–v)

I Know No Other Means but Love

Dear little Marie, as for myself, I know no other means of reaching perfection but "love".… Love, how well our heart is made for that!… Sometimes, I seek for another word to express love, but on this earth of exile words are powerless to express all the soul's vibrations, so we have to keep to this one word: "love!"…

But upon whom will our poor heart hungry for love bestow it?… Ah, who will be big enough for this…will a human person be able to understand it…and, above all, will he know how to return it? Marie, there is only one Being who can understand the profundity of this word: Love!… It is only our Jesus who knows how to return infinitely more than we give Him…. (LT 109, to Marie Guérin)

126

126. Carmel of Lisieux. General view of the cloister.

127. Carmel of Lisieux. Windows of the cells. The cell used by Thérèse after 1894 is marked by a white cross.

127

128

129

130

131

128. Carmel of Lisieux. The choir. There each day the community spent over three hours praying the Divine Office, two hours in mental prayer, and nearly one hour for Mass and thanksgiving.

129. Carmel of Lisieux. The choir. The cross marks the stall used by Thérèse.

130. Carmel of Lisieux. Corridor of St. Elias. The first door on the right is where Thérèse's cell was during her last three years.

131. Carmel of Lisieux. The recreation room, the only room with heat during the winter.

132. Carmel of Lisieux. The refectory.

133. Carmel of Lisieux. The chapter room where Thérèse pronounced her religious vows (cf. A 76v–77r).

134. Carmel of Lisieux. Garden. The walk under the chestnut trees; in the background the statue of St. Joseph.

132

133

134

1
3
5

136

137

138

135. Carmel of Lisieux. Garden. Natural beauty for whoever wants to view it.

136. Carmel of Lisieux. The monastery building seen from the garden.

137. Carmel of Lisieux. Hermitage of St. Mary Magdalene with the statue of Our Lady of Lourdes.

138. Carmel of Lisieux. The inside cemetery, once the burial place for the nuns.

139. Maurice Bellière (1874–1907), seminarian, Thérèse's first spiritual brother. He joined the White Fathers and became a missionary to Africa.

140. Adolphe Roulland (1870–1934), Thérèse's second spiritual brother. A member of the Paris Foreign Missions and missionary to China.

139

140

CHAPTER SIX

The Discovery of the "Little Way"

CONRAD DE MEESTER, OCD

In the preceding chapters, we followed young Thérèse through the apprenticeship of her Carmelite life. It was a new and often difficult experience, but she had desired it with all her heart. She knew that Jesus called her to this "desert" and she was ready to follow wherever he led her. No name resounded as deeply in her as "Jesus."

Just as it would be a serious mistake to think that Thérèse was born a saint, so it would be wrong to imagine that the young Carmelite only had to follow automatically a path that was clearly marked out. In Carmel, she had to find her own way, "a little way, totally new" (C 3v), of which she would be the vanguard. Bounding ahead at full speed, Thérèse had to devote more than seven years to the religious life before understanding that to love as deeply as she had imagined, her own efforts were not enough. Jesus alone must give her Jesus.

In Carmel, Thérèse had to live a unique spiritual adventure. It was only through a lot of reflection and questioning, wrestling with her conscience, making decisions, and prayerfully listening to her Lord, that she found her own way to realize her Christian and contemplative vocation in the church. Thérèse knew spiritual darkness and anguish. Her way often passed through the night. She suffered exteriorly, but even more so interiorly. And she felt the weight of her "poor nature," which is our "means of earning our bread" (LT 89). "With a nature such as my own…I would have become very bad and perhaps even been lost," she wrote (A 8v). As much for the individual Christian as for the entire church, and no less even in this age, Thérèse's walk in the desert, in search of a hidden source and guided by confidence in God, remains prophetic.

In a Jansenistic time—which viewed God as just judge and laid stress both on one's personal effort to assure oneself of salvation by good works and also on fearing sin that lies in wait everywhere—Thérèse developed a liberating view of God's merciful love. But the Christian must continually discover and love this God of love. Have we ever stopped "believing in love" (1 Jn 4:16) and surrendering ourselves to it, like Thérèse?

Therein lies the invitation of the Saint of Lisieux! Cardinal Pacelli, the future Pope Pius XII, said: "It is the same Gospel, the heart of the Gospel that Thérèse had rediscovered, but with how much charm and freshness." And John Paul II, while visiting Lisieux, said: "Of Thérèse one can say with conviction that the Spirit of God enabled her heart to reveal directly to the people of our times the fundamental mystery, the reality of the Gospel: the grace of having truly received 'a spirit of adoption which makes us cry *Abba, Father!*'" (Rom 8:15).

To Love, the Only Ideal and the Only Way

When Thérèse passed over the threshold of Carmel, she carried very few things with her. Her great wealth was within; it was the flame in her heart. The day before her entry she affirmed: "I want to give myself totally to Him, I want to live no longer but for Him" (LT 43 B). At last she would be able to love Jesus according to her unlimited dreams. This is why the "desert" of Carmel ravished her! It returned to the Essential. It hid a Presence. Her emptiness was her hope. And for Thérèse, the generous one, each sacrifice became a word of love, a smile, a flower to give. A very short time beforehand, while still living in the world, she had made up her mind to give to Jesus "a thousand proofs of my love" (A 47v).

We know that "suffering opened wide its arms to her" (cf. A 69v). To Sister Thérèse of St. Augustine she confessed: "I assure you that I have had many struggles and that I haven't been one single day without suffering, not a single day" (PA 337). All the better, thought the young novice Thérèse: suffering "is a gold mine to be exploited. Are we going to miss the chance?" (LT 82).

Thérèse approached her Carmelite life with the firm resolution to realize her ideal of sanctity, come what may. "I want to be a saint…. I am not perfect, but I want to become perfect" (LT 45). "To become a great saint" was her theme song (LT 52, 80). Her Lord "does not want to set any limit to [her] sanctity" (LT 83). The price would never be too high: "Jesus is asking ALL, ALL, ALL. As much as He can ask from the greatest saints"—and she underlined this word "ALL" respectively two, three, and five times (LT 57).

Thérèse wanted to break the world record for loving God! "I would so much like to love Him! …Love Him more than He has ever been loved!" (LT 74). She would love him "to folly" (LT 93, 96), "with a passion" (LT 94), "to infinity" (LT 127). She was really describing herself when she wrote to Céline: "Jesus' love for Céline can be understood only by Jesus!… Jesus has done foolish things for Céline…. Let Céline do *foolish things* for Jesus" (LT 85). Thérèse would go about it "with all her power to love" (LT 104). The day of her profession, she asked for "love, infinite love without limits other than Yourself; love which is no longer me but You, my Jesus" (Pri 2; SS 275).

How would it be possible to realize this ideal of perfect love? For Thérèse, in these first years of Carmel, there was no doubt: By love, by my very, very generous love, in response to the follies of Jesus' love! Because "love is repaid by love alone," she said, citing her great spiritual master, Saint John of the Cross (LT 85).

Thérèse was sure to accomplish this one day. "Love can do all things, and the most difficult things don't appear difficult to it" (LT 65). She didn't know any other way: "As for myself, I know of no other means of reaching perfection but 'love.'… Love, how well our heart is made for that!… Sometimes, I seek another word to express love, but on this earth of exile words are powerless to express all the soul's vibrations, so we have to keep to this one word: Love!" (LT 109). Her practical conclusion is this: "Let us profit, let us profit from the shortest moments; let us act like misers, and

let us be jealous of the littlest things for the Beloved!" (LT 101).

Suffering Crowned

It is certain that in these years of her life, suffering brought many course corrections. And suffering was there in abundance, continually, in numerous and varied arenas.

We are not speaking of the external austerity that the monastic life brought the young Martin girl, born of a family living in easy circumstances and surrounded by the comforts of their time. This austerity is what she had wanted, what she had embraced with an immense generosity and eagerness: all these deprivations in food, rest, space, health, accommodations, and the temperature of this unheated building. This was the arena in which she would realize her dream of sanctity, of love without end and without limit.

Most difficult of all was the emotional solitude. Pauline and Marie, who preceded her to Carmel, didn't want to re-create the familial climate of Les Buissonnets that she had left deliberately. Besides this, there was the prioress, Mother Marie de Gonzague, in whom Thérèse discovered very quickly a suspicious and touchy side, which tempered the radiance and warmth of her maternal heart in a sudden and unforeseen way. And Thérèse soon discovered the trying aspects of community life that she later described: "These sad sentiments of nature" (C 19r), these "struggles" and "faults" and "weaknesses" (C 23v) which she discovered in herself as in others; "these moral infirmities [that] are chronic"; the "lack of judgment, good manners, touchiness in certain characters; all these things which don't make life very agreeable" (C 28r).

More purifying still were the aridity, weariness, and distractions in the two hours of prayer each day and in the annual retreats. She often admits this. Alluding to the nameless suffering caused by the humiliating sickness of her father (of whom we will soon speak), Thérèse wrote: "My soul soon shared in the sufferings of my heart. Spiritual aridity was my daily bread and, deprived of all consolation, I was still the happiest of creatures, since all my desires had been satisfied" (A 73r–v).

Thérèse wrote this years after she had experienced it. Surely at the actual time the suffering was often pure, painful, and confusing. And she often reacted to it poorly, humbly, "weakly," "without joy, without courage, without strength," recognizing herself as "weak and very weak, and everyday she had a new experience of this weakness" (LT 109).

Thérèse's generosity gave unceasingly and didn't break. She was like a reed—the laundry mark used to identify her clothing—which bends but does not break (LT 55). In the second place, her suffering only stirred up generosity. Thérèse wanted to transform all weaknesses and all trials into love of Jesus: into loving him exclusively, more humbly, more purely, more frequently, lifting herself after each fall in order to begin again without ceasing. Using comparisons that were dear to her at the time, she gave herself to Jesus at his convenience as "a little ball" in his hand, humble and small like "a grain of sand," "unknown," and "forgotten" (LT 103), "ignored" and "under the feet of all," but "seen by Jesus" (LT 95).

All suffering to her was good. It was the money with which one pays for sanctity! Suffering was borne, in that period of her life, as a halo. Thérèse repeated with conviction the words of Fr. Pichon: "Sanctity! We must conquer it at the point of the sword; we must *suffer...*, we must *agonize!*" (LT 89).

Christ, Mirror of the Father

Thérèse was a realist. She didn't get carried away in an imagined suffering, but accepted what was present—and how much it was present! Thérèse was affected by her father's illness more than by all her other trials. During the first months that Thérèse was at Carmel, her father's illness went from being preoccupying and distressing to being heartrending and crushing for her.

On February 12, 1889, Thérèse's most tenderly cherished Papa was admitted into a psychiatric hospital under the most dramatic circumstances, suffering from an arteriosclerosis of the brain; Thérèse felt truly trampled underfoot. Years later, she wrote:

> I recall that in the month of June, 1888 [her father had run away to Le Hâvre for three days at that time], at the moment of our first trials, I said: 'I am suffering very much, but I feel I can still bear greater trials.' I was not thinking then of the ones reserved for me.... I didn't know that on February 12, a month after my reception of the Habit, our dear Father would drink the *most bitter* and *most humiliating* of all chalices. Ah! on that day I didn't say I was able to suffer more. (A 73r)

Monsieur Martin stayed at the Bon Sauveur of Caen for more than three years. Closed in her Carmel, as her father was kept in what was readily called a "lunatic asylum," Thérèse's heart bled abundantly, for a long time. She offered all her blood to Jesus.

During her father's illness, Thérèse's faith went through an intense purification. Let's keep in mind that Thérèse was only sixteen years old. Her Papa, who was so good, wise, and pious, had naturally been until then a mirror of the Heavenly Father to young Thérèse. Then, all of a sudden, he was doing impatient, incoherent, dangerous things. The mirror broke into a thousand pieces.

Thérèse held on tenaciously in the face of suffering. She wanted to give all, absolutely all! But between the lines, we seem to have a presentiment of how she had silently come face-to-face with the mystery of God. Hadn't she prayed so much for this not to happen? And here was the apparent failure of her prayer. Necessarily these questions made their way into the mind of a little thinker like Thérèse, even if she didn't let them come entirely to the surface, even if she immediately rejected them—even if she responded to them and affirmed her will to suffer, following Jesus, for him and for souls.

Why did God permit such trials to come to someone who had always served him so well? Indeed, they say (and Thérèse repeated it) that suffering is a privilege reserved for the friends of God, and in heaven all will be rewarded. But is there really a heaven? Thérèse, who silently passed over many things on purpose in her autobiography, made this admission in passing: "At the time, I was having great interior trials of all kinds, even to the point of asking myself whether heaven really existed" (A 80v). It was the question of the hereafter that came back to her at the end of her life with such cruelty, and to which Thérèse gave, in Jesus, the response of faith and of magnificent love.

During this period, and in part under this pressure, the very young religious of sixteen to seventeen years would approach Christ in a new way. She discovered the "Holy Face" of the agonizing Jesus, his bruised face, humiliated and covered with wounds and tears. Thérèse pondered how much the Resurrected One had first to suffer. As with his beloved Son, God doesn't prevent suffering and death. Then, for Thérèse, the incomprehensible mystery of suffering was no longer entirely absurd nor in contradiction with the Father's goodness. And she saw how Jesus accepted his own death with a love that gave, forgave, and abandoned itself to God in redemptive confidence.

From a rather traditional faith, Thérèse crossed over to a personal faith, a fully accepted and responsible faith. Her faith became fundamentally "Christian." Jesus became her great argument and her certitude; she didn't want to know anyone better than she knew him. In her Offering to Merciful Love, she invoked with happiness the "Face" of Jesus just as she invoked the "crucible of suffering through which she had passed" (Pri 6; SS 277).

The Beauty of Jesus

And her Christ shines in the night. During her years between sixteen and twenty, Thérèse discovered more and more the depths of the Gospel and the ineffable beauty of Jesus, value beyond all value. "There is only Jesus who *is;* all the rest *is not.…* Let us love Him, then, unto folly" (LT 96). "He alone is ravishing in the full strength of the term.… beauty itself!" (LT 76). He is "the beautiful Lily of our souls" (LT 105).

Who else would speak of "the hidden beauties of Jesus" (L108)? Faith could hardly veil them: "Yes, the Face of Jesus is *luminous,* but if in the midst of wounds and tears it is already so beautiful, what will it be, then, when we shall see it in heaven? Oh, heaven… heaven. Yes, to see one day the Face of Jesus, to contemplate eternally the marvelous beauty of Jesus, the poor grain of sand desires to be despised on earth!"(LT 95). Even in darkness, she saw "a half-veiled light, the light that was diffused by the lowered eyes of my Fiancé's Face" (LT 110).

The beauty of Jesus, the Word Eternal, was also the beauty of his love for humans. He loves us indescribably: "Jesus is on fire with love for us…look at his adorable Face!… Look at His eyes lifeless and lowered! Look at His wounds.… Look at Jesus in His Face.… There you will see how He loves us" (LT 87). Thérèse would pray: "Your Face is my only Homeland. It's my Kingdom of love" (PN 20).

Abandonment to God's Work in Her

After "three years of martyrdom" (A 73r), on May 10, 1892, Monsieur Martin returned home to his family, henceforth paralyzed in his limbs and very gentle and harmless. For Thérèse, "the very sad trial of Caen" (LT 137) had passed. What's more, on February 20, 1893, Sister Agnes, her "second mother" of Les Buissonnets, became prioress. Psychologically, it was a new stage in Thérèse's life. The "five years" of suffering (A 70r) had ended; now "with *love,* not only did I advance, I actually *flew*" (A 80v).

Spiritually also, she entered into a new stage. Already in October, 1892, during her annual retreat, she understood that "the exterior" had been reduced to nothing by means of the trials of Caen, and now Jesus invited her to work more intensely at "interior" detachment: she must totally "humble" that which could still be exalted in her own eyes (LT 137).

In a letter of July 6, 1893 (LT 142), for the first time in her writings she used the noun "abandonment" (*abandon*), summarizing her new attitude. Suffering and one's own effort lost their prime importance, giving way to loving adherence not only to the will of God, but above all to his divine action in Thérèse.

Our Carmelite asserted in this letter that "merit does not consist in giving much, but rather in receiving, in loving much." She no longer wanted "to amass spiritual riches" (LT 91), but now to abandon her spiritual "business" to the Lord. In this letter to Céline she wrote:

> Your Thérèse is not in the heights at this moment, but Jesus is teaching her to learn 'to draw profit from everything, *from the good* and *the bad* she finds in herself' [St. John of the Cross]. He is teaching her to play at the bank of love, or rather He plays for her and does not tell her how He goes about it, for that is His affair and not Thérèse's. What she must do is abandon herself, surrender herself, without keeping anything, not even the joy of knowing how much the bank is returning to her.... Jesus teaches me not to count up my acts. He teaches me to do *all* through love…. But this is done in peace, in *abandonment,* it is Jesus who is doing all in me, and I am doing nothing. (LT 142)

Thérèse, the daughter of two shopkeepers, would naturally use economic and financial language to speak of her spiritual progress, just as warrior language was familiar to her. Combative and earnest, she loved to direct her own quest, to gather up spiritual riches, desirous of soon reaching "the summit of the mountain of Love" (LT 112). Progressively she came to understand that it would never be possible for her to love as her heart commanded her to love, unless the Lord himself came to love in her. She gradually learned to disarm and to no longer seize and count, but to open her hands in order to receive God from God.

Irreparable Weakness

Formerly, she wanted to return love for love equally, if possible; she wanted to reciprocate the infinite love of God by doing "foolish things for love" of Jesus who had done "foolish things for love" of us (LT 85) and by loving God "more than He has ever been loved" (LT 74). After six years of religious life, she confessed: "We shall never be able to carry out the follies He carried out for us, and our actions will never merit this name, for they are only very rational acts and much below what our love would like to accomplish" (LT 169).

She would remain unavoidably short of this dreamed love. Toward the end of her brief life, Thérèse spoke about the true dimensions of the two loves:

> Your Love has gone before me, and it has grown with me, and now it is an abyss whose depths I cannot fathom. Love attracts love, and, my Jesus, my love leaps towards Yours; it would like to fill the abyss which attracts it, but alas! it is not even like a drop of dew lost in the ocean! For me to love You as You love me, I would have to borrow Your own Love, and only then would I be at rest. (C 35r)

Thérèse would always confess her "weaknesses," her "faults" and "unfaithfulness," very small and trifling though they be, and quite invisible to the eyes of others, but real and perceptible to her who had "the eyes and the heart" of an eagle (B 4v). These were irreparable weaknesses just the same, of which she later wrote without hesitation: "All our justice is stained" (Pri 6; SS 277), "no human life is exempt from faults" (LT 226), even "the most holy souls will be perfect only in

Heaven" (C 28r). Likewise, in Carmel, Thérèse again experienced scruples and anguish concerning her faults and her state of grace, so sensitive was she to the perfect love that God deserves. It happened that she was "in such a night that I no longer knew whether God loved me" (A 78r). Her meeting with Fr. Prou, in October 1891, proved to be liberating for Thérèse on this point; Father Prou explained to her that there are "faults that don't cause God any pain" (cf. A 80v). One year earlier, Thérèse had already had a presentiment of these "faults that *don't offend* Him but serve only to humble and to make love stronger" (LT 114).

The Carmelite had carefully observed this slow clearing away of her misery in one of the most profound and most human passages she ever wrote:

> When I think of the time of my novitiate, I see how imperfect I was. I made so much fuss over such little things that it makes me laugh now. Ah! how good the Lord is in having matured my soul and in having given it wings.... Later on, no doubt the time in which I am now [three months before her death] will appear filled with imperfections, but now I am astonished at nothing. I am not disturbed at seeing myself *weakness* itself. On the contrary, it is in my weakness that I glory and I expect each day to discover new imperfections in myself. (C 15r)

Thérèse accepted her human weakness and the great necessity of God's grace, which is our only harbor of salvation. This is what she was soon going to explore: the wonderful mercy in God's love.

When the Way Is Not Yet Very Clear

Her own irreparable weakness and the greatness of God's love are what led Thérèse to adopt her attitude of abandonment. This attitude is characteristic of the period between 1893 and 1894, that is to say, after five or six years of religious life.

Is this already her famous "Little Way"? Thérèse no longer expected merits and progress from herself, but

from God. She developed a profound awareness of her own incapacity. Henceforth, she sought less to transform her weakness in love by herself than to let the Lord act. She took account of the priority of God's love, which is not only the source of our acts of love, but also the source of our perfection. Isn't this already the "Way of Spiritual Childhood"?

Most certainly, this is already to live like a child of the Father. Nevertheless, it isn't yet the fullness of Thérèse's "little way." We must take the Saint seriously when she states that at a given moment—and this would be only during the course of the autumn of 1894—she made her discovery of a "little way, totally new."

Let's express it using the terminology of her letter of July 6, 1893. At that time, Thérèse wrote about a divine "game" in her journey toward sanctity, but she didn't yet understand "how Jesus would go about" increasing her love. At the time of her discovery of the "little way," the Lord revealed to her precisely *how* he goes about making her advance. Then, Thérèse was able to adapt herself perfectly to God's game. She saw a perfectly lighted path before her. Previously she had been walking in a good way, but in obscurity, like a blind person, with all the hesitations, delays, and mistakes. How much faster and more confidently she would now run on a clear path!

According to what Thérèse explains to us about her "little way, totally new," her great discovery was centered on God, on the divine mercy *precisely as* mercy. Of course, previous to this, Thérèse was also aware of divine goodness and how helpful it was. But now she learned to recognize that God's love is not only real, first, and faithful, but that it is a love that descends toward the little, that seeks the little ones *because* they are little, and *how great God is* for the little. Littleness, instead of being principally *humility*, would from then on become principally *confidence*.

Wanting to be little and to become more and more little, Thérèse earnestly desired, above all, a completely childlike confidence. What "pleases God in my little soul," she later wrote, "is *that He sees me loving my littleness* and *my poverty, the blind hope that I have in His Mercy.…* It is confidence and nothing but confidence that must lead us to Love" (LT 197). In a clear and deliberate way, she entrusted herself to the grace working in her, cooperating with it and surrendering to it.

The Discovery of the "Little Way"

It is only in Manuscript C of her autobiography, written three months before her death, that Thérèse told of her discovery of her "little way, a way that is very straight, very short, and totally new" (C 2v). She had noticed in comparing herself to the saints that on the one hand she was like a grain of sand at the foot of a mountain, and on the other hand that "it is impossible for me to grow up" (that is to say, to grow up all by herself, but that didn't mean that God couldn't make her grow!). Thérèse began "searching the Scriptures" for a solution, for an "elevator" that would lift her to the summit of the mountain of sanctity.

Here we need to know that on September 14, 1894, one and a half months after Monsieur Martin's death, Céline herself was also consecrated to the Lord at the Carmel in Lisieux. Upon her entry, she carried with her a little notebook in which she had copied the most beautiful passages of the Old Testament. At that time, young Carmelites were not allowed to read the Old Testament in its entirety. Eager to grasp the Word of God, Thérèse plunged herself into Céline's little notebook. It was there that she experienced her important "eureka" one day in the autumn of 1894.

She was at first struck by these initial words: "Whoever is a little one, let him come to Me." (Prv 9:4). Here she felt that she was being addressed personally: Littleness was precisely her difficulty on the way to becoming a

great saint. And there she was being invited to approach God as a "little one," even as a "very little" one.

Guided by the Spirit, she pursued her search in a very personal and penetrating interpretation. Something stirred her in reading the promise of God: "As one whom a mother caresses, so will I comfort you; you shall be carried at the breasts, and upon the knees they shall caress you" (Is 66:12–13).

Let us pause for a moment. Thérèse cited this passage twice, and twice she revealed the emotion that it evoked in her. Here is what she said about it: "Ah! Never did words more tender and more melodious come to give joy to my soul" (C 3r). And again: "After having listened to words such as these…there is nothing to do but to be silent and to weep with gratitude and love" (B 1r–v).

Why such a deep emotion? Because, for the very first time, Thérèse read in the Bible that God is like a *mother* to her child! And Thérèse was ultrasensitive to the love of a mother! Hadn't she lost her "matchless mother" (A 4v) to cancer when she was only four years and eight months old? This brutal loss, at the age when a child has such need for maternal affection to mold her personality, caused in Thérèse a deep trauma from which she only recovered at fourteen with "the grace of Christmas." Then, after her mother's death, Thérèse became strongly attached to her sister Pauline, her "second mother," who soon left for Carmel. It was a new tear at her heart when her other sister, Marie, her third "mother" so to speak, also left for the monastery.

And there Thérèse, the orphan, read that God is *like a mother* for her very little child! Thus, she concluded: "I had to remain little and become this more and more"—until she became a "very little one" to be filled with God's motherly love.

Her conclusion is clear: this "little way, a way that is very straight, very short," which leads to the summit of love and sanctity, this "elevator" she was searching for "is Your arms, O Jesus!"

Thérèse Speaks

The Apostolate of Prayer

Céline, the vast solitudes, the enchanting horizons opening up before you must be speaking volumes to your soul? I myself see nothing of all that, but I say with Saint John of the Cross: "My Beloved is the mountains, and the lonely, wooded valleys, etc." And this Beloved instructs my soul, He speaks to it in silence, in darkness.... Recently, there came a thought to me which I have to tell my Céline. It was one day when I was thinking of what I could do to save souls, a word of the gospel gave me a real light. In days gone by, Jesus said to His disciples when showing them the fields of ripe corn: "Lift up your eyes and see how the fields are already white enough to be harvested," and a little later: "In truth, the harvest is abundant but the number of laborers is small, ask then the master of the harvest to send laborers." What a mystery!... Is not Jesus all-powerful? Are not creatures His who made them? Why, then, does Jesus say: "Ask the Lord of the harvest that he send some workers"? Why?... Ah! it is because Jesus has so incomprehensible a love for us that He wills that we have a share with Him in the salvation of souls. He wills to do nothing without us. The Creator of the universe awaits the prayer of a poor little soul to save other souls redeemed like it at the price of all His Blood. Our own vocation is not to go out to harvest the fields of ripe corn. Jesus does not say to us: "*Lower* your eyes, look at the fields and go harvest them." Our mission is still more sublime. These are the words of our Jesus: "*Lift* your eyes and see." See how in my heaven there are empty places; it is up to you to fill them, you are my Moses praying on the mountain, ask me for workers and I shall send them, I await only a prayer, a sigh from your heart!...

Is not the apostolate of prayer, so to speak, more elevated than that of the word? Our mission as Carmelites is to form evangelical workers who will save thouands of souls whose mothers we shall be.... Céline, if these were not the very words of our Jesus, who would dare to believe in them?... I find that our share is really beautiful, what have we to envy in priests? (LT 135)

Maintain Love

Now I want to tell you what is taking place in my *own* soul; no doubt, it is the same things as in yours. You have rightly said, Céline, the cool mornings have passed for us, there remain no more flowers to gather, Jesus has taken them for Himself. Perhaps He will make new ones bloom one day, but in the meantime what must we do? Céline, God is no longer asking anything from me...in the beginning, He was asking an infinity of things from me. I thought, at times, that since Jesus was no longer asking anything from me, I had to go along quietly in peace and love, doing only what He was asking of me.... But I had a light. St. Teresa says we must maintain love. *The wood* is not within our reach when we are in darkness, in aridities, but at least are we not obliged to throw little pieces of straw on it? Jesus is really powerful enough to keep the fire going by Himself. However, He is satisfied when He sees us put a little fuel on it. This *attentiveness* pleases Jesus, and then He throws on the fire a lot of wood. We do not see it, but we do feel the *strength* of love's warmth. I have experienced it: when I *am feeling* nothing, when I am INCAPABLE *of praying,* of practicing virtue, then is the moment for seeking opportunities, *nothings,* which please Jesus more than mastery of the world or even martyrdom suffered with generosity. For example, a smile, a friendly word, when I would want to say nothing, or put on a look of annoyance, etc., etc.

Céline, do you understand? It is not for the purpose of weaving my crown, gaining merits, it is in order to please Jesus.... When I do not have any opportunities, I want at least to tell Him frequently that I love Him; this is not difficult, and it keeps the *fire* going. *Even though* this fire of love would seem to me to have gone out, I would like to throw something on it, and Jesus could then relight it. Céline, I am afraid I have not said what I should; perhaps you will think I always do what I am saying. Oh, no! I am not always faithful, but I never get discouraged; I abandon myself into the arms of Jesus. (LT 143)

CHAPTER SEVEN

The Offering to Merciful Love

CONRAD DE MEESTER, OCD

We have just followed Thérèse to the final months of 1894, when she made the discovery of her "little way" (later referred to by Mother Agnes as "the Way of Spiritual Childhood"). Let us now see how she was led to make the offering of herself to the merciful love of God.

Under the Light of Mercy

Since the discovery of her "little way," the "mercy" of God had become for the young Carmelite the sunshine of her life! If the word "mercy" was up to that point absent in her vocabulary, henceforth it would emerge spontaneously and repeatedly. When Thérèse was asked to retell her childhood memories (Manuscript A of her autobiography) in January 1895, just months after the discovery of her "little way," the central theme was readily apparent: "the Mercies of the Lord." The three exclamation points that follow in Thérèse's manuscript, like the ten suspension points, suggest how much these words spoke to her heart.

In the prologue of this autobiographical manuscript, Thérèse describes the gratuitous mercy of the Lord as "the mystery of my vocation, my whole life, and especially the mystery of the privileges Jesus showered on my soul," the explanation of the "totally gratuitous gifts of Jesus," the "preferences" of his mercy alone. "Since the nature of love is to humble oneself," Thérèse writes, thus showing how much she was referring to a *merciful* love, God "would not descend so low" if he didn't care deeply about the littlest ones. "By coming down in this way, God manifests His infinite grandeur," "just as the sun shines simultaneously both on the tall cedars and on each little flower as though it were alone on the earth" (A 2r–3v).

The word "mercy" would have appeared even more often in her writings if Thérèse hadn't understood some months later that the love of God is always and so essentially *merciful* that we can limit ourselves to the single word "love": to add "merciful" would be redundant, saying in two words what can be said in one. And when Thérèse mentions her oblation or "Offering to Merciful Love" at the end of her Manuscript A, she refers to it very succinctly as an "offering to Love."

A Long Written Meditation

From January 1895 until the end of the year, Thérèse would regularly write about certain aspects of her past. Her "memories of childhood?" Of course! But in fact she spoke first about the role of her merciful Beloved in her life. She could then see the golden thread of his mercy running everywhere through the fabric of her life.

Now she saw and understood. All was clear. To write was to pray, to see in depth, to sing God's mercies, in thanksgiving. Her writing assignment was a long meditation that took hold deeply in her. And no doubt partly under the effect of this long written meditation, on June 9, 1895, the morning of the feast of the Holy Trinity, Thérèse received "the grace to understand more than ever before how much Jesus desires to be loved" (A 84r). The passive form, to be loved, coincides in reality with the active form, to love: Jesus wants to love us mercifully, to flood us with "waves of His infinite tenderness." And Thérèse offered herself to him entirely.

Before entering into the details of her "offering," let us stop for a few moments to see the role that the image of her Papa, Louis Martin, played in this new vision.

We are all aware of the lasting bond that united father and daughter. Thérèse called him her "king," and he called her his "queen." We have mentioned the nameless suffering that Thérèse experienced when she saw her king fall prey to mental illness, which separated him from his family and put him in a psychiatric hospital in 1889. For Thérèse, when Monsieur Martin died in 1894, it was the end of a long period of mourning.

Three weeks after the death of her Papa, on July 29, 1894, she wrote to Céline: "How much these little delicacies make us feel that our dear father is close to us! After a *death* of five years, what a joy to find him once more always the same, seeking out ways to please us as he did in days gone by" (LT 169). And the next day, to her sister Léonie, who reentered the convent of the Visitation:

> Papa's death does not give me the impression of a death, but of a real *life.* I am finding him once more after an absence of six years. I feel him around *me,* looking at me and protecting me.... Now...we gaze on the heavens to find there a Father and a Mother who offered us to Jesus.... Soon their desires will be accomplished, and all the children God gave them are going to be united to Him forever. (LT 170)

Thérèse recalls this same vision of the future life—Papa and Mama reunited soon with all of their children for all eternity in heaven—at the beginning of her autobiography (A 3r–3v).

From the first line, Papa is present in this "springtime story of a little white flower": Thérèse named herself after the "little white flower" that she received from her father on the evening of Pentecost in 1887 when he gave her permission to enter Carmel. She then placed this little white flower—a symbolic gesture, and how suggestive!—in her *Imitation of Christ,* in the chapter entitled: "One must love Jesus above all things" (A 50v).

These "parents without equal" (A 4r) are present all through these childhood memories. What's more, Thérèse brought her personal memories to life again in rereading her mother's touching correspondence. In writing, Thérèse reflected on the heart of her father, who had died recently and who was then "watching over her and protecting her." "Our Father's *very affectionate heart* seemed to be enriched now [after

Madame Martin's death] with a truly maternal love!" (A 13r). She unceasingly emphasized his shining presence in the paternal home or during their long walks: "his handsome face said so much to me" (A 17v). Sitting "on Papa's knees," listening to "his handsome voice" when he sang or recited poetry or prayed, Thérèse had "only to look at him to see how the Saints pray" (A 18r). She vividly remembered how Papa, on the day of Pentecost 1887, "took my head and placed it on his heart," then walked slowly with her in the garden "while still holding my head on his heart" (A 50r). Similar gestures spontaneously reminded Thérèse of "the caresses [God] will bestow on me" one day in heaven (A 73r; cf. B 2r).

In this existential context after the death of Monsieur Martin, who had reunited with his spouse in heaven and watched over Thérèse, we can better understand why the Carmelite was deeply touched, at the moment she discovered her "little way," by the passage from Isaiah comparing God to a mother who carries her child on her knees and covers her with caresses.

Also, we better understand that, influenced by the remembrance of her father, Thérèse received on the following June 9 "the grace to understand more than ever before" how much the "Heart" of Jesus is rich in "waves of infinite tenderness," happy to "lavish" them on those who dare to "throw themselves into [God's] arms and accept [God's] infinite Love" (cf. A 84r). By inextricable bonds and to an extent we cannot exactly define, the grace and light of God came through the recollection of all the blessings received during her lifetime, not least by means of her parents who were the image of divine goodness to her.

The posthumous life of Monsieur Martin played a great role during his daughter's last years! As her Papa had been an image of God for Thérèse as a child, so, later, the humiliated face of her father had resembled the Holy Face of Jesus, the suffering servant of Yahweh. Thus the face and the memory of Papa who had entered into God's glory became for Thérèse, more than before, a mirror where Jesus' resplendent face and wonderful heart received a coloring still more human and concrete.

In 1896, in her poem *Jesus Alone,* Thérèse wrote some words that gently echoed to the very happy and vital experience she had with her own father:

O You Who knew how to create the mother's heart

I find in you the tenderest of Fathers!

My only Love, Jesus, Eternal Word,

For me Your Heart is more than maternal. (PN 36)

Two weeks after her Offering to Merciful Love, in her poem *To the Sacred Heart of Jesus,* Thérèse revealed herself wonderfully human in her faith in the Incarnate Word as she confessed:

I need a heart burning with tenderness

Who will be my support forever

Who loves everything in me, even my weakness…

And who never leaves me day or night.

I could find no creature

Who could always love me and never die.

I must have a God who takes on my nature,

and becomes my brother and is able to suffer! (PN 23)

How Much Jesus Desires to Love Us

Never before had Thérèse experienced the love of Christ more deeply than on this springlike morning of June 9, 1895, the summit of light. In the early hours of the day (we don't know whether it was during the hour of silent prayer or during the Eucharist), she was suddenly seized by the reality and the beauty of the merciful love of the Trinity, of the Three Divine Persons, who in Jesus want to communicate with us to the point of inundating the depths of our being and our daily existence.

"You have loved me so much as to give me Your only Son as my Savior and my Spouse," she exulted, fascinated by the light that flowed from the summit of love who is Jesus (cf. A 83r–84r; Pri 6; SS 276). On this feast of the Holy Trinity, her heart sounded the heart of God and she was completely renewed by it. Thérèse again experienced the grace she received as a privilege, a divine choice. "*Love* has chosen me as a holocaust, me, a weak and imperfect creature." "It is my weakness that gives me the boldness of offering myself as *VICTIM of Your Love, O Jesus!*" (B 3v).

She then contemplated her Christ, who seeks the poor and sinners, and is consumed with love for all. And what did she see? So much indifference on the part of humanity! "On every side" the love of Jesus "is unknown, rejected," "disdained." "Seeking happiness," human beings "turn to creatures." Yet there is an "infinite love" that has "need" to "lavish" itself and "overflow" in a torrent of grace.

And the heart of Thérèse, the tender and faithful heart of a spouse, again experienced a *poignant sorrow* at the loneliness of Jesus, who was constrained, wanting to find open doors, but had to "hold back the waves of infinite tenderness" within himself. She longed to release them, "throwing [herself] into Your arms and accepting [Your] infinite *Love.*"

But more than sorrow she again felt a *holy inebriation* in view of Jesus who "would be happy" finally to find a heart given without reserve and without restrictions. And the young religious of twenty-two wrote: "O my Jesus! Let me be this happy victim; consume Your holocaust with the fire of Your Divine Love!"

The Offering

Thérèse was going to surrender herself entirely, as an "offering," as a "victim" (to use her expressions). In an initial reflex, her spirit turned toward a form of "victimhood" familiar to her, particularly in relation to God's "justice." In the church and also at Carmel, souls offered themselves to this justice. In the same monastery where Thérèse lived, they had received on the eve of June 9 the obituary of one French Carmelite who died in suffering and terrible anguish after offering herself as a "victim" to the justice of God.

During Thérèse's time, Christians were readily shaped by the fear of God as just judge, a God from whose eyes nothing escaped, who rewarded or punished according to merit and demerit, to whom one paid the price of heaven with the small change of good works, sacrifices, and prayers. Likewise, in order to pay ransom for others, certain souls—let's listen to Thérèse—"offer themselves as victims of God's justice in order to turn away the punishments reserved to sinners, drawing them upon themselves."

Thérèse sincerely appreciated this offering. She found it "beautiful and very generous": "beautiful" because the offering recognized God's greatness and holiness, remembering all that his Son had suffered for us; "generous" because these souls laid themselves open to take on and expiate the consequences of sin.

Thérèse appreciated it, but kept her distance from this offering: "I was far from feeling attracted to making it." She, so weak and small, who "felt her helplessness," this helplessness that for more than seven years in Carmel she never stopped experiencing and probing, how could she take equal responsibility upon her fragile shoulders?

But it was not these negative considerations that were most decisive. On the springlike morning of the feast of the Holy Trinity, the light was all positive. It stirred her to "understand how much Jesus desires to be *loved*"—not out of fear. It is his immeasurable mercy, and not his exacting and severe justice, which comes to the fore. It is not divine justice that has the greatest "need" of comprehension and response, but God's "infinite tenderness," God's "Merciful Love." It is not a question of "drawing punishments upon herself," but of

letting herself be drawn by divine tenderness. Jesus didn't want "to release" his justice, but to "set us aflame" with the fire of his love.

It had been eight months since Thérèse had discovered her "little way," and at the beginning of her prayer of Offering she touched on the great points around which all else turned: the ideal of sanctity ("I desire, in a word, to be a saint"), the reality of her own helplessness ("but I feel my helplessness"), and the reconciliation of the ideal and the helplessness in her confident surrender to God's sanctifying work within her ("and I beg you, O my God! to be Yourself my *Sanctity!*"). But on this morning she "understood more than ever" how intensely the Lord's merciful love was searching, for her and for us, at the heart of our littleness. The *Offering to Merciful Love* is situated, historically and by its very nature, within the perspectives opened by this "little way." The Offering is the logical consequence of it, the prayerful expression and the ultimate consecration. The thesis of the desire of sanctity and the antithesis of helplessness are reconciled together in the synthesis of confident surrender to the work of the thrice holy God, Merciful Love.

Thérèse settled on the *fundamentals of her confidence:* 1) Through love of us, the Father gave us his Son: "His merits are mine. I offer them to You with gladness." In a similar gesture, Thérèse offered "the *Love* and the merits" of Mary, and of the angels and saints; 2) the promise of Jesus that he hears our prayers (Jn 16:23); and 3) the presence of these great desires in her, a sign that these longings would one day be fulfilled.

Then she reformulated her initial supplication of sanctity: "It is with confidence I ask You to come and take possession of my soul." She sought entire possession of such a "little host" similar to the Eucharistic host that becomes the Body of Christ! A little host, of which even the "weakness" and the "imperfections" would be "consumed" and "transformed" by the fire of divine love.

It was consequently to *merciful* love that Thérèse presented herself. The young Carmelite explained that there were "different types" of souls, but that it was her vocation, her vocation particularly, "to honor in a special way" the mercy of God and "*through it* to contemplate and adore the other divine perfections," which all "appear to be resplendent with *love.*"

Oh no, she didn't want to rely upon her own "merits" at all: she avoided the least appearance of pharisaic arrogance before God and depended solely on pure divine kindness, to which she would give praise for all eternity. Her "one purpose" was not to "lay up merits" but to "work for [God's] love alone," permitting him to "flood her soul with the waves of His infinite tenderness."

Her goal was to comfort and relieve the heart of God and to make her own life a song of praise to the mercy of God, who, in her view, desired to be the hinge on which our sanctification turns—the whole New Testament testifies to this. Thus it would be God as Merciful Love who would realize her dream of love within her! Thérèse was going to "accept" love, "to receive from Love" her own "justice" and her "heaven."

Thérèse qualified her position relative to mercy as an "offering." What reverence there was in this offering! What total dependence on the goodness of Jesus that she anticipated unquestionably, having caught a glimpse in his heart of his strong desire to give of himself. For nothing in the world would Thérèse force Jesus to accept such an offering if she didn't know that it was the same desire that God had: that she offer herself.

And, from this moment on, the offering became a true gift of self, a total commitment. Thérèse put all this faithfulness at the disposal of Jesus—this faithfulness that she was accustomed to living for a long time, as she tried to fulfill his least desires. But this generosity would no longer be, like before, the money with which to assure herself of sanctity, but instead the living expression of her openness to Jesus' life within her.

What changed exteriorly in Thérèse's generosity after the discovery of her "little way" and her "Offering to Merciful Love"? Nothing and everything! Nothing, because she was going to continue like before to be very faithful to "strewing flowers," to "profiting by all the smallest things," to scattering her "nothings" with love (cf. B 3v–4r). And everything, because she did it solely as a sign of her care for the God of love, as an expression of her unceasing openness to his grace, to this "immensity of love...which it has pleased You to give me freely, *without any merit on my part*" (C 35r).

She then fervently begged to be "consumed" and "transformed" by the fire of merciful love. With determination she wanted to throw all into the fire, to receive all from the fire. So she would say elsewhere: "To love is to give everything. It's to give oneself" (PN 54). Since the feast of the Trinity in 1895 she understood, more than ever, that the gift of self is before all else the fruit of free and overflowing divine action: to love is to receive everything and to be received oneself by the mercy to which one opens oneself, to which one offers oneself.

Martyr of Love

Thérèse then articulated a sort of *vow of spiritual poverty.* "In the evening of this life, I shall appear before You with empty hands, for I do not ask you, Lord, to count my works." After many years she had discovered that all our efforts are imperfect and bear "stains": good motives get easily entangled with more egotistical ones. But overall, Thérèse was inspired by the desire, indeed by the firm will ("I want...I don't want at all"), to render all homage to the redeeming love of Christ. It wasn't she who would build her throne, her crown: Jesus would be her only "Throne" and her only "Crown." All praise would converge toward "You, O my Beloved!"

Thérèse offered herself as a "victim." The word generally refers to a situation in which one is unjustly subjected to violence and involuntary suffering. Unable to say it better, the young contemplative used this term of her era, but in a mystical and loving sense. Involuntary? Oh, how much Thérèse begged for it with all her being and opened all her freedom to it in order that love would come to "take possession of my soul." Completely open like Mary and following her example (it was to Mary that Thérèse chooses to "abandon my offering, begging her to present it" to her Son), she offered herself to be flooded with the "waves of infinite tenderness" and to become a "martyr" to the action of love in her, to which each movement of her being was offered.

If there is *injustice* here, it can only be the disproportion between our "helplessness," our "weakness," and the magnificence of the forgiveness and the work of God. Such *injustice,* such selection as "victim," was the object of all Thérèse's desires: "O my Jesus! let me be this happy victim."

So Thérèse reached the decisive moment of her offering. She took the leap into the infinite tenderness of God who was going to realize her dream of sanctity: "in order to live in one single act of perfect Love, I offer myself."

"Perfect love," Thérèse dreamed only of that: "to accomplish Your Will perfectly," "sanctity." And all that "in one single act." A single one! Continuous! From morning to evening, and from evening to morning, all through the night. "Living on Love" (PN 17)! "I sleep, but my heart keeps watch!" Because Thérèse *gave a mission to her heart* "to renew this offering at each beat." Her heart would be her delegate. So she would stay vigilant at every moment, hanging onto the heart of Jesus, who desires, oh "how much," to love us. She would be his "martyr of love."

The Fire of the Spirit of Love

Thérèse qualified her state of being at God's disposal as like that of a victim "of holocaust." The word conceals the image of a consuming fire. The Carmelite was acquainted with the burning sacrifices of the Old Testament, but here she addressed herself to the "Fire" of Pentecost (in her time the feast of the Holy Trinity closed the octave of Pentecost), to the spiritual fire, that of divine love, by which she eagerly desired to be "consumed incessantly" until she was "transformed into [the Fire] itself." Some months earlier, in her poem *Living on Love* (PN 17), Thérèse had expressly invoked this action of the Spirit in herself: "The Spirit of Love sets me aflame with his fire."

Offering herself to merciful love, Thérèse newly surrendered herself to the fire of the Spirit, plunging herself in the waves of love of the Holy Trinity who had flooded her soul on the day of her baptism. It is revealing that the Saint, quite exceptionally, signs her Offering with her religious name preceded by her baptismal names, "Marie Françoise Thérèse." To plunge herself knowingly in the fire of the Spirit of love, to open herself without reserve to the life of Christ in us, is the final consequence of her baptism and ours.

As another eloquent gesture, henceforth she would always carry on her heart the Gospel, the formula of her religious vows, and the text of her Offering (the autograph is all worn out and patched!): Christian baptism, religious profession, and the Offering to Merciful Love were symbolically united there.

As a "victim," she desired to be without defense before the fire of the Spirit of love and this divine flood which nothing must curb. Thérèse offered herself, begging her Lord to "consume her incessantly," to "fill her soul to overflowing with the waves of infinite tenderness that are concealed within Him." As a torrent! Or as an ocean, which floods a shell, fills it, and carries it out to eternity.

The Fruits

On the following Friday, July 14, 1895, while making her Way of the Cross, the Carmelite experienced a "real flame that was burning her." It was as if, in an exceptional manner, Love acknowledged the receipt of this Offering that, in faith, she knew to be so agreeable to him. Mother Agnes received Thérèse's account of the experience:

> I was beginning the Way of the Cross; suddenly, I was seized with such a violent love for God that I can't explain it except by saying that it felt as though I were totally plunged into fire. Oh! What fire and what sweetness at one and the same time! I was on fire with love, and I felt that one minute more, one second more, and I wouldn't be able to sustain this ardor without dying. I understood, then, what the saints were saying about these states which they experienced so often. As for me, I experienced it only once and for one single instant, falling back immediately into my habitual state of dryness. (DE 7.7.2; HLC 77)

But if an extraordinary experience of this kind was infrequent, Thérèse experienced the very great benefits of her Offering in a more diffuse way. Six months later, she told of its wonderful impact on her life. "You know the rivers or rather the oceans of graces which flooded my soul. Ah! Since that happy day, it seems to me that *Love* penetrates and surrounds me, that at each moment this *Merciful Love* renews me, purifying my soul and leaving no trace of sin within it" (A 84r). She was then "flooded with light" (A 32r). "I feel that [Jesus] is within me at each moment; He is guiding and inspiring me with what I must say and do" (A 83v). And we know very well that Thérèse became luminous and incandescent for those around her, a burning lamp in the whole church.

Indeed, since Easter 1896, after her first hemoptysis when she was certain she would die soon, she entered into a mysterious night concerning the hereafter. Although the simple and abundant light disappeared, how much Thérèse still felt sustained by merciful love

to which she offered herself! Her faith remained unshakable, Jesus was very near: "At each new occasion of combat…I run towards my Jesus…. Never have I felt before this…how sweet and merciful the Lord really is, for He did not send me this trial until the moment I was capable of bearing it" (C 7r–v).

Now the merciful work of the Lord imbued all areas of her life. Her virtues, joy, interior freedom, humble truthfulness, patience? Thérèse had the feeling that she received these from the hand of God. When others complimented her on her patience, she answered: "I haven't even one minute of patience. It's not my patience! You're always wrong!" (DE 18.8.4; HLC 153).

As for her prayer? Formerly, it had been more of a wonderful communication from a "me" to a "You." Now it was rather a communication, no less marvelous, from a "You" to a "me" full of confidence. Thérèse let Jesus live in her: "This is my prayer. I ask Jesus to draw me into the flames of His Love, to unite me so closely to Him that He lives and acts in me" (C 36r).

Her charity toward others? Thérèse would not stop "penetrating into the mysterious depths" (C 18v). "Yes, I feel it, when I am charitable," she wrote, "it is Jesus alone who is acting in me; and the more united I am to Him, the more also do I love my Sisters" (C 12v). It is enough to run to him!

Her apostolate? "I felt that the only thing necessary was to unite myself more and more to Jesus and that 'all these things will be given to you besides.' In fact, never was my hope mistaken, for God saw fit to fill my little hand as many times as it was necessary" (C 22v).

Her unavoidable faults? "If I had committed all possible crimes, I would always have the same confidence; I feel that this whole multitude of offenses would be like a drop of water thrown into a fiery furnace" (DE 11.7.6; HLC 89).

She would cling to mercy. "I want, O my Beloved, with each beat of my heart to renew this offering to You an infinite number of times." "Very often, when I am able to do so, I repeat my Offering to Love," she said in her last sickness (DE 29.7.9; HLC 117).

On September 30, 1897, the last day of her life, in the afternoon, Thérèse said, "I am not sorry for delivering myself up to Love... Oh! no, I'm not sorry; on the contrary!" (DE 30.9; HLC 205).

Here, until the last moment, she remained faithful to the Lord of merciful love who accomplished her former dream of sanctity. Not in any way that she had contemplated in her youth, but better! She attained this sanctity by the work of the thrice holy God himself, to whom she offered herself in a radical way.

Thérèse Speaks

Living On Love

On the evening of Love, speaking without parable,
Jesus said: "If anyone wishes to love me
All his life, let him keep my Word.
My Father and I will come to visit him.
And we will make his heart our dwelling.
Coming to him, we shall love him always.
We want him to remain, filled with peace,
     In our Love!…"

Living on Love is holding You Yourself.
Uncreated Word, Word of my God,
Ah! Divine Jesus, you know I love you.
The Spirit of Love sets me aflame with his fire.
In loving you I attract the Father.
My weak heart holds him forever.
O Trinity! You are Prisoner
     Of my Love!…

Living on Love is living on your life,
Glorious King, delight of the elect.
You live for me, hidden in a host.
I want to hide myself for you, O Jesus!
Lovers must have solitude,
A heart-to-heart lasting night and day.
Just one glance of yours makes my beatitude.
     I live on Love!…

Living on Love is not setting up one's tent
At the top of Tabor.
It's climbing Calvary with Jesus,
It's looking at the Cross as a treasure!…
In Heaven I'm to live on joy.
Then trials will have fled forever,
But in exile, in suffering I want
     To live on Love.

Living on Love is giving without limit
Without claiming any wages here below.
Ah! I give without counting, truly sure
That when one loves, one does not keep count!…
Overflowing with tenderness, I have given everything,
To his Divine Heart…. lightly I run.
I have nothing left but my only wealth:
     Living on Love.

Living on Love is banishing every fear,
Every memory of past faults.
I see no imprint of my sins.
In a moment love has burned everything…..
Divine Flame, O very sweet Blaze!
I make my home in your hearth.
In your fire I gladly sing:
     "I live on Love!…"

Living on Love is keeping within oneself
A great treasure in an earthen vase.
My Beloved, my weakness is extreme.
Ah, I'm far from being an angel from heaven!…
But if I fall with each passing hour,
You come to my aid, lifting me up.
At each moment you give me your grace:
     I live on Love.

Living on Love is sailing unceasingly,
Sowing peace and joy in every heart.
Beloved Pilot, Charity impels me,
For I see you in my sister souls.
Charity is my only star.
In its brightness I sail straight ahead.
I've my motto written on my sail:
     "Living on Love."

Living on Love, when Jesus is sleeping,
Is rest on stormy seas.
Oh! Lord, don't fear that I'll wake you.
I'm waiting in peace for Heaven's shore….
Faith will soon tear its veil.
My hope is to see you one day.
Charity swells and pushes my sail:
     I live on Love!…

Living on Love, O my Divine Master,
Is begging you to spread your Fire
In the holy, sacred soul of your Priest.
May he be purer than a seraphim in Heaven!…
Ah! glorify your Immortal Church!
Jesus, do not be deaf to my sighs.
I, her child, sacrifice myself for her,
     I live on Love.

Living on Love is wiping your Face,
It's obtaining the pardon of sinners.
O God of Love! may they return to your grace,
And may they forever bless your Name.....
Even in my heart the blasphemy resounds.
To efface it, I always want to sing:
"I adore and love your Sacred Name.
         I live on Love!…"

Living on Love is imitating Mary,
Bathing your divine feet that she kisses, transported.
With tears, with precious perfume,
She dries them with her long hair…
Then standing up, she shatters the vase,
And in turn she anoints your Sweet Face.
As for me, the perfume with which I anoint your Face
         Is my Love!….

"Living on Love, what strange folly!"
The world says to me, "Ah! stop your singing,
Don't waste your perfumes, your life.
Learn to use them well…"

Loving you, Jesus, is such a fruitful loss!…
All my perfumes are yours forever.
I want to sing on leaving this world:
         "I'm dying of Love!"

Dying of Love is a truly sweet martyrdom,
And that is the one I wish to suffer.
O Cherubim! Tune your lyre,
For I sense my exile is about to end!…
Flame of Love, consume me unceasingly.
Life of an instant, your burden is so heavy to me!
Divine Jesus, make my dream come true:
         To die of Love!…

Dying of Love is what I hope for.
When I shall see my bonds broken,
My God will be my Great Reward.
I don't desire to possess other goods.
I want to be set on fire with his Love.
I want to see Him, to unite myself to Him forever.
That is my Heaven… that is my destiny:
         Living on Love!!!…..

141. An autograph of Thérèse's poem "Living on Love," February 2, 1895.

142. Thérèse at age twenty-two.

164

142

143. The cell of St. Stanislaus, with door opened, where Thérèse lived during the first years of her religious life.

144. The staircase for the corridor with the cells. Cf. C 3r on the "rough stairway of perfection" and the "elevator" of "the little way."

145. Staircase that leads to the corridor of St. Elias. Thérèse climbed it several times a day with much exhaustion during her last illness.

146. Entrance to her cell in the corridor of St. Elias where Thérèse lived from August 1894 on.

147. "Jesus is my only Love": inscription carved by Thérèse over the lintel of the door of her cell during her trial of faith (April 1896 to September 1897).

145

146

147

148

149

150

148. Thérèse's cell. Antechamber where she painted and received the novices for spiritual direction. Our Lady of the Smile can be seen. Céline brought it with her at the time of her entry into Carmel on September 14, 1894, a month and a half after the death of Louis Martin. Here, kneeling before the statue, the two sisters made their Offering to Merciful Love on June 11, 1895 .

149. Inside Thérèse's cell. On the bench an oil lamp and an hourglass. She had no table or chair; she wrote using a little wooden stand which rested on her knees. Over the bed, consisting of a straw mattress on a board supported by wooden horses, is a picture of Jesus knocking at the door.

150. A view of the cloister from Thérèse's cell.

SAINTE THÉRÈSE.

DIEU SEUL ! et puis rien, qu'amour et sacrifice...
«... Il y en a, Seigneur, qui vous servent mieux que moi, mais qu'il y en ait qui vous
aiment plus et désirent plus ardemment votre gloire, je ne le souffrirai jamais ! ...»

151. Our Lady, a holy picture in Thérèse's cell.

152. St. Teresa of Avila, a picture in Thérèse's cell.

153. A jug used by Thérèse.

154. Thérèse's work basket.

155. An hourglass for Thérèse's use.

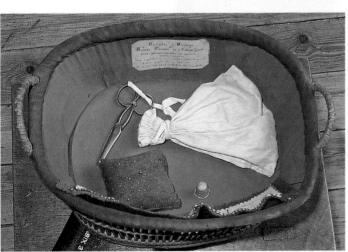

156

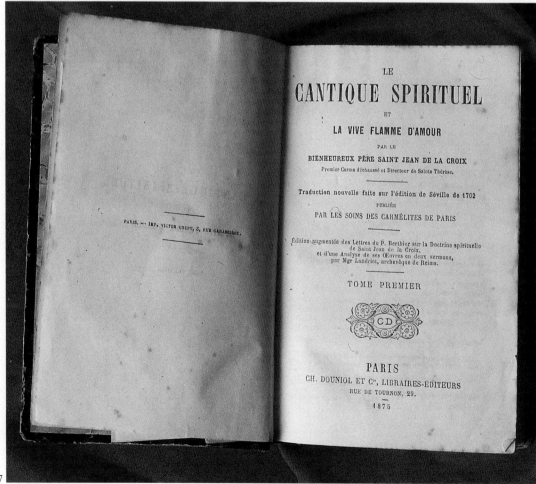

157

156. An 1870 breviary and other books used by Thérèse in Carmel.

157. *The Spiritual Canticle* by St. John of the Cross, 1875 edition, one of the few books Thérèse kept in her cell for personal use (cf. A 83r). She was still reading it during her last illness.

jusqu'à ce que les ombres s'étant évanouies je puisse vous redire mon Amour dans un Face à Face Éternel!....

Marie, Françoise, Thérèse de l'Enfant Jésus et de la Sainte Face

rel. carm. ind.

Fête de la très Sainte Trinité le 9 Juin de l'an de grâce 1895.

158

158. The final part of the autograph of her "Offering of Myself as a Victim of Holocaust to God's Merciful Love" (cf. A 84r–v; Pri 6; SS 276–277).

159. Chartres. Visitation Monastery. The dream of the Child Jesus. Oil painting done by Thérèse for feast of the prioress (her sister, Mother Agnès) on January 21, 1894. The shadow of the night of suffering (cross, chalice, Holy Face) weighs upon the sleeping Child who holds in his hand lilies, roses, and bachelor's buttons, Thérèse's favorite flowers.

159

160

161

160. The "Rose Child Jesus" (cf. A 72v). On the day of her clothing Thérèse beheld this statue and behind it the cloister garden covered with snow. One of Thérèse's assignments in Carmel was to decorate this statue with flowers.

161. The Infant Jesus of Prague, much venerated in the Carmel, placed in the corridor of St. Elias, near Thérèse's cell.

162. Lisieux. Carmel. The cloister covered with snow. "The monastery garden was in white like me" (A 72v).

162

CHAPTER EIGHT

Thérèse, Listening to the Word

ROBERTO FORNARA, OCD

Had I been a priest I would have studied Hebrew and Greek to be able to read the Word of God in the same human language in which God deigned to express it. (CSG 80; MSG 107–08)

By confiding the above ideal to Céline, Thérèse introduces us to her love for the Word of God. She longed to deepen her knowledge of it, even though she had to do without the many tools today's readers have at their disposal. For Thérèse—and also Céline as they shared their secrets—Scripture represented Carmel's "greatest treasure." She quoted it often in her writings with an originality that was the fruit of reading and meditation, not of what she heard from preachers. She often opened it at random—in a prayerful mood—looking for an answer to her doubts or questions. It served as the foundation of her prayer and the privileged means of her encounter with God.

Thérèse Discovers the Bible

Only gradually did Thérèse arrive at the discovery of Scripture as the privileged fount of her spiritual life. Along the way she had read much that helped form her, such as *The Imitation of Christ,* a decisive influence in her spiritual growth, or the works of St. John of the Cross. All her readings led her to a realization that only the Word of God—the Gospels in particular—could provide her with the nourishment she needed.

When seventeen and eighteen years old, already living in Carmel, she found primarily in St. John of the Cross one who could stir the fire within her and be her companion on her journey. At the same time he introduced her to meditation on the Bible and an understanding of some of its passages, above all from the Old Testament. Sacred Scripture became her only sure reference point, her soul's basic need: "But it is especially the *Gospels* that sustain me during my hours of prayer,

for in them I find what is necessary for my poor little soul. I am constantly discovering in them new lights, hidden and mysterious meanings" (A 83v).

She was continually searching the Scriptures. She drew on them for her prayer. She became so familiar with the Word of God that while speaking with her sisters she frequently quoted from the Bible. Sister Marie of the Trinity said that her conversations resembled commentaries on Scripture (cf. PO I, 462). She knew different passages by heart and always carried about a copy of the four Gospels. In a letter to Père Roulland she speaks of "the book of the Gospels which never leaves me" (LT 193).

Nonetheless, it wasn't easy in the kind of environment in which Thérèse lived for her to approach and deepen her understanding of the Word of God. Today we can count on a wide range of translations, resources, and publications that did not exist at the end of the last century. For preaching and the spiritual life, Scripture was not the center and axis about which everything else revolved. Thérèse's love and passion for the Bible, then, is something extraordinary.

Before entering Carmel, the young Martin girl shows no signs of any direct turn to Scripture. Although the Guérin family possessed at least two copies of the Bible, it was improbable because of her age that she had access to it. A first contact with the Word of God, even though sporadic, was made possible through reflection on Dom Guéranger's *Liturgical Year.* Her familiarity with biblical texts also grew through the various edifying works she read during this period: lives of saints, lives of Jesus, catechisms, and *The Imitation of Christ* itself.

Without permission from the prioress, it was impossible in the monastery—at least for the youngest sisters—to consult the complete Bible reserved in the library. Another Bible (in Le Maistre de Sacy's translation) was accessible at the entrance to the choir. The fact that Thérèse made use of it is evident in her writings. In addition, every nun had *The Christian Manual* for her use, which included, besides the ordinary parts of the Mass and the main Hours of the Divine Office, the psalter, the New Testament, and the *Imitation of Christ.* From September 1894, Thérèse was able to use a new source, although a limited one. Her sister Céline on entering Carmel was allowed to bring with her a little notebook in which she had copied out different passages from the Old Testament. According to Céline's testimony, after she had entered Carmel and taken the name Sister Geneviève, "Saint Thérèse of the Child Jesus made use of this little notebook with enthusiasm and was unable to let it go, so Marie of the Eucharist began to make a copy for her." Likewise, the liturgical life of her community enabled the young Carmelite to draw abundant riches from the Word. Her personal readings and those done in community contributed as well to the help she received along this path. In a special way St. John of the Cross inspired her with a love for the Song of Songs, on which she would have liked to write a commentary.

Her Teaching on How to Read the Bible

Writing to Céline on July 7, 1894, Thérèse underscored these words of Jesus: "If anyone loves me, he will keep my word, and my Father will love him, and we will come to him, and we will make in him our abode" (Jn 14:23). She comments: "To keep the *word* of Jesus, that is the sole condition of our happiness, the proof of our love for Him. But what, then, is this word?… It seems to me that the *word* of Jesus is *Himself.…* He, *Jesus,* the *Word,* the *Word of God!"* (LT 165).

The Word of Jesus is Jesus himself. This is the key to understanding Thérèse's reading of the Bible. In harmony with the patristic reading, Thérèse searched on every page for Christ's countenance. Her reading of the Word of God had no other purpose than to foster an encounter with him, to establish a personal contact with him.

In the last days of her life, while concluding the third manuscript of her autobiography, she still had this to say: "Since Jesus has reascended into heaven, I can follow Him only in the traces He has left; but how luminous these traces are! how perfumed! I have only to cast a glance in the Gospels and immediately I breathe in the perfumes of Jesus' life, and I know on which side to run. I don't hasten to the first place but to the last; rather than advance like the Pharisee, I repeat, filled with confidence, the publican's humble prayer. Most of all I imitate the conduct of Magdalene; her astonishing or rather her loving audacity" (C 36v).

Attentive listening to the Gospel was therefore a search for Jesus, for an encounter with him, and Scripture was the means that made this encounter possible. But for Thérèse her contact with the Word did not represent merely the first encounter with Jesus, a discovery of him; rather, it was a confirmation, a verification of what she was already living. In moments of difficulty, crisis, or trial, as also in moments of growth and new discovery, the Bible became her point of reference because it represented a confirmation of what the Master had already taught her in the depths of her soul. In reading the Bible, then, she did not seek to satisfy a curiosity to learn something new about her relationship with God; rather, the reading allowed her to recognize the truth that she was already living and experiencing. Often, the Word of God came out and met her first, to direct, console, and confirm her. The encounter with Jesus as Word of the Father permitted her to say in regard to all that was going on in her life: "It's true, it's so, I am sure!"

God had already revealed himself to her, he had taken up his abode in her. Recourse to the Word simply permitted her to listen better to an inner voice of which she was already aware. There was no separation or split between daily life on the one hand and the life of prayer and meditation on the Word of God on the other. Everything was brought back into unity, thanks to this inner Presence. Thérèse knew that the kingdom of God was within her (Lk 17:2) as the Presence who led and enlightened her. She in fact confessed: "I find just when I need them certain lights that I had not seen until then, and it isn't most frequently during my hours of prayer that these are most abundant but rather in the midst of my daily occupations"(A 83v).

It was this sense of the presence of Jesus and his Spirit within that guided her to the discovery and understanding of the Scriptures, a discovery that was not the fruit of human effort and conquest, but a gratuitous gift revealed to little ones, which increases without our being aware of it: "I have frequently noticed that Jesus doesn't want me to lay up *provisions;* He nourishes me at each moment with a totally new food; I find it within me without my knowing how it is there" (A 76r).

She comprehended the Bible in the measure that she lived it, letting herself become like Christ. We are always dealing with a personal experience of Scripture. It is the Word "for her, " for the moment in which she is living, for the problems she is being called on to confront. The severe judgment Hans Urs von Balthasar made when he branded Thérèse's reading of Scripture as subjectivist seems overstated: "Thérèse had read the Scriptures most ardently and even knew sections by heart; but it was almost exclusively in the light of her own life and her personal mission that she allowed them to affect her. No matter how strange it may sound it is true that Thérèse never acquired a genuine contemplation of the Scriptures…. In authentic contemplation the Word of God has to be heard *as it is,* and not as I would like to hear it, or I imagine it is *in relation to me"* (Hans Urs von Balthasar, *Two Sisters in the Spirit: Thérèse of Lisieux and Elizabeth of the Trinity* [San Francisco, CA: Ignatius Press, 1992], 92–93). If it is true that Thérèse did not have the tools for deepening her study of the Bible, it is just as true that her approach to the Word of God was not that of one who listened for what "she would like to hear." Rather, her humble and constant desire was to encounter Christ, intuit-

ing that this encounter involved and transformed one's whole life.

The poem "Why I Love You, Mary" (PN 54), composed a few months before her death, shows, for example, that her view of the Blessed Virgin was much more "objective" and grounded in the Gospels than that of so many preachers of her time, all of whom were prone to exaggerated rhetoric in recounting the privileges and special graces of Mary, expounding on her life with flowery and disagreeably sweet and useless details. Basing herself on the biblical data, Thérèse was instead all taken up with Mary's poverty, simplicity, and journey in faith. Indeed, despite her personal limitations and those of her times, Thérèse was a master in the spiritual reading of the Word of God.

The Song of Songs: A Way of Encounter

Although it was natural that Thérèse's attention turned chiefly to the Gospel texts, the important biblical foundation for her doctrine and spirituality was more the result of her frequent recourse to the Old Testament. As for the books of the Old Testament, she frequently quoted from the psalter, which she had continually at hand thanks to liturgical prayer and books of meditation. The reader is nonetheless surprised that the second most often quoted Old Testament book in Thérèse's writings is the Song of Songs. The quotations do not refer simply to this or that passage of the book; they are taken from all the chapters, an evident sign that Thérèse read and meditated at length on the entire work. A help to her in this regard were the different passages of the book transcribed in Céline's notebook, but before having this notebook, Thérèse had already drawn abundantly from the Song of Songs, as shown in her letters written before Céline's entrance to Carmel. Thérèse's references to the Song of Songs illustrate well her approach to Scripture and her way of making it a privileged vehicle for encountering God.

A faithful disciple of St. John of the Cross, Thérèse lived the life of prayer as a spousal encounter with the Beloved. It was probably from the Spanish mystic that she derived her love for the Song of Songs as the expression and fount of this way of union. Her quotations from the biblical poem scattered, above all, throughout her correspondence are directed toward describing God's jealous love for his creature. She wrote to her sister Léonie in May 1894: "You are very much blessed, dear little Sister, that Jesus is so jealous of your heart. He is saying to you as to the spouse of the Canticle: 'You have wounded my heart, my sister, my spouse, by one of your eyes and by one strand of your hair fluttering on your neck'" (LT 164; cf. Song 4:9).

His invitation continually reechoes within the soul that has set out in search of her Beloved, moved by an increasing desire to find him. This call is an expression of infinitely greater love and desire. "Open to me, my sister, my beloved, for my face is covered with dew, my locks with the drops of night"; this she writes to Céline (LT 108), borrowing the words of the Song of Songs (5:2). The Beloved is he who stands at the door and continually invites us to open, impatient to share moments of communion (Song 2:10–13; 8:1 in LT 158).

The way of union is not without difficulty. It is again the Song of Songs that awakened Thérèse to this reality. Sometimes the Spouse hides and for a long time does not allow us to perceive his voice and enjoy his presence. He communicates himself only by "looking through the lattices." This is the expression Thérèse took from the Song of Songs 2:9 to describe her situation to Mother Agnes of Jesus (LT 230). Speaking of her trial of aridity, Thérèse found inspiration again in a passage from the Song of Songs, "which expresses perfectly what a soul is when plunged into aridity and how nothing delights or consoles it. 'I went down into the garden of nuts to see the fruits of the valley, to look if the vineyard had flourished, and if the pomegranates had budded.... I no longer knew where I was...my soul was all troubled because of the chariots of Aminadab" (Song 6:11–12; LT 165).

In the same letter she also uses the words from the Song of Songs 7:1 ("Return, return, my Sulamitess; return, return, that *we may look at* you!") to indicate the condition of the soul that feels the Lord's merciful and benevolent gaze directed toward it despite the experience it has of its own poverty: "What a call is that of the Spouse! And we were no longer daring even *to look at ourselves* so much did we consider ourselves without any splendor and adornment; and Jesus calls us." The Song of Songs, as with all of Scripture, was for Thérèse a way leading to an encounter with God. The Word read and pondered does nothing else than repeat unceasingly the mystery of a belonging that arises from the initiative of God's love: "Fear not, for I have redeemed you; I have called you by name: you are mine.... Because you are precious in my eyes and glorious, and because I love you...fear not, for I am with you" (Is 43:1, 4–5). And because of this Thérèse can apply the words of Ezekiel 16:8–13 to herself and her own experience:

> Passing by me, Jesus saw that the time had come for me to be *loved*, He entered into a covenant with me and I became *His own*. He spread his mantle over me, he washed me with precious perfumes, He reclothed me in embroidered robes, He gave me priceless necklaces and ornaments. He nourished me with purest flour, with honey and oil in *abundance*. Then I became beautiful in His eyes and He made me a mighty queen. (A 47r)

Each one of the words resonated in her, took flesh in her life. Thérèse's final comment in this regard is eloquent: "Yes, Jesus did all this for me. I could take each word and prove it was realized in me" (ibid.).

The way mapped out by the Word of God is not just something private and personal. The young bride of Christ draws the whole church along with her. Commenting on the verse "Draw me, and we shall run," she writes: "I understand, Lord, that when a soul allows herself to be captivated by *the odor of your ointments,* she cannot run alone, all the souls whom she loves follow in her train; this is done without constraint, without effort, it is a natural consequence of her attraction for You" (C 34r).

The Biblical Basis of the "Little Way"

In reading God's Word, Thérèse drew out the cues and confirmations necessary for her spiritual life; her "little way" has a profoundly biblical flavor about it. Certainly, we cannot say that Thérèse of Lisieux elaborated a systematic theological doctrine derived from Scripture, but her writings allow the knowledge she drew from continual meditation on the Word of God to shine through. From the themes Thérèse assimilated to a greater degree, let us reflect especially on humility and poverty, the mercy of God, and the spirituality of abandonment.

Awareness of Our Own Poverty

One of the recurring biblical texts in Thérèse's writings is Jesus' prayer of praise to the Father: "I give you praise, Father, Lord of heaven and earth, for although you have hidden these things from the wise and the learned you have revealed them to the childlike. Yes, Father, such has been your gracious will" (Lk 10:21). Thérèse read and meditated also on the apostle Paul's words to the Corinthians:

> Consider your own calling, brothers. Not many of you were wise by human standards, not many were powerful, not many were of noble birth. Rather, God chose the foolish of the world to shame the wise, and God chose the weak of the world to shame the strong, and God chose the lowly and despised of the world, those who count for nothing, to reduce to nothing those who are something, so that no human being might boast before God. (1 Cor 1:26–29)

The fundamental discovery that guided Thérèse on her journey was this very awareness of her own poverty. We do not draw near to God through our own efforts and merits, but by accepting and offering him our own nothingness. Thérèse included herself among the ranks of the *anawim,* the "poor of Yahweh," who constituted the faithful remnant in the course of Israel's history, culminating in Mary, the daughter of Sion who recognized and sang of her own nothingness before God. "What is man that you should be mindful of him, or the son of man that you should care for him?" sang the author of Psalm 8 with amazement. And Mary was the one who magnified and exulted in the Lord because he had "looked upon his handmaid's lowliness" (cf. Lk 1:48). The Greek term *tapeinosis,* which is translated as lowliness or humility, means precisely "poverty, extreme misery, indigence." Mary recognized before God her own nothingness. Everything she had was a gift of grace, and she is "full of grace" (cf. Lk 1:28).

In her spirituality Thérèse uproots the pharisaical temptation to lay claim to merits before God, serenely accepting this poverty found in lowliness. She writes to Marie Guérin in July 1890:

> You give me the impression of a little country girl to whom a powerful king should come and ask her to marry him, and she would not dare to accept under the pretext that she is not rich enough and schooled enough in the ways of the court, without realizing that her royal fiancé is aware of her poverty and weakness much better than she is herself.… Neither ought you desire to see the fruit gathered from your efforts.

And going on to speak of herself, she adds:

> You are mistaken, my darling, if you believe that your little Thérèse walks always with fervor on the road to virtue. She is weak and very weak, and everyday she has a new experience of this weakness, but, Marie, Jesus is pleased to teach her, as He did St. Paul, the science of rejoicing in her infirmities [cf. 2 Cor 12:5]. This is a great grace, and I beg Jesus to teach it to you, for peace

and quiet of heart are to be found there only. When we see ourselves as so miserable, then we no longer wish to consider ourselves, and we look only on the unique Beloved!" (LT 109).

Experience of God's Mercy

The awareness of her own poverty was not for Thérèse a source of discouragement; it kept pace with the discovery of God's merciful love. At the beatification process, Sister Geneviève related that Thérèse of the Child Jesus examined the Scriptures so as "to know the character of God" (PO I, 275). God revealed himself to her precisely as love and mercy. Quoting from Psalm 118, which celebrates the Lord "because his mercy endures forever," Thérèse concluded that mercy is the fundamental and proper attribute of God. "Through it," she writes, "I contemplate and adore the other divine perfections" (A 83v). In tune with the Old Testament, she comprehended that the justice of God coincides with his mercy. Precisely because he is just does the Lord show tenderness and pity toward his children, according to the expressions of Psalm 103: "He crowns you with mercy and compassion.... He secures justice and the rights of all the oppressed.... He is compassionate and filled with gentleness, slow to punish, and abundant in mercy.... As a father has tenderness for his children, so the Lord has compassion on those who fear him. For he knows how we are formed; he remembers that we are dust" (vv. 4, 6, 8, 13–14; cf. LT 226). Perhaps recalling Paul's expressions in the Christological hymn of Philippians (2:6–11), Thérèse welcomed the gift of this mercy above all in Jesus, going so far as to accuse the Son of God of foolishness for renouncing the prerogatives of his divine nature out of love for us, and for going in search of lost humanity (cf. LT 169).

Among the Old Testament images that struck her, two had particular significance. The first was that of the shepherd in Isaiah 40:11, who "shall gather the lambs with his arm, and shall take them up in his bosom." The other was the word of comfort of Isaiah 66:12–13: "As one whom a mother caresses, so will I comfort you; you shall be carried at the breasts and upon the knees they will caress you." Commenting on these texts, Thérèse writes with complete amazement: "After having listened to words such as these, dear godmother, there is nothing to do but to be silent and to weep with gratitude and love" (B 1r–v).

In addition to the parable of the prodigal son, the Gospel icon of divine mercy, there is for Thérèse the sinner who welcomes Jesus' forgiveness and shows him her own gratitude and love with gestures of affection and tenderness (cf. Lk 7:36–50). Thérèse imitated her and felt close to her because "*her heart* has understood the abysses of love and mercy *of the Heart of Jesus*" (LT 247).

For Thérèse, the experience of God's mercy also entailed gratuitousness. It is significant that the autobiographical manuscripts begin by quoting the passage from Mark's Gospel on the call of the twelve: "And going up a mountain, he called to him men of his *own choosing,* and they came to him" (Mk 3:13). Thérèse comments: "This is the mystery of my vocation, my whole life, and especially the mystery of the privileges Jesus showered upon my soul. He does not call those who are worthy but those whom He *pleases*" (A 2r). Examining the Word of God more closely, Thérèse discovered the mystery of this eternal, free design of the Father who "chose us before the foundation of the world...predestining us for adoption to himself through Jesus Christ...for the praise of the glory of his grace that he granted us in the Beloved" (Eph 1:4–6). Our life does not depend on our own strength or will but on God and his merciful love, "or as St. Paul says: God will have mercy on whom he will have mercy, and he will show pity to whom he will show pity. So then there is question not of him who wills nor of him who runs, but of God showing mercy" (A 2r; cf. Rom 9:15–16).

Thérèse discovered and penetrated deeply into this reality until she realized that every path along which the Lord had led her was steeped in mercy (cf. A 71r). If she had never committed any mortal sins, she knew she owed it to the providence of God who, by removing from her path the occasions for falling, "forgave me *in advance* by preventing me from falling." Thérèse knew that she had been "preserved…only through God's mercy" (cf. 38v). She was saved by him "who has not sent His Word to save the *just,* but *sinners.* He wants me *to love* Him because He *has forgiven* me not much but ALL" (A 39r).

Confidence, Abandonment, and Hope

Sister Geneviève testified that Thérèse had been fond of a picture depicting a child seated on Jesus' knee reaching up to kiss him. This was the constant attitude of Thérèse. The awareness of her own littleness and poverty and the experience of the divine mercy flowed of necessity into the trusting abandonment of a child who feels secure in the arms of its father or mother: "Jesus deigned to show me the road that leads to this Divine Furnace, and this road is the *surrender* of the little child who sleeps without fear in its Father's arms" (B 1r). If she did not quote from it explicitly, Thérèse did make the trusting expression of Psalm 131 her own: "O Lord, my heart is not proud, nor are my eyes haughty; I busy not myself with great things, nor with things too sublime for me. Nay, rather, I have stilled and quieted my soul like a weaned child on its mother's lap, so is my soul within me."

Thérèse's writings take as their point of departure two wisdom texts. The first is from Proverbs 9:4: "Let whoever is a little one come to me"; the other is from Wisdom 6:7: "To the one who is little, mercy will be shown." These texts, together with those quoted from Isaiah (40 and 66), were copied down in Céline's little notebook that Thérèse always had for her use. The entire doctrine of spiritual childhood is founded on these simple quotations. We are not dealing then with a theological elaboration based on the most celebrated Gospel texts treating of spiritual childhood (cf. Mt 11:25–27; Mk 9:35–37; 10:13–16). The two passages from Proverbs and Wisdom, moreover, are chosen at random. Thérèse does not show concern for their literal meaning or the context in which they appear, but recognizes in these passages that speak of littleness a reflection of the experience that is developing within her, thanks to a life of prayer.

Nonetheless, if this appropriation of some biblical texts seems a bit risky, we should remember that, after all, she is translating some fundamental theological affirmations of the New Testament into a language entirely her own. When St. Paul speaks of our filial adoption, he is describing a condition that is given to the Christian as a pure gift of God. "When the fullness of time had come," he writes to the Galatians, "God sent his Son, born of a woman, born under the law, to ransom those under the law, so that we might receive adoption" (Gal 4:4–5). The interior presence of the Holy Spirit is the guarantee and fount of the dynamism of this filial life: "As proof that you are children, God sent the spirit of his Son into our hearts, crying out, 'Abba, Father!' So you are no longer a slave but a child, and if a child then also an heir, through God" (Gal 4:6–7).

Thérèse lived the practical consequences of this filial condition from day to day. The Pauline dynamism of Christian morality (being a child of God through grace) finds in the "little way" its logical and concrete application. Her self-discovery as a daughter of God leads her to the perception of her vital dependence on God and to the path of confidence and abandonment. It is the way of theological hope. It is the poverty of spirit that for Jesus is the first of the beatitudes (cf. Mt 5:3). In the same context, the Sermon on the Mount, Jesus teaches his disciples to call God "Father" in their prayer (cf. Mt 6:9). The Holy Spirit present within shapes us ever more into children of God. Thérèse confessed that a slow and meditative recitation of the Our Father recollected and helped nourish her soul. Through prayer and intimacy with God she was fashioned into a daughter after the image of the Son, who lived in her. Little Thérèse, hardly eleven years old, often repeated the words of St. Paul to the Galatians (Gal 2:20), and one of the first times she approached the Eucharist she applied them to herself (A 36r).

The way of confident abandonment—culminating in her Offering to Merciful Love made in June 1895—is the surest proof of all that Thérèse lived out as a daughter in the Son. The life of faith, for Thérèse as for "the poor" and "the humble" of Scripture, consists simply in placing one's trust in the One who is worthy of it. To abandon oneself is to believe absolutely in God's love for us, and that only this love can save:

> Knowing that a person is not justified by works of the law but through faith in Jesus Christ, we have believed in Christ Jesus that we may be justified by faith in Christ and not by works of the law.... I have been crucified with Christ; yet I live, no longer I, but Christ lives in me; insofar as I now live in the flesh, I live by faith in the Son of God who has loved me and given himself up for me. (Gal 2:16, 20)

When the young nun was entrusted with the responsibility of caring for the novices (a charge that was hers until her death), she felt the burden of it deeply, but did not despair or trust exclusively in her own strength. She simply trusted, aware also of her own limitations, knowing that "all these other things will be given besides" (Cf. Mt 6:33). She thus had the experience of a Presence dwelling in her, acting and speaking in her. Often she realized that she was saying words that were not coming from her. Once she intuited some deep suffering in the heart of a novice: "Her astonishment was so great that it even took hold of me, and for an instant I was seized with a supernatural fright. I was really sure I didn't have the gift of reading souls, and this

surprised me all the more because I had been so right. I felt that God was very close, and that, without realizing it, I had spoken words, as does a child, which came not from me but from Him" (C 26r).

The New Commandment

A final topic demanding consideration is Thérèse's practice of charity. In this case, too, the Saint comprehended the importance and significance of "meditating on Jesus' words" and testimony (cf. C 12r). Among the biblical texts important for Thérèse, chapters 12 and 13 of the apostle Paul's first letter to the Corinthians merit a special place. The apostle Paul helped her discover in charity both the essence of her vocation and her place within the church. The whole of Manuscript C can be considered a detailed commentary on the theme of charity; not an exegetical commentary on various passages—Thérèse did not have the intention or the adequate preparation to do so—but an attempt to make the commandment proposed to every Christian concrete within the context of a religious community.

Jesus' command in John (13:34) captured Thérèse's attention: "I give you a new commandment: love one another. As I have loved you, so you also should love one another." Her attention fell on the comparison so new and demanding: Jesus asks us to love one another *as* he loved us. For Thérèse this represented what was new about the commandment. It meant that the Lord did not give her an external law, but asked her to allow him to be and love in her:

> It is no longer a question of loving one's neighbor as oneself but of loving him as *He, Jesus, has loved him,* and will love him to the consummation of the ages. Ah! Lord, I know you don't command the impossible.... You know very well that never would I be able to love my Sisters as You love them, unless *You,* O my Jesus, *loved them in me....* Oh! how I love this new commandment since it

gives me the assurance that Your Will is *to love in me* all those You command me to love!" (C 12v)

The prophet Jeremiah foretold the new covenant in these same terms: "I will place my law within them, and write it upon their hearts…. All shall know me… for I will forgive their evildoing and remember their sin no more" (Jer 31:33–34). And the new covenant is realized in the gift of the Spirit, this divine presence within that forgives human beings, renders them children and enables them to love with God's very own love "because the love of God has been poured out into our hearts through the Holy Spirit that has been given to us" (Rom 5:5). Without explicit theological investigation, Thérèse penetrated the Pauline doctrine of justification, underlining not only the negative aspect of pardon and liberation but above all the positive aspect. She comprehended that God himself gives us gratuitously what he asks us to do through this commandment.

The greatest love is "to lay down one's life for one's friends" (Jn 15:13). For Thérèse this meant, in the concrete circumstances of her monastic experience, translating her desire for martyrdom into daily life, in a struggle against every imperfection, in forbearance, and in reciprocal esteem and acceptance of others (cf. C 12r). Charity ought to become total availability, openness toward everyone without distinction, the capacity to take initiative and the first step. The new commandment is a call to give your cloak (cf. Lk 6:29): "To give up one's cloak is, it seems to me, renouncing one's ultimate rights; it is considering oneself as the servant and the slave of others. When one has left his cloak, it is much easier to walk, to run" (C 16v).

Among the aspects of charity presented in the Gospels, Thérèse is particularly attentive to its gratuitousness:

> For if you love those who love you…if you do good to those who do good to you…if you lend money to those from whom you expect repayment, what credit is that to you?… But rather, love your enemies and do good to

them, and lend expecting nothing back; then your reward will be great and you will be children of the Most High, for he himself is kind to the ungrateful and the wicked. (Lk 6:32–35)

This gratuitousness is the distinctive sign of the presence of God's love in us, the basic characteristic of the children of God. Consequently, this was the invitation that represented the logical conclusion to Thérèse's experience: "Be merciful, just as your Father is merciful" (Lk 6:36). That mercy in which Thérèse felt herself enfolded and saved became a living presence that transformed her, urged her on, and sent her forth continually to be a sign and witness. For Thérèse it was a prerequisite of charity to in fact shine forth rather than remain hidden:

> But I understood above all that charity must not remain hidden in the bottom of the heart. Jesus has said: 'No one lights a lamp and puts it under a bushel basket, but upon the lampstand, so as to give light to ALL in the house.' It seems to me that this lamp represents charity which must enlighten and rejoice not only those who are dearest to us but 'ALL who are in the house' without distinction. (C 12r; cf. Mt. 5:14–16)

Under the guidance of the Word, encountering the living Christ who loved within her, Thérèse had the vocation—as does every Christian and even more every contemplative—to shine forth, to be light. The surroundings in which she lived were not important. What was important was to be light! If the Word of God is a lamp to our feet, a light to our path (Ps 119), it is so in the measure that we allow ourselves to be illumined and warmed. The Word of God cannot be transmitted in a cold, detached manner. Our hands must be burned by this gift, as one of Bernanos's characters asserts. The Word is called to become, as it was for Jeremiah, "like a burning fire, imprisoned in my bones," on account of which he admits "I grow weary holding it in, I cannot endure it" (Jer 20:9). In Thérèse's teaching this is how to approach the Word of God: not as an object of study, but as a conversion encounter in love.

Thérèse Speaks

I Take Up Holy Scripture

I do not understand, Brother, how you seem to doubt your immediate entrance into heaven if the infidels were to take your life. I know one must be very pure to appear before the God of all Holiness, but I know, too, that the Lord is infinitely just; and it is this justice which frightens so many souls that is the object of my joy and confidence. To be just is not only to exercise severity in order to punish the guilty; it is also to recognize right intentions and to reward virtue. I expect as much from God's justice as from His mercy. It is because He is just that "He is compassionate and filled with gentleness, slow to punish, and abundant in mercy, for He knows our frailty, He remembers that we are only dust. As a father has tenderness for his children, so the Lord has compassion on us!" …It is true that no human life is exempt from faults; only the Immaculate Virgin presents herself absolutely pure before the divine Majesty. Since she loves us and since she knows our weakness, what have we to fear? Here are a lot of sentences to express my thought, or rather not to succeed in expressing it, I wanted simply to say that it seems to me all missionaries are *martyrs* by desire and will and that, as a consequence, not one should have to go to purgatory. If there remains in their soul at the moment of appearing before God some trace of human weakness, the Blessed Virgin obtains for them the grace of making an act of perfect love, and then she gives them the palm and the crown that they so greatly merited.

This is, Brother, what I think of God's justice; my way is all confidence and love. I do not understand souls who fear a Friend so tender. At times, when I am reading certain spiritual treatises in which perfection is shown through a thousand obstacles, surrounded by a crowd of illusions, my poor little mind quickly tires; I close the learned book that is breaking my head and drying up my heart, and I take up Holy Scripture. Then all seems luminous to me; a single word uncovers for my soul infinite horizons, perfection seems simple to me, I see it is sufficient to recognize one's nothingness and to abandon oneself as a child into God's arms. Leaving to great souls, to great minds the beautiful books I cannot understand, much less put into practice, I rejoice at being little since children alone and those who resemble them will be admitted to the heavenly banquet. I am very happy there are many mansions in God's kingdom, for if there were only the one whose description and road seem incomprehensible to me, I would not be able to enter there.…

…While awaiting this blessed eternity that will open up for us in a short time, since life is only a day, let us work together for the salvation of souls. I can do very little, or rather absolutely nothing, if I am alone; what consoles me is to think that at your side I can be useful for something. In fact, zero by itself has no value, but when placed next to a unit it becomes powerful, provided, however, that it be placed on the *right side,* after and not before!… That is where Jesus has placed me, and I hope to remain there always, following you from a distance by prayer and sacrifice. (LT 226 to P. Roulland, her missionary brother)

CHAPTER NINE

Thérèse and Love of Neighbor

PIERRE DESCOUVEMONT

When Thérèse recalled the fundamental grace of her life, the grace of her "complete conversion" on Christmas Eve 1886, she affirmed that from that moment on she felt "charity enter her heart" and the "need to forget herself and to please others" (A 45v). Actually, she did not wait for that occasion to begin living profoundly the Gospel precept of love of neighbor. From very early on, Thérèse formed the habit of self-forgetfulness in order to please others, a mode of conduct she adopted all the more easily because she had a spontaneously generous heart: She could not bear to see a member of her family suffering.

We know, however, that Thérèse was burdened for too long a time by an obsessive preoccupation: Is Pauline pleased with my work? Is Papa happy with me? As a result, she lived in constant fear of displeasing them, and burst into tears whenever she was sure that she had done so.

Cured for good of her "extreme touchiness" (A 44v) on Christmas Eve, 1886, Thérèse was thereafter capable of serving others and being concerned about them without constantly wondering whether they were happy with her or not. Sure of pleasing Jesus, she was no longer thrown by the opinions of others in her regard. Thus she also boldly entered into action to obtain the necessary permission to enter Carmel near the time of her fifteenth birthday.

When she entered Carmel on April 9, 1888, Thérèse had already acquired great self-mastery and, without batting an eye, she put up with the difficulties of community life, notably the "pinpricks" inflicted on her by Sister St. Vincent de Paul. Very skillful with her hands, this Lay Sister scolded Thérèse for being so slow in performing her manual tasks, and gave her the nickname "grande biquette" (big kid goat). This was her way of letting the young middle-class fifteen-year-old know that she should be working faster! Thérèse did not flinch. In the bittersweet remarks of Sister St. Vincent de Paul she perceived the "gentle hand" of Jesus giving her the opportunity to perform sacrifices for the salvation of sinners. With a generous heart she offered her sacrifices to him.

It was likewise with joy that Thérèse, during the time of her novitiate, offered to accompany the crotchety invalid, Sister St. Pierre, to the refectory each evening. In her last manuscript she would write: "I did not want to lose such a beautiful opportunity for exercising charity, remembering the words of Jesus: 'Whatever you do to the least…, you do to me'" (C 29r). Thérèse ended up by "gaining her entire good graces." How? "I learned later," she declares, "that it was because, after having cut her bread, I gave her my most beautiful smile before leaving her alone" (C 29v).

This heroic charity, of which Thérèse gave proof from the very first years of her religious life, is in reality a cheerful charity, for Jesus had already made her understand the reasons for being filled with love for her Sisters. Her great strength of soul was rooted in the inner conviction that Jesus was there, very near her, that he was asking this sacrifice of her, and that on the Last Day he would reward her a hundredfold for all the efforts she made in this life to obey his commandment of love.

When Mother Agnes asked her, in February 1893, to help Mother Marie de Gonzague with the formation of the novices, Thérèse was content with teaching them the little ways she had already discovered for surmounting the thousand-and-one difficulties of community life. This is what we will explain first of all. Then we will look at the new lights she received during the last months of her life on the subject of love of neighbor, especially those about which she speaks so abundantly in Manuscript C.

A Thoroughly Evangelical Charity

Thérèse's charism was not to compose a systematic treatise on prayer or love of neighbor. The teaching she dispensed to her novices was a series of very practical counsels. All the same, they are supported by precise Gospel principles that we need to identify if we wish to enter Thérèse's soul and become, in her school, hearts burning with tenderness.

Let us closely examine the arguments Thérèse put before her novices to help them avoid becoming disheartened by the difficulties inherent in all community life. She had, in fact, understood that these difficulties could not be overcome by the mere repetition of generous acts, but by continually going back to the Gospel truths, which alone are capable of attacking the problem at its roots.

We are going to verify this by closely studying the way Thérèse counseled her novices when they confided to her their temptations of jealousy and impatience. All who live in community are familiar with these fundamental temptations.

My Neighbors and Their Talents

In all simplicity Sister Geneviève discloses to us the way Thérèse helped her in this area. Actually, when she joined her younger sister in Carmel in 1894, she could not help being jealous of her. Thérèse was far outdoing her in generosity!

In reading Sister Geneviève's *Conseils et Souvenirs* (A Memoir of My Sister, St. Thérèse) we clearly see the principles Thérèse invoked to help her older sister not succumb to these temptations of jealousy. The same principles are found in Manuscript C.

Like a good psychologist, Thérèse had observed the existence of two forms of jealousy, depending on the goods we envy in our neighbor. Sometimes what we envy is a particular quality, more or less brilliant, that we do not possess and the lack of which saddens us. And sometimes it is the very fervor of the charity animating the heart of a brother or sister which highlights by contrast our own mediocrity.

We are often, in fact, tempted to envy in our neighbor the presence of talents that we do not have. If, for example, remarks Thérèse, some Sisters receive in their prayer lights concerning the Gospel that we ourselves do not receive, we catch ourselves being jealous of them. We are tempted to consider this difference as a sign that the Lord loves us less, and this makes us sad (C 20r).

What are the principles Thérèse puts forward for overcoming this first form of envy or jealousy?

The first principle is that the *essential worth of persons* does not come from the *quantity* of talents that God has entrusted to them but from the way these individuals make them bear fruit, and in the final analysis from the *quality* of their love. God alone knows the true worth of a soul:

> [Jesus] willed to create great souls comparable to Lilies and roses, but He has created smaller ones and these must be content to be daisies or violets destined to give joy to God's glances when He looks down at his feet. Perfection consists in doing His will, in being what He wills us to be. (A 2v)

Our worth, therefore, is not measured by the number of talents received or acquired, nor by the brilliance of our intellect, nor even by the splendor of our apostolic works, but solely by the quality of our love.

Thérèse often harked back to this primacy of charity, quoting St. Paul: "If I speak with human tongues and angelic as well, but do not have love, I am a noisy gong, a clanging symbol" (1 Cor 13:1). And she, in her turn, says: "I do not hold in contempt beautiful thoughts which nourish the soul and unite it to God, but for a long time I have understood that we must not depend on them and even make perfection consist in receiving many spiritual lights." If, on the contrary, a soul "takes delight in her *beautiful thoughts* and says the prayer of the Pharisee, she is like a person dying of hunger at a well-filled table where all the guests are enjoying abundant food and at times cast a look of envy upon the person possessing so many good things" (C 19v).

To put it briefly, supernatural lights are not a criterion of sanctity. Like all riches, they are even a danger, since the soul receiving them runs the risk of becoming complacent and of thus falling into pride.

The second principle is as much indebted to St. Paul as the first. It is *for the benefit of the entire Body* that the Lord grants charisms to this or that member. Thérèse returned to this truth often. She knows, for example, that if she has been chosen by the prioress to care for the novices, that does not give her any extra worth in God's eyes: "I understand that it is not for my sake but for that of others that I must walk this road [of honors] which appears so dangerous. In fact, if I were to pass in the community for a religious filled with faults, incapable, without understanding or judgment, it would be impossible for you, Mother, to have me help you. This is why God has cast a veil over all my interior and exterior faults" (C 26v).

When Céline used to claim that Thérèse's responsibility for the novices gave her more worth, Thérèse often repeated to her:

> I'm really only what God thinks of me. As for loving me more because he has given me charge of souls, to be his interpreter to a little group of novices, I do not share your opinion. I think he has made me rather your servant. It is *for you* and not for myself that he has bestowed those virtues which make me pleasing in your eyes. (CSG 161; MSG 202)

And to make herself understood on this subject, Thérèse multiplied her comparisons: "Isn't the interior of a peach more important than the pretty pinkish color of its skin? Then why be jealous of others because of their exterior qualities?" (cf. LT 147). And she asked: "Isn't the canvas on which the artist paints his masterpiece more important than the brushes he uses in his work? Then why be jealous of the instruments God uses to realize his work in souls?" (cf. C 20r).

In short, when we are tempted to be envious or jealous of others because of the brilliance of their talents, we should immediately recall the relative worth of these gifts and that they have been bestowed for the good of all.

My Neighbor's Gifts Are Mine!

But are we able to resist the "holy jealousy" that takes hold of us when we witness heroic charity and holiness in others? We are then face to face with true wealth, with authentic worth. How can we keep from envying such a good?

This second manner of feeling jealous of others is often present among souls striving for sanctity. They have such an intense desire to make progress in the way of love that they fret and fume to see themselves "outstripped" by others. Or they become discouraged and imagine that God is no longer pleased to show his face to them; or else they seek, on the contrary, to cleverly reassure themselves, by attributing to the other person's self-love or hypocrisy what they were at first inclined to admire in their neighbor. What means does Thérèse propose to us for conquering this second form of jealousy?

Let us observe, first of all, that Thérèse was preoccupied from childhood with this mystery of inequality among souls. When she was very young, she was astonished "that God didn't give equal glory to all the Elect in heaven" and was afraid that all would not be perfectly happy (A 19r–v). By setting a large tumbler next to a thimble and filling them both to the brim with water, Pauline thus explained to her little sister that all the elect would have as much glory as they could take and therefore the last would have nothing to envy in the first.

Thérèse brought up this mystery at the beginning of her first manuscript. We must accept the fact that God does have preferences. Let us be content to be daisies or violets in "Jesus' garden," if that is our vocation, and not envy the lot of the lilies and the roses.

Such is, we might say, the "aesthetic" solution to the problem of inequality among souls: It takes all kinds to make a world! This is just as true in the spiritual world as it is in the material one: "I understood," writes Thérèse, "that if all flowers wanted to be roses, nature would lose her springtime beauty, and the fields would no longer be decked out with little wild flowers. And so it is in the world of souls, Jesus' garden. He willed to create great souls…, but He has [also] created smaller ones" (A 2v).

As valid as this solution might be, it still deals only with individual souls, placed side by side; it does not take into account the mystery of the Communion of Saints, which permits each soul to participate in the riches of the entire Mystical Body. Thérèse insists that this is the truth on which we must stand in order to overcome at its roots the temptation to be jealous of others because of the excellence of their charity.

It is again to Sister Geneviève that Thérèse most clearly reveals her thoughts on the subject. The novice came to her younger sister on another occasion to tell her about her temptations of jealousy: "What I envy in you are your special talents. I should be so happy if I, too, could compose beautiful poems to inspire others with the love of God!" Thérèse responds, first of all, with the principle stated above, namely, that we should realize that the composition of spiritual works is by no means the sign of a higher degree of sanctity, nor is the fact that one has been chosen by God as an instrument to make his message known the sign of being more loved by him. "We should become utterly detached from such things, and not set our hearts on doing good to others by means of poetry, art or by literary works."

Thérèse then raises the argument to a new level. Supposing that these works are inspired by a true charity and that they thus possess a supernatural value in the eyes of the Lord, we must offer them to him and in this way participate in their merits. It is the mystery of the

Communion of Saints: "When faced by our limitations," Thérèse affirms, "we must have recourse to the practice of offering to God the good works of others. That is the advantage of the Communion of Saints. Let us never grieve over our powerlessness but rather apply ourselves solely to the science of love" (CSG 62; MSG 71).

And Thérèse goes on to quote Tauler, the spiritual author in whom she found the most perfect expression of this astounding mystery:

> If I love the good that is in my neighbor more than he himself loves it, this good becomes mine more than it is his. If, for instance, in Saint Paul I love all the favors God bestowed on him, all these by the same title belong to me. Through this communion, I can become enriched by all the good that is in heaven and upon earth, in the angels and in the saints; in a word, by all the good in everyone who loves God.

Thérèse had understood that such an assurance transforms the way we look at others. Instead of wasting time being jealous of the good they do, instead of looking for weak points, we take pleasure in admiring all the good that is accomplished in the world and consider it as a "family possession" and offer it to God.

That is precisely what Thérèse often did. When she was in choir, she used to offer to God the prayers of her Sisters: "I feel then," she writes, "that the fervor of my Sisters makes up for my lack of fervor" (C 25v). When she received Communion, she offered Jesus the love and the merits of the Blessed Virgin, the angels and the saints (A 79v–80r).

During the last months of her life, Thérèse often expressed her hope of participating in the merits of her spiritual brothers and sisters. Very significant, for example, is her letter to Abbé Bellière in which she wrote about her confidence of participating in the palm of martyrdom through him: "Since the Lord seems to will to grant me only the martyrdom of love, I hope he will permit me, *by means of you,* to gather the *other palm* we are striving after" (LT 224). In the same vein, she told

Mother Agnes that she certainly hoped to participate in heaven in the glory of all the saints: "Just as a mother is proud of her children, so also we shall be proud of each other, having not the least bit of jealousy.... With the virgins we shall be virgins; with the doctors, doctors; with the martyrs, martyrs, because all the Saints are our relatives" (HLC 11.7.4, 13.7.12; DE 88, 93).

While being the chief antidote for jealousy, the assurance of participating in the merits of the saints likewise promotes the honest acceptance of our neighbor's worth. We can more easily discover the good qualities and merits of our sisters and brothers when we consider them in advance as a "family possession." And when we have discovered these good qualities and merits, they make us very happy. Thérèse could say in all truth, without stretching it: "True happiness can only be found in believing that others are virtuous and that we are the imperfect ones.... There is nothing sweeter than the inward joy that comes from thinking well of others!" (CSG 25; MSG 27–28).

The confidence Thérèse had of participating in the riches of the Mystical Body also helps us to better understand her love of spiritual poverty. If she did not hesitate to appear before the Lord "with empty hands," it was not only because she wished to count on his mercy in order to go to heaven, but also because she knew that she could present herself before God clothed in the infinite merits of Jesus Christ and, through him and in him, in the spiritual riches of the Virgin, the angels and all the saints!

Love Is Patient

Love is patient, it endures all things (1 Cor 13:4, 7). These two expressions encompass the Pauline description of *agape,* so true is it, both for the Apostle and for good common sense, that patience is the first and last word when it comes to love. Thérèse knew this from experience. She often had to make valiant efforts to remain patient in community. How did she go about it? How did she help her novices to display patience as well?

For dealing with impatience, Thérèse finally arrived at two distinct approaches: first, an approach in the "heat of anger," applicable at the onset of the temptation, at the first involuntary stirrings of our sensitivity wounded to the quick, for example, by someone's unkind remark (in other words, this is the remedy applied while we are emotionally upset); and second, an approach after we "cool off," applicable later, once the emotions have calmed down.

Like a discerning psychologist, Thérèse had quickly perceived that we should not be too hasty to apply the second approach. It is only to be used, she explained, after we have recovered our peace. As long as we are still feeling "traumatized" by someone's word or behavior, we must be content to weather the storm by simply applying the first treatment. Thérèse's wisdom in this regard is a very important element of her "little way."

In the Heat of Anger

Needless to say, Thérèse exhorted her novices to refrain from any angry word or gesture when they felt their tempers flaring up. But she invited them, above all, to carry out this self-mastery, as she herself did, in a great spirit of faith, which gave her patience a marvelous freedom and flexibility.

In those moments, there are only two things to carry out: an act of faith and an act of love. Thérèse believes that we should consider the person irritating us as a *providential instrument,* whose presence God is permitting on our journey in order that we might have a new occasion to prove our love for him and to win souls for him.

Thérèse based her argument on the famous words of Saint Paul: "God makes all things work together for the good of those who love him" (Rom 8:28). Instead of letting herself be controlled by the ill-will or the disagreeable character of a Sister, she thought instead of Jesus present in this trial. Had she not resolved to abandon herself, like a little ball, in the hand of Jesus?

Thérèse was a past master in the art of smiling right while she was being sorely tempted to impatience. And her smile was indeed the outward expression of her vibrant faith in the apostolic effectiveness of her renunciations of self-love. Opportunities for renunciation were many! It was not pleasant to hear the whispering around her, even within the walls of the monastery, that she had destroyed her father's health by entering Carmel too young—especially when her father was confined to an insane asylum! The following year, when Monsieur Martin's health seemed to have somewhat improved, it was thought at first that he might be able to attend his daughter's veiling on September 24, 1890. But at the last moment Thérèse's uncle, Monsieur Guérin, prudently decided that the moving ceremony would be too much for his brother-in-law. Thérèse was deeply disappointed by her uncle's decision and could not hold back her tears. But in the midst of her weeping, her faith-reflex intervened. On the very eve of her veiling, she wrote to Céline: "How can I tell you what is taking place in my soul?… It is torn apart, but I feel that this wound is made by a friendly hand, by a *divinely jealous hand!*… It is Jesus alone who is conducting this affair, it is He, and I recognized His touch *of love."* So much so that Thérèse ends her letter to her sister: "Ah! if I were able to convey to you the peace Jesus placed in my soul at the height of my tears, this is what I am asking Him for you who are myself!" (LT 120).

This significant example shows that profound *peace of soul can coexist with wounded sensitivity.* Thérèse absolutely does not reproach herself for having shed tears. She knows that her emotional upheaval is not under the direct control of her will, that it is part of the "weaknesses" about which the Apostle speaks and of which she must "boast" (2 Cor 12:9). They are the opportu-

nity for her to experience her poverty and her fragility, and oblige her to put herself entirely into the hands of God, her fortress and her refuge in the time of temptation.

Thérèse loves to recall, in fact, that she is only a "very little soul" incapable of "surmounting" the difficulties presented to her. She must leave the joy of easily "triumphing over" difficulties to the "great souls."

Thérèse was explaining this one day to Sister Geneviève, who was once again telling her of the difficulty she had in remaining patient: "This time it is impossible," Sister Geneviève said, "I simply cannot rise above this trial." Thérèse immediately responded:

> This does not surprise me, for we are too small to *rise above* our difficulties. Therefore let us pass *under* them. Remember the day, in Alençon, when we slipped under the horse who was blocking the entrance to the garden, while the grownups were trying to find some way to pass by it in order to enter. That is the advantage of staying small. There are no obstacles for little ones; they can slip in unnoticed anywhere. Great souls can rise above their trials. They can surmount human obstacles either by reasoning things out or through the practice of virtue. But in our case, because we are so little, we must never attempt to use such means. Let us, rather, always pass *under* our difficulties. (CSG 43–44; MSG 49–50)

Let us note well the Gospel inspiration that animates Thérèse's practice of this approach in the "heat of anger." Thérèse does not forget the lesson of Gethsemane. Since Jesus himself knew sadness and anguish and was shaken in his sensibility to the point of sweating blood, we must not try to do better than he! The disciple is not above his Master. Thérèse came to understand this shortly after she entered Carmel, while she was recopying some notes from a retreat preached by Père Pichon: Since Jesus suffered with sadness and without courage, we must not be surprised to experience the same hesitancy as he did in the face of suffering.

She understood that in order to suffer according to God's heart, it is totally unnecessary to appear as if we were not suffering at all, like a stoic hero. It is enough to accept our sufferings as they come and as we are, by offering them to the Lord with all our heart and trusting that they are of benefit for the salvation of the world. For Thérèse, the fact of suffering with sadness, far from being an imperfection, is a choice grace, a more intimate participation in the Passion of Christ: "What a grace," she writes, "when, in the morning, we feel no courage, no strength to practice virtue" (LT 65).

To exhort her novices to patience, Thérèse continually returned to the same truth: Consider those who wound you as God's *instruments*. Let yourself be humiliated: it is God himself who is humbling you. She used to say to Sister Geneviève, for example: "When you are exasperated with someone, the way to recover your peace is to pray for that person and to ask God to reward her for giving you the opportunity to suffer" (PO 284).

Notice Thérèse's psychological common sense. When her novices used to share with her their difficulties in being kind to this or that Sister, Thérèse counseled them not to stop at appearances but to look for the good qualities in the persons who were not so nice to them. But she knew by experience that this method, although excellent when our emotions are not involved—as we will see later—is impossible when we are emotionally upset with someone. Our mind is then so "obsessed" with this person's exasperating conduct that it is impossible to think of anything else, much less of any good qualities the person might have. The only thing we can do under these circumstances is to regard the person as an instrument of the Lord.

This patience must not degenerate, however, into passive resignation in the face of human maliciousness. To remain Christian, patience must be accompanied by a courageous and aggressive attitude before human malice and injustice. Without this effort, our patience would no longer conform to that of Jesus Christ. Christ in fact did not just have himself put on the cross by his enemies. He fought against the sin of the Pharisees; he denounced it. Thérèse knew this and never hesitated to correct the faults of the novices in her charge. "You see, I must die with my weapons in hand," she said in this regard, during the last months of her life (CSG 10; MSG 5).

Yet this did not prevent Christ Jesus from recognizing the will of his Father behind the hand of his executioners nailing him to the cross. A mysterious will, needless to say! It is the very mystery of the redemption, the compelling necessity of which escapes us, although the Risen Jesus declared it so strongly to the disciples on the way to Emmaus: "Did not the Christ have to suffer in order to enter into his glory?"

After Cooling Down

The moment arrives when our inner emotional upheaval calms down and we are no longer as exasperated as we were at the onset of our temptation to impatience. "Cool" reflection will often reveal that we were wrong in being so quick to denounce the actions of others as unjust or malicious, when in fact their true motives were unknown to us.

Here again, let us be guided by Thérèse who shows us that our impatience with others is frequently due to *ignorance* on our part. A better understanding of our neighbor keeps us from many useless outbursts of anger; above all, it permits us to achieve a definitive victory over our temptations to impatience by leading us to regard others as the Lord does, with a view that is both clear-sighted and indulgent.

Let us be attentive to Thérèse's enumeration of the various unknowns that often keep our judgments of others from being just. We are often unaware of our neighbor's motives. In Manuscript C of her autobiography, Thérèse relates a personal experience that made her understand, once and for all, that an action done with the best of intentions could be misinterpreted. In the course of a rather dull recreation, the portress came to ask for help. Thérèse wanted very much to have an excuse to leave, but out of charity she pretended not to be in a hurry to untie her apron, and let her neighbor, who also wanted to go, get ahead of her. One of the Sisters in the community misinterpreted Thérèse's act of charity as a lack of generosity (C 13r).

It is true that the intention of others often appears as clear as day to us, and is not always exemplary! In such a case, how do we keep ourselves from holding a grudge? Thérèse suggests that we think of all the attenuating circumstances that often excuse our neighbors' faults. She invites us not to forget all the graces that we have already received and to ask ourselves: What would others have become if they had received one-half of the graces of light and strength that we ourselves have received? Much better, perhaps (cf. LT 147).

Thérèse bore in mind, for example, that the neurasthenic character of Sister Marie of St. Joseph, whom she helped in the linen room, excused her nasty temper. Far from judging her severely, Thérèse pitied her with all her heart: "It is not her fault if she is badly endowed," she said to Marie, her sister and godmother. "She is like a poor clock that has to be wound every fifteen minutes" (DE 659). Being charitable, Thérèse thus remained clear-sighted.

Thérèse also made it a point to look for others' good qualities: "When especially the devil tries to place before the eyes of my soul the faults of such and such a Sister who is less attractive to me, I hasten to search out her virtues, her good intentions" (C 12v). She confided one day that she went beyond Sister Teresa of St. Augustine's stern appearance and rigid behavior in order to admire God's handiwork in her: Instead of dwelling on the exterior qualities of this Sister who was repugnant to her, Thérèse penetrated into her heart in order to admire her beauty and generosity. "Each time I met her I prayed to God for her, offering Him all her virtues and merits. I felt this was pleasing to Jesus, for there is no artist who doesn't love to receive praise for his works" (C 13v).

One day while walking in the garden with Sister Geneviève, Thérèse was trying to make her see that we are frequently so focused on the natural imperfections of others—which are for the most part superficial—that we forget the essential: their profound worth, their love of God. She pointed to a fruit tree:

> Those pears aren't a bit attractive at present, are they? In the fall, however, when they are served to us in the refectory, we shall find them to our taste, and it will be hard to connect them with the fruit which we are looking at now. That is a good reminder of the truth that on the Last Day, when we shall be delivered from our faults and imperfections, those Sisters, whose natural qualities may now be displeasing to us, might appear to us as great saints. And we shall perhaps gaze on them open-mouthed in wonder. (CSG 107–108; MSG 139)

In the same spirit, Thérèse used to say to herself, whenever she saw one of her Sisters frequently falling into an habitual fault: "Who knows whether the efforts she is making to correct her faults are not more pleasing to the Lord than certain acts of virtue accomplished openly by others?" (cf. C 12v).

But the deepest motivation for Thérèse's patience was *her communion with the very patience of God*, with that forbearance of the Lord who never grows weary of waiting for the conversion of sinners and does not become annoyed with their slow progress. Thérèse never forgot that on Christmas Eve 1886, Jesus had "in an instant" accomplished in her soul the work that she herself had not even been able to accomplish "in ten years"; she knew that in God's eyes a single day is like a thousand years and that he can, in the twinkling of an eye, convert the hardest hearts.

And that is how we can understand Thérèse's patience with her novices, who were so slow in profiting from the lessons and example of their mistress. Sister Martha, for instance, was never completely cured of her spirit of contradiction. As for Sister Madeleine of the Blessed Sacrament, she never had complete confidence in Thérèse. Later she would say: "I used to escape her glance, for fear that she could read my mind" (*Circulaire*, 2).

Far from establishing a distinction between "good" subjects and those who were not, Thérèse attended to all her novices with the same solicitude. As she left concern about results to God, the young mistress never became discouraged or resentful on seeing the novices' slow progress. Her patience was untiring. "Charity hopes all things," says St. Paul. It knows that nothing is impossible with God. Thérèse does not encourage us at any time to turn a blind eye to our neighbor's faults, but urges us instead to remember the Lord's all-powerful mercy, which never ceases to envelop these faults and can transform them in an instant.

Patience With Oneself

However, an important observation must be made in conclusion. We would be seriously mistaken to imagine that Thérèse overcame all her temptations to impatience by the systematic application of this "cool" approach. To the end of her life, there were still times when she was so sorely tempted to be disagreeable with Sister Teresa of St. Augustine that she felt it more prudent just to leave the room in which they were working together. Thérèse remains a "very little soul" who must, in order to overcome her temptations of impatience, pass "under" the difficulty, instead of trying to rise above it through reasoning and virtue.

Thérèse had remarked, moreover, while caring for her novices, that sometimes it is necessary to change our tactics in our struggle with impatience. Sister Geneviève explains:

> At the beginning of her responsibility as novice mistress, our dear little Sister used to strive to put an end to our interior conflicts either by reasoning with us or by trying to convince us in our little difficulties in the novitiate that our companions were not at fault. She soon realized that this method only served to open up long discussions,

with no profit whatsoever to our souls, so she adopted another means. Instead of trying to close the issue by denying that there was any cause for complaint, she would urge us to face reality" (CSG 10; MSG 8).

In other words, in the beginning Thérèse used to encourage her novices immediately to overcome a temptation to impatience by trying to reason with themselves: "Why get upset? It's ridiculous!" Thérèse quickly saw that this approach was ineffective. When our exasperation against someone is at its peak, the best thing to do is to bow humbly under the storm, to humbly put up with this movement of impatience while waiting for it to pass, and to offer to God this sacrifice of silence and patience.

"It wasn't long," continues Sister Geneviève:

> …before I found myself rejoicing that I had been imposed on, and I even began to desire that all the Sisters should utterly disregard me and show me no consideration at any time. I felt springing up in me very generous desires to be scolded and to bear alone the blame whenever my companions neglected any duty—or even to be reproached for some careless piece of work in which I had no part whatsoever. It was by such methods that Thérèse would have me soon established in an attitude of mind that was close to perfection. Afterward [note the importance of this word], when the victory was assured [that is, when the approach in the "heat of anger" was completed], she would relate in detail the countless acts of hidden virtue which the novice in question had often practiced [essential procedure in the "cool" approach]. A warm admiration would then replace my critical thoughts and I would believe that all the Sisters were more virtuous than I.

But in order to react so quickly to temptations of impatience, remarked Thérèse, we must "soften our heart in advance" (CSG 152), that is to say, prepare ourselves in prayer for the encounters that we must have with others; we must be prepared in advance for their sudden mood changes, pray for them, even ask God to reward them for giving us the opportunity to offer him a new sacrifice. This is certainly heroic conduct, but it is a heroism built on faith: faith in the unceasing tenderness of God for us and faith in the redemptive value of the least sacrifice.

Thérèse of the Child Jesus, doctor of the "little way," does not forget that it is difficult always to be faithful to this line of conduct. But we must never get discouraged. In order to be patient with others, we must first have patience with ourselves. We know how often Thérèse insisted on this point: "The foundation of her teaching," affirms Sister Geneviève, "was that we should not lose heart at the sight of our weakness but rather glory in our infirmities" (CSG 20; MSG 21).

This indicates how much Thérèse's love of neighbor was a reflection of the love she bore for herself. If she was so indulgent with others, it was because, first of all, she was very indulgent and patient with herself. This has often been called to our intention, that before putting up with others, we must first know how to put up with ourselves.

Bernanos has perfectly assimilated this aspect of Thérèsian thought, when, in the *Dialogues of the Carmelites* he puts these words into the mouth of the elderly prioress welcoming the young novice: "Oh! my daughter, be always soft and yielding in His hands! The saints did not stiffen themselves against temptations, did not revolt against themselves, for revolt is always of the devil. Above all, never despise yourself! It is very difficult to despise ourselves without offending God in us" (Georges Bernanos, *The Carmelites,* tr. Gerard Hopkins [London: Fontana Books, 1961], 53).

A Charity That Grows Deeper

It would be impossible to insist too strongly on the grace that made Thérèse, at the end of her life, better understand the precept of love of neighbor. She began composing Manuscript C of her autobiography precisely to make known the lights that she had received on this subject.

It seems while she was in the linen room helping Sister Marie of St. Joseph, a neurasthenic religious who had nothing especially attractive about her, Thérèse was led to discover all the Gospel demands of charity. Thérèse did not bother to enumerate the different "lights" that she received at this time, but by following the text of her last manuscript, we can distinguish *four* of them. Thérèse does not use the word "discovery" here, but let us remember that in her writing the verb *comprendre* (to understand), which she uses fourteen times on fourteen pages, always evokes a grace of light.

The Importance of the Second Commandment

What struck Thérèse first of all was that Jesus said: "The second commandment is like the first: You must love your neighbor as you love yourself." Thérèse underlined the word "like," which she had never noticed before. She had never "fathomed the meaning of these words of Jesus" (C 11v). Now she understood that the second commandment was *as important* as the first, that she must apply herself to pleasing others with as much attention as she had up to that time given to pleasing God. Or to put it better, that the essential way of pleasing God was by observing his second commandment: "I applied myself especially to *loving God* and it is in loving Him that I understood my love was not to be expressed only in words, for: 'It is not those who say: "Lord, Lord!" who will enter the kingdom of heaven, but those who do the will of my Father in heaven.'"

What does this mean? Is it possible that Thérèse had to wait until the end of her life to know that love must not be expressed in words alone? We need not pause to refute such a supposition. Didn't Thérèse say a few months earlier that "*Love* is proved by works" (B 4r)? And she was performing them: depriving herself of her share of beverage in the refectory so that her neighbor could have it all, seeking the companionship of the less agreeable Sisters during recreation, etc. But up to that point, Thérèse had not yet been so profoundly aware of the importance of the "second commandment."

One example would suffice to show this. In August 1893, commenting for Céline's benefit on the page of the Gospel where Jesus states that we will be judged on the effective love that we have had for others, Thérèse sees only one thing in this grand fresco of the Last Judgment: Jesus is begging us for our love. "He made Himself poor that we might be able to give Him love." And here it is not a question of the love Jesus is begging from us on behalf of our suffering brothers and sisters, but the love that we must "reserve" for Jesus and "refuse" others: "Let us give, let us give to Jesus; let us be miserly with others but prodigal with Him" (LT 145).

Recall that, in her first manuscript, Thérèse uses the term "charity" only once (A 45v). In her letter to Sister Marie of the Sacred Heart, she uses it twice, but in the sense of love for God. In the last manuscript, on the contrary, she uses the word "charity" twenty-six times and the word "charitable" four times—always in the sense of love for neighbor. It is only at the end of her life that Thérèse understands what great importance Jesus give to the commandment of love of neighbor.

She finds three other signs of this in Scripture: "on almost every page of his Gospel," Jesus speaks to us about charity; "at the Last Supper," after having given himself to his disciples "in the ineffable mystery of his Eucharist," he gives them a new commandment, to love one another; "he makes of this mutual love the distinctive mark of his followers."

In June 1897, Thérèse expressed to Mother Agnes, in a concise formula, the importance of love of neighbor: "On earth, love of neighbor is everything. We love God in the measure in which we practice it" (*Summarium* 652, p. 525).

As Jesus Has Loved Us

Thérèse also discovers the manner in which the Lord commands us to love others. It is no longer enough to love others as we love ourselves, according to the law of Leviticus, but we must love them as Jesus himself loves them, as much as he loves them!

"How did Jesus love his disciples and why did he love them?" she asks herself. The interrogative form of this sentence is not a simple figure of style. Thérèse is truly searching for the answer to *how and why* Jesus loved his disciples, "Ah! it was not their natural qualities that could have attracted Him, since there was between Him and them an infinite distance. He was knowledge, Eternal Wisdom, while they were poor ignorant fishermen filled with earthly thoughts. And still Jesus called them his *friends, His brothers"* (C 12r).

It would be wrong to see this discovery as a totally new beginning. Thérèse has understood for a long time that God loves us despite our wretchedness. Is not this the key to her bold confidence? At the beginning of her first manuscript she wrote: "The nature of love is to humble oneself" (A 2v). And in September 1896 she repeated: "Yes, in order that Love be fully satisfied, it is necessary that It lower Itself to nothingness and transform this nothingness into *fire"* (B 3v).

In the last months of her life, however, Thérèse realizes even more the *merciful* nature of this love: She is struck by the contrast between the Wisdom of Jesus and the slowness of the apostles to comprehend his teaching. From that time on, Thérèse understands more clearly that she must love her Sisters in spite of their imperfections : "Ah! I understand now that charity consists in bearing with the faults of others, in not being surprised at their weaknesses, in being edified by the smallest acts of virtue we see them practice" (C 12r).

The nuns of the Lisieux Carmel were not aware that Thérèse was, at that time, practicing greater patience in their regard. But by handing herself over unreservedly to the merciful love of the Lord, Thérèse's heart became very loving and her spirit more indulgent.

"Charity Must Not Remain Hidden in the Bottom of the Heart"

The third element of discovery, contrary to the first two, had visible repercussions on Thérèse's conduct: "But I understand above all that charity must not remain hidden in the bottom of the heart. Jesus has said: '*No one lights a lamp and puts it under a bushel basket, but upon the lampstand, so as to give light to ALL in the house.*' It seems to me that this lamp represents charity which must enlighten and rejoice not only those who are dearest to us but '*ALL who are in the house,*' without distinction" (C 12r).

Thérèse understands even more clearly the importance of making humor reign in community gatherings. She will in the future put as much enthusiasm and ingenuity into giving pleasure to her Sisters as she had formerly put into pleasing the Lord. She must, like a lamp, enlighten and make happy *all* who are in the house. In other words, the Sisters who are the least amiable, she must not only sit beside during recreation (she was already doing that!) but she must seek to make them happy in as many ways possible. She offers to her Sisters "a spiritual banquet of a loving and joyful charity" (C 28v).

In the last months of her life, Thérèse began to actually express her love of neighbor with a marvelous tenderness and spontaneity. Her love had become so pure that she no longer feared loving her Sisters in "too human a fashion." This is borne out in Sister Marie of the Trinity's remembrance of a June day in 1897 when Thérèse came to console her by sitting beside her on a tree trunk and resting her novice's head on her heart.

Since "that sweet flame" of charity "expanded her heart" (C 16r), Thérèse felt that the love she evoked in her Sisters' hearts in this way was only reinforcing their love for God. That is what she explained to the same Sister Marie of the Trinity, who was wondering whether she loved her mistress too much. On the back of a holy card that she gave her on May 7, 1896, Thérèse had copied this thought from Saint John of the Cross: "The affection for a creature is purely spiritual if the love of God grows when it grows, or if the love of God is remembered as often as the affection is remembered, or if the affection gives the soul a desire for God—if by growing in one, the soul grows also in the other."

It is likewise in the light of this third discovery that we should read all Thérèse's testimonies on *cheerfulness* during her last illness. Expression of her love for God, of the joyful acceptance of his will, this cheerfulness also manifested her desire to console those around her, saddened by the prospect of her approaching death.

We should not forget, however, that Thérèse imposed many sacrifices upon herself before being able to show her love with such beautiful simplicity. She wrote a splendid text on this subject:

> Love is nourished only by sacrifices, and the more a soul refuses natural satisfactions, the stronger and more disinterested becomes her tenderness.... How happy I am now for having deprived myself from the very beginning of my religious life! I already enjoy the reward promised to those who fight courageously. I no longer feel the necessity of refusing all human consolations, for my soul is strengthened by Him whom I wanted to love uniquely. I can see with joy that in loving Him the heart expands and can give to those who are dear to it incomparably more tenderness than if it had concentrated upon one egotistical and unfruitful love. (C 21v–22r)

Participation in the Love of Christ

Thérèse finally understands, and most profoundly, that it is impossible for her to realize this magnificent program if Jesus does not come into her to love all those whom he asks her to love. From this comes the exclamation that she places at the heart of her account: "Oh! how I love this new commandment since it gives me the assurance that Your Will is *to love in me* all those you command me to love!" (C 12v). We would certainly believe that on April 10, 1896, Thérèse already understood Jesus' will to love in her all her Sisters. On that day she writes to Léonie: "Dear little sister, I cannot tell you all the deep thoughts my heart contains concerning yourself; the only thing I want to say is this: I love you a thousand times more tenderly than ordinary sisters love each other, for I can love you with the *Heart* of our celestial Spouse" (LT 186). Thérèse is thinking in fact that on the next day—her sister's feast day—she will be able to receive Holy Communion and thus be united to the very love of Jesus for Léonie. But she still is not aware that this possibility of loving others with the very Heart of Jesus is offered to her *at every moment*. Only several months later will this light be given to her.

This ultimate Thérèsian discovery was in line with the series of deepenings that the Lord had realized in her in the preceding years. On June 9, 1895, understanding more than ever "how much Jesus desires to be loved," she had offered herself as a victim to merciful love. The following Friday, while making the Way of the Cross, she suddenly felt herself wounded by such an ardent flame of love that she understood that God was fully ratifying her oblation and was letting the floods of his love break upon her. She then understood perfectly that she could love God with the very heart of God. But it was only in the last months of her life that she received the grace of understanding that she could likewise love her *neighbor* at every moment with this same heart of God, present in her heart.

Thérèse Speaks

A Lamp on a Lampstand

How happy I am now for having deprived myself from the very beginning of my religious life! I already enjoy the reward promised to those who fight courageously. I no longer feel the necessity of refusing all human consolations, for my soul is strengthened by Him whom I wanted to love uniquely. I can see with joy that in loving Him the heart expands and can give to those who are dear to it incomparably more tenderness than if it had concentrated upon one egotistical and unfruitful love. (C 22r)

It is not always possible in Carmel to practice the words of the Gospel according to the letter. One is obliged at times to refuse a service because of one's duties; but when charity has buried its roots deeply within the soul, it shows itself externally. There is such a delightful way of refusing what cannot be given that the refusal gives as much pleasure as the gift itself. (C 18r)

Ah! I understand now that charity consists in bearing with the faults of others, in not being surprised at their weakness, in being edified by the smallest acts of virtue we see them practice. But I understood above all that charity must not remain hidden in the bottom of the heart. Jesus has said: *"No one lights a lamp and puts it under a bushel basket, but upon the lampstand, so as to give light to ALL in the house."* It seems to me that this lamp represents charity which must enlighten and rejoice not only those who are dearest to us but *"ALL who are in the house"* without distinction. (C 12r)

Luminous Beacon of Love

Charity gave me the key to my *vocation.* I understood that if the Church had a body composed of different members, the most necessary and most noble of all could not be lacking to it, and so I understood that the Church *had a Heart and that this Heart* was BURNING WITH LOVE. I understood it was Love alone that made the Church's members act, that if *Love* ever became extinct, apostles would not preach the Gospel and martyrs would not shed their blood. I understood that LOVE COMPRISED ALL VOCATIONS, THAT LOVE WAS EVERYTHING, THAT IT EMBRACED ALL TIMES AND PLACES.... IN A WORD, THAT IT WAS ETERNAL!

Then, in the excess of my delirious joy, I cried out: O Jesus, my Love .... my *vocation,* at last I have found it.... MY VOCATION IS LOVE!

Yes, I have found my place in the Church and it is You, O my God, who have given me this place; in the heart of the Church, my Mother, I shall be *Love.* Thus I shall be everything, and thus my dream will be realized.

Why speak of a delirious joy? No, this expression is not exact, for it was rather the calm and serene peace of the navigator perceiving the beacon which must lead him to the port.... O luminous Beacon of love, I know how to reach You, I have found the secret of possessing Your flame.

I am only a child, powerless and weak, and yet it is my weakness that gives me the boldness of offering myself as *VICTIM of Your Love, O Jesus!* In times past, victims, pure and spotless, were the only ones accepted by the Strong and Powerful God. To satisfy Divine *Justice,* perfect victims were necessary, but the *law of Love* has succeeded to the law of fear, and *Love* has chosen me as a holocaust, me, a weak and imperfect creature. Is not this choice worthy of *Love?* Yes, in order that Love be fully satisfied, it is necessary that It lower Itself, and that It lower Itself to nothingness and transform this nothingness into *fire.* (B 3v)

O Jesus! why can't I tell all *little souls* how unspeakable is Your condescension? I feel that if You found a soul weaker and littler than mine, which is impossible, You would be pleased to grant it still greater favors, provided it abandoned itself with total confidence to Your Infinite Mercy. But why do I desire to communicate Your secrets of Love, O Jesus, for was it not You alone who taught them to me, and can You not reveal them to others? Yes, I know it, and I beg You to do it. I beg You to cast Your Divine Glance upon a great number of *little* souls. I beg You to choose a legion of *little* Victims worthy of Your LOVE! (B 5v)

CHAPTER TEN

Apostle and Missionary

CAMILLO GENNARO, OCD

As St. Thérèse entered into deeper contact with the mystery of divine love that was revealed in Christ, she felt consumed by a desire to collaborate with Jesus in the salvation of souls. She pondered the figure of Jesus, "the man for others," who though innocent was weighed down by the sin of humanity, atoning for it on the cross. The impression left by this image soon deepened, resulting in an ardent desire to participate personally in Christ's Passion. When the Lord called Thérèse to Carmel to make her his bride, she received her destiny of being "one consecrated for others," leading many to salvation.

Thérèse and the "Thirst for Souls"

On Christmas in 1886, the Lord satisfied this desire greatly, but then enkindled it further through an experience she defines as her "conversion." After having recounted the miracle worked by the little Child Jesus, in which he cured her forever of the shyness she contracted when her mother died, Thérèse adds: "More merciful to me than He was to His disciples, Jesus *took the net Himself,* cast it, and drew it in filled with fish. He made me a fisher of *souls.* I experienced a great desire to work for the conversion of sinners, a desire I hadn't felt so intensely before" (A 45v).

On that Christmas night, by a divine grace, Thérèse was already substantially the Carmelite nun who would turn her life into an unceasing canticle of divine love for the sake of the coming of God's kingdom and paradise. It was a time for the conquest of souls.

A few months later, and precisely on a Sunday in July, Thérèse received a strong impulse to make use of the grace she had received of being a fisher of souls. Her first manuscript puts it like this:

> One Sunday, looking at a picture of Our Lord on the Cross, I was struck by the blood flowing from one of the divine hands. I felt a great pang of sorrow when thinking

this blood was falling to the ground without anyone's hastening to gather it up. I was resolved to remain in spirit at the foot of the Cross and to receive the divine dew. I understood I was then to pour it out upon souls. The cry of Jesus on the Cross sounded continually in my heart: 'I thirst!' These words ignited within me an unknown and very living fire. I wanted to give my Beloved to drink and I felt myself consumed with a thirst for souls. As yet, it was not the souls of priests that attracted me, but those of *great sinners;* I *burned* with the desire to snatch them from the eternal flames" (A 45v).

With her resolve to remain at the foot of the cross to receive grace and pour it out on souls, she proposed to herself a remedy against a heresy of both her times and ours: the indifference of many toward the redemption accomplished by Christ.

The Lord soon offered Thérèse the chance to carry out her desires, and the criminal Pranzini was the first to experience the apostolic efficacy of the ardor of Christ's youthful assistant. His conversion fired Thérèse with enthusiasm and convinced her that she could save still many others if she were to consecrate herself to God in a life of prayer and sacrifice. Thérèse called Pranzini "my first child"(A 46v), revealing thereby that her relationship with sinners had deepened. She was experiencing motherhood because she wished to bring forth sinners into glory.

Nonetheless the thirst for souls was only the beginning. After two months a qualitative leap took place. Not only did the souls of sinners attract Thérèse; she became aware as well of the need priests had for her help. This concern she carried with her to Carmel.

"Souls, and Especially Priests"

On April 9, 1888, Thérèse Martin crossed the threshold of Carmel, and on that day a profound spiritual revolution began for the monastery of Lisieux and for all the others in France. Thérèse entered a cloistered monastery that in 1861 had established a missionary foundation in Saigon. By this means the Carmel was reaching out in the fullest sense for the salvation of souls, a salvation sought through a very particular style of spiritual life. This way of life was set down in a book entitled *The Treasure of Carmel,* in which one reads among other things:

> The purpose of the Carmelite order is to honor the Incarnation and Passion of the Savior, to unite oneself strictly with the Word made flesh, and to glorify God through the imitation of his hidden life of suffering and immolation. Its purpose is also to pray for sinners, to offer oneself for them to the divine justice, and to make up for the penance they do not perform, through an austere and crucified life. In this way a Carmelite nun is charged with continuing and completing in some way Christ's work of mediation. This order calls for mortified and large-hearted souls who will generously and courageously take the place of our divine Master—now impassible—to be immolated with him for the glory of the Father and the salvation of souls.

Thérèse Martin entered Carmel with this spiritual ideal, arrived at through humble but heroic love and confident prayer: "I had declared at the feet of Jesus-Victim, in the examination preceding my Profession, what I had come to Carmel for: 'I came to save souls and especially to pray for priests' " (A 69v).

Thérèse, Céline recalled, referred to this daily mission of apostolic prayer for priests as a "wholesale business," because by working for the sanctification of those directly responsible for the Christian faith, she could more easily reach the souls of those entrusted to them. Looking back as a religious on the experience of her trip to Rome, she wrote to Céline:

> Oh, Céline, let us live for souls...let us be apostles...let us save especially the souls of priests; these souls should be more transparent than crystal.... Alas, how many bad priests, priests who are not holy enough.... Let us pray, let us suffer for them, and, on the last day, Jesus will be grateful. We shall give Him souls!... Céline, do you understand the cry of my soul? (LT 94).

And in October:

> Ah! Céline, I feel that Jesus is asking *both of us* to quench *His thirst* by giving Him souls, the souls of *priests* especially. I feel that Jesus wills that I say this to you, for our mission is *to forget* ourselves and to reduce ourselves to nothing.... There is only one thing to do during the night, the one night of life which will come only once, and this is to love, to love Jesus with all the strength of our heart and to save souls for Him so that He may be *loved*.... Oh, make Jesus loved! (LT 96)

A little afterward she writes still more to Céline on the same theme: "Céline, if you wish, let us convert souls; this year, we must form many *priests* who love Jesus! and who handle Him with the same *tenderness* with which Mary *handled* Him in His cradle!" (LT 101).

In a letter to Céline who herself had decided to enter Carmel, Thérèse courageously defends the vocation of those who were soon to receive her into their community:

> We are not *idlers,* squanderers, either. Jesus has defended us in the person of the Magdalene. He was at table, Martha was serving, Lazarus was eating with Him and His disciples. As for Mary, she was not thinking of taking any food but of *pleasing* Him whom she loved, so she took a jar filled with an ointment of great price and poured it on the *head* of Jesus, after *breaking the jar,* and the whole house was scented with the ointment, but the APOSTLES *complained* against Magdalene.... It is really the same for us, the most fervent *Christians, priests,* find that we are *exaggerated,* that we should *serve* with Martha instead of consecrating to Jesus the *vessels* of our *lives,* with the ointments enclosed within them.... And nevertheless what does it matter if our *vessels* be broken since Jesus is *consoled* and since, in spite of itself, the world is obliged *to smell* the perfumes that are exhaled and serve to purify the empoisoned air the world never ceases to breathe in. (LT 169)

"Our Brother," the Lost Père Loyson

Thérèse's spiritual intuition was confirmed by one of her Carmelite confreres, Père Hyacinthe

Loyson. Born in Paris in 1827, he entered the seminary of Saint Sulpice and was ordained a priest in 1851. Attracted by the religious life, he joined the Discalced Carmelites and made his religious profession in 1860. In 1863 he preached the Lenten sermons in the cathedral of Bordeaux. The archbishop of Paris then invited him to do the same at Notre Dame in Paris. A brilliant orator, Loyson repeated this ministry for three consecutive years. In 1868, he preached the Lenten sermons in Rome in the French church of Saint Louis and was received and congratulated by the pope in a special audience. Nonetheless, a trial of faith began disturb the friar. It threw him into a painful crisis, tempting him to leave the church, which appeared to him now as a residue from the Middle Ages. He did in fact leave in order to found the church of the future.

Among those who had followed him to Rome to hear him preach was a Protestant woman named Emilia Mériman, who had shortly before lost her husband. Moved by Père Hyacinthe's preaching, she took instructions in Catholicism and was converted. Some time later she went to the United States. Père Hyacinthe continued his preaching ministry, but after some turns of fortune and conflicts over church doctrine, he publicly announced his departure from the Discalced Carmelite Order on September 20, 1869. After three years in England, he married Mrs. Mériman. He became associated with a group of Old Catholics and tried to found a Gallican church. His behavior met with some approval, but most of all it generated severe condemnation by traditionalists. For Thérèse this brother of hers became a prototype of priests who withdraw from the church. On October 14, 1890, she wrote to her sister:

> Dear Céline, I *always* have the same thing to say to you. Ah! Let us pray for priests; each day shows how few the friends of Jesus are…. It seems to me this is what He must feel the most, ingratitude, especially when seeing souls who are consecrated to Him giving to others a heart that belongs to Him in so absolute a way. (LT 122)

A year later, and more explicitly, she wrote:

> Yes, dear Céline, suffering alone can give birth to souls for Jesus…. Is it surprising that we are so favored, we whose only desire is to save a soul that seems to be lost forever?… The details interested me very much, while making my heart beat very fast…. But I shall give you some other details that are not any more consoling. The unfortunate prodigal went to Coutances where he started over again the conferences given at Caen. It appears he intends to travel throughout France in this way…. Céline…. And with all this, they add that it is easy to see that *remorse* is gnawing at him. He goes into the churches with a huge Crucifix, and he seems to be making great acts of adoration…. His wife follows him everywhere. Dear Céline, he is really culpable, more culpable than any other sinner ever was who was converted. But cannot Jesus do once what He has not yet ever done? And if He were not to desire it, would He have placed in the heart of His poor little spouses a desire that He could not realize?… No, it is certain that He desires more than we do to bring back this poor stray sheep to the fold. A day will come when He will open his eyes, and then who knows whether France will not be traversed by him with a totally different goal from the one he has in mind now? Let us not grow tired of prayer; confidence works miracles. And Jesus said to Blessed Margaret Mary: '*One just soul* has so much power over my Heart that it can obtain pardon for a thousand *criminals.*' No one knows if one is just or sinful, but, Céline, Jesus gives us the grace of feeling at the bottom of our heart that we would prefer to die rather than to offend Him; and then it is not our merits but those of our Spouse, which are *ours,* that we offer to Our Father who is in heaven, in order that our brother, a son of the Blessed Virgin, return vanquished to throw himself beneath the mantle of the most merciful of Mothers. (LT 129)

On August 19, 1897, the day in which the church celebrated the liturgical feast of Saint Hyacinth, Thérèse received her last Communion and offered it for her confrère, for whom she had prayed so much. Hyacinthe Loyson died in Paris on February 9, 1912, assisted by a priest of the Armenian church, while whispering "My sweet Jesus" and kissing his crucifix.

Thérèse of Lisieux and Joan of Arc

In January of 1895, in her first manuscript, addressing her sister Pauline and narrating the first ten years of her childhood, Thérèse wrote:

> When reading the accounts of the patriotic deeds of French heroines, especially the *Venerable* JOAN OF ARC, I had a great desire to imitate them; and it seemed I felt within me the same burning zeal with which they were animated, the same heavenly inspiration. Then I received a grace which I have always looked upon as one of the greatest in my life, because at that age I wasn't receiving the *lights* I'm now receiving when I am flooded with them. I considered that I was born for *glory* and when I searched out the means of attaining it, God inspired in me the sentiments I have just described. He made me understand that my own *glory* would not be evident to the eyes of mortals, that it would consist in becoming a great *saint!* (A 32r)

In Carmel Thérèse was able to deepen her knowledge of this saintly sister of hers. Having access to the biography written by Henri Wallon, the best study then available in France, she was inspired in 1894 to write two plays for her religious community.

Thérèse wanted to imitate Joan of Arc, not by freeing her country from an enemy invader but by freeing souls from sin, the most dangerous enemy. In 1896 she composed this prayer:

> Lord, God of Hosts, in the Gospel You told us: 'I have not come to bring peace but the sword.' Arm me for battle; I burn to fight for Your glory but I beg You to strengthen my courage. Then with Holy King David I can exclaim: 'You alone are my sword, You, Lord train my hands for war.' O my Beloved! I know what combat You have in mind for me; the contest will not be on the field of battle. I am a prisoner of Your Love. I have freely forged the chain that binds me to You and separates me forever from that world which You have cursed. My sword is Love—with it I will chase the foreigner from the kingdom. (Pri 17)

In the last period of her life, when the trial of faith was assailing Thérèse's courage, she took her place willingly "at the table of sinners" so as to ransom them from their painful situation and bring them to God. Her thoughts turned spontaneously to Joan, who comforted her in the spiritual prison of aridity and solitude. "The saints encourage me, too, in my prison. They tell me: As long as you are in irons, you cannot carry out your mission; but later on, after your death, this will be the time for your works and your conquests" (DE 10.8.4; HLC 144).

The church, in proclaiming her a saint and patroness of the missions, fully confirmed Thérèse's intuition. For love of God and souls she made a daily sacrifice of her life as a religious. Joan of Arc wanted to liberate France from heretics and Thérèse wanted to liberate souls from sin. An identical love both for Christ and souls binds the two saints, making them one in their love and hope for a church menaced by evil.

Two Missionary "Brothers"

The year 1895 marked for Thérèse the important date of her Offering to Merciful Love. On October 15 the apostolic field that until then extended to all souls, and in particular to those of priests, acquired a specific focus: "For a very long time, I had a desire which appeared totally unrealizable to me, that of having *a brother as a priest.* I often thought that had my little brothers not flown away to heaven, I would have had the happiness of seeing them mount the altar; but since God chose to make little angels of them, I could not hope to see my dream realized. And yet, not only did Jesus grant me the favor I desired, but He united me in the bonds of the spirit to *two* of His apostles, who became my brothers" (C 31v).

The first was entrusted to her on October 17, 1895. Mother Agnes, prioress of the monastery, received a letter from a seminarian, Maurice Bellière, who asked for the support of a Carmelite nun who might both help him to persevere fervently in his priestly vocation and become his spiritual coworker in his future apostolic ministry.

Mother Agnes thought at once of Thérèse. So Maurice Bellière, a year younger than she, became her spiritual brother. In the period covering the years 1896–1897, Thérèse wrote him ten letters, addressing him in the end as "my dear little brother." She composed a long prayer for him in which she says in part:

> O my Jesus! I thank You for having fulfilled one of my greatest desires, that of having a brother, a priest, an apostle.... You know, Lord, that my only ambition is to make You known and loved. Now my desire will be realized. I can only pray and suffer, but the soul to whom You unite me by the sweet bonds of charity will go and fight in the plain to win hearts for You, while on the mountain of Carmel I will pray that You give him victory. (Pri 8)

In January of 1896 the providence of God, very generous toward Thérèse's good will, offered her again the chance to become spiritual sister to a missionary, Père Adolphe Roulland. Mother Marie de Gonzague, prioress at the time, asked Sister Thérèse if she would care to take on the obligation of praying for the young missionary. Thérèse discreetly pointed out that she was already offering her "poor merits" for a missionary and that there were other nuns in the monastery holier than herself. The prioress did not yield but told her that obedience would double her merits. She only cautioned her not to mention it to the community, letting them think Père Roulland was the "spiritual brother of the prioress."

Correspondence with the Missionaries

Thérèse's correspondence with her brother missionaries glows with a high spiritual quality in which she comforts them in their difficult and costly ministry. She shows the spirit and intention behind her gestures of sisterly love in the last chapter of her autobiographical manuscript:

> No doubt it is through prayer and sacrifice that we can help missionaries, but when it pleases Jesus to join two souls for His glory, He permits them to communicate their thoughts from time to time in order to incite each other to love God more. However, the *express permission* of authority is necessary for this, for it seems to me that this correspondence would do more harm than good, if not to the missionary, then at least to the Carmelite because of her type of life which tends to too much self-reflection. Instead of uniting her to God, this exchange of letters (even at long intervals) would occupy her mind, and imagining herself to be doing great marvels, she would be simply procuring useless distraction for herself under the cover of zeal. As for me, it is exactly the same with this matter as with all others, and I feel that if my letters are to do any good they must be written under obedience, and that I should feel repugnance rather than pleasure in writing them. (C 32r–v)

When Thérèse began to write to her spiritual brothers she could not help sharing with them all her spiritual maturity, her manner of approaching God and souls, what she called "a little way, a way that is very straight, very short, and totally new" (C 2v).

For an exact idea of what Thérèse communicated to her brothers some significant passages are helpful. These disclose three basic features of her thinking and spiritual stance: her view of herself in God, the style of her spiritual apostolate, and her thoughts about her mission after death.

Regarding her attitude before the Lord, she writes:

> It is true that you are not yet a Père de la Colombière, but I do not doubt that one day, you will be a real apostle of Christ like him. As for myself, the thought does not come into my mind to compare myself with Blessed Margaret Mary. I simply state that Jesus has chosen me to be the sister of one of His apostles, and the words that the "holy Lover of His Heart" addressed to Him out of *humility*, I repeat to Him *myself* in *all truth;* so I hope that His infinite riches will make up for all that I lack in accomplishing

the work He entrusts to me.... Oh, Brother! I beg you to believe me. God has not given you as a sister a *great* soul but a very *little* and a very imperfect one. Do not think that it is humility that prevents me from acknowledging the gifts of God. I know He has done great things in me, and I sing of this each day with joy. I remember that the one must love more who has been forgiven more, so I take care to make my life an act of love, and I am no longer disturbed at being a *little* soul; on the contrary, I take delight in this. That is why I dare to hope 'my exile will be short,' but it is not because I am *prepared*. I feel that I shall never be prepared if the Lord does not see fit to transform me Himself. He can do so in one instant; after all the graces He has granted me, I still await this one from His infinite mercy. (LT 224)

My way is all confidence and love. I do not understand souls who fear a Friend so tender.... I can do very little, or rather absolutely nothing, if I am alone; what consoles me is to think that at your side I can be useful for something. In fact, zero by itself has no value, but when placed next to a unit it becomes powerful, provided, however, that it be placed on the *right side,* after and not before! That is where Jesus has placed me, and I hope to remain there always, following you from a distance by prayer and sacrifice. (LT 226)

Regarding Thérèse's apostolic style, we read:

I am asking Him that you may be not only a *good* missionary but a *saint* all on fire with the love of God and souls; I beg you to obtain also for me this love so that I may help you in your apostolic work. You know that a Carmelite who would not be an apostle would separate herself from the goal of her vocation and would cease to be a daughter of the Seraphic Saint Teresa, who desired to give a thousand lives to save a single soul. (LT 198)

More than ever, I understand that the smallest events of our life are conducted by God; He is the One who makes us desire and who grants our desires.... When our good Mother suggested to me that I become your helper, I admit, Brother, that I hesitated. Considering the virtues of the holy Carmelites around me, I thought that our Mother would have better served your spiritual interests by choosing for you a Sister other than

myself; the thought alone that Jesus would have no regard for my imperfect works but for my good will made me accept the honor of sharing in your apostolic works. (LT 201)

I know there are some saints who spent their life in the practice of astonishing mortifications to expiate their sins, but what of it: "There are many mansions in the house of my heavenly Father," Jesus has said, and it is because of this that I follow the way He is tracing out for me. I try to be no longer occupied with myself in anything, and I abandon myself to what Jesus sees fit to do in my soul, for I have not chosen an austere life to expiate my faults but those of others. (LT 247)

Let us work together for the salvation of souls; we have only the one day of this life to save them and thus to give the Lord proofs of our love. The tomorrow of this day will be eternity, and then Jesus will restore to you a hundredfold the very sweet and very legitimate joys that you sacrificed for Him. (LT 213)

But Thérèse was also thinking of what awaited her beyond time and of how she intended to live in heaven:

Dear little Brother, perhaps when you read this note, I shall no longer be on earth but in the bosom of eternal delights! I do not know the future; however, I can tell you with certainty that the Bridegroom is at the door, and a miracle would be needed to keep me in the exile, and I do not think Jesus will perform this useless miracle. Oh, dear little Brother, how happy I am to die! Yes, I am happy, not at being delivered from sufferings here below (suffering united to love is, on the contrary, the only thing that appears to me desirable in this valley of tears). I am happy to die because I feel that such is God's will, and that much more than here below I shall be useful to souls who are dear to me, to your own in particular. (LT 253)

Never have I asked God to die young, this would have appeared to me as cowardliness; but He, from my childhood, saw fit to give me the intimate conviction that my course here below would be short. It is, then, the thought alone of accomplishing the Lord's will that makes up all my joy.... When I shall be in port, I shall teach you, dear little Brother of my soul, how you must sail the stormy sea of the world with the abandonment and the love of a child who knows his Father loves him and would be unable to leave him in the hour of danger. (LT 258)

You tell me that very often you pray also for your sister; since you have this charity, I would be very happy if each day you would consent to offer this prayer for her which contains all her desires: "Merciful Father, in the name of our gentle Jesus, the Virgin Mary, and the Saints, I beg you to enkindle my sister with Your Spirit of Love and to grant her the favor of making You loved very much." You have promised to pray for me *throughout your life;* no doubt your life will be longer than mine, and it is not permitted you to sing like me: "I have the hope my exile will be short!..." but neither are you permitted to forget your promise. If the Lord takes me soon with Him, I ask you to continue each day the same prayer, for I shall desire in heaven the same thing as I do on earth: To love Jesus and to make Him loved. *Monsieur l'abbé,* you must think I am very strange; perhaps you are sorry to have a sister who seems to want to go and enjoy repose and leave you working alone.... But rest assured, the only thing I desire is God's will, and I admit that if in heaven I were no longer to work for His glory, I would prefer exile to the homeland. I do not know the future; however, if Jesus realizes my presentiments, I promise to remain your little sister up above. Our union, far from being broken, will become more intimate. Then there will no longer be any cloister and grilles, and my soul will be able to fly with you into distant missions. Our roles will remain the same: yours, apostolic weapons, mine, prayer and love. (LT 220)

Brother, I shall go soon to offer your love to all your friends in heaven, begging them to protect you. Dear little Brother, I would like to tell you many things that I understand now that I am at the door of eternity; but I am not dying, I am entering into Life, and all that I cannot say to you here below, I will make you understand from the heights of heaven.... *A Dieu,* little Brother, pray for your little sister who says to you: *A bientôt, au revoir au Ciel!* (LT 244)

A Carmel in the Missions

Wanting to consecrate her own existence to God, Thérèse chose to live an intense spiritual life so as to give Christ every proof of her love and to offer the merit of her own life of communion with God for sinners. For this purpose she chose a most difficult path, entering a cloistered monastery where an austere rule was observed without much human consolation.

In her writings we find another desire emerging: to live in a Carmel in a mission land where life, far from the holy and normal experiences of family affection, could offer more opportunities to reach the goal she had set for herself. Thérèse often expressed this desire; only obedience and her precarious health stood in the way of this burst of heroic generosity.

Reading her writings, we find revealed all the enthusiasm of her young heart, ready to give herself to God and souls in an immeasurable generosity. "Ask Jesus, too, that I may always do His will; for this I am ready to traverse the world.... I am ready also to die!" (LT 225).

Thérèse had entered a community characterized by a highly developed missionary awareness. In 1861 the Carmel of Lisieux had founded a monastery in Saigon, the first in a mission country. Thérèse had always felt a certain desire to depart one day for a Carmel in the missions. She had eagerly read the biographies of missionaries and listened attentively to news about missionary expansion. In the last years of her life, her desire was reenkindled when there was talk of helping the new foundation in Hanoi.

She wrote in Manuscript C:

However, I am prepared to fight on another battle field if the Divine General expresses His desire that I do so. A command would not be necessary, only a look, a simple sign. Since my entrance into the blessed ark, I have always thought that if Jesus did not bring me swiftly to heaven, my lot would be the same as that of Noah's little dove: the Lord would open the window of the ark one day, telling me to fly very far, very far, toward infidel shores, carrying with me the little olive branch. Dear Mother, this thought has matured my soul, making me soar higher than all created things. I understood that even in Carmel there could still be separations, and that only in heaven will the union be complete and eternal; so I wanted my soul to dwell in the heavens, and that it look upon the things of earth only from a distance. I accepted not only exile for myself among an unknown people.... If I have to leave my dear Carmel some day it would not be without pain, for Jesus has not given me an indifferent heart. And precisely because my heart is capable of suffering I want it to give Jesus everything possible.... But *here,* above all, I am loved by you and all the Sisters, and this affection is very sweet to me. This is why I dream of a monastery where I shall be unknown, where I would suffer from poverty, the lack of affection, and finally, the exile of the heart. (C 9r–10r)

Her desire to live in a Carmel in the missions, far from the holiest family affections, arose solely from the desire to imitate Christ in his earthly exile and to share in his human suffering and his humility as the Word made flesh. Thérèse wanted to share to its very depths in the existential situation of Christ her spouse. Authentic love in fact demands a total likeness and fusion with the loved one so as to become one thing only with the object of its love. Thérèse, who had lived always and only for total love of Christ, also desired this total and definitive identification.

But she lived abandoned to the will of God. She wrote to Père Roulland in March of 1897:

Perhaps you want to know what our Mother thinks of my desire to go to Tonkin? She believes in my vocation (for really it has to be a special vocation, and every Carmelite does not feel called to go into exile), but she does not believe my vocation may ever be realized. For this it would be necessary that the sheath be as solid as the sword, and perhaps (our Mother believes) the sheath would be cast into the sea before reaching Tonkin.... I am not at all worried about the future; I am sure God will do His will, it is the only grace I desire. (LT 221)

The Lord was pleased with Thérèse's good will, but wanted her in heaven as patron of the missions, surpassing

her deep and immense desires, making her an apostle not only for some short years but for as long as human beings exist on earth.

Thérèse in the Heart of the Church

Thérèse of the Child Jesus, entrusted by the prioress with the charge of offering her prayers and sacrifices for the apostolate of two missionaries, felt in her heart a great desire for sanctity: "I would be a missionary, not for a few years only but from the beginning of creation until the consummation of the ages" (B 3r). If Thérèse by herself could not attain these desires "which reach even unto infinity," they were realized through the One who can bestow an infinite value on the acts of those who trust in him.

Profoundly convinced of this reality, she said, "I opened the Epistles of St. Paul to find some kind of answer." Chapters 12 and 13 of the First Letter to the Corinthians came into view. In them, the Apostle, after having spoken of charisms in general, celebrates in a crescendo the excellence of charity, highlighting its necessity, merits, and everlasting supernatural character. The reading provided Thérèse with peace, for she finally understood how all her desires could be realized. Spurred on initially by a compelling force that made her desire all vocations, she stopped for a moment in her searching. St. Paul said clearly in fact that one cannot be at the same time both prophet and doctor, since the church is made up of different members. "Without becoming discouraged, I continued my reading, and this sentence consoled me: 'Yet strive after THE BETTER GIFTS, and I point out to you a yet more excellent way.'" And the Apostle explained how the most perfect gifts are nothing without love, that charity is the excellent way that leads most surely to God.

The Apostle's explanation of the perfection of charity offered Thérèse the means of penetrating deeply into the mystery of this virtue and of comprehending its fruitfulness. Analyzing the doctrine of the Mystical Body of Christ, she discovered in the heart of this body the fount of love that is transformed into fervent activity for the church.

> *Charity* gave me the key to my *vocation.* I understood that if the Church had a body composed of different members, the most necessary and most noble of all could not be lacking to it, and so I understood that the Church *had a Heart and that this Heart was BURNING WITH LOVE. I understood it was Love alone* that made the Church's members act, that if *Love* ever became extinct, apostles would not preach the Gospel and martyrs would not shed their blood. I understood that LOVE COMPRISED ALL VOCATIONS, THAT LOVE WAS EVERYTHING, THAT IT EMBRACED ALL TIMES AND PLACES.... IN A WORD, THAT IT WAS ETERNAL! Then, in the excess of my delirious joy, I cried out: O Jesus, my Love.... my *vocation,* at last I have found it.... MY VOCATION IS LOVE! Yes, I have found my place in the Church and it is You, O my God, who have given me this place; in the heart of the Church, my Mother, I shall be *Love.* Thus I shall be everything, and thus my dream will be realized. (B 3v)

Without intending to do so, Thérèse offers here a brief outline of ecclesiology, expressing her thought about the church. Following the trail of the apostle Paul she saw in the church the Mystical Body of Christ; and in love, that is, in the Holy Spirit, she saw the soul of this body, without which everything would become paralyzed.

Enlivened with enthusiasm by her new discovery, Thérèse intensified her fervor, and the communion of love increased ever more. The letters to her missionary brothers provide authentic testimony to her deepening spiritual life. In these, Thérèse pours out all her desire to make God's love known and to have it triumph over all obstacles, to sanctify every moment of her life, and to be more useful to the church. In her act of oblation, the Offering to Merciful Love written in 1895, she exclaims: "O My God! Most Blessed Trinity, I desire to *Love* You and make You *Loved,* to work for the glory of Holy Church by saving souls" (Pri 6; SS 276).

"To Spend My Heaven Doing Good On Earth"

In a manner consistent with her own desires, the apostolic vocation that Thérèse received from God and that situated her in the heart of the church was not limited by time barriers. In contrast to the majority of saints who wanted to work hard on earth so they could then "rest" in heaven, Thérèse saw eternity as a time for conquest, and felt that her charity and zeal for the members of the Mystical Body would continue as long as there is a creature on earth in need of being joined to its Head.

The desire to work in heaven out of love for souls appears clearly in Thérèse's writings in 1896. She expresses this particularly to her missionary brothers. On March, 19, 1897 she wrote to Père Roulland:

> I would like to save souls and forget myself for them; I would like to save them even after my death. So I would be happy if you were to say then, instead of the little prayer you are saying and which will be always realized: "My God, allow my sister to make you still loved." (LT 221)

On July 17 she expressed the same idea to Mother Agnes with a full awareness of her mission in the world:

> But I feel especially that my mission is about to begin, my mission of making God loved as I love Him, of giving my little way to souls. If God answers my desires, my heaven will be spent on earth until the end of the world. Yes, I want to spend my heaven in doing good on earth.... I can't rest as long as there are souls to be saved. But when the angel will have said: "Time is no more!" [Rv 10:6] then I will take my rest; I'll be able to rejoice, because the number of the elect will be complete and because all will have entered into joy and repose. (DE 17.7; HLC 102)

A few days later she asserted as Céline read a passage to her on the happiness of heaven: "That's not what attracts me.... Oh! it's Love! To love, to be loved, and to return to the earth to make love loved" (DE 18.7.4; HLC 217).

Through the Prayer and Self-Offering of Love

Thérèse was beginning to comprehend that, for her, saving souls had all the characteristics of a "vocation." She immediately started seeking the most suitable means of attaining her goal. Wanting to satisfy entirely the will of the Lord who was seeking souls of her, she took the most direct route, choosing as her means the interior apostolate.

Through her two sisters who preceded her into Carmel, Thérèse was well acquainted with the character and spirituality of this order reformed by St. Teresa of Avila. Céline asserts: "From age fourteen, after what Thérèse calls her 'conversion,' the religious life appeared to her most of all as a means of saving souls. The servant of God herself disclosed the conclusion she came to about such a life: so as to suffer more and thereby win souls for Jesus. She considered it harder for human nature to labor without seeing the fruit of one's own labor, to labor without encouragement, without any kind of diversion; and the effort most trying of all was the conquest of self. So this life consisting in a death, more profitable than all others for the salvation of souls, was the one she wanted to embrace, longing to become a prisoner as soon as possible so as to give souls the beauties of heaven." In renouncing an apostolic activity, Thérèse did not enclose herself in a painful and sterile egoism, but penetrating deeply into the apostolic value of total renunciation, she delivered herself into the hands of God to become a docile instrument of God's grace. Thérèse had learned from St. Paul that charity is everything in the church because the church has a heart, which is the exclusive and sufficient principle of every apostolic activity. Thus, to be an apostle she will above all love. With this love the young Carmelite nun went out to conquer souls.

> Well, I am the *Child of the Church* and the Church is a Queen since she is Your Spouse, O divine King of kings. The heart of a child…asks for…Love. She knows only one thing: to love You, O Jesus. Astounding works are forbidden to her; she cannot preach the Gospel, shed her blood; but what does it matter since her brothers work in her stead and she, *a little child,* stays very close to the *throne* of the King and Queen. She *loves* in her brothers' place while they do the fighting. But how will she prove her *love* since love is proved by *works?* Well, the little child *will strew flowers.* (B 4r)

Thérèse knew that in the church everything comes from Christ and every grace is distributed by him; as a result she exclaimed:

> O Jesus, of what use will my flowers be to You?… This Church in heaven, desirous of playing with her little child, will cast these flowers, which are now infinitely valuable because of Your divine touch, upon the Church Suffering in order to extinguish its flames and upon the Church Militant in order to gain the victory for it! O my Jesus! I love You! I love the Church, my Mother! I recall that "the smallest act of PURE LOVE is of more value to her than all other works together." (B 4v)

Christ's mediation was the means Thérèse adopted to succeed in her apostolic vocation. She knew that in the church only Jesus can do everything; others can only collaborate with him. As at the wedding feast of Cana, they can prepare what he both transforms and makes fruitful through his divine action.

Love driven to heroism gave Thérèse the means of becoming within the church a mother of souls. Suffering, which had extended its arms to her from the first years of her life, had now become her inseparable companion. She had grasped the perennial efficacy and decisive importance of Christ's passion of love.

But Thérèse is logical and affirms: "When one wishes to attain a goal, one must use the means; Jesus made me understand that it was through suffering that He wanted to give me souls, and my attraction for suffering grew in proportion to its increase" (A 69v). To her sister Céline she wrote:

> Let us really offer our sufferings to Jesus to save souls, poor souls!… They have less grace than we have,

and still all the Blood of a God was shed to save them.... And yet Jesus wills to make their salvation depend on one sigh from our heart.... What a mystery! If one sigh can save *a soul*, what can sufferings like ours not do? (LT 85)

On her deathbed she exclaimed: "Never would I have believed it was possible to suffer so much! never! never! I cannot explain this except by the ardent desires I have had to save souls" (DE 30.9; HLC 205). The desires grew to the point of impelling Thérèse to push forward in her suffering even to the threshold of martyrdom, to give her life out of love for souls. The supreme salvific gesture of Christ attracted her as she grew in the desire to identify herself perfectly with her Spouse.

Thérèse was convinced of the apostolic fruitfulness of the prayer of a soul that had given itself completely. On this theme she left passages written with simplicity and depth:

> A scholar has said: "Give me a lever and a fulcrum and I will lift the world." What Archimedes was not able to obtain, for his request was not directed by God and was only made from a material viewpoint, the saints have obtained in all its fullness. The Almighty has given them as *fulcrum: HIMSELF ALONE*; as *lever: PRAYER* which burns with a fire of love. And it is in this way that they have *lifted the world;* it is in this way that the saints still militant lift it, and that, until the end of time, the saints to come will lift it. (C 36r–v)

"Ah! it is prayer, it is sacrifice which give me all my strength; these are the invincible weapons which Jesus has given me" (C 24v). "How great is the power of *Prayer!* One could call it a Queen who has at each instant free access to the King and who is able to obtain whatever she asks" (C 25r).

To her sister Céline she wrote in 1892:

> Our own vocation is not to go out to harvest the fields of ripe corn. Jesus does not say to us: *"Lower* your eyes, look at the fields and go harvest them." Our mission is still more sublime. These are the words of our Jesus: *"Lift* your eyes and see." See how in my heaven there are empty places; it is up to you to fill them, you are my Moses praying on the mountain, ask me for workers and I shall send them, I await only a prayer, a sigh from your heart!... Is not the apostolate of prayer, so to speak, more elevated than that of the word? Our mission as Carmelites is to form evangelical workers who will save thousands of souls whose mothers we shall be.... Céline, if these were not the very words of our Jesus, who would dare to believe in them?... I find that our share is really beautiful, what have we to envy in priests? (LT 135)

And so through love, suffering, and prayer, Thérèse collected the blood that streams from the Crucified One and poured it out on the church. Suffering: love stirred to an heroic inner martyrdom. Prayer: a cry of confidence and love for the spiritual needs of all people, her one preoccupation. Love: the deep and sole reality that synthesizes everything.

Thérèse Speaks

To Our Lady of Victories
Queen of Virgins, Apostles, and Martyrs

You who fulfill my hope,
O Mother, hear the humble song
Of love and gratitude
That comes from the heart of your child.....

You have united me forever
With the works of a Missionary,
By the bonds of prayer,
Suffering, and love.

He will cross the earth
To preach the name of Jesus.
I will practice humble virtues
In the background and in mystery.

I crave suffering.
I love and desire the Cross....
To help save one soul,
I would die a thousand times!........

Ah! for the Conqueror of souls
I want to sacrifice myself in Carmel,
And through Him to spread the fire
That Jesus brought down from Heaven.

Through Him, what a ravishing mystery,
Even as far as East Szechuan
I shall be able to make loved
The virginal name of my tender Mother!...

In my deep solitude,
Mary... I want to win hearts.
Through your Apostle, I shall convert sinners
As far as the ends of the earth.

Through Him, the holy waters of Baptism
Will make of the tiny little newborn babe
The temple where God Himself
Deigns to dwell in his love.

I want to fill with little angels
The brilliant eternal abode...
Through Him, hosts of children
Will take flight to heaven!...

Through Him, I'll be able to gather
The palm for which my soul yearns.
Oh what hope! Dear Mother,
I shall be the sister of a Martyr!!!

....

After this life's exile,
On the evening of the glorious fight,
We shall enjoy the fruits of our apostolate
In our Homeland.

For Him, Victory's honor
Before the army of the Blessed.
For me... the reflection of His Glory
For all eternity in the Heavens!....

The little sister of a Missionary
(PN 35)

163. The Martin sisters and Mother Marie de Gonzague. From left to right, seated: Mother Marie de Gonzague, Sister Marie of the Sacred Heart (Marie), and Thérèse, who is about twenty-two; standing: Céline, still a postulant but wearing the habit of a novice for the occasion, and Mother Agnes of Jesus (Pauline).

164. The community in the walkway beneath the chestnut trees. Thérèse, who is twenty-two, is at the left with the statue of the "Rose Child Jesus" and a painter's palette.

163

164

165

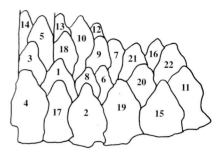

165. The community (not complete) in the cloister. Present are: 1. Sr. Thérèse of the Child Jesus and the Holy Face; 2. Sr. Marie of the Sacred Heart (Marie); 3. Mother Agnes of Jesus (Pauline); 4. Sr. Geneviève of the Holy Face (Céline); 5. Mother Marie de Gonzague; 6. Sr. St. Stanislaus of the Sacred Hearts; 7. Mother Hermance of the Heart of Jesus; 8. Sr. Marie of the Angels and of the Sacred Heart; 9. Sr. St. John the Baptist of the Heart of Jesus; 10. Sr. Teresa of Jesus of the Heart of Mary; 11. Sr. Marguerite-Marie of the Sacred Heart of Jesus; 12. Sr. Teresa of St. Augustine; 13. Sr. Marie Emmanuel; 14. Sr. Marie of St. Joseph; 15. Sr. Marie of Jesus; 16. Sr. Marie Philomena of Jesus; 17. Sr. Marie of the Trinity; 18. Sr. Anne of the Sacred Heart (on July 2, 1895 she returned to her monastery in Saigon); 19. Sr. Marie of the Incarnation; 20. Sr. St. Vincent de Paul; 21. Sr. Martha of Jesus; 22. Sr. Marie-Madeleine of the Blessed Sacrament.

166. The community doing the wash. From left to right: Sr. Marie of the Trinity (the only one younger than Thérèse in the community, she is twenty-two), Sr. Thérèse (twenty-two and a half years), Sr. Geneviève (Céline), and Sr. Marie of Jesus.

167. Thérèse and the novices. Thérèse, at age twenty-two and four months, holds an hourglass in her hand. At the window Mother Marie Gonzague, mistress of novices, and Mother Agnes of Jesus, prioress.

168. The four Martin sisters and Marie Guérin (Marie of the Eucharist, the novice on her knees), photographed on the walk beneath the chestnut trees. Standing are Marie and Céline; seated Pauline and Thérèse, who is twenty-three and already afflicted by her mortal illness. A few months later she will experience her first hemoptysis (April 3, 1896).

169. The community gathering the hay. Thérèse who is twenty-three is in the center near the tree with a pitchfork in hand.

170. Thérèse in the cloister at twenty-three. She carries a scroll with words from her patroness and spiritual mother Teresa of Avila: "I would give a thousand lives to save one soul." Her right hand rests on L. Guiot's book, *La mission de Su-Tchuen au XVIIIe siècle: Vie et apostolat de Mgr Pottier,* published by Téqui in 1892, and given to her by her spiritual brother, Father Adolphe Roulland.

167

168

169

CHAPTER ELEVEN

Thérèse and the Mystery of Mary

FRANÇOIS-MARIE LETHEL, OCD

In May 1897, shortly before her death, Thérèse revealed in its entirety the place Mary held in her life, in a long poem entitled: "Why I Love You, O Mary" (PN 54). It was her last poem, and was like her Marian testament, written at the request of Sister Marie of the Sacred Heart, her own sister Marie, for whom she had already drafted her masterpiece, the second autobiographical manuscript, some months earlier (September 1896).

There is a deep relationship between these two texts. They are prayers addressed to Jesus (Ms B) and to Mary (PN 54); they are animated by the same great refrain: "I love you." This act of love, which Thérèse desired to renew "with every beat of her heart...an infinite number of times" (cf. Pri 6; SS 277), was her last word, expressed in a last breath. Thérèse died while saying to Jesus: "My God, I love you." This fundamental "Jesus, I love you," which illumined all of Thérèse's writings, isn't a sentimental expression but the same act of charity by which the Holy Spirit introduces her into the inner life of the Holy Trinity. It was thus that she wrote: "Ah! Divine Jesus, you know I love you. / The Spirit of Love sets me aflame with his fire. / In loving you I attract the Father" (PN 17).

Inseparable from this "Jesus, I love You" is the same act of love addressed to Mary: "I love You, O Mary." Such is the great refrain of Thérèse's Marian poem. Already expressed in the title, and repeated untiringly in the threads of the stanzas, the other refrain is clear: "I am your child." This poem is thus like the Marian complement of her autobiography, and it is from there that one can try to discover the place of Mary in the life of Thérèse and in her spiritual teaching.

The Relevance of Thérèse's Marian Teaching

Hers is a true Marian doctrine, a great event of our time, because she is in line with the teachings of the Second Vatican Council (*Lumen Gentium,* ch. 8)

and Popes Paul VI (*Marialis Cultus*) and John Paul II (*Redemptoris Mater*). Deeply rooted in the Marian spirituality of Carmel, Thérèse's teaching was also in harmony with those of other saints, particularly Saint Francis, Saint Clare, and Saint Louis-Marie Grignion de Montfort. Jesus is always at the center, and Mary is entirely relative to him as his Mother. Such is Mary's greatest title: "She is more Mother than queen," affirmed Thérèse (DE 21.8.3; HLC 161).

It is a doctrine founded on the Gospel, emphasizing the littleness, poverty, and simplicity of Mary; and above all, it is a doctrine oriented entirely toward sanctity, the maternal mission of Mary being to lead all her children "to the summit of the mountain of Love."

It is also important to notice the balance of this teaching, which carefully avoided the two opposing excesses denounced by the Council as it simultaneously urged theologians and preachers to abstain from "all false exaggeration as from too summary an attitude" on the subject of Mary (LG 67).

Poverty and Love

The preachers of Thérèse's time generally fell into the first Mariological excess, that of "false exaggeration," according to her own testimony reported by Mother Agnes:

> She was telling me that all that she had heard preached on the Blessed Virgin hadn't touched her: 'Let the priests, then, show us practicable virtues! It's good to speak of her privileges, but it's necessary above all that we can imitate her. She prefers imitation to admiration, and her life was so simple! However good a sermon is on the Blessed Virgin, if we are obliged all the time to say: Ah!... Ah!... we grow tired. How I like singing to Her: "The narrow road to Heaven you have made visible (*she said: easy*) / When practicing always the most humble virtues." (DE 23.8.9; HLC 166)

Thérèse, citing two lines of her poetry here, was resolutely opposed to "triumphalistic" preaching that spoke only of Mary's greatness and privileges and that often stressed apocryphal gospels filled with the marvelous and the extraordinary. The Carmelite responded to this excess with the Gospels, which show us on the contrary that Mary was very simple, very small, near to us, and imitable. She discovered in this way the great privileges forgotten by these preachers: the privileges of poverty and littleness that characterize the entire earthly lives of Jesus and Mary. In that, she coincided exactly with what Saint Francis wrote in his last testament to Saint Clare: "As for me, Brother Francis, very little, I want to follow the life and poverty of our very great Lord, Jesus Christ, and of his very holy Mother." For little Saint Thérèse as well as for the "Poverello," the words "littleness" and "poverty" fundamentally expressed the same reality: it is the heart of the Gospels, the meeting place and the most intimate communion with Jesus and Mary.

Although preachers rendered Mary distant and inimitable in showing only her "sublime glory," Thérèse on the contrary found her to be very near to us in the Gospels—near to us in her littleness and poverty:

> In pondering your life in the holy Gospels,
> I dare to look at you and come near you.
> It's not difficult for me to believe that I'm your child,
> for I see you as human and suffering like me. (PN 54)

Thérèse would then re-read all the passages of the Gospels where Mary is present, always using the act of love as a key for reading: "I love You." In this way, the Holy Spirit allowed her to dwell in the Gospels, making her immediately attentive to all the mysteries that are revealed there, from the Incarnation to the cross. These are precisely the mysteries of poverty, where "the poor Virgin embraces the poor Christ," "loving Him totally," according to the expressions of Saint Clare.

It is from this viewpoint of love that Thérèse rediscovered the true meaning of the proverb *numquam satis*

de Maria, that is, "Of Mary, there is never enough." She gave us a wonderful expression during her novitiate when she wrote to her cousin Marie Guérin, who was very scrupulous: "Have no fear of loving the Blessed Virgin *too much,* you will *never* love her enough, and Jesus will be very pleased since the Blessed Virgin is His Mother" (LT 92). Such was exactly the response that Saint Louis de Montfort gave to the "scrupulous devout" who were afraid of displeasing Jesus by loving Mary too much: one never loves Mary enough because it is always Jesus whom one loves in her and with her. Such, then, is the meaning of this "never enough." It's a matter of love, and not of inventing new privileges.

Symbols of Mary's Maternal Love

So, after having read the last passage of the Gospel portraying Mary near the cross of Jesus, Thérèse ended her poem by saying to her:

> Soon I'll go to beautiful Heaven to see you,
> You who came *to smile at me* in the morning of my life,
> Come smile at me again… Mother,… It's evening now!…
> I no longer fear the splendor of your supreme glory.
> With you I've suffered, and now I want
> To sing on your lap, Mary, why I love You,
> And to go on saying that I am your child! (PN 54)

These lines were written in May 1897. Days later, in the first pages of Manuscript C, Thérèse wrote about her terrible test of faith which began more than a year beforehand, and which touched upon the existence of heaven. While speaking of her poems, she wrote: "When I sing of the happiness of Heaven…I sing simply what I WANT TO BELIEVE" (C 7v). Such was the heroic affirmation of heaven that we find here. Thérèse affirmed that in the glory of heaven, she would remain always the child of Mary, on her knees singing eternally this "I love You." At the same time, she summed up all her own life on earth, from the morning to the evening, as lived under Mary's maternal smile. For Thérèse, Mary was truly the smiling Virgin, and Thérèse's own smile that came to light up the whole world is one of the most beautiful reflections of Mary's smile.

In her Manuscript A, the Carmelite told of this "smile" of Mary "in the morning of her life." Deeply affected in her childhood by the death of her mother, then by the loss of her "second mother," her sister Pauline who left her to enter Carmel, Thérèse was cured by the maternal smile of Mary, a cure that became complete with the "grace of Christmas" and with her final confirmation at Our Lady of Victories in Paris:

> The Blessed Virgin made me feel that *it was really herself who smiled on me and brought about my cure.* I understood that she was watching over me, that I was *her* child. I could no longer give her any other name but *'Mama'* as this appeared ever so much more tender than Mother. How fervently I begged her to protect me always, to bring to fruition as quickly as possible my dream of hiding *beneath the shadow of her virginal mantle!* This was one of my first desires as a child. When growing up, I understood it was at Carmel I would truly find the Blessed Virgin's mantle, and toward this fertile Mount I directed all my desires. I prayed Our Lady of Victories to keep far from me everything that could tarnish my purity. (A 56v–57r)

So, without any new extraordinary manifestation, Thérèse experienced Mary's maternal love in the most profound way, and she responded to it with all her filial love. This love of a child who preferred the name of "Mama" to that of Mother wasn't in any way sentimentalism or infantilism. It was the same love with which Thérèse called God "Papa," and spontaneously rediscovered all the power of Jesus' word "Abba."

In order to express this intimacy between the child and her Mother, Thérèse used the symbol of Mary's mantle or veil. She entered Carmel in order to hide herself beneath the shadow of the virginal mantle of Mary. She was going to live that most intensely during the course of several days during the time of her novitiate: "I was entirely hidden under the Blessed Virgin's veil" (DE 11.7.2; HLC 88). A little while afterward, she invited her sister Céline to entrust herself totally to Mary: "Hide yourself well in the shadow of her virginal mantle in order that she may virginize you!" (LT 105).

The Most Intimate Union with Jesus

For Thérèse, this life hidden under the mantle of Mary was the occasion for the most intimate union with Jesus in the simplicity of daily life. She expressed this beautifully in one of her first poems:

> O Immaculate Virgin! You are my Sweet Star
> Giving Jesus to me and uniting me to Him.
> O Mother! Let me rest under your veil
> Just for today. (PN 5)

In the same sense, it was Mary herself who said to Céline:

> I will hide you under the veil
> Where the King of Heaven takes refuge....
> But to shelter you always
> Under my veil beside Jesus,
> You must stay little. (PN 13)

Like a Mother, Mary gives Jesus to us and gives us to Jesus. Here again, Thérèse's teaching coincides with that of St. Louis de Montfort in showing how Mary is always relative to Jesus. She never keeps her children to herself, but "She unites them to Him with a very intimate bond" (*Treatise of True Devotion,* 211).

From Her Profession to the Offering to Merciful Love

It was precisely in this Marian climate that Thérèse made her religious profession on September 8, 1890, the feast of the Birth of Mary. After telling how Mary had helped her to prepare her bridal "dress" for the great day of her wedding, she cried out: "Mary's nativity! What a beautiful feast on which to become the spouse of Jesus! It was the *little* Blessed Virgin, one day old, who was presenting her *little* flower to *little* Jesus" (A 77r).

With childlike simplicity, these words of Thérèse express the most essential aspect of her spirituality, which is evangelical littleness. Thérèse repeated and underlined the word "little" three times, showing how her own littleness was enveloped by the littleness of Jesus and Mary. It was the "little" Mary who presented her to Jesus so that she could become his spouse. Thus, it was with Mary that Thérèse could truly espouse the littleness of Jesus, just as Saint Francis and Saint Clare had espoused his poverty, intimately partaking in the Mysteries of his abasement from the Incarnation to the cross. With Mary, all these saints have shared in this staggering mystery of God's poverty and littleness. Thérèse contemplated Jesus as "a God who makes Himself so little for me" (LT 266). Likewise, Saint Clare recognized in him "the love of this poor God who was laid in a manger as a poor child, lived poor in this world, and hung naked and poor on the Cross."

So she who called herself *Thérèse of the Child Jesus and of the Holy Face* was going to identify always more deeply with this love whose "nature it is to humble itself" (cf. A 2v), from the poverty of the Incarnation to the total privation of the cross.

In living hidden under the mantle of Mary, Thérèse was going to enter more and more into the mystery of Jesus' littleness and poverty, because the discovery of evangelical littleness has a progressive character.

After her profession, in her letters to her sister Céline, the young Carmelite above all revealed her spousal heart, this fundamental spousal dimension of her love for Jesus. In this light, littleness identified itself in a practical way with *virginity*. We find the most beautiful expression of this in her letter of April 25, 1893. Through the symbol of the flower of the fields, which represents Jesus in his earthly life, and that of the drop of dew, which represents his spouse in the same condition, Thérèse showed how littleness is the indispensable condition of this virginal union between the bride and her Spouse. In order to be for Jesus and for him alone, "one must remain little, little like a drop of dew!" (L 141). It is virginity of heart, like undivided love, which led Thérèse to espouse the littleness of Jesus by giving herself totally and exclusively to him, like this little drop of dew that alone could respond to his thirst for love.

Close to Mary, Thérèse learned "to live on love," and it was in contemplating her that she would give the best definition of love: *"To love is to give everything. It's to give oneself"* (PN 54). And it was precisely in this dynamic of total giving that Mary was present at the heart of the Offering to Merciful Love on June 9, 1895. Thérèse offered herself then to the love of Jesus in which she came to discover the entire Trinitarian reality: "This year, June 9, the feast of the Holy Trinity, I received the grace to understand more than ever before how much Jesus desires to be loved" (A 84r). In giving herself totally "as a victim of holocaust" to the fire of his love, which is the Holy Spirit, she abandoned her offering into the hands of Mary (cf. Pri 6; SS 276). Here, Thérèse joined particularly with Louis-Marie de Montfort, who invited the poor and the little ones to live fully the grace of their baptism in giving themselves totally to Jesus by the hands of Mary. The symbol he used, that of "the slave of love," had in its depths the same sense as the Thérèsian symbol of the "holocaust to love," each one signifying the same extremity of love, the same total gift of self.

Communion in the Mystery of the Incarnation

At the same time that she gave herself entirely to Jesus, Thérèse received Jesus who gave himself entirely to her, in the infinite greatness of his love, symbolized by the ocean. She wrote to her prioress: "You permitted me, dear Mother, to offer myself in this way to God, and you know the rivers or rather the oceans of graces that flooded my soul" (A 84r). So, Thérèse, like Mary, "can contain Jesus, the Ocean of Love" (PN 54).

Evangelical littleness then took on a maternal nature, typically feminine. It was in this way that Saint Clare invited Agnes of Prague to "attach herself to the very gentle Mother," who carried at her breast "him whom the heavens couldn't contain," to share her maternity: "Just as the glorious Virgin of virgins carried him maternally, so you also, following her footsteps of humility above all and of poverty, you can always without any doubt carry him spiritually in a body which is chaste and virginal, holding him in whom you and all things are contained."

Thérèse expressed this beautifully in her Marian poem in which she contemplated the same mystery of Mary carrying Jesus in her maternal breast. Thérèse was not only the child of Mary, but even more profoundly, she was mother with Mary, sharing her maternal intimacy with the child whom she carried. Like Francis and Clare, Thérèse referred to the Eucharist:

> O beloved Mother, in spite of my littleness,
> Like You I possess the All-Powerful within me.
> But I don't tremble in seeing my weakness:
> The treasures of a mother belong to her child,
> And I am your child, O my dearest Mother.
> Aren't your virtues and your love mine too?
> So when the white Host comes into my heart,
> Jesus, Your sweet Lamb, thinks He is resting in You!
> (PN 54)

One of Thérèse's deepest desires was to keep the presence of the Body of Jesus within her. This is what she asked Jesus in the Act of Oblation: "Remain in me as in the Tabernacle" (Pri 6; SS 276). In this way, she asked to be like Mary, "the Tabernacle who veils the Savior's divine beauty!" (PN 54).

In her littleness, Mary carried Jesus, and it was in poverty that she gave birth to him in Bethlehem. It was there that Thérèse contemplated all of Mary's greatness, her greatness as the Mother of God close to her Child:

> No one wants to take in poor foreigners,
> There's room for the great ones.…
> There's room for the great ones, and it's in a stable
> That the Queen of Heaven must give birth to a God.
> O my dearest Mother, how lovable I find you,
> How great I find you in such a poor place!…
> When I see the Eternal God wrapped in swaddling clothes,
> When I hear the poor cry of the Divine Word,
> O my dearest Mother, I no longer envy the angels,
> For their Powerful Lord is my dearest Brother!…
> How I love You, Mary, you Who made
> This Divine Flower blossom on our shores! (PN 54)

For Thérèse, as for Francis, this mystery of the manger always remained very present; in it was manifested the union of the Mother with her Son in poverty, exemplifying our union with him in the Eucharist, where He is again "much more little than a child!" (RP 2). In this light, Thérèse wrote to Céline: "This year we must form many *priests* who love Jesus! and who *handle* Him with the same *tenderness* with which Mary *handled* Him in His cradle!" (LT 101). This was exactly what she asked Mary on behalf of a future priest, the seminarian Maurice Bellière, her first spiritual brother: "Teach him even now how lovingly you handled the Divine Child Jesus and wrapped him in swaddling clothes, so that one day he may go up to the Holy Altar and carry in his hands the King of Heaven. I ask you also to keep him safe beneath the shadow of your virginal mantle" (Pri 8).

Mary's Pilgrimage of Faith

This intimate relationship between Mary and her child was lived in faith. Thérèse emphasized this point very much, like Saint Louis de Montfort before her. Following the Second Vatican Council, Pope John Paul II developed this particular theme of "Mary's pilgrimage of faith": "Happy are those who have believed" (*Redemptoris Mater*, 1220). Jesus was at the same time her child and her God, the fruit of her womb and her creator and savior. Thus, the relationship between Mary and Jesus is inseparably the relationship between the mother and her child, and the relationship between the believer and her God. While preachers, stressing apocryphal legends, filled the life of Mary with extraordinary graces, Thérèse by contrast showed the spiritual poverty of Mary in the Gospels while affirming that "she lived by faith just like ourselves" (DE 21.8.3; HLC 161). And for her as for us, faith was obscure and sometimes sorrowful, put to the test by Jesus himself. Thérèse affirmed this with respect to the Gospel episode in which Jesus is lost and found again in the Temple:

Mother, your sweet Child wants you to be the example
Of the soul searching for Him in the night of Faith.
(PN 54)

For Thérèse, this was the climate of Mary's spiritual life in Nazareth:

Mother full of grace, I know that in Nazareth,
You lived in poverty, wanting nothing more.
No rapture, miracle, or ecstasy,
Embellish your life, O Queen of the Elect!...
The number of little ones on earth is truly great,
They can raise their eyes toward You without trembling.
It is by *the ordinary way,* incomparable Mother,
That you like to walk to guide them to Heaven. (PN 54)

This verse is particularly important, because it reveals the Marian nature of the "little way." Thérèse went to the heart of the mystery of Mary's poverty as a spiritual poverty of faith, stripped of all extraordinary graces.

With Mary Near the Cross

This poverty reached its height in the total privation of the cross. It was there that Thérèse ultimately identified with Mary, reading the last text of the Gospel where she is present close to Jesus:

Mary, at the top of Calvary standing beside the Cross
To me you seem like a priest at the altar. (PN 54)

As a mother, she participated in the redeeming sacrifice of her Son in a unique way. Like Abraham, she consented to the sacrifice of her only son; and her son Jesus Christ then extended her motherhood to all humanity redeemed by his blood.

Thérèse shared very deeply in this mystery while sharing in Mary's motherhood near the cross. She experienced it for the first time before her entry into Carmel. While looking at an image of Jesus Crucified, contemplating his blood poured out, she had made one of the most fundamental decisions of her life: "I was resolved to remain in spirit at the foot of the Cross to receive the divine dew. I understood that I was then to pour it out upon souls" (A 45v). Her spiritual motherhood began immediately with this decision; she obtained eternal salvation for the man she called "my first child" (A 46v): the criminal Pranzini, who was sentenced to death and guillotined.

In Thérèse's feminine heart, which she often compared to a lyre, this "lyre-string" of motherly love was essential, vibrating with that of her spousal love: "To be *Your Spouse...*, and by my union with You to be the *Mother* of souls" (B 2v). For Thérèse, these are the two most beautiful aspects of this "treasure" of love which is virginity: to be spouse and to be mother. Her virginity became fruitful by her communion with the blood of Jesus poured out in his passion. In contemplating this "dew of love" in his agony, Thérèse said to Jesus:

Remember that your fruitful Dew
Made the flowers' corollas virginal
And made them able even in this world
To give birth to a great number of hearts.
I am a virgin, O Jesus! Yet what a mystery,
When I unite myself to You, I am the mother of souls.
(PN 24)

We notice above all the beauty and the power of the affirmations: "I am a virgin.... I am a mother." Like Mary, Thérèse was inseparably virgin, spouse, and mother, and her motherhood found all its strength, all its fruitfulness, in the most intimate communion with Jesus Crucified. For Thérèse as for Mary, this communion with the annihilation of Jesus, with his total privation on the cross, characterized the very deep trial of faith that Pope John Paul II was not afraid to call a "Kenosis [i.e., total self-emptying] of Faith" (*Redemptoris Mater*, 18) Clearly it isn't a question of the loss of faith, but on the contrary of a more heroic faith that continues to endure even in the most total privation, in the deepest obscurity, supported by love and hope.

In fact, the passion of Thérèse, which began during Paschaltide in 1896, was above all characterized by this very difficult "test of faith." It was while Thérèse shared in Mary's most extreme spiritual poverty that she also shared in her universal motherhood. Thérèse's spiritual motherhood extended then to all people; she then became entirely missionary, "adopting" in a very special way the atheists of the modern world. With the greatest confidence she interceded for them, she prayed for their eternal salvation.

Thus, Thérèse lived her maternal love in a sorrowful faith and in a hope without limits, not only for herself but for others, for all. Like the poet Charles Peguy, her contemporary, Thérèse joined Mary in all the beauty of her motherly hope: the hope of a mother for the salvation of all her poor children.

Mary Is the Greatest Because She Is the Least

As Thérèse contemplates her, Mary is very simple in her faith and hope. She is "all Mother" by being "all hope," and she is that fundamentally because she is very little, the "very little" one par excellence, "overflowing with graces" in an unsurpassable manner, even more than Thérèse, because she was even more little.

Thus, Thérèse spoke of Mary without naming her when she said to Jesus, at the end of Manuscript B: "I feel that if You found a soul weaker and littler than mine, which is impossible, You would be pleased to grant still greater favors provided that it abandoned itself with total confidence to Your Infinite Mercy" (B 5v).

These lines were written on September 8, 1896, on the feast of the Birth of Mary, in the grace of the littleness of the one who became the Mother of God.

Thérèse Speaks

Why I Love You, O Mary!

Oh! I would like to sing, *Mary, why I love you,*
Why your sweet name thrills my heart,
And why the thought of your supreme greatness
Could not bring fear to my soul.
If I gazed on you in your sublime glory,
Surpassing the splendor of all the blessed,
I could not believe that I am your child.
O Mary, before you I would lower my eyes!...

If a child is to cherish his mother,
She has to cry with him and share his sorrows.
O my dearest Mother, on this foreign shore
How many tears you shed to draw me to you!....
In pondering *your life in the holy Gospels,*
I dare look at you and come near you.
It's not difficult for me to believe I'm your child,
For I see you human and suffering like me....

When an angel from Heaven bids you be *the Mother*
Of the God who is to reign for all eternity,
I see you prefer, O Mary, what a mystery!
The ineffable treasure of *virginity.*
O Immaculate Virgin, I understand how your soul
Is dearer to the Lord than his heavenly dwelling.
I understand how your soul, *Humble and Sweet Valley,*
Can contain Jesus, the Ocean of Love!...

O beloved Mother, despite my littleness,
Like you I possess The All-Powerful within me.
But I don't tremble in seeing my weakness:
The treasures of a mother belong to her child,
And I am your child, O my dearest Mother.
Aren't your virtues and your love mine too?
So when the white Host comes into my heart,
Jesus, your Sweet Lamb, thinks he is resting in you!...

Later in Bethlehem, O Joseph and Mary!
I see you rejected by all the villagers.
No one wants to take in poor foreigners.
There's room for the great ones….
There's room for the great ones, and it's in a stable
That the Queen of Heaven must give birth to a God.
O my dearest Mother, how lovable I find you,
How great I find you in such a poor place!....

The Gospel tells me that, growing in wisdom,
Jesus remains subject to Joseph and Mary,
And my heart reveals to me with what tenderness
He always obeys his dear parents.
Now I understand the mystery of the temple,
The hidden words of my Lovable King.
Mother, your sweet Child wants you to be the example
Of the soul searching for Him in the night of faith.

Since the King of Heaven wanted his Mother
To be plunged into the night, in anguish of heart,
Mary, is it thus a blessing to suffer on earth?
Yes, *to suffer while loving is the purest happiness!...*
All that He has given me, Jesus can take back.
Tell him not to bother with me.....
He can indeed hide from me, I'm willing to wait for him
Till the day without sunset when my faith will fade away.....

Mother full of grace, I know that in Nazareth
You live in poverty, wanting nothing more.
No rapture, miracle, or ecstasy
Embellish your life, O Queen of the Elect!....
The number of little ones on earth is truly great.
They can raise their eyes to you without trembling.
It's by *the ordinary way,* incomparable Mother,
That you like to walk to guide them to Heaven.

You love us, Mary, as Jesus loves us,
And for us you accept being separated from Him.
To love is to give everything. It's to give oneself.
You wanted to prove this by remaining our support.
The Savior knew your immense tenderness.
He knew the secrets of your maternal heart.
Refuge of sinners, He leaves us to you
When He leaves the Cross to wait for us in Heaven.

Soon I'll hear that sweet harmony.
Soon I'll go to beautiful Heaven to see you.
You who came *to smile at me* in the morning of my life,
Come smile at me again... Mother.... It's evening now!...
I no longer fear the splendor of your supreme glory.
With you I've suffered, and now I want
To sing on your lap, Mary, why I love you,
And to go on saying that I am your child!......

(PN 54, sts. 1–3, 5. 9. 15–17, 22, 25)

CHAPTER TWELVE

Thérèse in the Night of Faith

EMMANUEL RENAULT, OCD

"One who has never had trials knows little." This saying from the Book of Sirach (34:10) expresses a fact of human experience: We cannot attain true knowledge of ourselves or of others, or fulfill God's plan in our regard, without consenting to pass through the fire of trials, in the footsteps and pattern of Christ.

Scripture, therefore, speaks of "trials" as a necessary passage to life and as an indispensable condition for proving the quality of our faith (1 Pt 1:7), for manifesting the truth (1 Cor 11:19), and for exercising humility (1 Cor 10:12–13). But trials can become "temptations" when Satan exploits them (cf. Acts 5:3; 1 Cor 7:5; 1 Thes 3:5). God is not the author of temptations, but permits them as so many tests imposed on us, that we might penetrate into the divine mystery through the mystery of the cross.

These are the "trial-temptations" that Thérèse had to undergo, particularly at the end of her life, by suffering simultaneously a double confrontation with death: a physical death that was steadily destroying her young body, and a spiritual death that was threatening the life of her soul. To better evaluate the conditions of the battle that she had to wage in this final great test of her faith, we will have to situate it in the context of her fatal illness, a context evoked in the following chapter.

Profile of Her Trial

In June 1897, three months before her death, Thérèse declared: "During those very joyful days of the Easter season, Jesus made me feel that there were really souls who have no faith, and who, through the abuse of grace, lost this precious treasure, the source of the only real and pure joys" (C 5v).

It must be noted that this awareness of a group of souls without faith was not given to her as an illumination of the spirit intended to open up new perspectives for stirring her apostolic zeal. Such had been the case

for Saint Teresa of Avila when a visit from a Franciscan returning from Mexico, Father Maldonado, had inflamed her with zeal at the news of "millions of souls that were being lost there for want of Christian instruction" (*Foundations* 1, 7).

Thérèse was not unaware of the fact that there were "impious people without faith," since a niece of her aunt Madame Guérin, Marguerite Maudelonde, had married a well-known atheist, Monsieur Tostain, Deputy of the President of the Republic in Lisieux. But in her faith, which was "so alive and clear," Thérèse believed "that they were actually speaking against their own inner convictions when they denied the existence of heaven" because, for her, heaven was so evident that it was impossible for an upright and sincere mind not to acknowledge it: "The thought of heaven made up all my happiness" (C 5v).

And now suddenly she was given, not an exterior, but an inner, experiential knowledge of this world of souls without faith, by finding herself plunged into it: "[God] permitted my soul to be invaded by the thickest darkness, and that the thought of heaven, up until then so sweet to me, be no longer anything but the cause of struggle and torment" (C 5v). It was not that she shared the sentiments of these atheists and renegades, since it was only reluctantly that she found herself in their company and that Jesus "made her feel," only *feel*, that there truly are souls who find themselves in these darknesses of the spirit. The awareness of this drama of unbelievers would go on deepening in the heart of Thérèse, week after week and month after month, for her "trial was not to last a few days or a few weeks." When writing these words, she did not know that her trial would indeed last exactly sixteen months and twenty-five days, namely, until the hour of her death!

It was not simply a trial of a moral, affective, or psychological order, that is to say, of a passing crisis such as many Christians experience in our day, but truly a trial of a theological order, imposed by God to purify her faith of whatever was "too natural," as she herself will recognize. It was meant to take away, she says, "everything that could be a natural satisfaction in her desire for heaven" (C 7v).

For Thérèse, as for every Christian, the motivations of faith are not all supernatural; there are, more or less and almost always, some natural elements mixed in that take away some of its purity, its strength, and therefore its capacity for "seizing" God as he is, whence arise those necessary purifications that Saint John of the Cross has so masterfully described in the *Ascent* and *Dark Night*.

But the Lord, in his pedagogy full of wisdom and mercy, only imposes these purifications on those who consent to them, and does it only after a long and patient preparation. That is what Thérèse understood when she wrote: "He did not send me this trial until the moment I was capable of bearing it," adding, "A little earlier I believe it would have plunged me into a state of discouragement" (C 7v). Notice that she does not say "of doubt" but only "of discouragement"!

That is because her "faith, living and clear" was already so firmly established that she would not have risked sinking into unbelief. Nevertheless, according to God's designs for her, she must undergo an ultimate purification like gold in the furnace (cf. 1 Cor 1:12–13), as Mary the Mother of God herself was purified.

For this reason we must affirm that, if her trial of faith arose suddenly like a tempest on calm waters, or a violent storm in a blue sky, it was preceded by some warning signs, just as her first hemoptysis (i.e., expectoration of blood) on the night of April 2 or 3, 1896, was preceded by numerous sore throats and chest pains. It is evidently not by mere chance that the manifestation of her tuberculosis practically coincided with her entry into the night of her doubts (the following night of April 5)! It was as if her physical sufferings, which were going to increase to the point of being altogether unbearable, were supposed to accompany and double her spiritual sufferings right up to the moment of her death, in order to lead her, through heroic patience, to an attitude of faith totally stripped of every trace of "natural satisfaction."

The Darkness

How strange and incomprehensible it is!" (DE 3.7.3; HLC 72). This exclamation of the Saint warns us from the outset that we cannot pretend to understand perfectly the nature and the diverse forms of the trial of faith in a soul. They remain a mystery even for the soul itself.

The life of faith is a reality both simple and complex. Simple in its movement stretched out toward God. Complex in the elements of which it is composed: the interior and exterior world of the person. When the temptation of doubt arises in a soul, faith is attacked at its roots, and this radical calling into question has its repercussions in all of life, and all the more strongly in cases where the tree of faith has spread its roots and branches more deeply into all existence. It is not surprising that these temptations, since they follow the movement of life, appear to develop without any logical order. Not surprising either is the impression of incoherence and difficulty for those suffering through them, who are trying to understand and to make others understand what they are going through. "This spiritual trial…is impossible to understand," insists Thérèse (DE 21/26.5.10; HLC 48). So it is with prudence and modesty that we will attempt to describe and then to analyze the personal combat the Saint lived through.

In Manuscript C, composed in June 1897, three months before her death, Thérèse uses a comparison to try to explain her state: "I imagine I was born in a country that is covered in thick fog. I never had the experience of contemplating the joyful appearance of nature flooded and transformed by the brilliance of the sun" (C 5v). This is sound theological doctrine, proposed in simple terms. Faith is already by itself a night for the intellect, which cannot have evidence of divine realities. They, "these marvels" of which we have heard people speak, are not "an invented story" but "a reality, for the King of the Fatherland of the bright sun actually came and lived for thirty-three years in the land of darkness" (C 5v). Thus the inherent obscurity of faith is enlightened by a certitude comparable to a "bright torch" (C 6r). Saint Peter spoke of a "lamp shining in a dark place" (2 Pt 1:19). The trial consists then of this night of faith being transformed into total night: the temptations against faith have the effect of hiding the little flame or obscuring its light by the thick veil of doubts: "Then suddenly the fog which surrounds me becomes more dense; it penetrates my soul and envelops it" explains Thérèse (C 6v).

In a letter to Sister Marie of the Sacred Heart, the Saint had described the same phenomenon by comparing herself to a "little bird assailed by the storm." "It seems it should believe in the existence of no other thing except the clouds surrounding it," but "it knows that beyond the clouds its bright Sun still shines on" (B 5r).

Faith is still there, but the soul has ceased to perceive its "Invisible Light" (B 5r) and no longer has "the joy of faith" (C 7r). She has the impression of having entered into a deeper night, another night. It is striking to see how much Thérèse has insisted on the depths of this new obscurity. She speaks of "thick darkness," of a "dark tunnel" (C 5v); it is not a question any longer of a "veil, but of a wall which reaches right up to the heavens" (C 7v).

In the notes collected by her sisters during her illness, we will find the same characteristic reference: "The heavens are so black that I see no break in the clouds" (DE 27.5.6; HLC 51). Thérèse speaks of a "black hole…where one can see nothing…. Ah! What darkness!" (DE 28.8.3; HLC 173). The poems she composed from April 1896 to June 1897 speak clearly: "Without support yet with support, / Living without

Light, in darkness" (PN 30); "My Jesus smiles at me when I sigh to Him. / Then I no longer feel my trial of faith" (PN 32), "When in my heart the storm arises" (PN 36).

The confidences that stand out as landmarks in the *Last Conversations* show us that Thérèse will undergo this trial until she breathes her last. She notes, however: "It is true that at times a very small ray of the sun comes to illumine my darkness, and then the trial ceases for *an instant*" (C 7v), only to return a moment later, doubled in intensity.

These lulls in the storm are due to the momentary disappearance of the tyranny of her doubts: "It seems to be suspended" (DE 9.6.2; HLC 62). At other times they are due to her sudden perception of God's tenderness, as in her chance encounter in the garden with a hen sheltering her chicks under her wings (cf. DE 7.6.1; HLC 60); a dream in which Mother Anne of Jesus reassures her of the importance of her "little way" (cf. B 2r–v); and the tender care with which she is surrounded: "It's like a ray, or rather a flash of lightning in the midst of darkness" (DE 22.7.1; HLC 106). She had fleeting moments of joy: praying to the Holy Virgin (cf. DE 1.5.2; HLC 41), listening to Sister Teresa of St. Augustine tell of the dream in which she saw Thérèse behind a "heavy black door" (DE 1.5.2) or hearing "music in the distance" (DE 13.7.17; HLC 95).

But these brief consolations never brought back the interior sweetness that she had formerly known. For instance, weeping with gratitude over a sheaf of wild flowers that a Sister had brought to her for the anniversary of her profession, Thérèse clearly states: "It's all God's tenderness towards me; exteriorly, I am loaded with gifts; interiorly, I am always in my trial" (DE 8.9; HLC 186).

Another note: if this trial had basically no let-up, it did vary in intensity. Apparently it grew progressively more intense until it reached at times a maximum force: "I'm admiring the material heavens; the other is closed against me more and more" (DE 8.8.2; HLC 141). We note two crucial moments in particular: the night of August 15 to August 16, 1897, during which Thérèse's own sisters, very upset, feared that she would succumb to her temptations and prayed explicitly for her in this regard; and also, during the final hours of her life, when Thérèse exclaims: "It's the agony, really, without any mixture of consolation" (DE 9.30; HLC 204).

One imagines that the feelings the Saint experienced at the outset of her trial were those of astonishment and surprise. She did not expect it. It happened so "suddenly" (C 6v). Feelings of strangeness, of its incomprehensibility to herself and others, and then of solitude: "God alone can understand me" (DE 11.7.1; HLC 87). Feelings of discouragement (cf. DE 4.8.4; HLC 132), of anguish (DE 20.8.10; HLC 157). Seated at "a table filled with bitterness," she eats "the bread of sorrow" and suffers an unspeakable inner torment (cf. C 6r).

Temptations

If we now seek to question her on the exact nature of her "spiritual trial," we hear her respond that it consisted mainly of "thoughts," of doubts against faith (cf. DE 7.8.4; 10.8.7; HLC 140, 145). We must assuredly include those "extravagant thoughts" (DE 4.6.3; HLC 57) about which she gives no explanation. Although Thérèse shows a great reserve, she does give us some examples of those suggestions looming up from the darkness: "You are dreaming about the light, about a fatherland embalmed in the sweetest perfumes; you are dreaming about the *eternal* possession of the Creator of all these marvels; you believe that one day you will walk out of this fog that surrounds you! Advance, advance; rejoice in death which will give you not what you hope for but a night still more profound, the night of nothingness" (C 6v). She probably was more explicit still with her confessor, Abbé Youf,

who answered her: "Don't dwell on these, it's very dangerous" (DE 6.6.2; HLC 58).

We cannot compare one soul with another, especially in the area of faith where each individual journeys toward God by ways proper to him or her. The points about which the voice from the darkness provokes doubt are certainly those closest to Thérèse's heart, those in which she had, so to speak, invested her entire confidence. Otherwise, the suspicions of doubt would not have been able to gnaw at her. It would be interesting to confirm how well the themes evoked here, in brief, correspond to Thérèse's privileged universe: light, the "fatherland," perfumes, eternal possession of God, creation and its marvels, earthly "exile" and its sadness.

"Advance, advance," the voice whispers to her. The entire Thérèsian dynamism of life conceived as a march and even a "race" toward God is here taken up again with cynicism in an invitation to joy, to the false joy of a proud heart that does not want to hope in anything and is satisfied with nothingness: "Rejoice in death which will give you not what you hope for but a night still more profound, the night of nothingness." In this diabolical counsel, we also note a parody on Thérèse's habitual way of being, which knew how to transform her failures, her disappointments, and her pains into victories through the humble and cheerful acceptance of God's will.

All things considered, the main thrust of the temptation was aimed at destroying completely the profound movement of the "little way" by renouncing the unconditional trust that is its foundation. Thérèse understood this by remarking that the accursed voice was "mocking her." We should probably rather speak here of cynicism, of malicious irony. Elsewhere the Saint will compare these suggestions to "ugly serpents…hissing in my ears" (DE 9.6.2; HLC 62).

Mother Agnes gives the following account:

> One evening, in the infirmary, she was drawn to confide her troubles to me more than she usually did. She had

not yet opened up in this way on this subject. Up until then, I had known of her trial of faith only vaguely: "If you only knew what frightful thoughts obsess me! Pray very much for me in order that I do not listen to the devil who wants to persuade me about so many lies. It's the reasoning of the worst materialists which is imposed upon my mind: Later, unceasingly making new advances, science will explain everything naturally; we shall have the absolute reason for everything that exists and that still remains a problem, because there remain very many things to be discovered, etc., etc. I want to do good after my death, but I will not be able to do so! It will be as it was for Mother Geneviève: We expected to see her work miracles, and complete silence fell over her tomb." (DE II,10.8.7; HLC 257–258)

Here we perceive that Thérèse was not so cut off from the world that she was completely unaware of the discussions raised about scientific progress in her day. This temptation took aim at the Saint's conviction that here below, it is impossible to arrive at "seeing" the truth about everything (cf. DE 11.8.5; HLC 146). Not that she denied science unlimited power in the discovery of the secrets of the universe, but she repudiated the notion that this progress must dispense with faith. It is this insinuation that Thérèse rejects both as a lie and as violence perpetrated against her freedom: These "frightful thoughts" are in fact presented to her in an obsessive manner, through persuasion, under the form of a reasoning that "is imposed" on her mind.

Another negation, attempting to touch her to the heart, is that her desire to do good on earth after her death would be in vain. As proof, the "saintly" Mother Geneviève, foundress of the Lisieux Carmel, did not give any sign of her being in heaven: complete silence at her tomb! What good, then, all these sacrifices, her entire youth lost for a generous plan that is only a dream! To pretend to come back to help others, what an illusion!

Mother Agnes reports another confidence of Thérèse about the contents of her thoughts against faith: "Last evening, I was seized with a veritable anguish and my darkness increased. I do not know what

accursed voice said to me: 'Are you sure of being loved by God? Did he come and tell you? It is not the opinion of creatures that will justify you before him'" (DE p. 572). This temptation did not have the mocking tone of the first but, like the others, touched a sensitive point with Thérèse: God's love for her. In the same vein, Père Godefroy Madelaine, who heard the Saint's confession in June 1896, testifies: "Her soul was passing through a spiritual crisis in which she believed that she was damned" (PA 595).

According to this confessor, what was thrown into question for Thérèse was God's love, to the point where she felt herself rejected by him and "damned." But damnation presupposes an afterlife, an eternity of pain concurrent with an eternity of blessedness! That means she still believed in the existence of heaven. Yet according to Manuscript C this is precisely what Thérèse was tempted to deny. What awaits her is the "night of nothingness" (C 6v). If after death there is nothing, there will no longer be a heaven or a hell. How then to reconcile these contradictory statements?

We should note that the testimonies of Père Madelaine and Mother Agnes refer to times before the writing of Manuscript C (June 1897), in which the Saint explains what she means. We have already noted that Thérèse's trial of faith has evolved progressively while growing in intensity. We have an example of it here. With time, the temptation becomes more radical. In July 1897, she will say: "It's upon heaven that everything bears" (DE 3.7.3; HLC 72). What exactly does heaven mean for her? It seems it is essentially eternal blessedness, life with God. But doesn't that include the very existence of God? Certain considerations lead us to believe that she did not suffer doubts about God's existence, but only about life after death.

In brief, God would exist, but would not be concerned about human beings! "But if my suffering was really unknown to You, which is impossible…" (C 7r). This may appear illogical. How can she affirm that it is impossible? One day she said to Mother Agnes: "It's impossible for me to confide to you everything about the anguish I'm suffering; I would be afraid of offending the good God by expressing such thoughts in words. I who love him so much! But all this is incoherent" (DE p. 451). The incoherence of her inner state appears in a deposition of Sister Teresa of St. Augustine at the Diocesan Process: "'If you only knew,' she said to me, 'in what darkness I am plunged. I do not believe in eternal life. It seems to me that after this mortal life, there is nothing anymore: Everything has disappeared for me; *nothing remains for me but love*' " (PO 402).

"Nothing remains for me but love!" Can God's love subsist without faith? How can a house remain standing when it no longer has any foundations? Yet it is all but certain that in this torment, Thérèse's love for God has undergone no eclipse. That provokes her astonishment: "Must one love God and the Blessed Virgin so much and have these thoughts!" (DE 10.8.7; HLC 145). She had to have been seeking an explanation for this phenomenon, since she proposes this response, found while reading a commentary on the *Imitation:* "Our Lord enjoyed all the delights of the Trinity when He was in the garden of Olives, and still His agony was none the less cruel. It's a mystery, but I assure you that I understand something about it by what I'm experiencing myself" (DE 6.7.4; HLC 75).

Was she aware that she had there the proof of the firmness and vitality of her faith? If it is true, as Mgr. Combes says, that "Thérèse's charity saved her faith," we can also reverse the proposition and say that Thérèse's faith saved her charity! It is her "living faith" in its existential unity that resisted the assaults of doubt. Perhaps it is fitting to say simply that we find ourselves in the presence of an aspect of the mystical character of every trial of faith, and in particular of the mystery of the Thérèsian soul.

The term "combat," used by Thérèse, defines well her reactions under the assaults of doubt. Not content with undergoing the torment passively, she struggled valiantly, adopting one after the other, or simultaneously, four "systems" of defense: resistance without concession, the "flight" tactic, affirmation of her faith, and abandonment to God.

Resistance without Concession

The image that spontaneously comes to mind when evoking the attitude of Thérèse during her night of doubts is that of a solidly defended fortress. It is first suggested to us by the military vocabulary that she uses so freely—soldier, war, arms, etc. (and we note this especially from the end of 1896 onward)—but most of all by the strength of soul that she manifests throughout this entire formidable trial. We could speak of an immovable fortress, set on a rock. Nothing will prevent her "from remaining there.... No, she will not change her place" (cf. B 5r).

Her steadfastness does not falter. At most, she one day reveals the violence of the attacks she is undergoing by letting rise to her lips, despite herself, the obsessive suspicion with which "the enemy" is tormenting her, saying to Sister Agnes: "If there was no eternal life.... but there is one perhaps... and *it's even certain!*" (DE 5.9.1; HLC 184). This is not a breach in her fortified wall, because she repudiates this insidious "perhaps" as soon as it slips out. She does not want to concede anything to her "adversary," not the smallest particle of truth received and held in faith. She resists with all the strength that is in her. One morning after a particularly distressful night she discloses: "I repelled many temptations" (DE 8.6.1; HLC 135).

Thérèse's resistance without concession appears all the more admirable since her trial of faith was long and violent and had come upon her so suddenly. She had not known that slow invasion of twilight in which the truths of faith are dimmed little by little, finally giving place to nightfall without the person being aware of it, as happened to the philosopher Renan. It was impossible that such a thing could happen unexpectedly to Thérèse: impossible because of her vigilance and the vigor of her faith. "I am like the watchman observing the enemy from the highest turret of a strong castle" (C 23r). Besides the trials of faith of which we have spoken, the numerous sufferings she had to face throughout the course of her life, especially her father's illness, trained her in spiritual combat and strengthened her more and more in her faith in God and in an unfailing trust in him.

True, Thérèse had the advantage of an exceptional faith milieu, but to be strengthened, to acquire the vigor and maturity we see in her, to remain "living and clear" (C 5r), how could her faith *not* have had to combat those endless temptations to doubt and unbelief, to which every life, even the most protected, is subject? She who "never sought anything but the truth" (DE 9.30; HLC 205) did not fail to encounter certain difficulties of which her observations of the world around her, her personal reflections on the teaching she had received, and her own discoveries had made her aware. It does seem that she discerned certain problems. For instance, she regrets that she herself cannot throw light on translations of Scripture that she judges to be defective (DE 8.4.5; HLC 132). We know how avidly she sought information about the faith throughout her life, even before the catechism lessons of Abbé Domin who used to call her "his little doctor" (A 37v). Abbé Arminjon's book brought her a deep knowledge of "the mysteries of the future life" (A 47r). But it was the Gospel above all that she never grew tired of assimilating.

This solid and substantial formation, exempt from mere curiosities or intellectual subtleties, constituted the living treasure that she defended with an uncompromising vigilance. The jealously guarded integrity of her faith corresponded to the totality of her commitment in faith. Thérèse had staked everything on God. Her faith, constantly fostered, became an integral part of her entire being and her very substance, and had acquired the vigor of a healthy organism, very alive and

in full flower. Not surprising, then, that it gives the impression of an impregnable citadel. Its deep rooting in Christ and its vigilance gave to her faith that stability of the house built on rock of which the Gospel speaks (cf. Mt 7:24–27).

Flight Tactic

A second "system" that Thérèse adopts in order to cope with her temptations against faith is that of flight. "At each new occasion of combat, when my enemy provokes me, I conduct myself bravely. Knowing it is cowardly to enter into a duel, I turn my back on my adversaries without deigning to look them in the face" (C 7r).

Why is it cowardice to fight in a duel? Ought it not to be, on the contrary, an act of courage to risk one's life? To understand Thérèse's thinking, we must put ourselves directly in her place. To accept the challenge to a duel, that is, to agree to take into consideration the doubts against faith, is to enter into the "enemy's" game, to recognize the validity of his reasonings, perhaps even to secretly satisfy "a death wish" that sometimes pushes individuals, sorely tried, to end their difficulties through suicide. To fight a duel is already to surrender, to offend God; it is already to deny God by refusing to give him one's total trust. Finally, to agree to fight a duel is cowardice because it is to betray God and to flee from the true combat that is far more grueling, since it affords nothing to nature and demands an unconditional gift of self. Is not the true combat that of Jacob wrestling with the angel? Thus Thérèse, at "every new occasion," resolutely determines to flee the compromise and inevitable surrender proposed to her. She wisely chooses "not to expose myself to combat when there was certain defeat facing me" (C 15r). In other words, she refuses to dwell on "these thoughts" (DE 10.8.7; HLC 145) that the "accursed voice" (DE p. 526) whispers to her; she "turns her back on them without deigning to look them in the face," realizing that it is not only useless but likewise "very dangerous" to examine them close up, or to discuss them in order to assess their validity. "Don't worry, I'm not going to break my 'little' head by torturing myself" (DE 6.6.2; HLC 58).

We can imagine that she had already used this "flight tactic" to protect herself from getting caught off guard by the imperceptible attacks on the integrity of her faith presented by seemingly harmless but insidious "ifs" and "perhapses." That did not keep her from passionately desiring to know more about her faith, she who never "sought anything but the truth." Her sure supernatural instinct, however, made her avoid the snares of intellectual research for its own sake, which is more captivated by its own progress than by the truth. With Thérèse there was no rashness nor bravado; she did not go out to meet the enemy, it was the enemy who came to "provoke" her. It would not have entered her head to feign her difficulties or to play a mental game, because she had a horror for "pretense" (cf. DE 7.7.4; 13.7.7: HLC 77, 92). "Ah! I am not pretending," she exclaims, "it's very true that I don't see a thing" (DE 15.8.7; HLC 150).

It is also noteworthy that her temptations never strayed into grounds external to the essence of the faith itself, such as incomplete information about revealed facts, distorted teaching, or a general calling of everything into question because of the situation of the church or society, or again because of particular cases of scandal. For a long time, her sense of faith had made her discern and grasp its substance. That is why, unable to use indirect means, her adversary challenges her directly on the essential. Thérèse knows that temptation is not a sin, that a difficulty, in order to be transformed into doubt, must pass through a free and conscious consent, through a positive acceptance. "A thousand difficulties do not make a doubt," Cardinal Newman used to say. The solicitude of the Saint not "to offend God" is such that she is even afraid to describe her inner torments: "I don't want to write any longer about

it; I fear I might blaspheme; I fear even that I have already said too much" (C 7r). "I would be afraid by expressing such thoughts in words to offend the good God" (DE p. 451).

We can see another reason for her silence and prudent reserve in her desire to spare those around her from the contagion of her doubt. Sister Geneviève will say at the Apostolic Process: "She spoke to nobody about it, for fear she would pass her own indescribable torment on to them" (PO 276). She answered Sister Marie of the Sacred Heart in a vague manner and then changed the subject of the conversation: "I understood then that she did not want to tell me anything for fear that she would make me share her temptations" (PO 813). To Père Madelaine she will say: "I tried not to make anyone suffer from my pains" (PA 559).

Finally, Thérèse was applying in this extreme case a principle that was part of her "little way": "This does us so much good, and it gives us so much strength not to speak of our troubles"(DE 5.8.10; HLC 135). She refused to feel sorry for herself or to look for pity because she was totally detached from herself.

Affirmation of Her Faith

Thérèse was not content with energetically resisting the assaults of the adversary, and she used her flight tactic only to counterattack once more, by deliberately affirming her faith in the truth that these "thoughts" were trying to lead her to deny. "At each new occasion of combat…I run toward my Jesus. I tell Him I am ready to shed my blood to the last drop to profess my faith in the existence of *heaven*" (C 7r).

Thérèse renews, as it were, the totality of her commitment to God and to Jesus, by making acts of faith, multiplied as often as necessary: "I believe I have made more acts of faith in this past year than all through my whole life" (C 7r). After a night when her temptations had been more oppressive than ever, she exclaims: "Ah!

how many acts of faith I made! (DE 6.8.1; HLC 135). Speaking to Mother Agnes about her "dark thoughts," she says: "I undergo them under duress but while undergoing them I never cease making acts of faith" (DE, p. 526; HLC 258).

During her agony, when her sufferings were at their peak, while still thwarting her temptation, we hear her make this admirable cry of faith and love: "My God! my God! You who are so good! Oh, yes, You are good! I know it" (DE 9.30; HLC 205).

At other moments when she is under less pressure Thérèse makes numerous acts of faith, whether implicit—by serenely affirming "when I am in heaven…" (cf. DE 27.6; HLC 68) or by telling God directly that she loves him (cf. DE 30.7.8; HLC 119)—or by making the sign of the cross, which demands considerable effort on her part (DE 8.31.3). She kisses her crucifix with great tenderness (cf. DE 2.8.5; 19.8.3; HLC 129, 154). She even gets to the point of "singing very strongly in her heart: *'After death life is immortal'* " (DE 15.8.7; HLC 150). She will insist on the reception of extreme unction (the sacrament of anointing the sick) and will manifest her joy in receiving it (DE 30.7.18; HLC 121). And with the same motive of exercising and strengthening her faith, she will be disappointed when Abbé Youf is unable, at one point, to come to hear her confession (DE 6.9.3; HLC 185). But her keenest suffering of all was to be deprived of the reception of the Eucharist from August 19 until her death, because of her inability to consume even the smallest particle of the host. And finally, she bears with her terrible physical sufferings and her "spiritual trial" in the thought, or rather the certitude, of working for the good of souls and also continuing this after her death: "I will come back" (DE 7.9.2; HLC 83).

Thérèse's reaction to her doubts is remarkable for its relevance and effectiveness. She knew that she could not have recourse to any outside assistance to help her to stand firm during this torment. Abbé Youf's response to her confidences, "Don't dwell on these, it is very dan-

gerous," she took with humor: "This is hardly consoling to hear" (DE 6.6.2; HLC 58). When one of the Sisters read some beautiful texts to her, thinking it would give her some comfort in her trial, she said straightforwardly: "It was as though you were singing!" (DE 23.7.2; HLC 106).

She understood that no explanation, no verification, no rational demonstration, no human proof could dispense her from the journey that only she could make: "obedience to the faith" (Rom 16:26) by renewing her total adherence to it, by resting solely on the Word of God. There was only one way of fortifying her faith, and that was by exercising it.

Far from deploring the uncomfortable situation required of every intellect to adhere to a truth for which we have no natural proof, Thérèse deliberately accepts the obscurity inherent in faith: "I've had a greater desire not to see God and the saints, and to remain in the night of faith, than others have desired to see and understand" (DE 11.8.5; HLC 146), or again: "It's only in heaven that we'll see the whole truth about everything. This is impossible on earth" (DE 4.8.5). So "while not having *the joy of the faith,*" she strives "to carry out its works at least" (cf. C 7r).

In this area, she is not able to rely on her feelings. She knows that they vary with circumstances and with our moods. Feelings, moreover, are inadequate for the encounter with God. In order to find him "in spirit and in truth," we must surrender to him in the depths of our being. In other words, the soul, through a movement of its freedom, must *want* to believe. This is the source of Thérèse's strongly determined will to welcome the gift of faith in the face of doubt's assaults: "I sing simply what I WANT TO BELIEVE" (C 7v), words that she underlined twice. Needless to point out here, she cannot be accused of "fideism."

Let us instead note two distinctive features of Thérèsian realism. In her combat, Thérèse does not equivocate. Her comeback each time is immediate: "At each new occasion of combat…I run towards my

Jesus" (C 7r). She is totally intent on this movement. Elsewhere, we see at work her capacity for making use of events and the smallest occasions for raising herself to God. She possesses the art of living in the present moment, by concentrating on it all the intensity of her being: "I'm suffering only for an instant. It's because we think of the past and the future that we become discouraged and fall into despair" (DE 19.8.10; HLC 155).

Finally, Thérèse escapes the accusation of pure voluntarism because the ultimate reason for her will to believe is nothing else but love. The revealing sign of this is the following reflection: "I'd become discouraged if I didn't have any faith! Or at least if I didn't love God!" (DE 4.8.4; HLC 132). In fact, we will discover there the secret of the indomitable energy Thérèse displayed in her combat against temptations. She struggled to keep a faith that she loved, because it had revealed love to her.

Abandonment to God

Resistance, flight, acts of faith and love, Thérèse is convinced in the depths of her being that she could not do any of them without the help of grace. She knows that faith itself is a grace, but also that God's aid is indispensable for preserving faith: "I never cease to say to God: 'O my God, I beg You, preserve me from the misfortune of being unfaithful' " (DE 7.8.4; HLC 140).

We have here a marvelous illustration of the "little way," which consists of remaining "little," that is to say, of not attributing any virtue to ourselves, of believing ourselves incapable of accomplishing by our own strength anything good whatsoever, but recognizing, on the contrary, our extreme weakness, and making use of it to look to God for everything: "I can depend on nothing, on no good works of my own in order to have confidence" (DE 6.8.4; HLC 137); "I never rely

on my own ideas; I know how weak I am" (DE 20.5.1; HLC 46).

To the degree that we remain in this attitude of poverty, of humility of heart, we are not at risk of any danger. The trials that we must necessarily undergo are always measured out by God, who does not permit us to be tempted beyond our strength in the present moment: "God gives me exactly what I can bear" (DE 25.8.2; HLC 168); "If I can't breathe, God will give me the strength to bear it" (DE 27.7.15; HLC 115).

On the other hand, catastrophe is certain from the moment we believe ourselves capable of surmounting any difficulty on our own: "I understand very well why St. Peter fell. Poor Peter, he was relying upon himself instead of relying only upon God's strength. I conclude from this experience that if I said to myself: 'O my God, you know very well I love you too much to dwell upon one single thought against the faith,' my temptations would become more violent and I would certainly succumb to them" (DE 7.8.4; HLC 140).

If she stands fast, it is solely because God is sustaining her. But this help is not felt, it is given moment by moment and in such a secret way that Thérèse has rather the impression of being completely abandoned in her night, in her physical sufferings, in her anguish of soul. She eats "the bread of sorrow" at "this table filled with bitterness at which poor sinners are eating" (C 6r). She experiences the feeling of God's absence *as if* she had fallen into unbelief. Without "the joy of faith" (C 7r), deprived of the supernatural joys of love formerly showered on her, she lives *psychologically* the dereliction of atheists. Heaven is totally closed to her. "Even the saints are abandoning me," she sighs (DE 3.7.6). Nothing her Sisters say or do to console her is able to alleviate this indescribable torment.

This interior darkness seems to question not only her adherence to the faith, but likewise the vigor of her hope, under the form of doubt about God's fidelity to his promises. That the happiness of heaven appears illusory is one facet of the temptation, but no less formidable is the other side, which consists in doubting that God is interested in the soul, in thinking that he is abandoning it to itself in its own ridiculous efforts to reach the promised goal.

What is threatened more profoundly still, in Thérèse's trial of faith, is her most precious possession: her trust in Merciful Love. This was the heart of her "little way." Thérèse had offered herself "as a victim of holocaust to God's Merciful Love" (cf. A 84r) and had received the pledge of divine acceptance in that "wound of love" (cf. DE 7.7.2; HLC 77) received shortly after (in June 1895) and by other signs. And now that reciprocity of total love seemed suddenly to cease. God withdrew into the silence of her double night. Thérèse understood that she must respond to the apparent abandonment of God by totally handing herself over, by a no less total abandonment into the hands of God: "God wills that I abandon myself like a very little child who is not disturbed by what others will do to him" (DE 15.6.1; HLC 65). This habitual disposition appears as a constant theme in her resolutions: "I abandon myself" (DE 10.6; HLC 63); "We must abandon ourselves" (e.g., DE 25.8.8; HLC 169).

It must be said that Thérèse arrived only gradually at this total abandonment to God: "This saying of Job: 'Although he should kill me, I will trust in him,' has fascinated me from my childhood. But it took me a long time before I was established in this degree of abandonment. Now I am there" (DE 7.7.3; HLC 77).

Such abandonment is not resignation but a definitive acceptance, without reservation, of God's will whatever it may be. It is a question therefore of the highest form of faith, of a naked faith stripped of any human motivation; above all, it is the purest form of a love that has reached its fullness and that expresses itself in a blind confidence in God's mercy in spite of everything that appears to contradict it. No, God is not abandoning her in the middle of her dark night, he cannot abandon her, he has never abandoned her:

"I love Him! He'll never abandon me" (DE 27.7.15: HLC 115). Thérèse repeated her certitude untiringly, and in doing this, she gave the most pertinent and most complete answer to her temptations against faith.

At no time does she give way to questioning the goodness of a God who permits her to suffer so. Instead of accusing him of indifference, or even of cruelty, as did Job, Thérèse finds a way of giving him thanks, of showing her gratitude to him for what she is going through. She makes this extraordinary exclamation: "Oh! how good God will have to be so that I can bear all I'm suffering" (DE 23.8.1; HLC 164). She knows that he is there, that it is he who is giving her the power to go so far in this "martyrdom," which is beautiful and the very "martyrdom of love" that she has so longed for. She understood that her perseverance in confidence was demonstrating her love and that God was expecting of her "further proofs...of my abandonment and love" (DE 10.7.14; HLC 87).

To a question about patience and about the saints who were present as observers in her combat, she responds: "They want to see...especially if I'm going to lose confidence...and how far I'm going to push my confidence" (DE 22.9.3; HLC 195). What motivates this total confidence are not her personal merits, nor an exemplary life, but rather the incomprehensible and infinite merciful love of God himself: "One could believe that it is because I haven't sinned that I have such great confidence in God. Really tell them, Mother, that if I had committed all possible crimes, I would always have the same confidence" (DE 11.7.6; HLC 89).

Is there need to say that Thérèse came out victorious from this long and unrelenting combat? To have proof, we need not have recourse to her influence and glory after her death. She gave us a preview of this happy outcome during the very time of her trial of faith, in her fierce resistance, her refusal to debate with her adversary, her acts of faith and love, and her unshakable confidence, as we have seen. But we have other signs from her that show she remained the mistress of operations and that in reality she was on top of the situation. Two characteristics of her conduct are particularly revealing: *her joy* and *her peace,* which are manifested in untold ways through her "playfulness," her puns, her jests, her calling up of songs from the past, her efforts to distract and amuse her Sisters. Certainly she suffered, and greatly, but as she writes to Mother Marie de Gonzague, "It is in joy and peace" (C 4v).

The *Last Conversations* are full of comments like the following: "My soul, in spite of this darkness, is in an astonishing peace" (DE 24.9.10; HLC 199). Astonishing indeed, considering the nature of the afflictions of body and soul that were crushing her. Joy and serenity radiated from her being to such a degree that her Sisters were struck by it and, sometimes forgetting that they were dealing with an extremely sick person, came to her to ask advice, to bother her with questions, or to be consoled. An astonishing peace, humanly speaking, because it had no other source than the grace present in the depths of Thérèse's heart. The result was that her last sigh, marking her triumph with a moment of ecstasy, appears as the completion of her ascent. It is understood, of course, that up to the last second she could fail, and Thérèse was well aware of this, she who mistrusted her weakness so much. But this failure was more than improbable, for, as they say, one dies as one has lived. Thérèse's death confirms her entire life, pausing on the final note that summarizes it entirely: "Oh! I love Him!... My God... I... love You!..." (DE 30.9; HLC 230).

CHAPTER THIRTEEN

The Final Illness

Bishop GUY GAUCHER, OCD

During Lent of 1896, Sister Thérèse entered the last stage of her life and a new condition: she became a patient. Certainly she knew what it meant to courageously drag herself through the day with a sore throat, persistent coughing, and bouts of fever that she endured without complaint. She had been treated for a persistent sore throat since 1894. They even consulted Doctor Francis La Néele, her cousin by marriage, even though the official physician was Doctor de Cornière, an old friend of the Martin family. However, she was not even examined.

She was treated with the means at hand. The Guérin family was seriously concerned, as the family correspondence indicates: "she [should] take care of herself *energetically*" (cf. Letter of October 21, 1894, following LT 171).

The real warning took place during Holy Week, 1896: two successive hemoptyses on Holy Thursday and Good Friday (C 4v). Rather than becoming frightened, Sister Thérèse, in the momentum of the glorious year of 1895 and of her Act of Offering of June 9, saw in this a "call of the Bridegroom." She had never wished to die young, yet always had the presentiment that she would. "I sense my exile is about to end!" she reveals in her canticle, "Living on Love" (PN 17), written spontaneously. In April 1895, she told Sister Teresa of Saint Augustine: "I will die soon" (PO, 1945).

After these incidents she was examined (through the grille) by Doctor la Néele, who detected nothing serious. In fact, tuberculosis was already at work. It was active in the monastery and elsewhere. The extern, Sister Marie Antoinette, had died from tuberculosis on November 4, 1896. After Thérèse, others would follow the same path, including the young Sister Marie of the Eucharist, Thérèse's first cousin and daughter of a pharmacist, who also died of tuberculosis on April 14, 1905, at the age of thirty-five, despite the most modern treatments of the time.

Tuberculosis was a fearful scourge that killed about 150,000 people each year between 1886 and 1906. The age group most affected was between twenty-seven and thirty-five. The province of Calvados was particularly afflicted. Each week the town of Lisieux saw the burial of another young person carried away by the terrible sickness that sowed terror and would not truly be arrested until appropriate antibiotics were discovered in 1944.

Progressively More Solitary

Beginning in Lent 1897, Sister Thérèse became seriously ill. On April 4, Sister Marie of the Eucharist wrote to her family (the Guérins) that her cousin had indigestion and fever every day until three o'clock in the afternoon. Doctor de Cornière came to see the sick woman, for now there was vomiting, intense chest pain, and episodic spitting up of blood. The long fits of coughing exhausted her.

Her solitude deepened. Gradually, she abandoned community exercises: in May she could no longer help Sister Marie of Saint Joseph in the laundry; she did some sewing to compensate for this. On Wednesday, May 26, she could no longer participate in the Rogation Day procession in the garden. She was relieved of her position as assistant to the novice mistress, Mother Marie de Gonzague. Thérèse was also obliged to renounce the choral recitation of the office. At the end of May, the beginning of June, she was no longer seen in the refectory. Nor was she able to attend the tiring periods of recreation.

She dragged herself to Mass, though not every day. One morning when she returned from it exhausted, she was found in her cell seated on her little bench; she said to Mother Agnes of Jesus: "This is not suffering too much to gain one Communion!" (DE II, 21/26.5.6; HLC 255). It sometimes took her a half-hour to return to her cell, and it required unheard of efforts for her to undress herself.

She was often seen in her cell trying to make good use of her time, and she went to the garden when the

The Léo Taxil — Diana Vaughan Affair

Bishop Guy Gaucher, OCD

On Easter Monday, April 19, 1897, during a press conference in the Geographical Society's hall in Paris, Charles Jogand-Pagès, alias Léo Taxil (1854–1907) confessed to a twelve-year hoax. It was the epilogue to a very strange and intricate story, involving the battles between the Catholic Church and Freemasonry, as well as the "genius" of a hoaxer from Marseilles who had feigned conversion to the Catholic faith.

Amazingly, this sad episode in the clerical and anticlerical battles of the second half of the nineteenth century drew a young and unknown Carmelite nun into the deception, and added to her severe trial of faith.

Jogand-Pagès began life as a deserter and thief, before inventing some spectacular hoaxes in Marseilles and Switzerland.

Under the name of Léo Taxil, he produced some 130 pamphlets in the "Anticlerical Library," and a newspaper, *l'Anticlérical.* In 1882 he was expelled from the Freemasons. Bankrupt, he converted in 1885 and wrote *Confessions d'un libre penseur* (Confessions of a Free Thinker), which went through 45 editions. In 1884, Pope Leo XIII published the encyclical *Humanum Genus,* against Freemasonry. The battles raged.

Then appeared the *Mémoires d'une ex-palladiste* (Memoirs of an Ex-Palatine), by a certain Diana Vaughan, who had been converted from Freemasonry and satanic practices through the influence of Joan of Arc. The Catholic press was fascinated with these revelations, as were many religious journals. Mother Agnes suggested to her sister Thérèse to write a poem for Diana Vaughan. No inspiration came, but Thérèse did send her a photograph of herself as Joan of Arc, with a few lines attached. Diana wrote back.

In June of 1896, Thérèse wrote a short play for her community, "The Triumph of Humility" (RP 7), which speaks of the devil and Diana Vaughan. During the summer, she read the convert's *Neuvaine eucharistique* (Eucharistic Novena).

But some were skeptical. At the end of September 1896 an anti-masonic congress was held at Trent. A Roman commission distanced itself from Taxil. Sister Thérèse expressed her reservations when Diana Vaughan attacked an Italian bishop.

Finally came the press conference of April 19, 1897. All awaited the first public appearance of Diana Vaughan. But it was Léo Taxil who arrived, revealing the deception: he had invented everything about Diana Vaughan, and fooled the Catholic Church for twelve years. His conversion was also another fraud.

The meeting was stormy and the next day Catholic newspapers denounced the imposter. A terse paragraph in the newspaper *Le Normand* threw the Lisieux Carmel into consternation, saying that during the meeting Taxil had projected a picture allegedly of a Carmelite nun dressed as Joan of Arc. For once, Taxil had not lied. It was Sister Thérèse!

One can imagine the Sisters' humiliation. Thérèse threw "Diana's" letter onto the garden's manure pile, and removed Diana Vaughan's name from all her writings (RP 7 and the beginning of Manuscript B).

To have been thus deceived (along with many bishops, priests, and religious) during her night of faith was very painful for her. She let none of it show through. But we can be sure that Thérèse gathered into her prayers "the impious" Léo Taxil, who had "abused graces" (cf. C 5v), just as she was willing to remain alone in the darkness so that unbelievers might receive light.

weather permitted. The prescriptions of May called for vesicatories, painful ignipunctures, sedatives, and cough syrup.

Her solitude left her time to compose what was dear to her heart: in this month of Mary, she wrote a long poem on the Virgin (PN 54). She did not want to die without saying what she thought of her Mother, "more Mother than Queen." She saw in Mary the Christian who faithfully followed her son Jesus, even in the night of faith, along the ordinary way. By now Thérèse herself was habitually living in this night of

faith, as certain discreet allusions to Mother Agnes indicate: "this spiritual trial…is impossible to understand" (DE 21/26.5; HLC 48); "I felt the agonies of death…and that with no consolation!" (DE 4.6.2; HLC 56).

In response to a challenge set by Mother Henriette of the Paris Carmel, she wrote "An Unpetalled Rose," a brief, poignant poem, and a kind of testament (PN 51, May 19, 1897). Like the rose that decorates the altar and embellishes Jesus' feast and then sheds its petals, Sister Thérèse gives herself "to be no more":

Jesus, for your love I have squandered my life,
My future.
In the eyes of men, a rose forever *withered,*
I must *die!* (PN 51, 4)

To her spiritual brothers, Fathers Bellière and Roulland, she spoke of her approaching death. All hope of a cure seemed lost. In early June the situation worsened.

To Write Again: Manuscript C

On the evening of May 30, Mother Agnes learned that her young sister had hemoptyses the preceding year. She was deeply shaken and went to see Mother Marie de Gonzague late on the night of June 2. Mother Agnes informed her prioress of the existence of a notebook written by Thérèse at her own request, and suggested to her that Thérèse complete the account of her life, for this would be useful when the time came to write her obituary. Mother Marie de Gonzague agreed, on condition that the text be addressed to her. The next day, Mother Agnes gave her sister a little black notebook with the order to write about love of neighbor, about her spiritual brothers, about whatever she wanted.

Once again Sister Thérèse obeyed. Her state, however, did not permit her great concentration. Sometimes in her cell, sometimes in the garden (constantly disturbed by her sisters in this case), often suffering, she would write a few pages each day, without outline or erasures, "as though I were fishing with a line; I write whatever comes to the end of my pen" (DE 11.6.2; HLC 63). She would have to stop after filling thirty-six pages in a handwriting that became progressively more difficult; she finished in pencil, exhausted. She then went into the infirmary on the ground floor; she would never leave it again.

She did not know that she had written a spiritual masterpiece that would travel around the world. It

ended with the words "with confidence and love," two key words of her spirituality. Hardly speaking of her illness, she gives us precious confidences about her past and her life at the time: her Offering to Merciful Love, her trial of faith and, later, the secret of community life lived in the truest charity. The pages on her way of exercising her responsibility as novice mistress show that her pedagogy was remarkable, and once again well in advance of her times.

On Saturday June 5, the community and family began a novena to Our Lady of Victories, as in May of 1883. On June 7, Sister Geneviève took three photographs as a final remembrance of her exhausted sister, but in spite of all efforts the sick woman, suffering with fever, could not smile.

Doctor de Cornière visited her at least on June 11, 12, and 24. On June 30, the sick woman met for the last time with the Guérin family in the speakroom; they were leaving on vacation for their property (la Musse) near Evreux. On July 2, the first Friday of the month, she adored the Blessed Sacrament in the oratory. This was the last time she would be able to do so, for her condition was deteriorating gravely and quickly.

Further Hemoptyses: July 6 to August 5

For twenty-nine days, with some respites, she lost blood at least twenty times, night and day. This situation was indeed agonizing for her and those around her. During this period, Doctor de Cornière visited her at least eighteen times. Curiously, on July 7, he declared: "It's not tuberculosis, this is a problem in the lungs, a real pulmonary congestion."

Did he make an erroneous diagnosis? According to the prescriptions, it does not seem so, for they suggest the ordinary remedies known at the time for this disease. It is possible, however, that the doctor, a longtime friend of the Carmelites, deliberately avoided saying the taboo word, "tuberculosis," the object of fear and sometimes also of scorn. At that time tuberculosis was considered the illness of the poor and less fortunate.

The doctor added that "only two percent" survive in the state Thérèse was in. In fact, she was extremely weak. She could not even bring her hand to her mouth; it would fall. She could no longer take nourishment on account of the vomiting.

They brought her to the infirmary on a mattress. Neither the doctor nor the superior thought the last sacraments were yet called for. Furthermore, Thérèse found the strength to continue to joke, so they thought she could not be dying.

From July 27 to 30, she experienced intense suffering. She was suffocating. They made her breathe ether, with no effect. Canon Maupas decided to give her extreme unction, for they did not think she would last the night. In the little neighboring cell everything was prepared for an imminent death.

These terrible sufferings would last until August 6; the tuberculosis invaded the right lung. Henceforth Sister Thérèse would no longer leave the first floor infirmary which measured five meters by four (about sixteen and a half by thirteen feet). Here, on August 5, her beloved picture of the Holy Face from the nuns' choir had been installed, much to Thérèse's delight (DE 7.8.7; HLC 134).

Her iron bed was set in a corner, next to the window covered by long brown curtains. Between two doors, one of which opened to the cloister, they placed the Virgin of the Smile who watched over her. The patient could see it in front of her.

Thérèse was cared for by Sister Saint Stanislaus, the official infirmarian. Given her advanced age, she often delegated Sister Geneviève, who was happy to take care of her sister even if she did not always have the desired sensitivity.

Mother Agnes of Jesus received from the prioress, Mother Marie de Gonzague, the permission to watch her sister during Matins, and she noted her words on little pieces of paper. She did not realize that they would be precious in the future, but her pain as "little mother" was relieved by the "crumbs" she affectionately gathered.

Other visits were relatively rare; they wanted to spare the sick woman, so it was necessary to close her door to the novices.

Obviously Thérèse could not continue to write her manuscript in the state she was in. The last pages were written in pencil, for she no longer had the strength to hold her pen. Nonetheless, out of love, she would yet write long letters to her spiritual brother, the seminarian Maurice Bellière, who was on vacation in Langrune-sur-Mer, a farewell letter to Father Roulland, the missionary in China, two letters to the Guérin family, and a few short notes to her sisters.

She no longer had the strength for reading. At her bedside were the Gospels, the *Imitation of Christ,* and a one volume work containing St. John of the Cross's *Spiritual Canticle* and *Living Flame of Love.* Thérèse would be satisfied to mark in pencil those passages where she saw herself.

Though they thought she was at death's door, her condition became stable for a few days, from August 6 to 15. It was vacation time. Doctor de Cornière left with his family for Plombières. He had noticed that the left lung was deteriorating, and prescribed some "little remedies." After hesitating and consulting the doctor, the Guérins left for Vichy where Uncle Isidore received treatment at the spas.

Intense Sufferings: August 15 to 27

Rapidly the patient's sufferings on the left side of the chest became intolerable; her feet swelled. Mother Marie de Gonzague agreed to send for Doctor Francis La Néele in Caen. By his marriage to Jeanne Guérin, he was first cousin to Thérèse. He would soon write to his father-in-law of his emotion in seeing his

The "Last Conversations"

Bishop Guy Gaucher, OCD

During the time Mother Agnes of Jesus watched over her sick sister, she would hastily note down her words, sometimes in a telegraphic style. First of all these were for her own consolation, because with great sadness the "little Mother" was watching her young sister die. When she realized that Thérèse was dying, she also thought about the obituary "circular letter." Because of this she asked questions about Thérèse's past, her thoughts, and her ideas about religious life.

In total, Mother Agnes collected about 850 sayings. In addition, Sister Marie of the Sacred Heart (Thérèse's godmother and oldest sister) and Sister Geneviève (Thérèse's sister Céline) also noted down some of her words.

After Thérèse's death, Mother Agnes, preparing the book that became *Story of a Soul,* used these notes in writing Chapter XII, which tells the story of the young Carmelite's final illness and death.

Around 1904–1905 she recopied and organized all these papers in a "large black notebook," later destroyed. She would draw from it to write five "green notebooks" that would be the basis of her deposition on this period in her sister's life for the Ordinary Process (i.e., the diocesan investigation in view of possible beatification) in 1909–1910.

Not until 1922 did Mother Agnes write a very complete "Yellow Notebook," undoubtedly for her own use. After St. Thérèse's canonization (1925),

she published a very abbreviated anthology of Thérèse's last conversations, entitled *Novissima Verba* (with 362 sayings), in 1927.

In 1971 a team of researchers with access to the Lisieux Carmel's archives published the *Derniers Entretiens* (Last Conversations) in their different versions (four in all), but giving priority to the "Yellow Notebook." This edition contains complementary materials very important for understanding Thérèse.

Certainly these texts were not taken down on a tape recorder, and they bear the stamp of Mother Agnes of Jesus. But the publication of a synopsis of the four versions, in the *Dernièrs paroles* volume of the *Nouvelle Edition du Centenaire* (1992), allows us to compare the texts and critically examine them.

We cannot give these sayings the same weight as the writings of St. Thérèse herself, but to deprive ourselves completely of them would diminish our knowledge of Thérèse as sick, human, suffering, jovial, praying, poor, and at times sublime in her complete simplicity. Mother Agnes would not have been able to invent many of the lines recorded in her "Yellow Notebook." On the contrary, she strongly censored *Novissima Verba,* not wishing to hand over to the general public in 1927 these "intimacies," these "little joys," which reveal the Saint's humanity and bring her closer to all those suffering sickness and distress.

cloistered cousin. "I kissed our little saint on the forehead for you, Mamma, and the whole family. I had asked permission, as a matter of form, from Mother Prioress, and without waiting for the answer that perhaps the Rule forbade it, I took what was your right.… The right lung is totally lost, filled with tubercles in the process of softening. The left lung was affected in its lower part" (letter of August 26, 1897; HLC 289–290). Sister Marie of the Eucharist, his sister-in-law, wrote to her father: "[Francis] told us that the tuberculosis has reached its last stage" (letter of August 17, 1897; HLC 286).

Thus the terrible taboo word had been pronounced: it left no illusion about a possible cure. On Thursday, August 19, the feast of Saint Hyacinth, Thérèse received Communion for the last time. She offered this Communion for the ex-Father Hyacinth Loyson (1827–1912), former provincial of the

Discalced Carmelite friars, who had left the church in 1869. He had denied papal infallibility (which would be proclaimed in 1870) and had married an American convert from Protestantism with whom he had a son. He founded a Gallican Catholic Church. The scandal had been enormous in France and in Europe, for he was very well known, a friend of Newman and Montalembert. His name was proscribed in all the Carmels. Nonetheless from 1891 on, Sister Thérèse called him her brother (LT 129). She prayed for him until her death and this last Communion was the proof of it.

At that time, the ceremonial for Communion of the sick was difficult and complicated. Thérèse was in such a state of weakness that she could no longer endure it, thus she could no longer receive Communion. Some of the sisters were scandalized by this. She spent the day of August 20 in anguish and tears.

Beginning Sunday, August 22, the patient entered an even more intense phase of suffering. She admitted: "We don't realize what it is to suffer like this. No, we must experience it" (DE 22.8; HLC 162). It was "a day of continual suffering" (ibid.).

Then began the terrible intestinal pain, the source of much humiliation for the patient. Later they would speak of "gangrene of the intestines" with all its consequences. These were pains to make one cry out and Thérèse could not hold back her sighs.

To make matters worse, at the time when she would have most needed a physician, Doctor La Néele went on a national pilgrimage to Lourdes with his wife and Léonie. It was no doubt during this period that the patient, who was suffering enough "to lose one's mind," stated that "if she did not have faith, she would not have hesitated a single moment to take her own life" (PA 204).

Nonetheless, on Friday, August 27, a sudden respite unexpectedly occurred. While previously everyone thought she was dying, now she experienced a new remission that would last nineteen days. To please her they moved her bed to the center of the infirmary, so she could see the splendor of the summer garden from her window.

The Last "Good" Period: August 28 to September 13

Although the intense sufferings ended, the fever, thirst, congestion, and weakness remained. On Monday, August 30, 1897, Thérèse was brought to the cloister on a rolling bed where Sister Geneviève photographed her. This would be the last photograph of Thérèse alive. Sister Geneviève rolled her bed to the door leading to the choir; Thérèse prayed and contemplated the Blessed Sacrament for the last time.

On the same day, Doctor La Néele, back from Lourdes, visited his cousin. She had only half a lung left

with which to breathe. With his typical directness, he reproached Mother Marie de Gonzague for not calling for a doctor every day, given Thérèse's condition. He returned the next day and again, for the last time, on September 5.

During these days of remission the gravely ill woman had renewed interest in life; she had unexpected desires for the meals the Guérin family tried to provide: roast with purée, charlotte, a chocolate éclair, artichokes, and cream cheese.

On Wednesday, September 8, they celebrated the seventh anniversary of her profession, and on September 11 she still had the strength to make two crowns of cornflowers, which she offered to the Virgin of the Smile.

Doctor de Cornière returned from vacation on Friday, September 10. He admitted that Sister Thérèse's condition concerned him. The next day she was worse.

The Last Days and Death Agony: September 17 to 30

Doctor de Cornière judged correctly. On September 14, he thought that Sister Thérèse would live only two weeks more. In order to remake her bed, the robust Sister Aimée of Jesus lifted her under her arms; Thérèse was so weak they thought she would die immediately.

On September 20, Mother Marie de Gonzague noticed how emaciated the young Carmelite was; this condition so frightened her that she exclaimed: "How thin this girl is...." "A skeleton!" replied Thérèse, who took advantage of every opportunity to make those around her smile and to make the situation less dramatic. On the following days she could not breathe. Her lungs did not function. She was suffocating: "Mamma [her sister Pauline]!...earth's air is denied me, when will God give me the air of heaven?" (DE 28.9.1; HLC 200–201).

The two last days, Wednesday, September 29, and Thursday, September 30, were literally the days of her death agony. On Wednesday, the death rattle began. At six o'clock in the morning the community, pressed into the little infirmary, intoned the prayers for the dying.

The patient remained lucid. She was given—by way of unusual relief—a spoonful of morphine syrup from time to time. Doctor de Cornière visited her for the last time. Thérèse asked Mother Marie de Gonzague: "Mother, is this the agony?... Never will I know how to die!" (DE 29.9; HLC 201).

That evening Father Faucon, the Carmel's extraordinary confessor, heard Sister Thérèse's last confession, since the regular chaplain, Father Youf, was himself seriously ill. (He would only survive his penitent by a week). As he was leaving the infirmary, Father Faucon said to the prioress: "What a beautiful soul! She seems to be confirmed in grace."

That night, the patient could not be left alone. Sisters Marie of the Sacred Heart and Geneviève watched over her. Thérèse slept very little. She prayed to the Holy Virgin and, rather than disturb her sisters, held a glass in her hand.

Mother Agnes of Jesus slept in the neighboring cell. In the morning, the three Martin sisters surrounded their young sister who gasped: "This is the death agony with no mixture of consolation."

The afternoon of September 30 was dramatic. Around 2:30 P.M., Thérèse raised herself on her bed with great strength. Her voice was "clear and strong." Her hands were blue. She prayed: "O my God! Have pity on me!... O Good Blessed Virgin, come to my aid!... My God, I am suffering!... The chalice is filled to the brim!... I will never know how to die!" (DE 309; cf. HLC 203–207).

Around 4:30 P.M., a terrible rattle pierced her chest and every part of her body trembled. Her cheeks and clothing were soaked with perspiration. She uttered little cries.

About seven o'clock, Mother Marie de Gonzague sent away the community who had been assembled around Thérèse for two hours, praying. Mother Agnes of Jesus, frightened by the death agony of her little sister, withdrew and went to pray before the little statue of the Sacred Heart in the stairwell, asking that her sister not despair.

The prioress saw the end was near. She had the infirmary bell rung and cried out; "Open all the doors!" The sisters knelt around the bed. The dying woman, holding her crucifix, pronounced distinctly: "O! I love Him." Then: "My God, I love you!"

Suddenly she raised her eyes and her face became very beautiful. For the space of a Creed, she looked up at the statue of the Virgin, then fell back, eyes closed, leaning on her side, a mysterious smile on her lips. She breathed her last breath; it was 7:20 P.M. We can contemplate the beauty of her peaceful face thanks to the photograph taken by Sister Geneviève.

Friday afternoon, according to the Carmelite custom, her body was transported to the choir to be laid out in front of the grille. It was to remain there until Sunday evening. The signs of decomposition were already present, however, so the casket was closed that night.

The Carmelite cemetery had no space for any more bodies, according to the opinion of the municipal authorities. The Guérin family, distinguished benefactors, had bought a cemetery plot for the Carmel on a hill overlooking Lisieux.

On Monday, October 4, thirty people climbed this hill, following the hearse. Léonie Martin herself led the funeral procession; Uncle Guérin was unable to attend because of an attack of gout.

The following day, the infirmary was put back in order. The straw mattress and Thérèse's very worn alpargatas (cord sandals) were burned, and daily life returned to its normal rhythm.

Even an account as brief as this indicates that her twenty-four-year-old body was ravaged by this illness.

We must put aside all of Epinal's images evoking the death "of a little saint with a rose in her hand." These words describe another woman from Normandy, the Lady of the Camellias, dead of tuberculosis at twenty-three, surrounded by lovers, a camellia in her hand.

All this is only fiction. Sister Thérèse suffered terribly from this implacable illness. But how did she suffer? Let us now try to look at and listen to this sick woman who reached, by grace, the fulfillment of her life, by the very logic of her total self-gift: that of her baptism, her religious profession, and her Offering to Merciful Love.

A Most Human Woman

We find her astonishingly human. Thérèse was a sick woman like many others; she suffered, sighed, wept, had nightmares, and had difficulty praying, so great was her weakness.

Memories came back to her and she would often think of her past life—at Les Buissonnets, at the Benedictine school, then her nine years in Carmel. She revealed herself as she was, in her love of nature with its flowers, fruits, and many animals.

Throughout these months, she revealed herself to be affectionate and sensitive. Her physical weakness made it impossible for her to hold back her tears, but she sometimes cried for joy, in gratitude to God and to her Sisters. There were also tears of love!

We wonder how she could manifest so much cheerfulness in such a situation. "She made all who came near her laugh. From the manner in which she recounts things, where you would expect to cry, you burst out laughing, for she is so amusing.... I think she will die laughing, she is so cheerful" wrote her cousin, Sister Marie of the Eucharist.

She was often playful, even in the midst of the most tragic circumstances. She was especially fond of Théophane Venard, the young martyr and missionary to Vietnam (1829–1861), because he was always joyful. Thérèse gave evidence of much humor, sometimes very dark, as when she saw the materials required for her burial—she found them very ugly!

She did not hesitate to use plays on words if they would bring joy to her sisters who were saddened at the thought of her leaving. Often enough, she would use the Norman expressions of her childhood, with their distinctive accent. She even made fun of her good doctor whose hesitation she did not appreciate. She nicknamed Doctor de Cornière "Clodion le Chevelu" (Clodion the Hairy, nickname of a fifth century Frankish chieftain)!

Though Thérèse sometimes used childlike language, she did not play a childish role or regress into infantilism. It is true that, just as at Les Buissonnets in 1883, she was sick and surrounded by her sisters. But what progress had occurred over those fourteen years! From the time of the Christmas grace of 1886, she put aside, as she wrote, the "swaddling clothes of a child" with its defects (A 44v). She would not fall back into it at the moment of her death.

Far from sinking into sentimentality, she used these childlike words to make her Sisters smile (and first of all the three Martins). We must see in this an act of courage and especially of love. When one is in the state we have described, it is not easy to forget oneself to think of the sufferings of others.

This joy was even more far reaching. In June she wrote in her last manuscript: "What banquet could a Carmelite offer her sisters except a spiritual banquet of loving and joyful charity?... The Lord *loves a cheerful giver*" (C 28v). "Whenever I can, I do my very best to be cheerful" (DE 6.9.2; HLC 185).

"Make My Life an Act of Love" (LT 224)

For a long time, Thérèse's whole life was "to love Jesus and make him loved" (LT 224, 225, 226,

254), as she wrote in her act of Offering to Merciful Love.

Love of Jesus, love of neighbor. As a testament, in her last manuscript she wrote sublime pages on love of neighbor. In the "Last Conversations," she lived it in daily life: "When I am charitable, it is Jesus alone who is acting in me" (C 12v).

How rapidly she matured! She was only twenty-four years old, yet known for her wisdom. Father Youf said to Mother Marie de Gonzague one day: "You have a second Mother Geneviève." Remember that Mother Geneviève was considered the saint of Lisieux Carmel. It was not without reason that Mother Marie de Gonzague entrusted the five novices to Sister Thérèse. She thought Thérèse would one day be prioress.

With Mother Agnes of Jesus, the roles were reversed. Throughout her life, Pauline was "the little Mother," the teacher, the spiritual advisor and the prioress. Yet in the infirmary, her little sister advised her, even corrected her.

According to Sister Geneviève's testimony, even some of the older sisters secretly went to Thérèse to ask her for spiritual counsel. In her correspondence with her two spiritual brothers, until the end, she continued proposing to them her little way, to be followed with confidence and love. To Father Bellière, she wrote: "I follow the way [Jesus] is tracing out for me.... I hope that one day Jesus will make you walk by the same way as myself" (LT 247). She insisted some time later: "I feel it, we must go to heaven by the same way, that of suffering united to love" (LT 258). "You are *forbidden* to go to heaven by any other way except that of your poor little sister... the way of simple and loving confidence is really made for you" (LT 261).

Nonetheless the sick woman did not play the role of "teacher" in the state she was in. In the *Last Conversations* collected by Mother Agnes, we find scarcely eight words concerning the little way. First and foremost, she lived it.

To Live the "Little Way"

First of all, Thérèse continued to recognize her imperfections and weaknesses: "I am not disturbed at seeing myself *weakness* itself.... I expect each day to discover new imperfections in myself" (C 15r). She admitted to Father Bellière: "Oh, Brother! I beg you to believe me. God has not given you as a sister a *great* soul but a *very little* and a very imperfect one" (LT 224).

At the time of a little incident with Sister Saint John Baptist, witnessed by Mother Agnes of Jesus, Thérèse dared to write to her: "I am indeed happier to have been imperfect than if, sustained by grace, I had been a model of meekness" (LT 230).

This weakness, so often recognized and accepted, became the privileged place of divine mercy. If Thérèse wanted to "remain little," it was not out of sentimentality, but to curl up in the arms of Jesus, "the elevator" that would lift her to the Father, especially in the humanly desperate situation she experienced in the infirmary. "For a long time I have not belonged to myself since I delivered myself totally to Jesus, and He is therefore free to do with me as He pleases" (C 10v). Abandonment alone guided her: "After all, it's the same to me whether I live or die" (DE 15.5.7; HLC 45).

This is the paradox that so struck her witnesses: in the midst of her worst sufferings, Thérèse remained peaceful and joyful. Even in her trial of faith, which knew almost no respite, she declared: "Ah! what darkness! But I am in peace" (DE 28.8.3; HLC 173).

The Great Desire for a Universal Mission

At the end of her last manuscript, she wrote: "A soul that is burning with love cannot remain inactive" (C 36r). The mission to "make Jesus loved" continued to haunt her. She prayed and sacrificed for Monsieur Tostain, "a relative who did not have faith." Her last

Communion was for the Discalced Carmelite Father Hyacinth Loyson who had left the church.

This was not enough for her, for her horizon was vast, even universal. She could not conceive that her missionary task came to an end with her life. Why not continue it? A great desire took hold of her: to do good after her death. She found that God had fulfilled all her desires. Why then not this one too, "the greatest desire of all?" She prayed for this and made "the novena of grace," from March 4 to 12, to Saint Francis Xavier, patron of the missions.

Her reasoning was based on the example of the angels. She confided to Father Roulland: "I really count on not remaining inactive in heaven. My desire is to work for the Church and for souls. I am asking God for this and I am certain He will answer me. Are not the angels continually occupied with us without their ever ceasing to see the divine Face and to lose themselves in the Ocean of Love without shores? Why would Jesus not allow me to imitate them?" (LT 254).

Three days later, Mother Agnes of Jesus wrote down these words on a little piece of paper:

> My mission is about to begin, my mission of making God loved as I love Him, of giving my little way to souls. If God answers my desires, my heaven will be spent on earth until the end of the world. Yes, I want to spend my heaven in doing good on earth. This isn't impossible, since from the bosom of the beatific vision, the angels watch over us.... I can't rest as long as there are souls to be saved.... But when the angel will have said: "Time is no more!" then I will rest; I'll be able to rejoice, because the number of the elect will be complete and because all will have entered into joy and repose. My heart beats with joy at this thought. (DE 17.7; HLC 102)

Later these words would have universal repercussions.

From time to time, during this last period of her life, Thérèse uttered these mysterious words: "I will come back.... I will send graces.... Later on, I'll go to little baptized children just like this" (DE 25.6.1; HLC 67), and then this astonishingly bold statement:

"God will have to carry out my will in heaven because I have never done my own will here on earth" (DE 13.7.2; HLC 91). All this was said in profound humility, for she knew that "everything is a grace" (DE 5.6.4; HLC 57) and that "everything comes from God" (DE 11.7.3; HLC 88).

Although tested by trial—some evenings she sensed the presence of the devil—her faith led her to make another memorable statement: "I really don't see what I'll have after death that I don't already possess in this life. I shall see God, true; but as far as being in His presence, I am totally there here on earth" (DE 15.5.7; HLC 45).

The Obituary

During these last weeks, a decision was made that had incalculable consequences. Mother Agnes of Jesus was thinking about her sister's obituary, according to the custom in Carmel. After the death of a Carmelite nun, an obituary was sent to all the monasteries of the Order. Sister Thérèse agreed on this.

To this end, the "little Mother" thought she would use Thérèse's own writings, so she asked Mother Marie de Gonzague to order the sick woman to complete her first manuscript.

The plan was made to publish these pages. Thérèse agreed, but in her state, it was impossible for her to take part in this project. Thus she was satisfied to make recommendations to her sister. She had complete confidence in her: "I didn't have the time to write what I would have wanted, so whatever you think good to delete or add to the notebook of my life, it is I who delete or add. Remember this later and have no scruples, no doubts on this subject" (DE II, 11.7.3).

Thérèse made her recommendations: "Don't forget to tell the story of the sinful woman! That will prove that I'm not mistaken" (DE 20.7.3; HLC 104). "After my death, you mustn't speak to anyone about my manuscript before it is published; you must speak about it only to Mother Prioress. If you act otherwise, the devil will make use of more than one trap to hinder the work of God, a very important work!" (DE 1.8.2; HLC 126).

Once Mother Agnes asked Thérèse to reread a passage from her manuscript that seemed incomplete to her. Her sister replied: "What I am reading in this copybook reflects my soul so well! Mother, these pages will do much good to souls. They will understand God's gentleness much better" (DE II, 1.8.2; HLC 126).

She was only an instrument of mercy: "How well they will understand that everything comes from God; and what I shall have of glory from it will be a gratuitous gift from God that doesn't belong to me; everybody will see this clearly" (DE 11.7.3). "Ah! I know it; everybody will love me" (DE II, 1.8.2; HLC 126).

Five days before her death, Sister Thérèse would give a kind of conclusion to her writings and also a key to their reading: "I really feel now that what I've said and written is true about everything" (DE 25.9.2; HLC 200).

"To Climb Calvary with Jesus" (PN 17)

In June, Thérèse reread her second play on Joan of Arc. She said to Mother Agnes: "You will see there my sentiments on death; they are all expressed" (DE 5.6.2; HLC 57). One sentence in particular must have struck her: "How consoled I am to see that my agony is like my Savior's" (RP 3.2.5).

Such was the ultimate secret concerning Sister Thérèse's illness and death. Certainly, from a medical point of view, she died of tuberculosis. Yet to the eyes of faith, she wanted to "die of love" for and with the Beloved whom she always followed, to the very end, to the glorious cross. She was always moved by the desire for martyrdom. After a hemoptysis, she declared: "I knew well that I would have the consolation of seeing my blood shed, since I am dying the martyrdom of love" (Geneviève, PO 307).

In general, she had no fear of death, but she did experience some difficult moments: "One morning, during my act of thanksgiving after Communion, I felt the agonies of death...and with it no consolation!" (DE 3.6.2; HLC 56). "I'm afraid I've feared death.... What is this mysterious separation of the soul from the body? It's my first experience of this, but I abandon myself to God" (DE 11.9.4; HLC 188).

Thérèse's Sisters, who had read these descriptions of the "death of love," imagined apparitions of angels, even the Virgin Mary and some extraordinary sign at the moment of their young Sister's death. She constantly brought them back to reality: "Don't be astonished if I don't appear to you after my death, and if you see nothing extraordinary as a sign of my happiness. You will remember it's 'my little way' not to desire to see anything" (DE 4.6.1; HLC 55).

She kept her eyes fixed on Jesus crucified: "Our Lord really died as a Victim of Love, and see what His agony was!" (DE 4.6.1; HLC 56). "Our Lord died on the cross in agony, and yet this is the most beautiful death of Love. This is the only one that was seen; no one saw that of the Blessed Virgin. To die of love is not to die in transports. I tell you frankly, it seems to me that this is what I am experiencing" (DE 4.7.2; HLC 73). She rejected all that was spectacular. She would not die "after Communion" or on a beautiful liturgical date, but rather on an ordinary day.

Most of all she was Sister Thérèse of the "Holy Face," which evokes the suffering servant of Isaiah 53 and Jesus at Gethsemane. On June 2, she wrote Sister Marie of the Eucharist: "Her Bridegroom is no longer a Bridegroom who must lead her into festivities but to Mount Calvary" (LT 234). She was never without her "dear little crucifix": she kissed it (on the cheek), unpetalled roses over it and would not let go of it during her death agony. All the little details of her experience of sickness directed her to the passion of Jesus. Her three sisters all fell asleep at her bedside. When they awoke, she called them: "Peter, James, and John!" When her shoulder hurt, she evoked the carrying of the cross.

After making the way of the cross so often in the chapel, now she was truly living it, without words. Thérèse's compassion responded to Jesus' passion. That is why she did not hesitate to apply to herself Jesus' priestly prayer (Jn 17). Her boldness finds its legitimacy in a healthy theology of the Mystical Body: "I can only borrow the words of Jesus at his Last Supper. He cannot take offense at this since I am His little spouse and, consequently, His goods are mine" (LT 258 and C 34v). The great passage of her last manuscript expresses her Holy Thursday. It is the key to the meaning of her sufferings. Scarcely had she finished writing this text when

Good Friday began. She too, Jesus' disciple and bride, is this grain of wheat that falls to the ground and dies, but only to bear much fruit. She quoted this verse of Saint John (12:24) on August 11.

She was placed in the earth on October 4, after an agony during which she said: "Never would I have believed that it was possible to suffer so much! never! never! I cannot explain this except by the ardent desires I have had to save souls" (DE 30.9; HLC 205).

Thérèse has been bearing much fruit for almost a hundred years.

Why should this surprise us? God has fulfilled all her desires because it was his Spirit that inspired them in her. Did she not write to Father Bellière: "I am not dying, I am entering into Life" (LT 244)?

Thérèse Speaks
To Sing the Mercies of the Lord

Ah! Brother, like me you can sing the mercies of the Lord, they sparkle in you in all their splendor.... You love Saint Augustine, Saint Magdalene, these souls to whom "many sins were forgiven because they loved much." I love them too, I love their repentance, and especially...their loving audacity! When I see Magdalene walking up before the many guests, washing with her tears the feet of her adored Master, whom she is touching for the first time, I feel that *her heart* has understood the abysses of love and mercy *of the Heart of Jesus,* and, sinner though she is, this Heart of love was not only disposed to pardon her but to lavish on her the blessings of His divine intimacy, to lift her to the highest summits of contemplation.

Ah! dear little Brother, ever since I have been given the grace to understand also the love of the Heart of Jesus, I admit that it has expelled all fear from my heart. The remembrance of my faults humbles me, draws me never to depend on my strength which is only weakness, but this remembrance speaks to me of mercy and love even more.

When we cast our faults with entire filial confidence into the devouring fire of love, how would these not be consumed beyond return?

I know there are some saints who spent their life in the practice of astonishing mortifications to expiate their sins, but what of it: "There are many mansions in the house of my heavenly Father," Jesus has said, and it is because of this that I follow the way He is tracing out for me. I try to be no longer occupied with myself in anything, and I abandon myself to what Jesus sees fit to do in my soul, for I have not chosen an austere life to expiate my faults but those of others. (LT 247 to P. Bellière, her missionary brother)

172

171. Thérèse in July 1896. She is twenty-three and a half, and is undergoing the trial of faith.

172–173. Thérèse at twenty-two, the protagonist in the play she wrote on Joan of Arc.

174. Louis Martin returned to Lisieux with paralyzed legs in May of 1892. He lived with his daughters Léonie and Céline in a rented house at 7 rue Labbey, where the photo was taken, close to the Guérins. From left to right: Marie Guérin, Léonie, Céline, the servant Désiré and his wife (at the window), Uncle Isidore Guérin, Aunt Céline Guérin, and her friend. Below is Thérèse's dog, Tom.

175. The manor "La Musse," located in the municipality of Saint-Sébastien-de-Morsent, near Évreux, property of Isidore Guérin. Here Louis Martin spent his summer months in 1893 and 1894, and here he died July 29, 1894.

176. The manor "La Musse." A commemorative monument to Louis Martin with Thérèse.

173

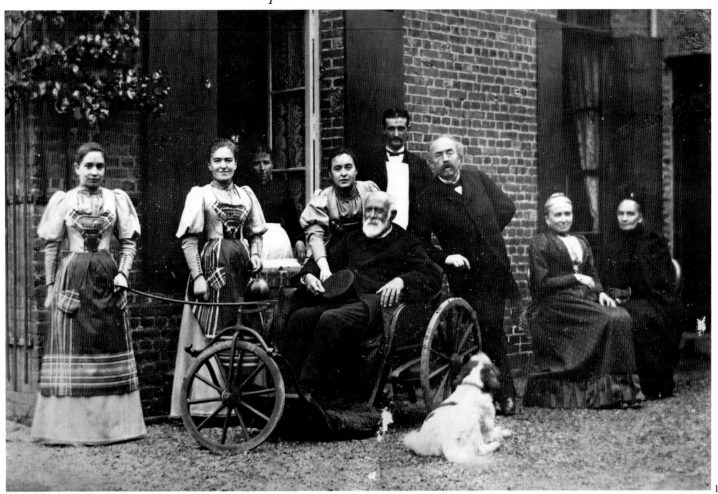

174

175

A LA MÉMOIRE
DE
MONSIEUR LOUIS MARTIN
PÈRE DE SAINTE THÉRÈSE
DE L'ENFANT-JÉSUS
DÉCÉDÉ LE 29 JUILLET 1894
AU CHÂTEAU DE LA MUSSE
ALORS PROPRIÉTÉ DE Mr GUÉRIN
SON BEAU-FRÈRE

176

177

178

179

177. The infirmary in the Carmel of Lisieux where Thérèse died on September 30, 1897.

178. Lisieux. Monastery garden. From her bed placed in the center of the infirmary Thérèse was able to see this grotto where there was a picture of the Holy Face. She alludes to the "black hole" where she feels she is "in body and soul," but where she remains "in peace" (DE 28.8.3; HLC 173).

179. Carmel of Lisieux. Infirmary. Inside.

180–181. Images of Our Lady of Mount Carmel and the Infant Jesus of Prague which Thérèse contemplated in her last moments.

182. A stalk of wheat prompting Thérèse to behold "the image of my soul," laden "with graces for myself and for many others" (DE 4.8.3; HLC 131).

DILECTUS MEUS MIHI
ET EGO ILLI

180

181

182

251

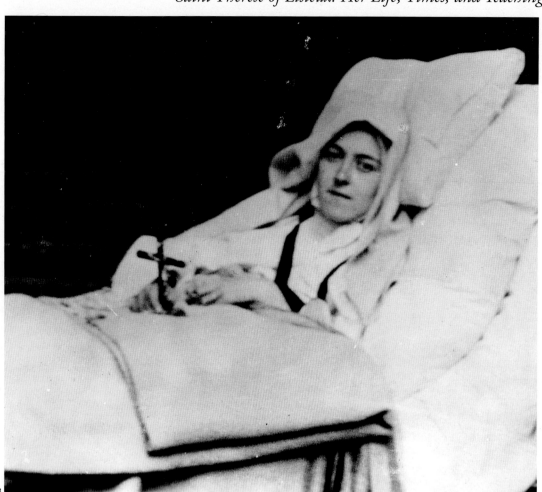

183. Thérèse in her last illness, near the door of the infirmary on August 30, 1897.

184. Lisieux. Carmel. The last prayer written by Thérèse on September 8, 1897.

185. Thérèse immediately after death. "I am not dying, I am entering into life" (LT 244).

O Marie, si j'étais la Reine du Ciel et que vous soyez Thérèse, je voudrais être Thérèse afin que vous soyez La Reine du Ciel !!!...... - - - - - - - -

8 Septembre 1897

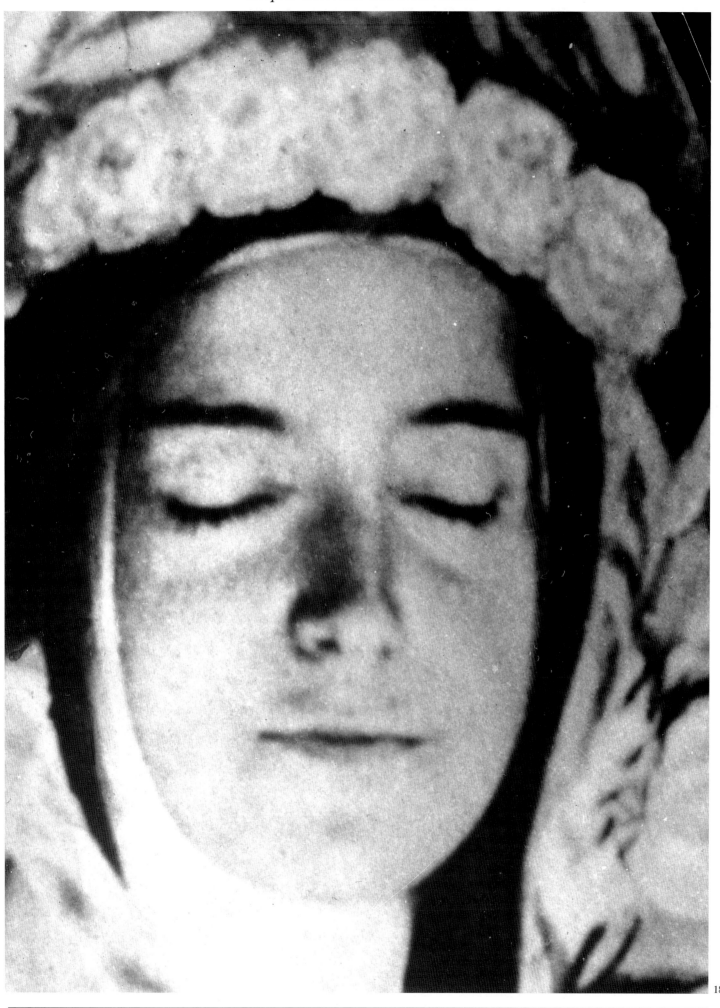

CHAPTER FOURTEEN

Thérèse's Universal Influence

PIERRE DESCOUVEMONT and RAYMOND ZAMBELLI

During the last century, when a Discalced Carmelite nun died, it was the custom for her prioress to send a death notice to the other Carmels summarizing the deceased nun's life and asking for prayers for her. As time went on, these notices became more detailed. This was the case for Sister Thérèse of the Child Jesus and the Holy Face, dead at Lisieux on September 30, 1897.

Her prioress actually used first-hand documentation, namely, the three autobiographical manuscripts Thérèse herself wrote. Toward the end of her life, Thérèse had a presentiment that, after her death, the reading of those pages would do much good. Souls would thereby understand that it is possible to attain holiness by a very simple "little way." Thérèse entrusted Mother Agnes with the work of editing, telling her not to hesitate to correct her prose!

At the time of her little sister's death, Mother Agnes set about completing the work. She divided the three manuscripts into eleven chapters and composed a twelfth, in which she related Thérèse's last months and death. The book concluded with some extracts from her letters, a good number of her poems, and the testimony of her novices.

The *Story of a Soul*

On October 29, Mother Marie de Gonzague wrote to the Norbertine priest, Godefroid Madelaine, prior of Mondaye Abbey and great friend of Carmel, to inform him that she had sent him Thérèse's manuscript, to correct it or have it corrected.

Father Madelaine was enthusiastic about it. On January 30, 1898, four months after Thérèse's death, he wrote: "I continue to read the wonderful manuscript; how refreshing, simple, and edifying it is! I hope to return it to you by the end of February with those observations I felt I could make. If I may use the term, I see this autobiography as a relic." The testimony

was important, for Father Madelaine, later to be elected Abbot of Frigolet, was an influential person. It was his idea to entitle Thérèse's obituary *Story of Soul,* a title suggested by what Thérèse herself had written at the beginning of the first manuscript. The title was not at all original since it was found on the cover of several works of that period. It was also Father Madelaine who worked to obtain the bishop's *imprimatur.*

When Bishop Hugonin heard Father Madelaine speak about the manuscripts left by Sister Thérèse of the Child Jesus, he knew exactly who she was: Thérèse Martin who had come to him in Bayeux ten years earlier to obtain permission to enter Carmel at an early age. The bishop's first reaction was not encouraging: "Father, be careful where the imagination of women is concerned!" he told him. Since Father Madelaine insisted on the value of these pages, the bishop ended by saying: "Then make me a report!"

On the following March 7, on the occasion of an academic session on the feast of Saint Thomas Aquinas when a significant number of ecclesiastics were gathered together, Father Madelaine presented his report. Bishop Hugonin granted the *imprimatur;* he died two months later.

Two thousand copies of the work were published on September 30, 1898, exactly one year after Thérèse's death. Monsieur Guérin received the proofs and financed the publication. How would they manage to sell them? "We will be stuck with these books," said one of the Lisieux Carmelites.

An Unexpected Reception

Contrary to all expectations, the work quickly sold out. Sent for the most part to the monasteries, it sparked a serious interest. Many lay people also began to read it and were moved. Many priests admitted that reading it had done them more good than all the previous priestly retreats they had made. At the major

Thérèse's Parlor

Raymond Zambelli

In the heart of the many pilgrims to Lisieux, there is the secret desire to enter one day into the interior of Thérèse's Carmel. This very legitimate desire is very rarely granted. It was not until the 150th anniversary of the foundation of this Carmel that the doors of the community, by way of exception, were opened to several hundred guests; that was in 1988.

There is, however, one place in this Carmel where the gaze of every pilgrim penetrates the cloister. It is Thérèse's resting place, the most venerated place of her tomb.

I love this place because of all it represents to me. There is, first of all, this grille that symbolically marks the inevitable distance between Thérèse and us, a distance imposed when one measures the separation between the holiness of her life and each of our poor existences. This distance, nonetheless, turns no one away. This distance is necessary to recall in its own way the indispensable respect that must surround each encounter.

This blessed place is truly a parlor. It is the parlor given to us where we can have, at any time of the day, an exchange with the one we have come to see, who waits for us, listens to us, and responds to us.

Ah! if this grille could speak. What prayers, supplications, confidences! What names whispered, what souls entrusted each day!

Here hearts are liberated, souls are opened. Here Thérèse receives our secrets and our promises. Here Thérèse replies with a word that enlightens, calms, reassures, and encourages.

Peaceful, silent, beneficial parlor. It is a true sanctuary where the story of our souls is easily communicated to the one who has revealed her own to us.

Each day is written here this other story of the pilgrimage to Lisieux that can never be printed, for it is the most secret, the most profound, the most mysterious, in a word, the most incommunicable.

There is the grille, the recumbent statue—and then there are the flowers, those armfuls of flowers. They also speak in their own way and give forth perfumes that are called affection, admiration and gratitude.

This language of the flowers of Thérèse's tomb is the loving language of so many faithful for the one who declared a month before her death: "I love very much flowers and roses, red flowers, and beautiful pink daisies" (DE 28.8.7; HLC 174).

It is also the evangelical language of the freely flowing perfume of Bethany that is inscribed in Thérèse's pure logic: "Ah! I give without counting, truly sure / That when one loves, one does not keep count!" (PN 17).

During Thérèse's time, there was always a third person in the parlor. We need only lift our eyes to identify her in the person of the Virgin Mary, represented under the features of the original and celebrated statue of the Virgin of the Smile. Thus, in the parlor of the Lisieux Carmel, there are really two women who truly welcome us, listen to us, and respond to us.

---

seminary in Bayeux, most of the students devoured the book, although some found the style too sentimental.

Furthermore, many contemplatives—men who were instinctively suspicious of all sentimentality—would express their admiration for "little Thérèse." At the Charterhouse, the religious "wrangled" over the two copies of *Story of a Soul,* even the one who was considered "the most knowledgeable theologian of the Order."

Beginning in 1899, letters arrived in Lisieux from Poland, England, and Spain asking for translations for each country. Father de Teil, who was working for the beatification of the Carmelites of Compiègne, guillotined in 1794, read *Story of a Soul* in 1899 and spoke very favorably of it.

Obviously not everyone shared this enthusiasm. Some Carmels expressed their reticence: "This very young religious should not have stated her views on perfection in so absolute a manner. Age and experience would most likely have modified them." One prioress found that the young Carmelite, in speaking of her graces, expressed herself with simplicity, but that one could also find pride in this. Another thought the *Story* was not virile enough, and an Italian Carmelite friar thought it was too childish.

Nonetheless, it soon became clear that a new edition was needed. On May 24, 1899, Mgr. Amette, the new bishop of Bayeux, who would soon become coadjutor and then archbishop of Paris, authorized the reprinting of 4,000 copies of *Story of a Soul.* From then on, it was necessary to repeat the operation every year. In 1900, the third edition of 2,000 copies was published; in 1901, the fourth printing of 2,000; in 1902, the fifth printing of 3,000; in 1903, the sixth of 3,000; and since then the printings have increased and the translations have multiplied. Today the work has been translated into more than fifty languages.

To make *Story of a Soul* affordable for everyone, a popular edition was published in 1902 under the title *Une Rose effueillée* (An Unpetalled Rose). It was also providentially decided to present a summary of her life and doctrine: *l'Appel aux Petites Ames,* or *Call to Little Souls,* was published for the first time in 1904. Later, a *Vie abrégée,* or abridged *Life,* would contain an even more succinct summary (first edition, 1913) and a collection of *Thoughts* (*Pensées,* first edition, 1915) would permit meditation on the different aspects of her spirituality.

A few statistics will suffice to show the popularity little Sister Thérèse enjoyed. From the time of her death until her canonization, that is, a period of less than seventeen years, the following books were published:

— 400,000 copies of *Story of a Soul* in French
— 800,000 copies of the *Call to Little Souls;*
— 300,000 copies of the abridged *Life;*
— 500,000 copies of the *Thoughts.*

Let us mention in passing the almost unheard of success of the pictures and relics. From 1898 to 1915, the Carmel distributed 8,046,000 pictures and 1,124,000 mementos.

Another statistic, no less significant, concerns the correspondence. Letters from around the world arrived daily in Lisieux asking the Carmelites to pray to little Thérèse for their special intentions: the conversion or cure of a child, of a spouse, reconciliation in the home, etc. There were requests for intercession, but also letters of thanksgiving.

Curiously enough, Thérèse had foreseen this kind of posthumous activity toward the end of her life. On June 9, 1897, after making the famous promise that after her death she would send a shower of roses, she added: "After my death, you will go to the mailbox and find consolation there."

The movement that began with a few daily letters accelerated progressively. In 1909, the average number of letters received was twenty to thirty each day. By 1911, it would be fifty. During the following years, the daily flow would increase to 200 and then to 400 in 1914. In 1923–1925, at the time of Thérèse's beatification and canonization, the number of letters was 500 to 1,000 each day. Even today, an average of fifty letters arrives each day at the Carmel or for the Director of Pilgrimages.

First Pilgrimages to Her Tomb and First Miracles

Thérèse's tomb was located on the Champs-Rémouleux, as the town cemetery was then called. The Carmelites would have preferred to bury her at the back of their garden, in the little cemetery located there, but at the end of the last century these burials "in town" were no longer permitted without exceptional authorization. The Carmel was obliged to buy a plot in the Lisieux cemetery. The site was considered too small and Thérèse's death was imminent; therefore Monsieur Guérin bought another enclosure, the one still used today for the burial of the Carmelites. Thérèse was thus the first Carmelite to be buried there.

Monsieur Guérin was ill the day of Thérèse's burial (Monday, October 4, 1897), so Monsieur Maudelonde, Madame Guérin's brother-in-law, led the funeral procession to the cemetery. He was accompanied by Léonie.

Shortly thereafter, and with increasing frequency after the publication of *Story of a Soul,* pilgrims began to visit Thérèse's tomb. Almost immediately, relics were taken from the cemetery: a sprig of grass, a flower, or a clump of dirt.

From 1899, requests were made to the Lisieux Carmel for Thérèse's relics—pieces of her clothing or a lock of her hair. Then from almost everywhere, numerous testimonies arrived in Lisieux of cures received during novenas in honor of the "Little Queen." These cures

The Basilica of Lisieux

Pierre Descouvemont

The Basilica of Lisieux was constructed in record time thanks to the generosity of the thousands of gifts received from around the world. Begun in 1929, it was solemnly blessed on July 11, 1937, by Cardinal Pacelli, legate of Pius XI and himself the future Pius XII.

The architect Louis-Marie Cordonnier opted for a neo-byzantine plan, similar to the Basilica of the Sacred Heart at Montmartre (Paris). Over a forty-year period, this internationally renowned architect had won first place in countless contests:

1885: The New Stock Exchange of Amsterdam;

1887: Laureate for the restoration of the Cathedral of Milan (the work was never undertaken for financial reasons);

1894: Ecole des Beaux Arts, Conservatory de Music in Lille;

1900: Grand Prix at the World Exposition of Paris;

1906: Peace Palace at the Hague.

The construction of this basilica was the express desire of Pius XI. In November 1929, he informed Monseigneur Suhard, the new bishop of Bayeux, that he wanted it to be "very big, very beautiful, and completed as quickly as possible!"

The total area of the edifice is 4,500 square meters (about 48,500 square feet); its length is 95 meters (about 312 feet) and the dome likewise reaches 95 meters.

The arch of the crypt, completed in July 1932, is completely covered with mosaics, in the style of the exhibit of the "Arts Decoratifs" of 1925. Its decoration illustrates Thérèse's interior life, while the mosaics of the upper basilica evoke her posthumous influence.

During World War II, the one hundred and fifty bombs and shells that fell around the basilica, and the two bombs that fell directly on the basilica itself, did not destroy it. During the ten years that followed the the town's liberation, the damage caused by the bombings was repaired and the mosaics and stained glass windows of the upper basilica were set in place. Once all the work was completed, it was solemnly consecrated on July 11, 1954.

were usually brought about by contact of the sick person with the Carmelite's relics.

Toward the Process of Beatification (1903–1909)

Despite the exceptional diffusion of *Story of a Soul* and the confidence quickly placed in the intercession of "little Sister Thérèse," no one thought, in those first years after her death, that she would one day be canonized.

Apparently Father Thomas Taylor, a young Scottish priest ordained in 1897, was the first to promote this idea. After reading *The Little Flower of Jesus,* he was conquered by the young French Carmelite. On his return from a pilgrimage to Lourdes, he stopped by Lisieux on May 15 and 16, 1903, and met Thérèse's three sisters (Marie, Pauline, and Céline), their cousin Marie Guérin, and Mother Marie de Gonzague. He told them directly that they must begin the steps toward the opening of a process. The prioress's response was unexpected: "But Father, how many Carmelites must we canonize?"

Gradually, nevertheless, the idea of a process of beatification took hold. From almost everywhere petitions requesting the opening of the cause of the "Little Flower," as she was called in English-speaking countries, arrived in Lisieux. She became exceptionally popular in Canada. Belgium, Italy, Spain, South America—and especially Brazil—already venerated her as a saint.

On June 6, 1905, Pius X promulgated the brief of beatification for the sixteen Carmelite martyrs of Compiègne. That very night, the Lisieux Carmel received from the seminary of Tournai in Belgium a petition containing fifty-three signatures asking for "the introduction, advancement, and success of the cause of the servant of God, Sister Thérèse of the Child Jesus." The Carmelites could not help but see a sign in this coincidence. It seemed to them that the Carmelites of Compiègne were asking them to work for the glorification of their little Sister! What the Carmelites did not know at the time was that Thérèse would later have the distinguished canonist Mgr. Roger de Teil, the same person who was responsible for the process of beatification for the Carmelites of Compiègne, to advance her cause. In February, 1909, he was named vice-postulator of her cause.

By a similarly curious coincidence, Father de Teil had come to the Lisieux Carmel in September 1886 to

Relics

Raymond Zambelli

Thérèse of the Child Jesus and the Holy Face was buried in the Lisieux municipal cemetery on October 4, 1897. She was the first to be buried in the new plot her monastery had purchased in response to the city's new legislative directives prohibiting interment inside the cloister. In view of what took place after Thérèse's death, we can now say that the new directives were providential, since they enabled hundreds of thousands of pilgrims to visit her grave over a period of twenty-five years. Had Thérèse been buried inside the cloister, this would never have been possible. Only in 1923 on the occasion of her beatification were her mortal remains transferred to the Carmelite chapel where they are kept to this day.

When speaking of Thérèse's relics, we must return to the initial stage of their veneration in the town cemetery. Everything began there, to the point that Thérèse's grave became the cradle of the pilgrimages. But isn't this the case with Rome, Compostela, and so many other shrines spread throughout the world?

Anthropologists have taught us that burial is an indubitable sign of the presence of human beings, because only humans bury their own. The church respects the custom of gathering to pray in the presence of the mortal remains of those we have known and loved. When each year millions of men and women of every culture and social condition visit cemeteries, they draw near the "relics" (that is, the remains) of their dear ones. We understand well enough that we do not really rejoin our loved ones there, but we are not pure spirits and we need signs.

The saints' relics are poor and fragile signs of what went to make up their bodies. When we are close to their relics we can more easily evoke their human condition; that with their own bodies they acted, thought, worked, and suffered.

At times God wishes to use such tenuous and seemingly foolish signs to manifest his presence and make his power and glory shine forth. It is God in fact who works through these signs. Here we enter into the perplexing divine logic, different from that of the world. The apostle Paul reminds the Corinthians of this: "Rather, God chose the foolish of the world to shame the wise, and God chose the weak of the world to shame the strong" (1 Cor 1:27). But the same apostle had just declared: "For the foolishness of God is wiser than human wisdom, and the weakness of God is stronger than human strength" (1 Cor 1:25).

To return to Thérèse's case, it is a fact that when people stand in the presence of her mortal remains or have some contact with her poor relics, as with petals from an unpetalled rose, God, who received through her humanity so many signs of love, is pleased in turn to manifest his love through her bodily remains.

From these poor signs, God's salvific power reveals and unfolds itself. To become convinced it is enough to read the many volumes recounting favors and cures obtained through contact with Thérèse's relics, as well as the abundant correspondence that arrives daily in Lisieux. And who can name all those who cherish in their wallets or among their personal papers an image bearing the words "cloth touched to the relics of the Saint"? Truly we find ourselves in another logic, arising from the words of Jesus: "I give you praise, Father, Lord of heaven and earth, for although you have hidden these things from the wise and the learned you have revealed them to the childlike" (Lk 10:21).

give a conference on the Carmelites of Compiègne. This conference greatly pleased Thérèse; it renewed within her heart the desire for martyrdom and led her to say, as she was leaving the speakroom, that with such a postulator the Carmelites of Compiègne would soon be beatified!

Note that Thérèse had special devotion to the martyrs of Compiègne. In 1894, she had joyfully participated in their centenary celebration and, while making banners in their honor, she confided to Sister Teresa of Saint Augustine: "What happiness if we had the same lot, the same grace!"

What especially struck the Carmelites in 1905 was the number of postulants who, deeply moved by the reading of *Story of a Soul,* sought entrance into the Lisieux Carmel. On March 1, Sister Marie of the Sacred Heart wrote to Léonie:

> A sixteen-year-old girl from a fine family has the consent of her parents to enter Carmel in August. She will come from the other end of France, from Metz, drawn by Thérèse of the Child Jesus. Just as with Thérèse herself, the permission of the bishop, who finds her somewhat young, is required. This week, three Italian girls made the same request to Mother, but you know it is impossible to satisfy everyone.

Given Teresa of Avila's desire for communities of only a limited number, it was necessary to direct many to other Carmels.

Astonishment and Reticence

This growing popularity of "their" little Thérèse did not impress the Carmelites of Lisieux. They had such little faith in her future canonization that they did not even think of keeping the immense amount of mail they were required to answer in as personal a way as possible. It was Father de Teil who advised them in 1909 to keep this correspondence. This argument alone would prove that Thérèse's process was not an affair instigated by the Lisieux Carmel. The life of the monastery continued, peacefully and fervently.

Although they were very happy to see the influence exerted by the reading of her manuscript, the Carmelites never imagined that one day Thérèse would be "on the altars." Her own sisters did not believe it! Even in 1910, when the Superior of the Visitation of Caen went to the monastery garden to inform Léonie, Thérèse's sister, that there was serious question of a canonization process, she continued to hang out the laundry and said: "Thérèse was very kind! But a saint! Really!"

Thérèse's uncle, Monsieur Guérin, was himself completely opposed to the idea of a process intended to canonize his niece. As much as he favored the publication of her manuscripts and rejoiced at their diffusion, to that extent was he opposed to the idea of a Vatican process! He had another idea of canonized holiness. He saw it crowned with extraordinary charisms and accompanied by sensational scourgings. If Thérèse were canonized, he reasoned, it would be necessary to canonize many others, including his daughter Marie who had also just died of tuberculosis at the Carmel after much suffering (April 14, 1905). Later, when the echo of the first "Thérèsian" miracles began to appear in the news, Monsieur Guérin was seriously annoyed. At one point, he even considered leaving Lisieux.

The see of Bayeux was vacant. Mgr. Amette, who was leaving for Paris, was not enthusiastic when he was asked to introduce the cause. He evasively responded that "time, personnel, and money were needed." Mgr. Lemonnier, the new bishop appointed on July 13, 1906, was no more anxious than his predecessor, especially since Mother Agnes was still prioress of the Carmel. He could see nothing in the life of this young religious that justified such "pretension" and he simply suspected the "Martin sisters" of wanting to have their youngest sister canonized. Nonetheless, on October 15, 1907, he asked the religious who knew Sister Thérèse of the Child Jesus to write down their memories and send them to their chaplain, Father Pitrou.

In 1907 Father Prévost often went to the Vatican because the pope had asked him to found a house in Rome. He asked Lisieux to prepare for him two copies of the *Story of a Soul,* one bound in white leather for the pope and the other in red for Cardinal Merry del Val, Secretary of State. On March 15, 1907, the volume was given to the pope who, that day, gave very little attention to the one he would later call "the greatest saint of modern times"!

The cause was moved along thanks to the election of a new prioress of the Lisieux Carmel: Mother Marie-Ange of the Child Jesus, elected on May 8, 1908, replacing Mother Agnes who had completed her second term. The very day of her election, Mother Marie-Ange wrote to Mgr. Lemonnier to ask him to open the cause. Despite the worldwide renown Thérèse already enjoyed, the bishop seemed little inclined to grant this authorization. On May 26, however, a rather spectacular miracle occurred in Lisieux: the instantaneous cure of a little four-year-old blind girl whom her mother had brought to Thérèse's tomb the previous day. This miracle caused quite a stir in Lisieux because this little "Reine" Fauquet was from modest surroundings and her age left little room for suspicion. Doctor La Néele, Thérèse's cousin by marriage, formerly so little in favor of the cause, was obliged to validate the cure. He signed the medical certificate on December 7. It is understandable that Sister Marie of the Trinity could write on August 12: "Her cult exploded throughout the world; there were letters and requests from everywhere."

Bishop Lemonnier had no recourse but to petition a process at the court in Rome. In January 1909, he agreed on the choice of a postulator, Father Rodrigue of St. Francis Paola, postulator general for the causes of Carmel. He appointed Mgr. de Teil as vice-postulator.

The Major Steps of the Glorification (1909–1925)

The process was under way. Nothing could stop it now. Begun in 1909, it would be completed in 1925 with the canonization. For those who are not familiar with the ordinary prudence of the church in matters of canonization, this time frame may appear rather long. In fact, Thérèse's process was completed in record time. *What were the reasons for this exceptional speed?*

First of all, Thérèse was literally *canonized by the people of God,* well before she was by the hierarchy. The hierarchy only gave official recognition to the veneration she already received throughout the world just a few years after her death. What Cardinal Vico, Prefect of the Congregation of Rites, permitted himself to say in 1919 in the privacy of the Lisieux cloister is understandable: "We must hasten to glorify the little saint, otherwise the voice of the people will precede us." He added: "If we were living in the early days of the church when beatifications of the Servants of God were done by acclamation, your little Sister would have been raised to the altars a long time ago." Thus Thérèse clearly contradicted what Renan foretold in 1858, when he wrote: "Holiness is a kind of finished poetry like so many others. There will be saints canonized in Rome, but there will be no more canonized by the people."

It would be equally false, however, to think that Thérèse was canonized so quickly only because of the popular fervor. The *three popes* under whom the process took place were deeply convinced of Thérèse's holiness and the importance of the "little way" she wanted to bring to the world. Thus, by special privilege, Benedict XV dispensed Thérèse from the time period of fifty years normally required between the death of the servant of God and the opening of the debate on the heroicity of her virtues. The same pontiff judged it useless to open a new process on Thérèse's reputation for holiness; it was so evident that there was no need to prove it.

The *miracles* finally were so abundant that the vice-postulator of the cause truly had difficulty limiting the choice of the miracles for closer study; he had many more than the two cures necessary for beatification and the two others necessary for canonization.

Furthermore, there was the "shower of roses" Thérèse had promised. Favors of all kinds obtained through the intercession of "little Sister Thérèse" became so numerous that seven volumes entitled *Pluie de roses* (Shower of Roses) would be published in succession to relate not all, but only the most spectacular conversions and miracles wrought by the famous "strewer of roses."

The first *Shower of Roses* had been inserted as an appendix at the end of the 1907 edition of *Story of a Soul.* The seven volumes published from 1907 to 1925 form a total of more than 3,000 densely printed pages and sold 400,000 copies.

The Development of the Pilgrimages

The miracles multiplied and the pilgrims who came to pray at Thérèse's tomb were ever more numerous. The silence of the way leading up to the Lisieux cemetery and the panorama discovered at the summit favored prayer. Once they arrived at the Carmelite enclosure, many prayed with their arms outstretched in the form of a cross. And as if the tomb were a "mailbox to heaven," they left requests, cards, and photographs to draw the attention of the one they already called "saint." They brought flowers, but also *ex votos:* crutches, canes, and devices of all kinds to attest to a cure obtained through Thérèse's intercession.

On August 24, 1913, an important military pilgrimage was organized at Thérèse's tomb. It was the prelude to the special role that soldiers were to play during World War I in the development of devotion to little Sister Thérèse.

The Lisieux cemetery became more and more a new "colline inspirée" (inspired hill) according to the title a journalist from *Democracy* gave it in an article of October 3, 1913, devoted to these pilgrimages. At the time this article was published, the first exhumation of Thérèse's body had already taken place. On September 6, 1910, in fact, the first official examination of her relics had been carried out in the presence of five hundred people. After thirteen years in the grave, only the remnants of a few bones covered with strips of cloth were found. This time the new casket was placed in a stone vault, two meters deep.

The Process

If Thérèse abundantly fulfilled the promise that she had made to spend her heaven doing good on earth, those who were in charge of her process did not rest either; very quickly they arrived at the conviction that, quite simply, Thérèse was truly a saint.

The Promoter of Justice, commonly called the *Devil's Advocate,* was especially competent; he was Théophile Dubosq, a Sulpician and superior of the seminary in Bayeux. Named "promoter of the faith" in July 1910 by Mgr. Lemonnier, he was immediately conquered by Thérèse and strove to present a dossier that was both clear and complete. Specialists consider Thérèse's process was a model of its kind because of this report.

The *vice-postulator,* Mgr. de Teil, who would not see the definitive result of his work since he died a year

before Thérèse's beatification, was a tireless worker, and at the same time a man filled with finesse and humor. He was clever enough to present to Pius X the arguments that would move him. During an audience on October 29, 1910, he read the letter Thérèse had written to Marie Guérin, her cousin, on May 30, 1889, to encourage her to receive Communion regularly, despite her scrupulosity. "Jesus is there in the Tabernacle expressly for *you,* for *you alone;* He is burning with the desire to enter your heart…. What offends Him and what wounds His Heart is the lack of confidence!… Dear little sister, *receive Communion often,* very often…. That is the *only remedy* if you want to be healed, and Jesus hasn't placed this attraction in your soul for nothing" (LT 92). Such a Eucharistic text could only please the pope who had just promulgated the decree on frequent communion.

In 1910–1911, the informative process occurred, called "ordinary" because it took place under the authority of Bishop Lemonnier, the Ordinary of Bayeux. Thirty-seven witnesses went to Lisieux or Bayeux to give depositions on Sister Thérèse's life, including nine Carmelites who had lived with her.

In 1915–1917 the Apostolic Process took place, once again at Bayeux and Lisieux, under the authority of the apostolic Holy See.

On August 9, 1917, Thérèse's body was exhumed a second time. The ceremony took place before an estimated crowd of 1,500 people. In a sheltered area, two doctors under oath identified the bones of Thérèse's body.

The Congregation of Rites in Rome constantly received letters from everywhere calling for little Thérèse's beatification by the church. There was no longer any doubt that her beatification would soon take place. In fact, on August 14, 1921, Benedict XV promulgated the decree on the heroicity of the virtues of the "Venerable" Thérèse of the Child Jesus. He gave an admirable discourse on "Spiritual Childhood" in which he named the essential characteristics of the evangelical doctrine the Lord wanted to bring to our attention through the intermediary of Thérèse. The year 1922 saw the procedure established for the examination of the two cures obtained by Thérèse's intercession and proposed to the Congregation of Rites in view of her beatification.

The solemn translation of her body took place on March 26, 1923. All those present in Lisieux on that day cherish an unforgettable memory. In the cemetery closed to the public, workers labored under the watchful eyes of the bishop and civil authorities to withdraw the casket from the grave. Outside, thousands of pilgrims prayed the rosary. Then the procession moved forward in magnificent sunshine, and a long line of pilgrims—probably 50,000—stretched out over a distance of two kilometers. There was no singing, no music, for Thérèse had not yet been beatified. Only the recitation of the rosary alternated with that of the psalms.

Thérèse's Beatification and Canonization

It was Pope Pius XI's privilege to proclaim the final glorification of Thérèse. He thanked God for placing this "star" at the dawn of his pontificate; her portrait and her relics were always on his desk.

On February 11, 1923, he signed the decree declaring the authenticity of the two miracles investigated in view of Thérèse's beatification, and he said on that occasion that the Carmelite of Lisieux was a "miracle of virtue" and a "prodigy of miracles."

On April 29, he presided at the beatification ceremonies. "The most beautiful day of my pontificate," he would say that evening to those close to him.

Finally, on May 17, 1925, Pius XI, surrounded by twenty-three cardinals and 250 bishops, canonized Thérèse. Five hundred thousand faithful had come to Rome for this occasion, but only 50,000 were able to enter Saint Peter's Basilica to hear the pope proclaim the solemn announcement, declaring that henceforth the

humble Carmelite of Lisieux could be addressed as "Saint Thérèse of the Child Jesus."

These last words had scarcely fallen from the lips of the Sovereign Pontiff when immediately, for the first time at such an event, enthusiastic and prolonged applause broke the crowd's silent recollection. And while the fanfares resounded in the cupola, the bells of Saint Peter's burst forth, to which all those of Rome replied in festive carillon.

In the homily of the Mass, the pope exalted the *spiritual childhood* that Thérèse had taught "by word and example," and he asked Christians to contemplate her in order to become in turn "children" in the evangelical sense of the term. "If this way of spiritual childhood were widely accepted," the pope concluded, "it is evident how easy the reform of human society would become."

Throughout his life, Pius XI never ceased to entrust to Thérèse his major apostolic initiatives, in particular the inauguration of Catholic Action and the development of the missions.

An Ever-Growing Influence

Although Christians did not wait for the canonization of Thérèse to come in pilgrimage to her tomb, it is evident that from 1925 on they came to Lisieux in even greater numbers to pray to Saint Thérèse of the Child Jesus.

On December 14, 1927, Pius XI proclaimed this little Carmelite principal patroness of the missions along with Saint Francis Xavier. If international tension in July 1937 had not impeded him, the pope would have come himself to dedicate the Basilica of Lisieux. He had to be satisfied with sending Cardinal Pacelli as legate.

When Cardinal Pacelli became pope, under the name of Pius XII, he proclaimed Thérèse secondary patroness of France along with Saint Joan of Arc. The proclamation was made on May 3, 1944, one month before the Allied forces landed in Normandy.

Some statistics will suffice to indicate Thérèse's influence on the church of the twentieth century. She is the patroness of more than seventy seminaries and a great number of schools. Around the world, more than 1,700 churches or chapels are dedicated to her. Among them are eight cathedrals—Niamey (Niger), Sokodé (Togo), Bouaké (Ivory Coast), Garoua (Cameroon), and Urawa (Japan)—as well as five minor basilicas: Rio de Janeiro (Brazil), Lisieux, Anzio, La Bombetta (Venice) and Choubrah (Cairo). This last edifice was given by Cairo's Muslims to the "little saint of Allah" to thank her for all the favors received.

About fifty religious congregations in the world have been placed under her patronage. Three of them were founded by Father Gabriel Martin, missionary from the Vendée who was won over to Thérèse while reading the *Call to Little Souls* and who was the preacher in Lisieux in 1923 and 1925 for the celebrations of beatification and canonization. In 1928 he founded the Congregation of the *Missionaires de la Plaine* to work for the evangelization of the Plain and the Marais of the Vendée; in 1933, the Congregation of the *Oblates of Saint Thérèse* who welcome pilgrims to her birthplace in Alençon, to Les Buissonnets, and to the Hermitage of Saint Thérèse in Lisieux; and in 1947, the Congregation of the *Missionaries of St. Thérèse*.

Note too the existence of a Thérèsian Secular Institute, *Deus Caritas,* founded by Father Puaud, chaplain of pilgrimages, whose statutes were approved by Rome in 1979. Its members (several hundred today) strive to live the Gospel in the spirit of Saint Thérèse while living as laity in the heart of the world.

Among the works that particularly benefit from the patronage of Saint Thérèse is the *Oeuvre des Orphelins*

Apprentis d'Auteuil (Work of the Orphan-Apprentices of Auteil [Paris]) to which Father Daniel Brottier dedicated the last twelve years of his life. One of Thérèse's novices, Sister Marie of the Trinity, often spoke to her novice mistress of this Work (the "Work of First Communion," soon after to become the "Work of the Apprentices") founded in the last century by Father Roussel to serve the poor children of the French capital. This novice's father, Victor Castel, a retired teacher, actually traveled throughout France to make Father Roussel's Work known. Whenever Marie Louise Castel in Carmel received a letter from her father, Thérèse was soon informed of the difficulties and developments of this Work and she would pray for these dear orphans.

In 1923, Father Brottier's superiors from the Congregation of the Holy Spirit gave him the responsibility to resume this great Work. The former military chaplain already had great devotion to the little Carmelite. At the time of his appointment in Auteil, he decided to build a chapel in honor of Thérèse, who had just been beatified a few months earlier, so that the orphans could pray to their "little mama" in a sanctuary worthy of her. One day he learned from the coal merchant, Joachim Léon Castel—one of Sister Marie of the Trinity's brothers—that, twenty-five years earlier, Thérèse had often prayed for the development of this Work. What joy! He immediately proposed to Sister Marie of the Trinity that she become the godmother of his orphans and asked Thérèse to shower on his houses "no more roses, but bank notes!" Father Brottier's confidence was not disappointed, for the gifts multiplied and the Work grew considerably.

Father Brottier was beatified by Pope John Paul II on November 25, 1984, along with another disciple of the "little way," Elizabeth of the Trinity, Carmelite of Dijon.

Thérèse Speaks

I Will Be More Useful in Heaven Than on Earth

When you receive this letter, no doubt I shall have left this earth. The Lord in His infinite mercy will have opened His kingdom to me, and I shall be able to draw from His treasures in order to grant them liberally to the souls who are dear to me. Believe, Brother, that your little sister will hold to her promises, and, her soul, freed from the weight of this mortal envelope, will joyfully fly toward the distant regions that you are evangelizing. Ah! Brother, I feel it, I shall be more useful to you in heaven than on earth, and it is with joy that I come to announce to you my coming entrance into that blessed city, sure that you will share my joy and will thank the Lord for giving me the means of helping you more effectively in your apostolic works.

I really count on not remaining inactive in heaven. My desire is to work still for the Church and for souls. I am asking God for this and I am certain He will answer me. Are not the angels continually occupied with us without their ever ceasing to see the divine Face and to lose themselves in the Ocean of Love without shores? Why would Jesus not allow me to imitate them? (LT 254 to Père Roulland, her missionary brother)

I Shall Be Able to Make Him Loved

Brother, you see that if I am leaving the field of battle already, it is not with the selfish desire of taking my rest. The thought of eternal beatitude hardly thrills my heart. For a long time, suffering has become my heaven here below, and I really have trouble in conceiving how I shall be able to acclimatize myself in a country where joy reigns without any admixture of sadness. Jesus will have to transform my soul and give it the capacity to rejoice, otherwise I shall not be able to put up with eternal delights.

What attacts me to the homeland of heaven is the Lord's call, the hope of loving Him finally as I have so much desired to love Him, and the thought that I shall be able to make Him loved by a multitude of souls who will bless Him eternally.

Brother, you will not have time to send me your messages for heaven, but I am guessing at them, and then you will only have to tell me them in a whisper, and I shall hear you, and I shall carry your messages faithfully to the Lord, to our Immaculate Mother, to the Angels, and to the Saints whom you love. I will ask the palm of martyrdom for you, and I shall be near you, holding your hand so that you may gather up this glorious palm without effort, and then with joy we shall fly together into the heavenly homeland, surrounded by all the souls who will be your conquest!

Au revoir, Brother; pray very much for your sister, pray for *our Mother,* whose sensitive and maternal heart has much difficulty in consenting to my departure. I count on you to console her.

I am your little sister for eternity,
Thérèse of the Child Jesus and the Holy Face

(LT 254 to Père Roulland, her missionary brother)

Thérèse Today

BISHOP GUY GAUCHER, OCD

The mystery remains: how did a young Carmelite nun, dying unknown in a little French provincial town, manage to conquer the world?

But it is a fact. Is there, throughout the church's 2000 year history of holiness, a more brilliant course or a more intense "storm of glory" (Pius XI)? And we are only a century removed from her her obscure death, as she suffered the pangs of tuberculosis and the night of faith. We are still far from measuring the impact of Thérèse's life and doctrine on the church and world. No serious study has yet been done on her posthumous life.

Certainly the church has honored her with an astonishing number of titles. She has been named patron of the universal missions (1927), secondary patron of France (1944), patron of all novitiates, and protector of Russia (1932), Mexico (1929), The French Mission (1941), the Catholic Worker Movement (1929), and so on.

Popes Saint Pius X and Pius XI respectively named her "the greatest saint of modern times" and "a word of God for the world." Cardinal Pacelli, the future Pius XII, called her "the greatest wonder-worker of modern times" (1938). We could prolong the list indefinitely, and on a worldwide scale.

What is important today, a century after her "entrance into life," is to note the constant impact of her life and spiritual message. At the close of this century in which skepticism and hidden despair have invaded all levels of society, in which the hopes raised by totalitarian ideologies have misfired, in which the world of technology no longer leaves room for simple humanity, the crisis of hope has come to full term.

The church's saints reemerge as masters of meaning, hope, and love, for "the saints virtually never grow old,… they never fall under 'prescription.' They continually remain witnesses of the youth of the Church. They never become characters of the past, men and women of 'yesterday.' On the contrary: they are always men and women of tomorrow, men of the evangelical future of man and of the Church, witnesses 'of the future world.'" It is no coincidence that the first pope to come on pilgrimage to Lisieux, John Paul II, spoke these words in the basilica's square. They fit this young Norman girl perfectly.

We notice, at Lisieux and elsewhere, that Thérèse's word and prayer frees wounded people, unchains drug-addicted or despairing youth, and constantly raises up priestly, religious, and lay vocations. She goes in search of distant people, insinuates herself into the most unlikely situations, plays an ecumenical role, attracts Muslims, and touches even strangers to the faith, sometimes through a simple look at her real face that photography has made available to us.

More than fifty apostolic congregations have named themselves after Saint Thérèse and claim her as their patroness. In France, the fast rising new communities are often rooted in the spirituality of this young saint, for whom weakness was a springboard to sanctity in ordinary life. Thérèse continues to gather around herself both the great intellectuals and the poor of every land.

Since 1932, many theologians and spiritual writers have seen that the doctrine of Saint Thérèse has universal application. More than 600 bishops and a vast number of lay people asked Pope Pius XI to declare her a Doctor of the Church. No woman up to that time had ever received this honor, and the pope refused to cross the line. But Pope Paul VI did in 1970 when he proclaimed two women as Doctors of the Church: Saints Teresa of Avila and Catherine of Siena. The way is now open. Saint Thérèse of Lisieux herself wrote: "Ah! in spite of my littleness I would like to enlighten souls as did the *Prophets* and the *Doctors*. I have the *vocation of the Apostle*" (B 3r) and "I feel the vocation of…THE DOCTOR" (B 2v).

God always granted her desires, and will grant this one when and how he wishes. The essential point remains that her life and her message, marked by her times but prophetically surpassing them (she announces what will be the great themes of Vatican II), are the most effective antidote to contemporary dispair. One day she may be the "Doctor of Hope." Certainly she is an important saint for the twenty-first century, "turned toward the future and a witness of the future world."

Under the inspiration of the Holy Spirit, she desired to be Love in the heart of the church. She is, and no one can rob her of that place, because "it is Jesus who has given it to her" (cf. B 3v).

186

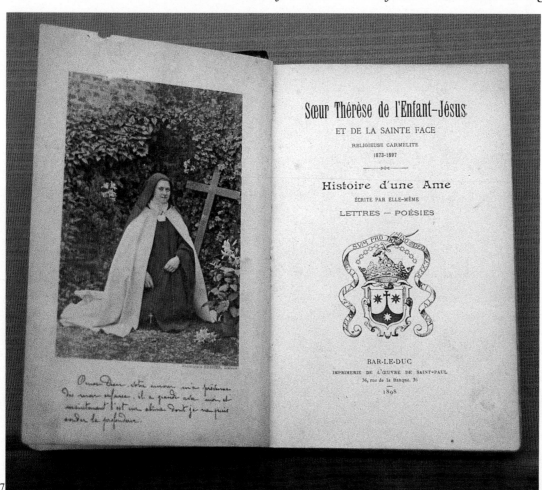

186. Lisieux. Carmelite chapel. Casket containing remains of Thérèse.

187. Frontispiece of *Histoire d'une Ame* (Story of a Soul), Thérèse's autobiography first published September 30, 1898, with a printing of 2,000 copies.

188. Father Rodrigo of Saint Francis of Paola, OCD, postulator general for the Discalced Carmelites, promoted Thérèse's cause for beatification and canonization.

189. Thérèse's canonization in St. Peter's basilica in Rome. Painting by Sr. Marie of the Holy Spirit from a photograph.

190. Pius XI blesses statue of St. Thérèse of the Child Jesus which he had placed in the Vatican gardens (May 17, 1927).

191. Vatican City. Gardens with the statue of St. Thérèse.

192. Statues of Thérèse in the Lisieux cemetery. In the background is the cupola of the basilica.

190

191

192

193

194

195

193. Daniel Brottier, founder of the Work for the Apprentice Orphans of Auteil (Paris), beatified by John Paul II on November 25, 1984 with the Carmelite nun from Dijon, Elizabeth of the Trinity.

194. Choubra (Cairo). Shrine offered by the Moslems of Cairo to the "little saint of Allah." St. Thérèse in the lower corner is from a fresco in the shrine.

195. Lisieux. Panorama. The Carmel in the foreground; in the background the Basilica of St. Thérèse.

196. Lisieux. The Basilica of St. Thérèse.

195

198

197. Lisieux. Interior of the basilica.

198. Lisieux. Mosaic in the apse of the basilica. With Mary, Thérèse leads us to Christ, the Good Shepherd.

199. Lisieux. The nave of the basilica.

199

200. Lisieux. Basilica. Pillar with a mosaic of the apostles.

201. Lisieux. Basilica. The cupola. Mosaic of Thérèse in glory.

202. Lisieux. Main altar and apse of the basilica.

203. Lisieux. Mosaic of St. Teresa of Avila and St. John of the Cross.

204. Lisieux. Basilica. Mosaic of Thérèse and the popes: Pius X, Benedict XV, Pius XI, and Pius XII approve her doctrine on the way of spiritual childhood.

205. Lisieux. Basilica. Chapel of the relics. The stained-glass window represents the grace received by Thérèse a few days after her offering to Merciful Love.

201

202

203

204

205

206

SA SAINTETÉ LE PAPE JEAN PAVL II
PÈLERIN DE SAINTE THÉRÈSE
A PRIÉ DANS CETTE BASILIQUE
ET CÉLÉBRÉ L'EUCHARISTIE
SUR L'ESPLANADE
LE 2 JUIN 1980
ENTOURÉ D'UNE GRANDE FOULE

207

208

209

206. Lisieux. The crypt of the basilica.

207. John Paul II, the first pilgrim pope to Lisieux. A commemorative plaque in the basilica.

208. Lisieux, September 24, 1994. At Carmel, Bishop Guy Gaucher, auxiliary bishop of Bayeux and Lisieux, presides at the annual procession with Thérèse's relics.

209. Lisieux, September 25, 1994. The procession leaves the basilica with Thérèse's relics.

210. Lisieux. Thérèse's relics being brought back to the Carmel.

211. Lisieux. Thérèse the teacher.

210

211

Thérèse: A Motive for Hope

ANASTASIO Cardinal BALLESTRERO, OCD

This volume reconstructs the story of a remarkable and mysterious event: the life and spirituality of St. Thérèse of Lisieux. Careful, full of fascinating details, rich in its authentic interpretation, yet not meant to substitute for her autobiographical writings, this reconstruction provides us with a precious introduction to Thérèse. This is the delightful story of a young girl whose rich human experiences of family life together with her vivacious personal talents were all deeply and mysteriously overtaken by the gifts of divine mercy.

This connection between personal story and mercy is one of the most remarkable aspects of Thérèse's life. She is conscious of this herself. She proclaims it with absolute conviction. And she convinces us by her reflections, in which the outpouring of divine mercy abounds and where we discover a transparent humanity, delightful and exemplary, fully open to the divine gift. We find the family remembrances, the early vocation, the response to her Carmelite call, the encounter in Carmel with teachers like Teresa of Jesus and John of the Cross. We find a ray of light illumining the life of the community, to the advantage above all of the new recruits. And after her precious death we find the quick and rapid outpouring of interest within the church, like an authentic miracle, leaving all those amazed who know how to see and understand the logic and consistency of God, who is essentially the Lord of mercy.

By the very fact of her unremitting proclamation of the mercy of God, Thérèse of the Child Jesus is a motive for hope, a hope that is not only her personal treasure but also a gift she gives to all those who know and listen to her.

To the one who listens to Thérèse of the Child Jesus, the fatherhood of God becomes not just a mystery to be believed but an experience to be lived forever. She is the daughter who recollects herself in the Father's heart and abandons herself to the embrace of God's paternal love, so mercifully great and supremely generous.

This declaration of God's fatherhood, this proclamation of the Savior's mercy that Thérèse lives, is not the dubious gratification of an infantile affectivity, but a courageously consistent thrust toward the mystery that transcends her, that overwhelms her, that renders her a "victim," brimming over at the same time with supreme blessedness and glory.

In this sense the experience of Thérèse of the Child Jesus is an authentic gospel event. That Gospel that the Saint carried on her heart, that Gospel on which she was nourished almost exclusively, is truly the Word of God, truly the mystery of Christ, Son of the Father, Spouse of virgins, Savior of the world, incarnation of Trinitarian love.

The message of Thérèse of the Child Jesus proclaims all this, and so can be interpreted as a new evangelization in which the substance of the Gospel comes alive through interior experience, contemplative prayer, filial and fraternal love, and the generosity of a charity that becomes heroic and oblational.

To this Lord Jesus, to whom she offers herself, Thérèse leads souls who follow her by means of the simplicity of the Gospel; hers is not a spiritual infantilism but an adherence to the word of the Lord: "Unless you become like little children, you will not enter the kingdom of heaven."

These words from the Gospel are the synthesis of a life, a spiritual experience, an evangelical doctrine, and they are also, we can say, the vocation of a creature who after having lived all of this in heroic fidelity on earth is now proclaiming it wonderfully from the glory of heaven.

Everything in the preceding pages can become living, transparent, and invaluable to us by approaching the Saint, listening to the message, and following the way that leads to salvation.

This is the hope we have for the book, and a grace we can request of the Saint, its exemplary protagonist.

Bibliography

A. Original Sources in French

Sainte Thérèse de l'Enfant-Jésus et de la sainte-Face. *Oeuvres complètes.* Paris: Cerf-DDB, 1992.

Sainte Thérèse de l'Enfant-Jésus et de la sainte-Face. *Nouvelle édition du Centenaire.* 2d ed. Paris: Cerf-DDB, 1992. Critical edition in eight volumes: 1. Manuscrits autobiographiques; 2. La première Histoire d'une âme (1898); 3. Correspondance générale I; 4. Correspondance générale II; 5. Poésies; 6. Récréations pieuses & Prières; 7. Derniers entretiens; 8. Derniers paroles (synopsis).

François de Sainte-Marie. *Visage de Thérèse de Lisieux.* 2 vols. Lisieux: Office central de Lisieux, 1961. English language reprint edition: *The Photo Album of St. Thérèse of Lisieux.* Trans. Peter-Thomas Rohrbach. Westminster, MD: Christian Classics, 1990.

Geneviève de la Saint-Face, *Conseils et Souvenirs,* Lisieux: 1952, 1973. English translation: *A Memoir of My Sister, St. Thérèse.* Trans. Carmelite Sisters of New York. New York: P. J. Kenedy & Sons, 1959.

Zélie Martin. *Correspondance familiale.* Lisieux: Office central de Lisieux, 1958.

B. Translations by ICS Publications

Story of a Soul: The Autobiography of St. Thérèse of Lisieux. Trans. John Clarke. 3d ed. Washington, DC: ICS Publications, 1996.

Letters of St. Thérèse of Lisieux: General Correspondence. Trans. John Clarke. 2 vols. Washington, DC: ICS Publications, 1982–1988.

The Poetry of Saint Thérèse of Lisieux. Trans. Donald Kinney. Washington, DC: ICS Publications, 1996.

The Plays of St. Thérèse of Lisieux: Pious Recreations. Trans. David Dwyer. Washington, DC: ICS Publications, 1997.

The Prayers of St. Thérèse of Lisieux. Trans. Aletheia Kane. Washington, DC: ICS Publications, 1997.

St. Thérèse of Lisieux: Her Last Conversations. Trans. John Clarke. Washington, DC: ICS Publications, 1977.

C. Studies

Baudouin-Croix, Marie. *Léonie Martin: A Difficult Life.* Dublin: Veritas, 1993.

Bro, Bernard. *The Little Way: The Spirituality of Thérèse of Lisieux.* Translated by Alan Neame. London: Darton, Longman and Todd, 1979.

————. *Thérèse de Lisieux: sa famille, son Dieu, son message.* Paris: Fayard, 1996,

Cadéot, Robert. *Louis Martin.* V.A.L., 1985.

Cadéot, Robert. *Zélie Martin.* V.A.L., 1990.

Chalon, Jean: *Thérèse de Lisieux: une vie d'amour.* Paris: Cerf, 1996.

Day, Dorothy. *Thérèse: A Life of Thérèse of Lisieux.* Reprint edition. Springfield, IL: Templegate Publishers, 1987.

D'Elbée, Jean du Coeur de Jésus. *I Believe in Love: Retreat Conferences on the Interior Life.* Chicago: Franciscan Herald Press, 1974.

De Meester, Conrad. *Dynamique de la confiance.* Paris: Cerf, 1995.

————. *With Empty Hands: the Message of Thérèse of Lisieux.* Homebush, New South Wales: St. Paul Publications, 1982; Tunbridge Wells: Burns and Oates, 1987.

Descouvemont, Pierre and Loose, Helmuth Nils. *Sainte Thérèse de Lisieux: la vie en images.* Paris: Cerf, 1995.

Descouvemont, Pierre and Loose, Helmuth Nils. *Thérèse and Lisieux.* Trans. Salvatore Sciurba. Grand Rapids, MI: Eerdmans, 1996.

Ducrocq, Marie-Pascale. *Thérèse of Lisieux: A Vocation of Love.* Translated by Robert Jollett from 2nd edition. Staten Island, NY: Alba House, 1982.

Emert, Joyce. *Louis Martin: Father of a Saint.* Staten Island, NY: Alba House, 1983.

Frost, Christine. *A Guide to the Normandy of Saint Thérèse.* Birmingham: Theresian Trust, 1994.

————. *A Life of St. Thérèse of Lisieux: The Little Flower.* Illustrated by Elizabeth Obbard. Wheathamptstead, Hertforshire: Antony Clarke, 1988.

Gaucher, Guy. *The Passion of St. Thérèse of Lisieux.* New York: Crossroad, 1990.

———. *Saint Thérèse of Lisieux: From Lisieux to the Four Corners of the World.* Strasbourg: Editions du Signe, 1994.

———. *The Story of a Life: St. Thérèse of Lisieux.* San Francisco: Harper & Row, 1987.

Görres, Ida F. *The Hidden Face: A Study of St. Thérèse of Lisieux.* New York: Pantheon; London: Burns and Oates, 1959.

Hollings, Michael. *Thérèse of Lisieux: An Illustrated Life.* London: W. Collins & Co., 1981; Ann Arbor, MI: Servant Publications, 1991.

Jamart, François. *Complete Spiritual Doctrine of St. Thérèse of Lisieux.* New York: St. Paul Publications (Alba House), 1961.

Lafrance, Jean. *My Vocation Is Love: Thérèse of Lisieux.* Translated by A.M. Brennan. Victoria, Australia and Middlegreen, Slough UK: St. Paul Publications, 1990.

Marie-Eugene of the Child Jesus. *Under the Torrent of His Love: Thérèse of Lisieux, a Spiritual Genius.* Staten Island, NY: Alba House, 1995.

O'Connor, Patricia. *In Search of Thérèse.* London: Darton, Longman & Todd; Wilmington, DE: Michael Glazier, 1987.

———. *Thérèse of Lisieux: A Biography.* Huntington, IN: Our Sunday Visitor, 1983.

O'Mahoney, Christopher, trans. and ed. *Saint Thérèse of Lisieux by Those Who Knew Her: Testimonies from the Process of Beatification.* Dublin: Veritas Publications, 1975, 1989; Huntington, IN: Our Sunday Visitor, 1976.

Piat, Stéphane-Joseph. *The Story of a Family: The Home of the Little Flower.* Reprint edition. Rockford, IL: TAN Publications, 1995.

Redmond, Paulinus. *Louis and Zélie Martin: The Seed and the Root of the Little Flower.* London: Quiller Press, 1995.

Renault, Emmanuel. *L'épreuve de la foi: la combat de Thérèse de Lisieux.* Paris: Cerf-DDB, 1991.

Rohrbach, Peter-Thomas. *The Search for Saint Thérèse.* Garden City, NY: Doubleday and Co., 1961.

Six, Jean-François and Loose, Helmuth Nils. *Teresa di Lisieux.* Rome: Edizioni San Paolo, 1981.

Sullivan, John, ed. *Carmelite Studies,* vol. 5: *Experiencing St. Thérèse Today.* Washington, DC: ICS Publications, 1990.

Teresa Margaret. *I Choose All: A Study of St. Thérèse of Lisieux and Her Spiritual Doctrine.* Tenbury Wells, England: Fowler Wright Books, 1964.

Ulanov, Barry. *The Making of a Modern Saint: A Biographical Study of Thérèse of Lisieux.* Garden City, NY: Doubleday, 1966.

Victor de la Vierge. *Spiritual Realism of Saint Thérèse of Lisieux: From the Original Manuscripts.* Milwaukee, WI: Bruce Publishing Co, 1961.

Vinatier, Jean. *Mère Agnès de Jésus.* Paris: Cerf, 1993.

von Balthasar, Hans Urs. "Thérèse of Lisieux." In *Two Sisters in the Spirit: Thérèse of Lisieux and Elizabeth of the Trinity,* 13–362. San Francisco: Ignatius Press, 1992.

———. *Thérèse of Lisieux: The Story of a Mission.* Translated by Donald Nicholl. London, New York: Sheed and Ward, 1953.

Chronology

1873
Thursday, January 2: Thérèse born in Alençon
Saturday, January 4: Thérèse baptized in Notre-Dame Church
Saturday, March 15 or Sunday, March 16: Thérèse sent to wet nurse in Semallé.

1874 — one year old
Thursday, April 2: Thérèse returns to Alençon.

1875 — two years old
Monday, March 29: Train trip with her mother to Le Mans, to see Thérèse's Visitandine aunt.
At age of two: "I too will be a religious" (A 6r).

1877 — four years old
Saturday, February 24: Death of Thérèse's Visitandine aunt.
Friday to Wednesday, June 18–23: Zélie Martin's pilgrimage to Lourdes, with Marie, Pauline, and Léonie, seeking a cure.
Wednesday, August 28: Death of Zélie Martin at 12:30 AM.
Thursday, November 15: Family moves to Les Buissonnets in Lisieux.

1878 — five years old
Monday to Tuesday, June 17 to July 2: Louis Martin in Paris with Marie and Pauline to see the Exposition. Thérèse stays with the Guérins.
Thursday, August 8: At Trouville, Thérèse sees the ocean for the first time.

1880 — seven years old
At the beginning of the year or end of preceding year: Thérèse makes first confession.

1882 — nine years old
Monday, October 2: Pauline, her "second Mama," enters the Carmel of Lisieux.

1883 — ten years old
Sunday, April 8: Death of Thérèse's paternal grandmother.
Sunday, May 13 (Pentecost): Thérèse cured suddenly by the Blessed Virgin's smile.
Monday to Thursday, August 20–30: Vacation in Alençon.

1884 — eleven years old
Thursday, May 8: Thérèse's First Communion, at the Abbey. Pauline's profession at the Lisieux Carmel.
Saturday, June 14: Thérèse confirmed by Bishop Hugonin at the Abbey.
August: Vacation in Saint-Ouen-le-Pin.

1885 — twelve years old
Sunday to Friday, May 3–10: Vacation by the sea in Deauville.
July: Vacation in Saint-Ouen-le-Pin.
Saturday, August 22 to Saturday, October 10 (17?): M. Martin's trip to Constantinople (seven weeks).

1886 — thirteen years old
February or March: Thérèse leaves Abbey school for good.
Beginning of October: Trip with her father and sisters to Alençon.
Friday, October 15: Marie enters Carmel of Lisieux.
Saturday, December 25 (Christmas): grace of "conversion."

1887 — fourteen years old
Sunday, May 29 (Pentecost): Thérèse receives her father's permission to enter Carmel.
Monday to Sunday, June 20–26: Vacation in Trouville.
Summer: "conversations in the Belvedere" with Céline.
Prayer for the conversion of Pranzini.
Monday, October 31: Thérèse visits Bishop Hugonin in Bayeux.
Friday, November 4 to Friday, December 2: Thérèse on pilgrimage to Paris, Switzerland, Italy, and Rome.

1888 — fifteen years old
Monday, April 9 (Annunciation): Thérèse enters Lisieux Carmel.
Saturday to Tuesday, June 23–27: M. Martin runs away to Le Havre.

1889 — sixteen years old
Thursday, January 10: Thérèse clothed in habit.
Tuesday, February 12: M. Martin confined to mental asylum in Caen.

1890 — seventeen years old
Monday, September 8 (Birth of Mary): Thérèse's final profession of vows.

Wednesday, December 25 (Christmas): Lease on Les Buissonnets ends.

1891 — eighteen years old
Monday, November 24: Third centenary of the death of St. John of the Cross.
Saturday, December 5: Death of Mother Geneviève, foundress of the Lisieux Carmel.

1892 — nineteen years old
Saturday to Thursday, January 2–7: Influenza epidemic takes lives of three nuns in the Lisieux Carmel.
Tuesday, May 10: After three years at Caen, Louis Martin returns to Lisieux an invalid, in the care of the Guérins.
Thursday, May 12: Louis Martin's last visit to his Carmelite daughters. His final words to them: "In heaven!"

1893 — twenty years old
Monday, February 20: Sister Agnes elected prioress.
September: Thérèse obtains permission to remain in novitiate.

1894 — twenty-one years old
January: Thérèse's writes her first theatrical work, on Joan of Arc, for the prioress's feast on January 21.
Sunday, May 27: Louis Martin's paralysis and extreme unction.
Saturday, June 16: Marie of the Trinity enters Carmel.
Friday, July 29: Louis Martin dies at Saint-Sébastien-de-Morsent, at La Musse.
Friday, September 14: Céline enters Lisieux Carmel.

1895 — twenty-two years old
During the year: Thérèse writes Manuscript A.
Sunday, June 9 (Trinity Sunday): Thérèse makes her Offering to Merciful Love.
Thursday, August 15: Thérèse's cousin Marie Guérin enters the Lisieux Carmel.
Thursday, October 17: Mother Agnes asks Thérèse to pray for Maurice Bellière, her first "spiritual brother."

1896 — twenty-three years old
Monday, February 24: Profession of Sister Céline, Thérèse's sister.

Saturday, March 21: Difficult election of Marie de Gonzague as prioress. Thérèse is confirmed in her office as assistant novice mistress.
Friday, April 3 (Good Friday): First hemoptysis, repeated in the evening.
Sunday, April 5 (Easter): Beginning of Thérèse's "trial of faith," which continues until her death.
Saturday, May 30: Mother Marie de Gonzague assigns Thérèse a second "spiritual brother," Adolphe Roulland.
Tuesday, September 8: Thérèse begins Manuscript B.
Saturday, November 21: Novena made for Thérèse's cure, in hopes that she can eventually depart for a Carmel in Indochina; final relapse.

1897 — twenty-four years old
Beginning of April: Thérèse falls seriously ill at the end of Lent.
Tuesday, April 6: Mother Agnes begins recording Thérèse's *Last Conversations.*
Monday, April 19: Léo Taxil reveals his Diana Vaughan hoax, which Thérèse believed for a long time.
Thursday, June 3: Thérèse begins Manuscript C.
Thursday, July 8: Thérèse is transferred to the monastery infirmary.
Friday, July 30: Thérèse experiences continued hemoptyses and feelings of suffocation. At 6 P.M. she receives viaticum and extreme unction.
Thursday, September 30: Thérèse dies at about 7:20 P.M. Her finals words are "My God, I love you."
Monday, October 4: Thérèse buried in the Lisieux cemetery.

After her death
1898, September 30: 2,000 copies of *Story of a Soul* printed. A new edition was necessary each year thereafter.
1910: Beatification process opened.
1923, April 29: Thérèse beatified by Pius XI.
1925, May 17: Thérèse canonized by Pius XI in St. Peter's Basilica, Rome.
1927, December 14: Pius XI declares St. Thérèse co-patroness of the missions with St. Francis Xavier.
1980, June 2: John Paul II's pilgrimage to Lisieux.
1997, September 30: First centenary of Thérèse's death.

Amilcare Pizzi S.p.A. - Cinisello Balsamo (MI)
Printed in Italy - 1997